...A SCHULTE-PEEVERS

DUBAI

CITY GUIDE

INTRODUCING DUBAI

Burj Khalifa soars above Dubai's cityscape

JEAN-PIERRE LESCOE

Aboard approaching airliners, passengers' eyes are glued to the view: traditional wind towers yield to space-age skyscrapers sprouting across an endless desert hemmed in by a glittering coastline.

Welcome to Dubai, the 21st-century Middle Eastern Shangri La powered by unflinching ambition and can-do spirit. The motto: 'If you can think it, it shall be done.' The world's tallest building? Check. Skiing in the desert? Check. Islands shaped like the entire world? Check.

Over the last decade, Dubai has grown into the most progressive and modern city in the Middle East. Under the leadership of its dynamic and daring ruler, Sheikh Mohammed bin Rashid al-Maktoum, Dubai has become a centre of finance, tourism and trade. Despite having been hit harder by the global financial meltdown than just about any other place on earth, the tiny emirate is still regarded as a major power player and *the* place to do business in the Middle East.

For visitors, the doom-and-gloom headlines matter little. Dubai is an exciting place to visit with lovely beaches, sophisticated restaurants and bars, world-class shopping, ultraluxe hotels, and skyscrapers that leave you gasping in awe – including, of course, the world's tallest building, Burj Khalifa. But there's more to the emirate than 21st-century glitz and glam. Despite appearances, Dubai's culture is solidly rooted in Islam and generations of Bedouin heritage. It's still alive along the Creek, in the historic Bastakia Quarter and the warren-like souqs. It's this juxtaposition of the traditional past and the hi-tech present that makes it such an intriguing and compelling place to visit.

CITY LIFE

Dubai's success has been shaped by forward-thinking governments, but the achievements wouldn't have been possible without the foreign workforce that has helped carry out their vision. While everyone in Dubai in some way shares in the city's accomplishments, expatriate workers – some of whom were born and raised in the emirate but haven't qualified for UAE citizenship – find it hard to escape the feeling that they're the 'hired help' in this grand experiment. While buying property in Dubai now allows expats to have an open-ended residency visa, it's still not citizenship – and effectively they have no political voice. Then again, the disparity of wealth in Dubai is colossal and only a minority of expats can even dream of owning a property here.

'Dubai has grown into the most progressive and modern city in the Middle East'

To local Emiratis, who make up between 5% and 10% of the city's population, Dubai's sudden acquisition of wealth has been a double-edged *khanjar*. The vast majority have a lot of faith in their leaders and appreciate the perks they receive: free health care, education, land, zero-interest loans, and marriage funds. However, Emiratis are facing challenges in the employment market. How can they compete when a foreigner will do the same job for a tenth of the price? Plus the segregated society means that many expat managers don't even know any Emiratis, let alone employ any.

There is also debate about whether the Emiratis' heritage and traditions are endangered as the city becomes increasingly multicultural, or if being a minority helps reinforce Emiratis' sense of identity; many display their roots, wearing national dress such as hijabs and *abeyyas* with pride.

Dubai today is friends with the West; for progressive Arabs it's a shining example of a modern Arab city. But conservative branches of Islam are less than impressed by the city's tolerance of alcohol and pork, and its failure to curb prostitution. How Dubai manages to balance all these factors is just as important as keeping up its spectacular growth. Given the track record of Dubai's leaders over the past few decades, it would be unwise to bet against them.

BRENT WINEBRENNER

Teenagers rollerblading along the boardwalk, Bur Dubai

MERTEN SNI

① Burj al-Arab

This landmark hotel, known throughout the world, floats on its own man-made island (p79)

② National Bank of Dubai

The awe-inspiring architecture makes the bank building a special feature of any journey along the Creek (p38)

③ Jumeirah Emirates Towers

A group in traditional dress stand beneath the iconic Jumeirah Emirates Towers (p160)

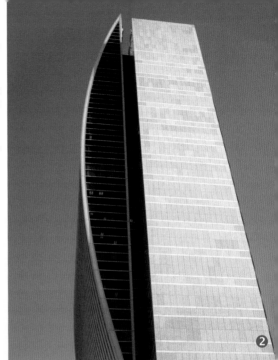

TONY WHEELER

FANTASTIC LANDMARKS

The world's tallest skyscraper, a giant indoor ski-slope and the earth mapped out on water – experiencing Dubai's fantastical next-gen architecture up close is a guaranteed highlight of every trip.

TERRY CARTER

TRADITIONAL DUBAI

Walk alongside the Creek and it's easy to imagine life in Dubai half a century ago. The wooden dhows, whirring abras, bustling souqs, stately wind towers and graceful mosques have barely changed over the decades.

تكنولوجيا الإضاءة الأل

1 Jumeirah Mosque
Breathtaking in its intricate beauty (p75)

2 Dhow Wharfage
The dhows transport goods across the Arabian Sea for importing and re-exporting (p56)

3 *Abra* passengers, Dubai Creek
Traditional *abras* provide a link between Bur Dubai and Deira (p60)

4 A wind tower in Bastakia Quarter
Traditionally, wind towers cooled buildings (p61)

5 Al-Ahmadiya School
Museum exhibit at Dubai's oldest school, which dates back to 1912 (p56)

RICHARD L'A

BACK STREETS

Dubai's otherworldly mega projects got you craving a dose of reality? Wander the bustling back streets to find the true heart of a city that's become home to hundreds of thousands of people from across the globe.

BRENT WINEBRENNER

❶ Bur Dubai Souq, Deira
Friday evenings see the souq get lively (p61)

❷ Spice Souq
Follow your nose to stock up on some spices (p51)

❸ Camel-skin sandals
Step out in some colourful footwear found in a local souq (p61)

BRENT WINEBRE

RICHARD L'ANSON

WATERWAYS

The Palm Islands are nothing new – Dubai was built on water. Pearlers, fishermen, oilmen and dhow captains worked the Gulf and the Creek in the city's formative years, and today tourists flock to see the canals, marinas, waterparks and beaches.

TERRY CARTER

MARK DAFFEY

❶ Dubai Creek
Historic Dubai flanks the Creek (p57)

❷ The lake at Ras al-Khor Wildlife Sanctuary
Flocks of people come to this nature reserve at Ras al-Khor to watch the pink flamingos and enjoy the serene surroundings (p72)

❸ Wild Wadi Waterpark
You won't notice the view as you hurtle down waterslides at speeds up to 80km/h (p80)

SOCIAL SCENE

The phrase 'work hard, play hard' could have been coined for Dubai. Whether it's at a nightclub, a sheesha cafe, a wine bar or a restaurant, the city lets its collective hair down on Thursday and Friday nights.

PHIL WEYMOUTH

TERRY C

❶ Band Boom
Dubai's live music scene is growing, with plenty of local and international talent (p134)

❷ Wicked Beats
DJs reign supreme in Dubai's popular club scene (p132)

❸ Basta Art Cafe
Enjoy the outdoors over a drink (p113)

PHIL WEY

❶ Deira Gold Souq
Jewellery lovers will drool over the shiny stuff in this local souq (p51)

❷ Ibn Battuta Mall
Take a quick trip around the ancient world at this themed mall (p85)

❸ Mall of the Emirates
A sparkle of light and colour to put you in the mood to shop (p85)

HOLGER LEUE

TERRY CARTER

SHOPPING

The mall-makers' game of one-upmanship – from City Centre to Mall of the Emirates to Mall of Arabia – has turned this town into one big spree for shopaholics. Dubai isn't only the name of the city – it's an instruction.

RICHARD L'ANSON

1 **Camel riding in the desert**
Develop a meaningful relationship with a camel on a sunset ride (p170)

2 **Camel road-crossing sign**
There are camel-crossing-sign fridge magnets at the souqs, but this sign is for real (p101)

3 **Sandboarding** A local enjoying a slippery scratchy board ride down the dunes (p170)

HOLGER LEUE

DESERT-SCAPE

If you're feeling fearless you can ski, snowboard or drive across the desert dunes in a 4WD. If you want somebody else to do the hard work, travel the old-fashioned way and take a ride on the back of a camel.

CHRIS MELLOR

CHRISTINE OS

CONTENTS

THE AUTHOR

Andrea Schulte-Peevers

Andrea has travelled the distance to the moon and back in her visits to over 60 countries, but she'll forever cherish the memory of first flying into Dubai. Seeing only the tops of Burj Khalifa and its neighbouring towers soaring above a billowing layer of cottony fog seemed to perfectly symbolise the mystery, surrealism and ambition of this mega city. When she's not gallivanting around the globe, Andrea divides her time living in Berlin and Los Angeles, where she graduated from UCLA. She's authored or contributed to more than 40 Lonely Planet titles and traces her passion for Arab countries back to the three months she spent in Tunisia in the 1980s. Being asked to update the *Dubai City Guide* was a special thrill because it allowed her to get a closer look at this complex destination that's tip-toeing so deftly between tradition and turbo-modernity. Andrea also recently overhauled the United Arab Emirates chapter of Lonely Planet's *Oman, UAE & Arabian Peninsula* guide.

ANDREA'S TOP DUBAI DAY

My perfect day starts with flicking through the newspaper over a leisurely breakfast in the tranquil walled garden of the Basta Art Cafe (p113) in the historic Bastakia Quarter. Afterwards, I pop into Majlis Gallery (p61) and XVA Gallery (p61) to check out the latest exhibits before making my way to the Creek via delightfully claustrophobic Hindi Lane (p66) and the breezy Bur Dubai Souq (p61). A quick *abra* (water taxi) ride later I'm in Deira, where I stock up on saffron in the Spice Souq (p51) and hopscotch around gaggles of tourists going ga-ga over sparkling baubles in the Gold Souq (p51). Time to take a break from the bustle and spend the hottest hours of the day with a luxuriant massage at the Amara Spa (p142) in the Park Hyatt, followed by a light lunch at Cafe Arabesque (p110). Dipping and nibbling from a plate of inventive mezze at my terrace table, I feel blissfully relaxed as the yachts and dhows plough up and down the Creek. Limbered up and fortified, I'm ready catch the Dubai Metro Red Line at City Centre and head to Dubai Mall (p72) in the shadow of the rocket-like Burj Khalifa. I say 'hi' to my favourite giant grouper at the Dubai Aquarium & Underwater Zoo (p72) before indulging in a healthy dose of retail therapy. When it's 'wine-o'clock', I cab it over to the Jumeirah Beach Hotel to meet friends for a glass of chilled Chardonnay at 360° (p130) with front-row views of the Burj al-Arab (p79). For dinner, I treat myself to a delicious meal at Eauzone (p121) before winding down the day languidly puffing away in the Sheesha Courtyard (p135).

No matter whether you're a trendy urban nomad, a cocky jetsetter, a three-button suit or travelling with the tots, you should find all your needs and expectations met in Dubai. Tiny but turbo-charged, the city-state is a highly developed tourism destination that offers world-class shopping, lodging, eating, sports and relaxation beneath nearly year-round sunny skies. Crime is rare, almost everyone speaks English, tourists are unlikely to be hassled or ripped off, and most of them can obtain a visa on arrival. Room reservations are a good idea anytime except at the height of summer (June to early September) and especially around major holidays and festivals. Otherwise you can keep your advance planning to a minimum (but do have a look at the boxed text, p18).

It's important to realise that the United Arab Emirates is an Islamic country and behaviour that's tolerated in Western countries – such as kissing in public, drunkenness or swearing – may cause offence, or worse, get you into trouble with the law. While it boasts countless settings tailor-made for romance and plenty of good bars and pubs, Dubai might not be the perfect destination if you're planning a honeymoon or a stag weekend. And here's another caveat: Dubai's drug laws are extremely strict and even a microscopic speck of a controlled substance could see you arrested (see p190).

WHEN TO GO

The eye-catching room rates advertised for July and August come with a catch: the scorching heat (up to 48°C) and extreme humidity (as high as 95%) make being outside for longer than 10 minutes extremely uncomfortable. The best time to visit Dubai is between November and April, when the weather is pleasant and there's lots going on. Flick over to p186 for more information on climate. The month of Ramadan (see p189) is a fascinating time to visit if you're interested in Islam, but those planning to indulge themselves in Dubai's restaurants and bars might find the conservative laws imposed for the month too restrictive.

FESTIVALS & EVENTS

As part of their efforts to lure tourists to the city, Dubai authorities have encouraged the development of several major sporting and cultural events. All of these, with the exception of Dubai Summer Surprises (DSS), take place between October and March. For details of major sporting events, see p149. For information about religious holidays, see p188.

January
DUBAI SHOPPING FESTIVAL
www.mydsf.com
Reports of Russian millionaires chartering passenger jets so they can return from the Dubai Shopping Festival (DSF) with planeloads of purchases are probably exaggerated, but the annual instalment of DSF certainly attracts plenty of tourists each year. Discounts can be as high as 70% and there's plenty of live music, kids' events, sporting activities and nightly fireworks over the Creek to supplement your spending spree. Also see boxed text, p95.

GLOBAL VILLAGE
www.globalvillage.ae
At the hugely popular Global Village you can take a trip around the world in a couple of hours. Running from late November to late February, it features three dozen or more nations (mostly from Asia) who introduce their cultures, customs, food and wares in beautifully decorated pavilions. This and a busy schedule of music, dance, fireworks and other performances draw around 4.5 million visitors every year. Also see boxed text, p95.

February
DUBAI INTERNATIONAL JAZZ FESTIVAL
www.dubaijazzfest.com
This increasingly popular event has doo-wopped in Dubai since 2003. Performances take place over nine days in the outdoor amphitheatre at Dubai Media City and

have featured such heavyweights as James Morrison, the James Taylor Quartet, John Legend and James Blunt.

March

ART DUBAI
www.artdubai.ae

The arrival of this ambitious international art fair in 2007 signalled that art is big business in the Gulf, and the growing number of galleries around town confirms the trend. Madinat Jumeirah (p79) provides a suitably glamorous setting for the artists, dealers and gallery owners to mingle in and show off their stuff.

BASTAKIYA ART FAIR
www.bastakiyaartfair.com

This six-day indie art fair comes courtesy of the tireless folks at XVA Gallery (p61) and runs parallel to Art Dubai in the atmospheric wind tower houses of the historic Bastakia Quarter. Great for keeping tabs on young, innovative up-and-comers.

SHARJAH INTERNATIONAL ART BIENNIAL
☎ 06-568 5050

Held every two years (next in 2011) in the neighbouring emirate of Sharjah, this is one of the most important art events in the Arab world. It has fostered the dialogue between artists, institutions and organisations since 1993 and exhibits works of around 80 artists from around the world from March to May.

AL-AIN CLASSICS FESTIVAL
www.aacf.ae

International top talent – from Zubin Mehta to the Vienna Philharmonic Orchestra – perform concerts, opera and plays in the restored Al-Jahili fort in Al-Ain, about a 90-minute drive south of Dubai (see p173).

April

DUBAI FASHION WEEK
www.dfw.ae

For the latest local trends hot off the sewing machine, pay attention to the runway during this glam showcase for regional designers. Names to keep an eye on include the fashion house HSY, wedding gowns by Mariam Al Mazro and

the feminine dresses by Zaeem Jamal. The spring/summer collection is presented at a second event in October.

June, July & August

DUBAI SUMMER SURPRISES
www.mydsf.com

Perhaps the most surprising thing about DSS is that it manages to attract any visitors at all. It takes place, after all, at the sweaty height of the sweltering summer. But a combination of free kids' entertainment and big sales in shopping malls draws in plenty of tourists from other Gulf nations. Also see boxed text, p95.

October

GITEX
www.gitex.com

Find out what gadgets everyone wants for Christmas and snap up some bargains at this international consumer electronics fair held over five days in the Dubai International Convention and Exhibition Centre (DICEC).

SWIM THE BURJ
www.swimburjalarab.com

Benefiting the non-profit organisation Médecins Sans Frontières (Doctors without Borders), this charity event draws hundreds of swimmers to complete the 1km circle around the iconic Burj al-Arab hotel. There's one competitive heat and two non-competitive heats for families and relay teams.

MIDDLE EAST INTERNATIONAL FILM FESTIVAL
MEIFF; www.meiff.com

Stars, starlets, directors, critics and cinephiles descend upon Abu Dhabi to meet, mingle and present the latest flicks from around the region in a warm-up to the Dubai International Film Festival.

November & December

DUBAI INTERNATIONAL FILM FESTIVAL
www.dubaifilmfest.com

This excellent non-competitive film festival has brought a touch of Hollywood glamour to Madinat Jumeirah since 2004. It's a great place to catch international indie flicks as well as new releases from around the Arab world and the Indian subcontinent.

SHARJAH INTERNATIONAL BOOK FAIR
www.swbf.gov.ae
The neighbouring emirate of Sharjah stages one of the region's most significant book fairs. The 10-day annual event sees about 750 publishers showcasing books (in Arabic, English and other languages) from nearly 42 nations, drawing over 400,000 visitors. Readings, workshops and symposia supplement the exhibits.

UAE NATIONAL DAY
The birth of a nation in 1971 is celebrated across the country every year on 2 December with all sorts of events, from boat parades to fireworks, concerts to horse shows, traditional dances to military parades.

COSTS & MONEY

Dubai is not an inexpensive place to visit, but how much you end up spending very much depends on what kind of traveller you are and what experiences you wish to have. The daily tab for a stay in a midrange hotel, two sit-down meals, using taxis, and spending some money on going to bars and clubs should be somewhere between Dh700 to Dh1300 (per person, travelling as an adult couple). For mere survival, you'll need to budget around Dh200 per day, but this will have you staying in a youth hostel dorm, taking public transport rather than taxis, eating at budget restaurants and limiting your entertainment and alcohol intake.

There are also quite a few things that are free or practically free. It costs nothing to wander through the cacophonous Deira souqs or among the wind towers and courtyard houses of Bur Dubai. Dubai Museum and other historic sites are either free or cost just a few dirham admission. An *abra* (wooden water taxi) ride on the Creek can be had for Dh1. The spectacular dancing Dubai Fountain is free and so are a tour of Jumeirah Mosque, flamingo watching in the Ras al-Khor Wildlife Sanctuary and gallery hopping in Al-Quoz. There are long stretches of open sandy beaches and big parks for picnics and frolicking for the kids. Malls provide plenty of entertainment

HOW MUCH?

1L petrol **Dh1.35**

1L bottled water **Dh1.50**

Pint of draught beer **Dh25**

Dubai Metro ride **Dh2 to Dh6.50**

Taxi from Gold Souq to Burj al-Arab **Dh70**

Admission to Wild Wadi Waterpark **Dh195**

Evening desert safari **Dh275**

Shwarma **Dh5**

Set meal at budget Indian restaurant **Dh15**

Main course in top restaurant **Dh120**

beyond the shops, especially Dubai Mall, Mall of the Emirates and Ibn Battuta Mall.

And there are ways to stretch your budget even further. To save money when going out, it's worth picking up *The Entertainer*, a book containing hundreds of two-for-one meal vouchers. You'll also save a few dirhams by asking for local water rather than expensive imported bottles. Women can also take advantage of ladies' nights (usually on Tuesdays), when they get free drinks just for turning up.

Of course, if you're a high roller, Dubai has no shortage of luxury hotels, ultraposh restaurants and fancy bars to help you part with your money. Preferred pampering choices include a gourmet dinner at Verre by Gordon Ramsey, a night in a fantasy suite at the Burj al-Arab, a cordoned-off VIP booth at Sanctuary nightclub, being pummelled into a state of bliss at a fancy spa such as the Amara or the Talise Spa, or teeing off at the prestigious Emirates Golf Club.

INTERNET RESOURCES

Dubai City Guide (www.dubaicityguide.com) Decent information on happenings in town.

Dubai Kids (www.dubaikidz.biz) Good source for kiddie stuff around Dubai, plus tourist information.

Lonely Plant (www.lonelyplanet.com.au) For succinct summaries on travelling to Dubai. The Thorn Tree forum allows you to ask questions before you go and dispense advice when you get back.

UAE Government (www.government.ae) Official government site with lots of good information.

UAE Ministry of Information and Culture (www.uaeinteract.com) Covers just about every aspect of life in the UAE.

ADVANCE PLANNING

Unless you're visiting during summer, it is essential you book accommodation at least a few weeks in advance, especially if you're keen on staying in a particular place. Dinner reservations are always a good idea, especially on Thursday and Friday nights as well as for Friday brunches. While one day's notice is enough at most restaurants, you should book as much as a week in advance at the most popular haunts.

If you're hoping to catch a major sporting event such as the final of the Dubai Tennis Championships, Desert Classic or Rugby Sevens, it's necessary to book tickets several weeks in advance as these sell out every year. Time Out Tickets (www.itp.net/tickets) and Box Office Middle East (www.boxofficeme.com) sell tickets for major events, including concerts.

Treatments at fancy spas such as the Amara at Park Hyatt Dubai should also be booked a couple of weeks in advance, especially on Friday and Saturday. Check the website for treatment menus; some also have a booking function.

Booking tee-off times at big clubs like the Dubai Creek Golf Club a few weeks before you get into town is also a good idea.

SUSTAINABLE DUBAI

Being environmentally responsible in Dubai can be a challenge. Hotel rooms and many offices don't have recycling bins for waste paper, newspapers routinely come wrapped in plastic for no apparent reason, it's impossible to live without air-conditioning for at least half the year, and efforts to reuse plastic bags in supermarkets are nearly always greeted by bemused stares. And unless you're travelling overland from Oman or Saudi Arabia, you'll be adding another shoe size to your annual carbon footprint just getting to and from Dubai. But there are a few things you can do while in the city to make your visit more sustainable.

Taxis may generally be the fastest and most comfortable way to get around, but since late 2009 riding the Dubai Metro, which is cheap, clean and fast, is definitely an alternative. Buses are another option, although while safe and well-lit, they're also quite slow and not always reliable. See p182 for details of public transport.

Recycling bins are increasingly popping up in malls and bus and Metro stations, but there is no household recycling, and recycling centres are badly publicised and often poorly maintained. Some of the better ones can be found at the Ramada, Trade Centre Rd and Umm Suqeim branches of Spinneys, and at Emarat service stations.

When it comes to sightseeing, build your itinerary around more than the major sites and impacted hot spots. Exploring Bur Dubai or Deira on foot, jogging on the beach or picnicking in a park are all fun yet low-impact experiences.

The Emirates Environmental Group (www.eeg-uae .org) runs several campaigns every year to try to increase environmental awareness. These include desert and city clean-ups, and tree-planting campaigns. If you can't spare a day to pick up litter – you're on holiday after all – you'll help by doing the simple things: turning off the air-con when you go out, switching off lights during the day and resisting the temptation to linger extra long under that rainfall showerhead.

BACKGROUND

HISTORY

EARLY SETTLEMENT

Little is known about the early history of the area that now forms the United Arab Emirates (UAE). However, archaeological remains found in Al-Qusais, on the north-eastern outskirts of present-day Dubai, show evidence of humans here as far back as 8000 BC, after the end of the last Ice Age.

Up until 3000 BC the area supported nomadic herders of sheep, goats and cattle; these early inhabitants camped on the coast and fished during winter, then moved inland with their herds during summer (not so very different to what the Bedu did here just a short time ago). The first signs of trade emerged with the discovery of pottery from Ubaid (in present-day Iraq) dating back to 5000 BC. Agriculture developed with the cultivation of the date palm around 2500 BC, which not only provided food and a range of materials for building and weaving, but also shelter for smaller plants grown for food.

Archaeological evidence also suggests that this area, together with present-day Oman, was closely associated with the Magan civilisation during the Bronze Age. The Magans apparently dominated the ancient world's copper trade, exploiting the rich veins of copper in the hills throughout the Hajar Mountains, and near Sohar, in Oman. It's also likely that they traded pearls with people in Mesopotamia (now Iraq), and with the Indus Valley civilisation in present-day Pakistan. However, all records of the Magan civilisation cease after the 2nd millennium BC, with some historians speculating that the desertification of the area hastened its demise.

There's little archaeological evidence of occupation of Dubai during the Iron Age, with the next major habitation of the area appearing to have been by the Sassanid empire. Archaeological excavations at Jumeirah reveal a caravan station dating from the 6th century AD, which is thought to have had links with the Sassanids. A dynasty that ruled in Persia from AD 224 to 651, the Sassanids wielded amazing power over the region during this time, until the Umayyads, an Islamic tribe, uprooted them. Archaeologists seem to think that the buildings at Jumeirah were restored and extended by the Umayyad dynasty, making it the only site in the UAE to span the pre-Islamic and Islamic periods.

With the Umayyads came the Arabic language and unification with the Islamic world. Christianity made a brief appearance in the form of the Nestorian sect, members of which had a monastery on Sir Bani Yas Island, west of Abu Dhabi, in the 5th century. However, it was the arrival of Islam that shaped the future of the region. Unfortunately the early Islamic period from the 7th to the 14th century hasn't been well documented in the UAE. All that's known is that during this period the area was loosely under the control of the Umayyads and their successors, the Abbasids. After the Baghdad-based Abbasid dynasty went into decline around AD 1000, the centre of power in the Islamic world shifted to Cairo, leaving the UAE on the periphery. In the absence of centralised control, the tribes of the Arabian Peninsula asserted themselves in the hinterlands, while the coastal regions were dominated by trading ports such as Julfar,

TIMELINE

c 3000 BC	AD 700	1580
The Dubai area is populated by nomadic herders of sheep, cattle and goats. The Magan civilisation dominates the world's copper trade and mines for metal near the Hajar Mountains.	From their capital in Damascus, the Umayyads introduce Arabic and Islam to the region. The Umayyad Caliphate was the first dynasty of Islam, and lasted from AD 650 to 750.	Gasparo Balbi, a Venetian jeweller, tours the region to investigate its potential for the pearling trade. He notes in his records that he visits a town in the Gulf called 'Dibeï'.

near present-day Ras al-Khaimah, and Hormuz, an island in the Strait of Hormuz. Trade soon became the backbone of the local economy as ships travelled as far as China, returning laden with silk and porcelain.

EUROPEAN PRESENCE

In the 16th century, Portugal became the first European power to take an interest in this part of the Gulf, attracted by lucrative trade routes to India and the Far East. The arrival of the well-armed Portuguese was a disaster for Muslim traders. The Portuguese wanted a monopoly on trade routes between Europe and India and tolerated no rivals. Local trade dried up to the extent that many coastal settlements were just about abandoned, with tribes taking refuge in oases far from the coast, such as Liwa and Al-Ain. While Portugal's occupation lasted until the 1630s, eventually extending as far north as Bahrain, the only evidence of their presence are the two cannons on display at the Dubai Museum (p60).

Next to arrive were the French and Dutch, who infiltrated the area in the 17th and 18th centuries and aspired to control the trading routes to the east. The British were equally intent on ruling the seas to protect the sea route to India, and in 1766 the Dutch finally gave way to Britain's East India Company, which had established trading links with the Gulf as early as 1616.

Throughout this time Dubai remained a small fishing and pearling hamlet, perched on a disputed border between two local powers – the seafaring Qawasim of present-day Ras al-Khaimah and Sharjah to the north, and the Bani Yas tribal confederation of what is now Abu Dhabi to the south. The region was also affected by the rivalries between bigger regional powers – the Wahhabi tribes (of what is now Saudi Arabia), the Ottoman Empire, the Persians and the British.

THE TRUCIAL COAST

At the beginning of the 19th century, Dubai was governed by Mohammed bin Hazza, who remained in charge until 1833, when the Al Bu Fasalah, a branch of the Bani Yas tribe from Abu Dhabi, came to dominate the town, severing it from Abu Dhabi. The Bani Yas were the main power among the Bedouin tribes of the interior. Originally based in Liwa, an oasis on the edge of the desert known as the Empty Quarter (Rub' al-Khali) in the south of the UAE, the Bani Yas engaged in traditional Bedouin activities of camel herding, small-scale agriculture, tribal raiding and extracting protection money from merchant caravans passing through their territory. At the end of the 18th century, the leader of the Bani Yas moved from Liwa to the island of Abu Dhabi on the coast.

About 800 members of the Al Bu Fasalah tribal branch settled by the Dubai Creek under the leadership of Maktoum bin Butti (r 1833–52), who established the Al-Maktoum dynasty of Dubai, which still rules the emirate today. For Maktoum bin Butti, good relations with the British authorities in the Gulf were essential to safeguard his small upstart sheikhdom against attack from the larger and more powerful sheikhdoms of Sharjah to the north and Abu Dhabi to the south.

In 1841 the Bur Dubai settlement extended to Deira on the northern side of the Creek, though throughout the 19th century it largely remained a tiny enclave of fishermen, pearl divers, Bedouin, and Indian and Persian merchants. Interestingly, the Indians and Persians (now Iranians) are still largely the custodians of the area and give much of the Creek its character today.

1833	1892	1930
Approximately 800 members of the Al-Maktoum family leave Abu Dhabi for Bur Dubai and establish power in the emirate under Maktoum bin Butti. When smallpox breaks out in 1841, people relocate to Deira, which soon becomes larger than Bur Dubai.	The sheikhdoms sign a treaty with Britain; they'd have no dealings with other foreign powers and receive protection from British armed forces in return. Sheikh Maktoum lures foreign traders to Dubai by declaring they would be exempt from paying taxes.	The worldwide Great Depression precipitated by the Wall Street Crash of 1929, paired with the arrival of a new method of creating pearls artificially, prompts Sheikh Rashid to conclude that the pearling industry is finished.

HISTORY BOOKS

There's lots of terrific stuff out there on Dubai history. While not all of these books are specifically about Dubai, there's some great reading here about the region's history.

- *Telling Tales: an Oral History of Dubai* by Julia Wheeler – A beautiful book of black-and-white photography and interviews with a cross-section of Emiratis reveals what life in Dubai was like before it started resembling a set from a science-fiction movie.
- *Father of Dubai: Sheikh Rashid bin Saeed al-Maktoum* by Graeme Wilson – A photographic and narrative tribute to Sheikh Mohammed's father.
- *From Trucial States to United Arab Emirates* by Frauke Heard-Bey – An insight into a society in transition, including the development of Dubai, by a leading scholar and long-term UAE expat.
- *Seafarers of the Emirates* by Ronald Codrai – This remarkable record recreates the lives of pearl divers, merchants, shipbuilders and seafarers, with photos taken in Dubai in the middle of the 20th century.
- *Arabian Destiny* by Edward Henderson – This wry memoir by a British colonial official includes perceptive observations of the society he lived in: Dubai hasn't simply changed since the 1950s, it's become a different place altogether.
- *Sheikhdoms of Eastern Arabia* by Peter Lienhardt and Ahmed al-Shahi – An insight into how oil wealth altered Arabia, tribal structure, gender relations, and the complex relationship between the ruling sheikhs and their subjects.
- *The Merchants: the Big Business Families of Saudi Arabia and the Gulf States* by Michael Field – A brief sketch of the rise of Dubai as a trading centre, and the role played by its powerful tribal relationships.
- *Dubai: Gilded Cage* by Syed Ali – A close (and highly critical) examination of Dubai's turbo-speed metamorphosis, the forces that made it happen and the brand created in the process.
- *City of Gold: Dubai and the Dream of Capitalism* by Jim Krane – Another take on Dubai's remarkable rags-to-riches story written by a locally based journalist.
- *Dubai: The Vulnerability of Success* by Christopher M. Davidson – This Dubai case study spans the arc of history from the pearling days to 21st century big-time boomtown.

Things really began to change around the end of the 19th century. In 1892 the British, keen to impose their authority on the region and protect their Indian empire, extended their power through a series of so-called exclusive agreements, under which the sheikhs accepted formal British protection and, in exchange, promised to have no dealings with other foreign powers without British permission. As a result of these treaties, or truces, Europeans called the area 'the Trucial Coast', a name it retained until the 1971 federation.

In 1894 Dubai's visionary ruler at the time, Sheikh Maktoum bin Hasher al-Maktoum (r 1894–1906), decided to give foreign traders tax-exempt status, and the free port of Dubai was born. Around the same time, Sharjah, the area's main trading centre, began losing its trade to Dubai, and Lingah (now Bandar-e Langeh), across the Strait of Hormuz in Iran, lost its status as a duty-free port. The Maktoums lured Lingah's disillusioned traders to Dubai and also managed to convince some of Sharjah's merchants to relocate.

At first the Persians who came to Dubai believed that it would just be a temporary move, but by the 1920s, when it became evident that the trade restrictions in southern Iran were there to stay, they took up permanent residence in the area of today's Bastakia Quarter (p61).

More good news for Dubai came in the early 20th century when the Maktoums, probably with the assistance of the Persian merchants, prevailed on a British steamship line to switch its

1940	1946	1951
There is a brief conflict between Dubai and Sharjah following a dispute in the Maktoum family. Hostilities ceased after the British cut off the supply lines and both sides ran out of gunpowder.	Sheikh Zayed bin Sultan al-Nahyan makes his political debut at the age of 38 when he is appointed ruler's representative in his hometown of Al-Ain.	The British government establishes the Trucial States Council, which brings together the leaders of the sheikhdoms that would later form the UAE. It was the first time the leaders had regularly gathered to communicate.

BOOKS: ARABS & THE ARAB WORLD

Dubai may get only the briefest of mentions in these books, but they'll give you a solid understanding of the region in which Dubai is a now a central focus.

- *The Arabs* by Peter Mansfield – This must-read book discusses Arabs, their characteristics, aspirations and future, from the pre-Islamic Arabian nomads, through the life of Prophet Mohammed, to the modern Arab renaissance.
- *Arabia and the Arabs: from the Bronze Age to the Coming of Islam* by Robert G Hoyland – From inscriptions, poetry, histories and archaeological evidence, you learn about Arabia, from ancient Sheba to the deserts and oases of the north.
- *A History of the Arab Peoples* by Albert Hourani – A bestseller when first published in 1991 (updated 2003), this superb book covers politics, culture, society, economy and thought.
- *Travellers in Arabia* by Robin Bidwell – Arabia as experienced by its earliest tourists: Burckhardt, Burton, Palgrave, Philby, Stark, Cox and Thesiger.
- *Arabian Sands* by Wilfred Thesiger – Fascinating accounts of five years spent with the Bedu of the Arabian Peninsula in the Empty Quarter (Rub' al-Khali) in the 1940s.
- *The New Gulf – How Modern Arabia is Changing the World for Good* by Edmund O'Sullivan – A cutting-edge look at how the growing affluence and influence of the Gulf States, including the UAE, will lead to greater economical, social and political stability in the entire region.

main port of call in the lower Gulf from Lingah to Dubai. This gave Dubai regular links with British India and the ports of the central and northern Gulf – Bahrain, Kuwait, Bushire and Basra. Dubai's importance to Britain as a port of call would remain in place for half a century, marking the beginning of Dubai's growth as a trading power and fuelling the prosperity that would follow.

THE EXPANDING CITY

By the beginning of the 20th century, Dubai was well established and had a population approaching 10,000. Deira was the most populous area at this time, with about 1600 houses, inhabited mainly by Arabs, but also by Persians and Baluchis, who came from parts of what are now Iran, Pakistan and Afghanistan. By 1908 there were about 350 shops in Deira and another 50 in Bur Dubai, where the Indian community was concentrated. To this day the Bur Dubai Souq (p61) shows a strong Indian influence, and Bur Dubai is home to the only Hindu temple in the city.

The development of Dubai as a major trading centre was, ironically, spurred on by the collapse of the pearling trade, which had been the mainstay of its economy for centuries. The pearling trade had fallen victim both to the worldwide Great Depression of 1929–34 and to the Japanese discovery (in 1930) of a method by which pearls could be cultured artificially. Sheikh Saeed al-Maktoum (r 1912–58), whose residence is now a museum (p60), concluded that the pearling industry was finished and started to look for alternative forms of revenue. This chain of events heralded a new era in Dubai's trade: re-exporting. Dubai's enterprising merchants began importing goods to sell them on to other ports. In practice, this involved the smuggling of goods, particularly of gold, to India. The goods entered and exited Dubai legally; it was the countries at the other end of the trade that saw it as smuggling.

1958	1966	1968
After almost 20 years of de facto leadership, Sheikh Rashid officially becomes ruler of Dubai. He had been regent since 1939 but could only assume the position of leader after his father's death.	Eight years after oil is discovered offshore in Abu Dhabi, Dubai makes its own discovery. The arrival of oil persuades traders from across the region to settle in Dubai, spurring a period of rapid economic growth.	The British announce that they will be ending their relationship with the Trucial States by 1971 and local leaders discuss the possibility of a future nation. In 1969, Dubai starts exporting crude oil and petrodollars flood in, reaching a peak in 1991.

WWII also played a role in the growth of the re-export trade. The war brought much of Dubai's trade to a standstill and this was compounded by a shortage of basic food supplies. The British government supplied the Trucial sheikhdoms with plenty of rice and sugar. Dubai merchants bought these goods cheaply and, finding themselves oversupplied, shipped them off to the black market in Iran.

In 1939 Sheikh Rashid bin Saeed al-Maktoum (r 1958–90) took over as regent from his father, Sheikh Saeed, but he only formally succeeded to the leadership when his father died in 1958. He quickly moved to bolster the emirate's position as the main trading hub in the lower Gulf, at the same time as the rulers of Sharjah made the costly mistake of allowing their harbour to silt up.

In 1951 the Trucial States Council was founded, for the first time bringing together the rulers of the sheikhdoms of what would become the UAE. The direct predecessor of the UAE Supreme Council, it met only twice a year, under the aegis of the British political agent in Dubai. It was around this time that modern Dubai began to take shape. Sheikh Rashid became one of the earliest beneficiaries of Kuwait's Fund for Arab Economic Development, created by the Kuwaiti government in 1961 to provide financial and technical assistance to developing Arab countries. Rashid used the money to dredge the Creek (it had become badly silted up, reducing the volume of Creek traffic) and to build a new breakwater near its mouth. But he caught the biggest break when oil was discovered in Dubai in 1966. The first cargo load left town three years later. The discovery of oil greatly accelerated the modernisation of the region and was a major factor in the formation of the UAE.

PEARLING

The heyday of pearling is laced with romanticism. But unfortunately for those who dove in the depths to collect pearls, it was a life of hardship and the rewards were no match for the dangers involved. Most of the divers were slaves from East Africa and the profits of the industry went straight to their master, the boat owner.

The only equipment the divers used was a rope tied around their waist, a turtle-shell peg on their nose and leather finger gloves to protect their hands from the sharp coral and shells. At certain times of the year they'd wear a muslin bodysuit to protect them from jellyfish stings. The best pearls were found at depths of up to 36m and divers would be underwater for around three minutes. To reach this depth, they held a rope weighted with a stone and tied to the boat, and then were thrown overboard.

The pearl-diving season lasted from May until September. On the ship there would be divers; men responsible for hauling up the divers after each job; a cook; and boys employed to serve food and water, and open the oyster shells. Each boat also had a singer, called the *naham*, whose job was to lead the crew in songs or lighten their mood by singing to them. Many of the songs were about lucky men who had become rich through diving, and the joys of returning home after the diving season.

Back on shore, pearl merchants would grade the pearls according to size using a number of copper sieves, each with different-sized holes. The greatest market for pearls was originally India, but in the early 20th century the UK and US also became keen buyers. The discovery of the means to make artificial pearls in the early 20th century triggered the demise of the industry. The Dubai Museum (p60) and the Diving Village (p66) feature informative displays on pearling.

1971	1973	1979
The Trucial States is re-established as the UAE. Qatar and Bahrain opt out of the union and declare independence. Sheikh Zayed of Abu Dhabi is named the new nation's first president.	The dirham replaces the riyal as the official unit of currency in Dubai. Until 1966, all the sheikhdoms had used the Gulf rupee. The dirham has been pegged to the US dollar since 1997.	Sheikh Rashid is declared prime minister of the UAE. The post had been held by his son, Sheikh Maktoum, who stepped aside to give his father more power.

THE ARCHITECTS OF MODERN DUBAI

Sheikh Rashid bin Saeed al-Maktoum

Remembered fondly as the 'Father of Dubai', Sheikh Rashid laid the foundations of the modern city. When he became ruler in 1958, Dubai was a small town with a very limited infrastructure. Within a few years of coming to power, he had dramatically improved the police force and school system, built a modern hospital and a network of roads, and established a steady supply of electricity and water. His decisions to dredge the Creek and construct an international airport provided a huge logistical boost to Dubai's trade-focused economy. The discovery of oil in 1966 enticed people from across the region to migrate to Dubai and tap into the petrodollar boom, doubling the emirate's population between 1967 and 1973. In the last two decades of his life, Sheikh Rashid oversaw the construction of the ports at Mina Rashid and Jebel Ali; the World Trade Centre; Al-Maktoum Bridge and Al-Shindaga Tunnel; and the city's first free zone, in Jebel Ali. In 1985 he helped establish Emirates Airlines, which has been instrumental in fashioning Dubai as a tourism destination.

Sheikh Maktoum bin Rashid al-Maktoum

When Sheikh Rashid passed away in 1990 after a prolonged illness, Sheikh Maktoum officially succeeded his father, although in reality he'd already been working hard to ensure that Dubai's next generation reaped the benefits of the burgeoning economy. Spreading the wealth through education, housing and greater job opportunities, and all the while diversifying Dubai's economic portfolio, his work set a solid platform for the phenomenal growth of Dubai today. In the later years of Sheik Maktoum's reign, his younger brother Mohammed began working on a more active (and economically aggressive) expansion of Dubai, succeeding him as ruler upon his death in 2006.

THE RECENT PAST

When Britain announced its departure from the region in 1968, an attempt was made to create a nation that included the seven emirates that made up the Trucial States (today's United Arab Emirates) as well as Bahrain and Qatar. While the talks collapsed with Bahrain and Qatar (who both moved on to their own independence), the leader of Abu Dhabi, Sheikh Zayed bin Sultan al-Nahyan (see boxed text, opposite), and his counterpart in Dubai, Sheikh Rashid bin Saeed al-Maktoum of Dubai, strengthened their commitment to creating a single state.

After persistent persuasion by Sheikh Zayed, the federation of the UAE was born on 2 December 1971, consisting of the emirates of Dubai, Abu Dhabi, Ajman, Fujairah, Sharjah and Umm al-Quwain, with Ras al-Khaimah joining in 1972. Impressively, the UAE remains to this day the only federation of Arab states in the Middle East.

Under that agreement, the emirs had approved a formula whereby Abu Dhabi and Dubai (in that order) would carry the most weight in the federation, but would leave each emir largely autonomous. Sheikh Zayed became the supreme ruler (or president) of the UAE, and Sheikh Rashid of Dubai assumed the role of vice-president.

Since federation, Dubai has been one of the most politically stable city-states in the Arab world; however, the fledgling nation has still had its teething problems. Border disputes between the emirates continued throughout the 1970s and '80s, and the level of independence that each emirate assumes has always been the subject of long discussions.

1990	1996	2006
Sheikh Rashid dies during the first Gulf War and his son, Sheikh Maktoum, takes over as ruler of Dubai. Five years later, Maktoum's brother Mohammed is made Crown Prince of Dubai, assumes de facto rule and is soon seen as the major figure in local politics.	Two major annual events, the Dubai Shopping Festival and the Dubai World Cup, are launched. American racehorse Cigar is the first winner of the Cup. The Burj al-Arab opens, enhancing Dubai's reputation as a tourist mecca.	Sheikh Mohammed becomes ruler of Dubai after Sheikh Maktoum's passing, and is also confirmed as Prime Minister and Vice-President of the UAE.

While Dubai and Abu Dhabi had an agreement to cooperate long before the nation was born, the relationship has not been without its difficulties. Achieving an equitable balance of power between the two emirates, as well as refining a unified vision for the country, was much debated until 1979 when Sheikh Zayed and Sheikh Rashid sealed a formal compromise under which each gave a little ground on his vision of the country. The result was a much stronger federation in which Dubai remained a bastion of free trade while Abu Dhabi imposed a tighter federal structure on the other emirates. Rashid also agreed to take the title of Prime Minister as a symbol of his commitment to the federation.

Sheikh Rashid, the driving force behind Dubai's phenomenal growth and 'father of (modern) Dubai', died in 1990 after a long illness, and was succeeded as emir by the eldest of his four sons, Sheikh Maktoum bin Rashid al-Maktoum. Maktoum had already been regent for his sick father for several years and continued to put his energies towards further expanding Dubai.

Overseeing Dubai's transformation into a 21st-century metropolis is the third son of the dynasty, Sheikh Mohammed bin Rashid al-Maktoum, who was the face of modern Dubai even before he succeeded his older brother as ruler in 2006. Having ruled Dubai as a de facto leader since the mid 1990s, Sheikh Mohammed has brought consistency and continuity to Dubai in a period of tremendous social, cultural and economic change. In February 2008 he named his son Hamdan bin Mohammed bin Rashid al-Maktoum, also known as 'Fazza 3', as the emirate's crown prince and his likely successor. The young prince is already tremendously popular – check out his fan videos on YouTube or friend him on Facebook.

FATHER OF THE NATION

Visitors to Dubai will no doubt see enormous posters of a smiling sheikh in a pair of Ray Ban–style sunglasses – this is Sheikh Zayed bin Sultan al-Nahyan, the first, and up until his death in 2004, the only president of the UAE. Revered by his people, and often called 'father' by Emiratis, he commanded huge respect across the Middle East.

Sheikh Zayed was born in Abu Dhabi in 1918, and his father was ruler of the emirate from 1922 to 1926. After his father's death in 1927, Sheikh Zayed relocated to Al-Ain and spent his time studying the Quran and learning from local Bedouin tribesmen; the knowledge he gained here was crucial to his ability to pull a nation together decades later.

His first taste of politics came in 1946, when he was appointed ruler's representative in Al-Ain, where he honed his famed negotiating skills. When the oil began flowing in Abu Dhabi in 1962, it soon became apparent that Sheikh Zayed had the right skills to handle the massive changes that were to come, and the sheikh soon took over from his older brother in managing Abu Dhabi's affairs. Seizing the opportunity, Sheikh Zayed built schools, hospitals and housing for his people, and when the British decided to withdraw from the Trucial States in 1968, he set out to federate the states and create a nation.

The act of pulling together these often-squabbling, sometimes-fighting seven states is key to Sheikh Zayed's legacy. Few thought it could be done, and fewer thought it would last, but for three years Sheikh Zayed negotiated, cajoled and convinced the other states that a United Arab Emirates was the only way forward.

After he became president in 1971 (and was continually re-elected to the post up until his death), the distribution of wealth to the poorer emirates, as well as his handling of an ambitious Dubai, were key in keeping the fledgling nation together.

Sheikh Zayed had an almost obsessive ambition to 'green' the Emirates and to keep tradition alive. Even though in the Middle East it's almost obligatory to praise leaders, both past and present, in the UAE even the most cynical students of Arab politics note that the affection the people have for this leader runs far deeper than that.

2008	2009	2010
The world financial crisis severely impacts Dubai's economy in late 2008, putting the brakes on its surging development and causing a plunge in real estate prices of up to 50%.	Stock markets worldwide tumble temporarily when Dubai's debt rises to US$80 billion dollars and only stabilise after a US$10 billion cash injection from the Abu Dhabi government to help pay off immediate obligations.	Burj Khalifa, at 828m the world's tallest building, opens on 4 January. Hamas official Mahmoud al-Mabhouh is assassinated in a Dubai hotel room, allegedly in retaliation for his suspected role in the 1989 killing of two Israeli soldiers.

ECONOMY

The UAE has the world's seventh-largest oil reserves (after Saudi Arabia, Iran, Iraq, Canada, Kuwait and Venezuela), but the vast majority of it is concentrated in the emirate of Abu Dhabi. It is thought that at current levels of production, reserves will last for only another century and, sensibly, the country is looking at other industries to take over from oil in the future. Dubai handled this with particular foresight, largely thanks to the vision and ambition of Sheikh Mohammed bin Rashid al-Maktoum. Its reserves of oil and gas were never huge, but it used its resources wisely towards financing a modern and efficient infrastructure for trade, manufacturing and tourism. Today, about 82% of the UAE's non-oil GDP is generated in Dubai, and about 95% of Dubai's GDP (US$81 billion in 2008) is not oil-based. Inflation slowed down significantly in 2009 and now hovers around 3.5%.

In fact, until September 2008 it looked as if Dubai had the Midas touch. But then the world financial crisis struck and the emirate's economy collapsed like the proverbial house of cards. Real estate was particularly hard hit, with prices plummeting as much as 50%. The bubble had finally burst and Dubai was left with a staggering debt of at least US$80 billion. When the government announced, in November 2009, that it would seek a six-month standstill to put off repayment of its debt, including a US$4 billion Islamic bond due in December, it sent worldwide stock markets into a tailspin. Markets stabilised quickly after the Abu Dhabi government rode to the rescue with a US$10 billion loan, which seems generous until you realise that oil-rich Abu Dhabi actually has a balance sheet of US$600 billion. Still, in January 2010, officially out of gratitude, Sheikh Mohammed named the world's tallest building – which had thus far been referred to as Burj Dubai – Burj Khalifa in honour of the UAE president and ruler of Abu Dhabi, Sheikh Khalifa bin Zayed al-Nahyan. It remains to be seen whether the loan was merely a stopgap measure or whether it will buy enough time for Dubai to restructure its finances and put itself on a slower but more sustainable growth path.

Dubai imports an enormous amount of goods, primarily minerals and chemicals, base metals (including gold), vehicles and machinery, electronics, textiles and foodstuffs; the main importers into Dubai are the US, China, Japan, the UK, South Korea and India. Exports are mainly oil, natural gas, dates, dried fish, cement and electric cables; top export destinations are the other Gulf States, India, Japan, Taiwan, Pakistan and the US. Dubai's re-export trade (where items such as white goods come into Dubai from the manufacturers and are then sent onwards) makes up about 80% of the UAE's total re-export business. Dubai's re-exports go mainly to Iran, India, Saudi Arabia, Kuwait, China and Afghanistan.

SHEIKH MOHAMMED – MR DUBAI

When in 2008, Dubai's current ruler, Sheikh Mohammed bin Rashid al-Maktoum, was named one of the world's 100 most influential people by *Time* magazine, it surprised no one. Having spent several years as a de facto ruler while he was crown prince, Sheikh Mohammed was the only candidate for the top job when his brother, Sheikh Maktoum, died in early 2006. Although he is surrounded by some of the greatest minds in the Gulf, as well as political and economic expertise imported from all over the world, there's no uncertainty about where executive power lies. 'Sheikh Mo', as he is affectionately called, has a flair for generating publicity for the city and was deeply involved in the planning and construction of landmark projects such as the Burj al-Arab, Palm Jumeirah and Burj Khalifa. For the Burj al-Arab project, it's said that the sheikh wanted a design that would be as resonant as the Eiffel Tower and the Sydney Opera House.

In addition to handling the day-to-day running of the emirate, in his capacity as Prime Minister and Vice-President of the UAE Sheikh Mohammed strengthens the bond between Dubai and the other six emirates, while his ownership of Dubai Holding gives him control of numerous businesses such as the Jumeirah Group (properties including the Burj al-Arab), Tatweer (Dubailand) and TECOM (Internet City). He's also a keen fan of falconry and equestrianism and runs the Godolphin Stables. He is believed to be worth at least US$10 billion.

Visitors from Western countries may feel uncomfortable with the large-scale portraits of the ruler on billboards and buildings around town. Yet these are not simply the propaganda tools of an autocratic regime; many people in Dubai revere their ruler. Few world leaders are able to drive themselves around town without a bodyguard and without any fear of being attacked. Although dissenting voices aren't tolerated and the local media is uncritical, most people admire the Emirates' leaders for creating a haven of peace and prosperity in a troubled part of the world.

Dubai is home to the world's largest man-made harbour and biggest port in the Middle East. Called Jebel Ali, it's at the far western edge of Dubai, en route towards Abu Dhabi. The Jebel Ali Free Zone, established in 1985, is home to 5500 companies from 120 countries and has contributed hugely to Dubai's economic diversification. Companies are enticed here by the promise of full foreign ownership, full repatriation of capital and profits, no corporate tax for 15 years, no currency restrictions, and no personal income tax. Other industry-specific free zones such as Dubai Internet City and Dubai Media City have added a hi-tech information and communication stratum to the city's economy. IT firms based here include Google, HP, Dell and Oracle. Reuters, CNN, CNBC, MBC, Sony, Showtime and Bertelsmann are among the media companies that have set up shop in town.

Meanwhile, near Jebel Ali, the world's biggest airport is taking shape. When completed, Al-Maktoum International Airport is expected to handle 120 million passengers and 12 million tonnes of freight per year (also see boxed text, p180). Meanwhile, the existing airport, Dubai International, is the busiest in the Middle East and is the base of Emirates, the region's biggest airline.

Dubai's tourism industry has also exploded. The city's relative tolerance of Western habits, profusion of quality hotels, long stretches of beach, warm winter weather, shopping incentives and desert activities have helped it become the leading tourist destination in the Gulf.

For Emirati citizens all this prosperity translates into benefits of which the rest of the world only dreams: free health care, free education, heavily subsidised utilities and, in some cases, free housing. Dubai's per capita income is around Dh80,000 per annum, while the monthly salary of an unskilled expat labourer is anywhere between Dh500 to Dh1000 per month.

But while the globalisation of the international labour market (read: cheap foreign labour) has made the phenomenal growth of Dubai so attainable, there is one hurdle in the economy that Dubai is seeking to overcome. Dubai is highly dependent upon this expat labour and, at the same time, its citizens are having trouble finding meaningful employment. While the government in the past had made some attempt to 'Emiratise' the economy by placing nationals in the public workforce and imposing local employee quotas on private companies, this hasn't been particularly successful. One of the problems is that private companies are reluctant to hire nationals, often due to the misguided notion that they are lazy. A more likely reason, though, is that nationals expect to start on a salary that's far above what the equivalent expat would receive. There is no doubt that Dubai will be dependent on foreign labour and expertise for a long time to come.

GOVERNMENT & POLITICS

Dubai is the second most powerful of the seven emirates that make up the UAE, with Abu Dhabi being both the capital and home to most of the country's oil wealth. In each emirate, power rests with a ruling tribe, which in Dubai's case is the Maktoum family. The term 'emirate' is derived from the word 'emir', which means ruler, although the rulers of the emirates are known as sheikhs. As yet, there are no political parties or general elections in Dubai and, even if there were, it would be hard to imagine the Maktoums being deposed, having been in power since 1833.

Despite Dubai becoming so strong over the last few years, it has had to fight long and hard to preserve as much of its independence as possible and to minimise the power of the country's federal institutions. Along with Ras al-Khaimah, it maintains a legal system that is separate from the federal judiciary.

Politically, the relative interests of the seven emirates are fairly clear. Abu Dhabi is the largest and wealthiest emirate and has the biggest population. It is, therefore, the dominant member of the federation and is likely to remain so for some time. Dubai is the second largest emirate by population, with both an interest in upholding its free-trade policies and a pronounced independent streak. However, its dependence on Abu Dhabi became abundantly clear during the financial turmoil of 2008/9 when the capital had to bail out Dubai on several occasions. The other emirates are dependent on subsidies from Abu Dhabi, though the extent of this dependence varies widely.

The seven rulers form the Supreme Council, the highest body in the land, which ratifies federal laws and sets general policy. New laws can be passed with the consent of five of the seven

THE ROAD TO DEMOCRACY

Slowly but surely, the UAE is taking tentative steps towards democracy. Since 2006, half the country's Federal National Council (FNC), a 40-person body established to review and debate legislation, has been elected; the other 20 are appointed by each emirate. But the FNC has no real power; it can only advise the government, and only 6689 people have been hand-picked to vote – less than 1% of Emiratis and a tiny fraction of the UAE's total population – for candidates on a list approved by the government. Eight women are FNC members, although only one was elected. While full democracy in the UAE may be decades away, there are plans to grant the FNC some legislative powers and eventually to give the vote to all UAE citizens.

rulers. The Supreme Council also elects one of the emirs to a five-year term as the country's president. After the death of the founder of the country and its first president, Sheikh Zayed, in late 2004, power passed peacefully to his son Sheikh Khalifa bin Zayed al-Nahyan.

There is also a Council of Ministers, or cabinet, headed by the prime minister, who appoints ministers from all the emirates. Naturally, the more populous and wealthier emirates like Abu Dhabi and Dubai have greater representation. The cabinet and Supreme Council are advised, but can't be overruled, by a parliamentary body called Federation National Council (FNC). Since 2006, half of its 40 members have been elected (also see boxed text, left).

IDENTITY & LIFESTYLE
IDENTITY

Dubai's population clocked in at 1.78 million in February 2010, a giant leap from 183,200 in 1975. Fewer than 10% of Dubai's total population are Emiratis; the expatriate community makes up the rest of the population – one of the most multicultural in the world. Three quarters of the population is male.

In stark contrast to neighbouring Saudi Arabia and nearby Iran, Dubai is a tolerant and easygoing society, with its cultural and social life firmly rooted in Islam. Most religions – Judaism is a noteworthy exception – are tolerated and places of worship have been built for Christians, Hindus and Sikhs. Day-to-day activities, relationships, diet and dress are very much dictated by religion (see boxed text, p40). Gender roles are changing, with more and more women wanting to establish careers before marriage. With successful Emirati women such as Sheikha Lubna al-Qasimi (who in 2004 became the first woman to hold a ministerial position in the UAE) and Dr Amina Rostamani (CEO of TECOM, a corporation that oversees several free trade zones) serving as role models, women's contribution to the workforce has grown considerably in the past decade.

Take comments you may hear about Dubai being fake and a 'shopping culture' with a pinch of salt – shopping is merely a pastime, albeit an extremely popular one. Emirati cultural identity is expressed through poetry, traditional song and dance, a love of the desert and nature, and of camels, horses and falconry, all of which remain popular activities. If you're lucky enough to be invited to a wedding (and you should take up the offer), it's a great way to see some of these cultural traditions in action.

Dubai has been quite active in preserving and publicly displaying many local sights and traditions. The Dubai Museum (p60), the Bastakia Quarter (p61), the Al-Ahmadiya School (p56), Heritage House (p56) and Sheikh Saeed al-Maktoum House (p61) all give insights into traditional and cultural life. The aim of such preservation efforts is not just to attract and entertain tourists, but to educate young Emiratis about the value of their culture and heritage. Families also make an effort to maintain their heritage by taking their kids out to the desert frequently and teaching them how to continue traditional practices such as falconry.

One matter of great concern to the authorities is the ongoing trend for Emirati men to marry foreign women. One reason for the trend is the prohibitive cost of a traditional wedding, plus the dowry the groom must provide – essentially, it's cheaper and easier to marry a foreign woman. Another factor is that as Emirati women are becoming better educated, they're less willing to settle down in the traditional role of an Emirati wife. The issue comes up frequently in the Arabic press – in a culture where women who are still unmarried at the age of 26 are referred to as spinsters, or even as slighting the family's honour, the growing numbers of single

THE MULTICULTURAL CITY

The majority of Dubai's expatriate population (comprising 90% of the emirate's population) is from India (about 60%), supplying the city with cheap labour as well as filling management and professional positions. Most of Dubai's construction workers and men in low-prestige positions (taxi drivers, hotel cleaners etc) come from Kerala, a southern Indian state, while there are also a lot of workers from the Indian states of Tamil Nadu and Goa. In contrast, most of the Indians in office jobs or managerial positions are recruited by agencies based in Mumbai, while IT guys come from Bangalore. All of the leading Indian mercantile communities – Jains, Sindhis, Sikhs and Marwaris – are also represented here.

About 12% of expats are from other Arab countries (mainly Lebanon, Syria, Jordan and Egypt), while there's also a substantial Iranian community. The first wave of Iranians built the Bastakia neighbourhood in the 1930s. They were mostly religiously conservative Sunnis and Shiites from southern Iran. After the 1979 Islamic revolution, a more affluent and often Western-educated group of Iranians settled in Dubai. There is also a growing community of Filipino expatriates, many of whom work in the hospitality sector, as well as some Chinese, Indonesian, Malaysian and Vietnamese residents. Western expats make up about 5% of the population, with at least 100,000 British citizens and increasing numbers of workers from Australia, Canada, South Africa, Ireland, Germany and France.

women is a hot topic indeed. The UAE Marriage Fund, set up by the federal government in 1994 to facilitate marriages between UAE nationals, provides grants to pay for the exorbitant costs of the wedding and dowry, and promotes mass weddings to enable nationals to save for a down payment on a house. These initiatives have reduced the rate of intermarriages between Emirati men and foreign women to a degree, but not sufficiently to ensure that every Emirati woman has a husband.

LIFESTYLE
Nationals

Don't be surprised if you hear expats make crude generalisations about Emiratis. You may be told they're all millionaires and live in mansions, or that they refuse to work in ordinary jobs, or that all the men have four wives. Such stereotypes simply reinforce prejudices and demonstrate the lack of understanding between cultures in Dubai.

Not all Emiratis are wealthy. While the traditional tribal leaders, or sheikhs, are often the wealthiest UAE nationals, many have made their fortune through good investments, often dating back to the 1970s. As befits a small oil-producing nation, all Emiratis have access to free health care and education as well as a marriage fund (although the budgets don't often meet the expenses of elaborate Emirati weddings). These types of social benefits, and charities operated by generous sheikhs, such as Sheikh Mohammed, are essential to the survival of poorer Emiratis in modern Dubai.

The upper and middle classes of Emirati society generally have expansive villas in which men and women still live apart, and male family members entertain guests in the *majlis* (meeting room). In all classes of Emirati society, extended families living together is the norm, with the woman moving in with the husband's family after marriage, although some young couples are now choosing to buy their own apartments for a little more privacy than the traditional arrangement allows.

Most Emiratis work in the public sector, as the short hours, good pay, benefits and early pensions are hard for young people (whose parents and grandparents still recall hard times) to refuse. The UAE government is actively pursuing a policy of 'Emiratisation', which involves encouraging Emiratis to work in the private sector, and encouraging employers to reject negative stereotypes and hire them. In the long term the government hopes to be much less dependent on an imported labour force.

Living with such a large proportion of expats, and an increasing number of Western cultural influences, has led to both growing conservatism and liberalisation. This is especially noticeable among young women: while some dress in Western fashion (usually ones with foreign mothers), others are sticking with traditional dress yet individualising it, while yet others are 'covering up'.

HAWALA: THE BUSINESS OF TRUST

Imagine a money transfer system with quick delivery and minimal or no fees, which is available to people in the poorest countries in the world. This is *hawala,* and Dubai is one of the key centres of this controversial practice.

Hawala is an Arabic term for a written order of payment. It works like this. You hand over your dirhams and the contact details of the recipient to your neighbourhood *hawala* trader. In return you get a code – say, a letter and four numbers. Then you ring up the recipient and give them the code. The trader contacts the people in his network. The next day, maybe two days later, the *hawala* trader's partner hands over the money, sometimes delivering it to the door of the recipient. The commission taken by the *hawala* traders might be as little as 1% or 2%, even zero if they can make a little profit on exchange-rate differences.

Some newspaper reports say as much as 90% of wages remitted to developing countries from the UAE were sent via this system until recently. Sending Dh100 to India via a bank would yield Rs 1050, while via a *hawala* trader it yields Rs 1130; while this is only US$2 difference, this amount still goes a long way in India's poorer regions and is a huge benefit to workers who can only afford to send home small amounts.

The *hawala* system has existed among Arab and Muslim traders for centuries as a defence against theft. It's a uniquely Islamic system, completely dependent on trust and honour. If a *hawala* trader breaks this trust, he'll be out of work, as his reputation is crucial to his business.

The *hawala* system in Dubai grew through gold smuggling in the 1960s. Once the gold was sold in India or Pakistan, the traders couldn't get the money back to Dubai. They found their solution in the growing number of expatriate workers. The workers gave their wages to the gold traders in Dubai, and the gold traders in India paid their relatives.

Since the attacks of September 11, the system is under increased pressure, as the USA – and its media outlets – has claimed that *hawala* is being used to transfer money to terrorists. *Hawala* operators in Dubai have been subject to further regulations, yet there's no sign that this long-standing alternative to Western Union and the other money transfer giants is under threat of ceasing anytime soon.

One aspect that's not going away is the importance of traditional dance, song and customs. All Emiratis know their traditional songs and dances, and activities such as falconry are being passed from father to son. So is the love of the desert – Emiratis are as comfortable in the sands as they are in Switzerland, where many of them take a summer break away from the heat.

Expats

As far as the foreign community goes, there are as many different lifestyles being played out in Dubai as there are grains of sand on Jumeirah Beach. Disposable income plays a big part in how people live. At the top end of the pay scale is the professional and wealthy management class. They can enjoy a good salary package, a nice car, a large villa with a maid and nanny, and a lifestyle that allows them to travel overseas for two months a year to escape the summer heat. Housewives left with little to do at home spend much of their time with other women in similar circumstances. These 'Jumeirah Janes', as other expats call them with a hint of derision, keep the cosmetics and spa industries alive and the coffee shops ticking over during the day. These residents are generally Western, but there are plenty of Indians, Iranians and Lebanese (mainly in business) that fall into this category too.

There is another category of professional expat – the academics, health professionals, media and IT people – who earn much the same as they would back home in gross terms, but with no tax, free or subsidised housing, great holidays and other benefits like schooling and health care, they come out ahead in financial terms. These expats are also generally Western, but there are a large number of Indians working in the IT field and Arabs working in the media, health and education sectors.

But not all Western expats are on big salaries. Many aren't paid enough to save money in Dubai, with much of their salary being eaten up by apartment rent and fairly high day-to-day living expenses.

Dubai has a vast army of service sector workers, most of them from India, Pakistan and the Philippines and, increasingly so, from other parts of Asia as well as Africa. Working as line cooks and servers and in supermarkets, these expats stand to make more money in Dubai than at home, usually working six days a week and sharing rooms in cheap accommodation.

There is a huge number of maids employed in Dubai. Indian, Pakistani, Indonesian, Filipina and Sri Lankan maids are generally paid between Dh500 and Dh800 a month and live in a tiny room in their employer's villa or share an apartment with friends. While the money earned is a fraction of a Western professional's starting salary, it's still more than unskilled work pays at home. Depending on the family, some of these maids become an integral part of their employer's family structure, forming close bonds with the children. Unfortunately, UAE labour law doesn't yet fully cover domestic workers, and a small but significant number of maids are exploited and subjected to violence and abuse.

WASTA

When visiting Dubai, you might hear expats talking about 'wasta'. The term translates loosely as 'influence high up' and having wasta can grease the wheels in just about every transaction in Dubai. Most Westerners get a little outraged at the thought of a select few receiving favours and special treatment because of powerful contacts – until, of course, they want some help themselves. Then being friends with a local who has wasta becomes a very desirable thing. But the funny thing is that those who claim to have wasta usually don't and those that do generally don't mention it.

Indians, Pakistanis and workers from other countries in the region go about the hazardous business of construction in Dubai. These men usually work six or six-and-a-half days a week on 12- to 14-hour shifts, earning as little as Dh2 per hour or Dh400 per month. Many are made to pay off large debts to the agents who initially arranged their employment. Many live in what are known locally as 'labour camps' (compounds) provided by the construction companies. Conditions in the labour camps vary enormously; while some are spacious and comfortable, others cram 10 to 15 people into small and filthy rooms.

Partly spurred by a slew of critical articles in the international press and a scathing report by the Human Rights Watch, the UAE government has taken some steps towards curbing abuse and improving labour rights. Three new institutions have been created to deal with the problems, including a Human Rights Department in the Ministry of Interior. In June 2009 the cabinet approved mandatory housing standards to improve workers' living conditions. Also in 2009, the Wage Protection Scheme was rolled out, under which workers' earnings are transferred directly to a bank account on time and without any deductions. The government has banned outdoor work in July and August between 12.30pm and 3pm, although some construction firms continue to ignore the ruling.

In its updated report (released in 2009), Human Rights Watch acknowledges that some improvements have been made but that much more needs to be done. As of now, it is illegal for workers to organise, bargain collectively or go on strike. Over the past few years, a number of riots have broken out on construction sites, with workers protesting against low pay and bad conditions. The report specifically cites an incident in 2009 in which police 'quickly dispersed a demonstration over low wages by as many as 2000 striking migrant workers'. Unsafe working environments and the practice of withholding workers' passports also continue to be a problem, according to the report.

The response of the expatriate community to the hardships suffered by construction workers has been apprehensive and slow. One non-political organisation trying to make a difference is Helping Hands UAE (www.helpinghandsuae .com). If you'd like to donate clothes, food, toiletries, books or CDs to construction workers, see Helping Hands' website for information on collection points.

RACISM IN DUBAI

Notice something weird about the job ads in the classifieds section of the newspaper? In the UAE, it's quite normal for employers to specify the preferred nationality or gender of applicants in advertisements. Ads often include phrases such as 'Arabs only', 'UK/US/AUS only', or even 'males preferred'. Some employers expect female candidates to send photographs with their application. The open discrimination you'll see in job ads is often reflected in pay. A European can expect to earn more than a Filipino or Indian doing the same job. When the *Xpress* newspaper sent four men, two from India and two from Britain, to nightclubs across Dubai, bouncers at several of the clubs turned away the Indian men while British men got in without any problems. Dubai may be one of the most multicultural cities in the world, but it has a very long way to go before it can be considered a true melting pot.

THINGS YOU ALWAYS WANTED TO KNOW ABOUT DUBAI

You can't buy alcohol? Partially true. When arriving by air, you can, as a non-Muslim visitor over 18, buy certain quanti-ties of booze in the airport duty-free shop upon arrival (see p187). With the exception of 'dry' Sharjah, where alcohol and even *sheesha* (water pipe) smoking is banned, you can also purchase alcohol in bars and clubs that are generally attached to four- and five-star hotels for on-site consumption. Expat residents can acquire an alcohol licence, which entitles them to a fixed monthly limit of alcohol available from alcohol stores. The only store where you can officially buy alcohol without a licence is at the Barracuda Beach Resort in the northern emirate of Umm al-Quwain, north of Sharjah, about an hour's drive north of Dubai. Note that you are not officially allowed to transport alcohol through 'dry' Sharjah, although most people just seem to take the risk anyway.

There's no pork? Pork is available for non-Muslims in a special room at some supermarkets (such as Spinneys and Carrefour). In many hotel restaurants, pork is a menu item and is usually clearly labelled as such. However the 'beef bacon' and 'turkey ham' that are commonly available are nothing more than a reminder of how tasty the real thing is…unless you're a vegetarian, of course.

Do women have to 'cover up'? All locals ask is that people dress respectfully, with clothes that are not too reveal-ing – especially outside of Dubai (Sharjah in particular). Emiratis *will* judge you on how you dress; men in shorts at shopping malls will be assumed to have forgotten their pants and women who dress like Paris Hilton will be assumed to have the same morals as the heiress.

Homosexuals are banned? Simply being homosexual is not illegal as such, but homosexual acts are – as are any sex acts outside marriage.

What about those guys holding hands? It's just a sign of friendship. It's OK for married couples to hold hands as well, but serious public displays of affection (whether married or not) are frowned upon and fines and jail terms can result.

Will you be kicked out if you're HIV positive? Yes. As a worker coming to live in Dubai you will be tested for HIV as well as other things such as diabetes. If you are proven to be HIV positive, you'll be deported.

FASHION

Emirati women have been showing a growing pride and renewed confidence in their own national dress, the *abeyya* (full-length black robe) and *shayla* (black veil), despite the ever-increasing Western influences in Dubai. The latest trend is for young women to wear *abeyyas* and *shaylas* playfully embellished with jewels, beads, sequins, embroidery, feathers, lace, tassels and tiny plastic toys. And while Emirati men are occasionally seen in Western dress (women very rarely are, unless travelling outside the country), most wear their *dishdasha* (man's shirt-dress), either in classic off-white or in smart new colours, such as slate, teal and chocolate, along with a white or red-and-white checked *gutra* (head cloth) with *agal* (a black headrope used to hold the *gutra* in place). Only older women still wear a black or gold burka on their face.

Hand in hand with this pride in national fashion is the exciting emergence of young Emi-rati and Dubai-based expat designers. One standout is Rabia Zargarpur, who was named the region's 'International Young Fashion Entrepreneur of the Year' in a competition sponsored by the British Council in 2008 and also made it into the Top 100 list of the World's Most In-fluential Arabs issued by the well-respected *Arabian Business* magazine. Creating fashion for young women, she blends Western styles with Arabic modesty, a trend that also extends to the swimming pool and the gym. Check out My Cozzie (http://mycozzie.com), a line of styl-ish full-body swimwear, and Capster, a bathing cap–style hood worn as an alternative to the *abeyya*. Other local labels include Sweet Lemon, Ice Lolly, Crazy Daisy and Pink Sushi (which makes bags and outfits from *gutras*).

Meanwhile, expats living in Dubai increasingly incorporate exotic Arabic (and Indian) dress into their own style and are wearing giant Bedouin earrings pendants and bangles; long, flowing, colourful kaftans; and floaty smocks featuring embroidery, beads, jewels and gemstones.

The latest designs are introduced twice annually during the invitation-only Dubai Fashion Week (www.dfw.com), which makes heads swivel in April and October. Names to watch during recent shows included Mariam Al Mazo or Mimi Fashion Designs, Hassan Sheheryar Yasin, Asma Chapti and Khalid Alhajri. Stores stocking local fashions include S*uce (p100), Luxecouture (p100), Ginger & Lace (p102) and Amzaan (p94).

SPORT

Given the fierce summer heat, obviously the best time to play or watch sport in Dubai is during the winter months, when all of Dubai's sports lovers make the most of the marvellous weather. Tennis and golf are extremely popular, as are all varieties of football, but water sports are more suitable as a year-round activity. Scuba diving, sailing and kitesurfing are all popular, as are skateboarding and surfing (when there are waves, that is). For more on these activities, see p140.

ENVIRONMENT & PLANNING

THE LANDSCAPE

Dubai is capital of the emirate of the same name and extends over 4114 sq km, making it the second largest of the seven emirates that compose the UAE. Prior to settlement, this area was flat *sabkha* (salt-crusted coastal plain). The sand mostly consists of crushed shell and coral and is fine, clean and white. The *sabkha* was broken only by clumps of desert grasses and a small area of hardy mangroves at the inland end of the Creek. Photographs of the area from the early 20th century show how strikingly barren the landscape was.

East of the city, the *sabkha* gives way to north–south lines of dunes. The farming areas of Al-Khawaneej and Al-Awir, now on the edge of Dubai's suburbia, are fed by wells. Further east the dunes grow larger and are tinged red with iron oxide. The dunes stop abruptly at the gravel fans at the base of the rugged Hajar Mountains, where there are gorges and waterholes. A vast sea of sand dunes covers the area south of the city, becoming more and more imposing as it stretches into the desert known as the Empty Quarter (Rub' al-Khali), which makes up the southern region of the UAE and the western region of Saudi Arabia. North of Dubai, along the coast, the land is tough desert scrub broken by inlets similar to Dubai Creek, until you reach the mountainous northern emirates.

PLANTS & ANIMALS

In Dubai's parks you will see indigenous tree species such as the date palm and the neem (a botanical cousin of mahogany), and a large number of imported species, including eucalypts. The sandy desert surrounding the city supports wild grasses and the occasional date-palm oasis. In the salty scrublands further down the coast you might spot the desert hyacinth emerging in all its glory after the rains. It has bright-yellow and deep-red dappled flowers.

Decorating the flat plains that stretch away from the foothills of the Hajar Mountains, near Hatta, are different species of flat-topped acacia trees. The *ghaf* also grows in this area; this big tree looks a little like a weeping willow and is incredibly hardy, as its roots stretch down for about 30m, allowing it to tap into deep water reserves. The tree is highly respected in the Arab world, as it provides great shade and food for goats and camels; it's also a good indicator that there's water in the vicinity.

As in any major city, you don't see much wildlife. Urbanisation, combined with zealous hunting, has brought about the virtual extinction of some species. These include the houbara

---

THE GULF – ARABIAN OR PERSIAN?

To avoid causing offence, you must not refer to the body of water off the coast of Dubai as the 'Persian Gulf'. This is an exceptionally sensitive issue in Arab Gulf countries, where the water is definitely, emphatically and categorically called the 'Arabian Gulf', even if the rest of world, including the UN, disagrees.

The term 'Persian Gulf' is banned in Dubai. It is ripped out of school textbooks and crossed out on maps (as is the word 'Israel'), and any newspaper or magazine using these words by mistake can expect to be severely reprimanded. Even historical maps in the city's museums have been altered so the original inscription of 'Persian Gulf' isn't legible.

It's an equally sensitive issue in Iran, which banned the *National Geographic* for using the term 'Arabian Gulf' on a map, although it was in parenthesis below a much larger 'Persian Gulf'. They even banned *The Economist* for using the neutral term 'The Gulf'. Tech-savvy Iranians have also taken their battle to the internet. Do a Google search for 'Arabian Gulf', click on the first result, and you'll see what we mean.

THE BIRTH OF A METROPOLIS

It may have taken Dubai a little longer than other major cities to get its own metro system, but let's keep a sense of perspective: until the 1960s donkeys and camels provided the only transport around town. As is the case today, *abras* (water taxis) were used to transport people across the Creek. The first roads were only built in the 1960s.

The development of a modern infrastructure started long before the discovery of oil in 1966, although this was the principal catalyst for rapid growth. The first bank, the British Bank of the Middle East, was established in 1946, and when Al-Maktoum Hospital was built in 1949 it was the only centre for modern medical care on the Trucial Coast until well into the 1950s. When Sheikh Rashid officially came to power in 1958, he set up the first Municipal Council and established a police force and basic infrastructure, such as electricity and water supply.

Construction of the airport began in 1958 and the British Overseas Airways Corporation (BOAC) and Middle East Airlines (MEA) launched regular flights to Dubai soon after. Even after oil revenues began coming in, trade remained the foundation of the city's wealth, though oil has contributed to trade profits and encouraged modernisation since its discovery. Work on the Port Rashid complex began in 1967, after it became obvious that the growing maritime traffic could no longer be managed by the existing facilities, and was completed in 1972. The mid-1970s saw the start of more massive infrastructural improvements, resulting in the opening of the Shindaga Tunnel in 1975 and the Al-Garhoud Bridge the following year. By the end of the decade, Jebel Ali Port, the largest artificial port in the world, and the adjacent free-trade zone had become reality, as had the World Trade Centre, the dry docks and a major desalination plant.

bustard, the striped hyena and the caracal (a cat that resembles a lynx). The Arabian oryx (also called the white oryx), however, is one success story. As part of a program of the Dubai Desert Conservation Reserve (see boxed text, p171), it has been successfully reintroduced. The Al-Ain Zoo (p174), which is being expanded into a wildlife park with a heavy focus on sustainability, also has a successful breeding program.

On the fringes of Dubai, where the urban sprawl gives way to the desert, you may see a desert fox, sand cat or falcon if you are very lucky. Otherwise, the only animals you are likely to encounter are camels and goats. The desert is also home to various reptile species, including the desert monitor lizard (up to a metre long), the sand skink, the spiny-tailed agama and several species of gecko. The only poisonous snakes are vipers, such as the sawscaled viper, which can be recognised by its distinctive triangular head. There are even two remarkably adapted species of toad, which hibernate for years between floods burrowed deep in wadis.

The city is a hot spot for birdwatchers; because of the spread of irrigation and greenery, the number and variety of birds is growing. Dubai is on the migration path between Europe, Asia and Africa, and more than 320 migratory species pass through in the spring and autumn, or spend the winter here. The city's parks, gardens and golf courses sustain quite large populations, and on any day up to 80 different species can be spotted. Species native to Arabia include the crab plover, the Socotra cormorant, the black-crowned finch lark and the purple sunbird.

Artificial nests have been built to encourage flamingos to breed at the Ras al-Khor Wildlife Sanctuary (see boxed text, p72), at the head of Dubai Creek. In addition to flamingos, ducks, marsh harriers, spotted eagles, broad-billed sandpipers and ospreys all call the sanctuary home – for birdwatchers this place is a must-visit.

The waters off Dubai teem with around 300 different species of fish. Diners will be most familiar with the hammour, a species of grouper, but the Gulf is also home to an extraordinary range of tropical fish and several species of small sharks. Green turtles and hawksbill turtles used to nest in numbers on Dubai's beaches, but today their nesting sites are restricted to islands. Although you won't see them around Dubai, the coastal waters around Abu Dhabi are home to the Gulf's biggest remaining population of dugongs, where they feed off sea grasses in the shallow channels between islands.

PROGRESS & SUSTAINABILITY

There's no shortage of sand in Dubai, so converting it into islands that cost several million dollars each looked like a very profitable venture. Today we know that this venture was largely a pipe dream. Worse, though, as environmentalists have long argued, Dubai's offshore projects such as the Palm Islands and The World will probably cause considerable long-term damage. To create The World, around 33 million cubic metres of sand and shell from the seabed of the

Gulf has been dredged and redistributed. Critics claim that this work has damaged the marine environment, with dredging destroying the seabed and plumes of sediment from the construction wrecking fragile coral reefs. Also see boxed text, p84.

Dubai consumes resources at a much faster rate than it can replace them, which is why its ecological footprint is so high (see boxed text, below). It won't be easy to reverse the trend and achieve environmental sustainability because the UAE relies so heavily on imported goods. Nearly everything on the supermarket shelves is brought into the country, and most of what you'll eat in restaurants has been transported from overseas too. There are a few farms in the UAE (including a couple of organic pioneers), but in a country where the economy – and the local mentality – is so urbanised, it will take some effort to entice UAE nationals or expatriates to work in the agricultural sector to lessen the nation's dependency on imported goods.

There will always be a huge demand for air-conditioning in such a hot climate. (For information on Dubai's climate, see p186.) Future residential buildings are likely to be more energy-efficient, but people have to become less wasteful too, and switch off the air-conditioning when they're not at home.

ENVIRONMENTAL AWARENESS

In terms of going green at the micro level, much work needs to be done. Water and energy wastage are major issues. At 133 gallons per day, the UAE has the highest per capita rate of water consumption in the world, and rainfall is infrequent. According to Dr Rashid bin Fahad, the UAE Minister of the Environment, the country relies on desalination for 98% of its drinking water needs, an expensive and energy-intensive process, but necessary to convert seawater into water clean enough to drink.

Littering is another problem, although recycling bins are increasingly popping up in malls and bus and metro stations. Abu Dhabi plans to make household recycling mandatory in 2010 and Dubai may follow soon. Meanwhile, public transport systems are proliferating. Dubai Metro inaugurated in 2009 and other emirates, such as Sharjah, have recently introduced public bus networks. Meanwhile, in Abu Dhabi, the most ambitious environmental project is taking shape: when completed, Masdar City will be the world's first carbon-neutral community.

It's estimated that a third of the cars on Dubai's roads are gas-guzzling sports utility vehicles (SUVs). But petrol is very cheap and many expatriates like to have a big car for reassurance on Dubai's volatile roads. Many drivers, of course, require 4WD vehicles for their off-road leisure pursuits.

While some Dubai residents come from countries where the environment isn't a pressing concern, many others are well informed on the topic of global warming but stop recycling after moving to the emirate. This may be because the facilities are inconveniently located, or perhaps because they're not concerned about the long-term health of a city they're only living in temporarily.

DUBAI'S ECOLOGICAL FOOTPRINT

Dubai's transformation from a small town into a major metropolis in the space of a few decades has been remarkable. But such rapid expansion has inevitably had a negative impact on the environment.

The Living Planet Report 2008, published by the WWF, shows that the UAE has the highest per capita ecological footprint in the world. If that's too abstract for you, ponder this little fact: if every human being in the world consumed natural resources like the average UAE resident, it would take 4.5 earths to sustain this level of consumption. The excessive usage of water and energy are largely to blame, accounting for 80% of the footprint. According to the Abu Dhabi Water & Electriticy Company, meeting this demand may be difficult beyond 2012 if current growth levels continue.

The good news is that Dubai and the UAE are taking more than baby steps towards improving the situation. Soon after the WWF's report was released, the government launched an initiative called *Al Basma Al Beeiya* (Ecological Footprint Initiative; www.agedi.ae/ecofootprintuae), which sets out a plan for both the public and private sector to make a greater effort to work towards sustainable development.

There's also the 'Heroes of the UAE' (www.heroesoftheuae.ae), a joint campaign launched by the Emirates Wildlife Society, the WWF and the Environment Agency – Abu Dhabi. The goal is to educate UAE residents on how to reduce their energy consumption and to get government institutions involved in leading by example.

Being environmentally responsible in Dubai can be a challenge. Many offices don't have recycling bins for waste paper, newspapers routinely come wrapped in plastic for no apparent reason, it's impossible to live without air-conditioning for half the year, and efforts to reuse plastic bags in supermarkets are nearly always greeted by bemused stares.

Local Environmental Organisations

The Federal Environmental Agency legislates on environmental issues and encourages communication on these issues between the emirates. There are also a number of NGOs concerned with the environment.

Emirates Diving Association (☎ 393 9390; www.emiratesdiving.com) This association is an active participant in local environmental campaigns, with an emphasis on the marine environment.

Emirates Environmental Group (☎ 344 8622; www.eeg-uae.org) This non-profit group organises educational programs in schools and businesses as well as community programs, such as clean-up drives.

Emirates Wildlife Society (http://uae.panda.org) Works in association with the WWF on implementing conservation initiatives to protect local biodiversity and promote sustainable lifestyles.

MEDIA
NEWSPAPERS

A few years ago the front pages of the local newspapers were reassuringly familiar. A sheikh said something wise, had a successful meeting or received a message of congratulations and hardly a day went by without a call for Arab unity in the op-ed columns. As an ever-increasing number of journalists leave countries with a free press to work in Dubai, this situation is slowly improving, although critical coverage of the government remains off limits.

Currently the most reputable among the UAE's English-language broadsheets is *The National* (www.thenational.ae), which was launched in 2008. Although owned by Abu Dhabi's ruling family, it maintains high journalistic standards and includes global news and analysis. Despite being toothless in its domestic reporting, Dubai-based *Gulf News* (www.gulfnews.com) features solid coverage of the Middle East and the Indian subcontinent. Its publisher, Al Nisr, also produces *Xpress* (www.xpress4me.com). In spite of its chatty, informal style and irritatingly spelt name, the weekly paper occasionally publishes stories other newspapers won't touch, such as investigating racist door policies at nightclubs (see boxed text, p31).

The other major English-language broadsheet is the *Khaleej Times* (www.khaleejtimes.com); it's popular with expats but its strapline, 'The Truth Must Be Told', is a regular source of amusement for resident cynics.

The government also owns the Arab Media Group, which publishes *Emirates Business 24/7* (www.business24-7.ae), the UAE's first business newspaper. The best free newspaper is *7 Days* (www.7days.ae), which amusingly is published only six days a week. Its reporting may not be so high calibre but its writers do occasionally demonstrate a bold independent streak.

If you're after something more internationally minded, both the *Times* and the *Financial Times* publish Middle East editions. Todaily (www.todaily.com) print same-day editions of many international newspapers including the *Guardian, Daily Telegraph, Le Monde* and *Sydney Morning Herald* – these are usually available in branches of Carrefour.

MAGAZINES

There are plenty of locally produced English-language magazines crowding Dubai newsstands. ITP, the region's biggest publisher, makes Middle East editions of *Grazia* and *Harper's Bazaar*, while Motivate puts out an ultra-gossipy local version of *Hello!* and an electronics mag *Stuff*. *VIVA* and *Emirates Women* are UAE-based women's monthlies. The main listings magazines are the weekly *Time Out* and the monthly *What's On*, while *Arabian Business* is considered the Middle East's best-selling weekly business magazine.

ONLINE

All the major newspapers and magazines have an online presence, but there are also some interesting online-only publications. Anyone interested in the business side of things should check out Kippreport (www.kippreport.com). Blogs worth skimming through include Secret Dubai (www.secretdubai.blogspot.com), An Emirati's Thoughts (www.aethoughts.blogspot.com) and The Emirates Economist (www.emirateseconomist.blogspot.com), which often address topics the mainstream press steer clear of. While *Secret Dubai* has a large following, and its comments pages host some of the most bitter debates in the city, it also has its detractors, with many arguing that it isn't respectful enough to the local culture.

TELEVISION

Dubai isn't a city accustomed to playing catch-up, but when it comes to TV news in the Gulf, Qatar has stolen a march on the opposition. Al Jazeera is the most popular news network in the Arab world and its English-language service has helped put this small country on the map.

There are a few English-language TV channels in Dubai, although only a couple – the amateurish City 7 (www.city7tv.com) and Dubai One (www.dubaione.ae) – produce their own shows. Dubai One also shows many popular programs from the US and the UK. For classic and contemporary movies, turn to MBC (www.mbc.net).

While Dubai's rulers, unlike their Qatari counterparts, haven't bankrolled a home-grown media superpower, they have attracted many of the big names in the broadcasting world to set up Middle East headquarters at Dubai Media City. CNN, Reuters, CNBC, BBC World and Showtime Arabia are all residents. Media City is meant to be free of government intervention, hence its motto 'Freedom to Create'.

THE CENSORSHIP QUESTION

Dubai is one of the key media hubs in the Middle East. It has multiple newspapers, magazines, radio and TV stations, as well as the largest number of internet users per capita among the Gulf countries. Many international news organisations, including CNN, Reuters and the BBC, have set up shop in Dubai Media City (DMC), a free zone created in 2000. What makes DMC so attractive is that within it the UAE's rather restrictive media laws do not apply. Such is not the case for domestic publishing outlets, or in fact anyone operating outside the zone.

According to a report issued by the Open Net Initiative (ONI), 'the government of the United Arab Emirates (UAE) censors political and religious content and pervasively filters Web sites that contain pornography or content relating to alcohol and drug use, gay and lesbian issues, or online dating or gambling. Online privacy and circumvention tools, as well as some sites belonging to Nazis or historical revisionists, are blocked'.

All journalists working in Dubai know that some topics, such as criticism of the UAE's rulers or anything that could be perceived as negative treatment of Islam, are completely off limits. It's also perilous to write about sex, drugs, alcohol, homosexuality or Israel. At other times the line isn't so clear. Can journalists write about prostitution, domestic violence, human trafficking or drug addiction in the emirate? Possibly, but very few, if any, Dubai editors are prepared to take the risk. Most follow the golden rule – don't write anything negative about Dubai if you want to keep your job.

It's usually self-censorship, rather than direct government interference, that hinders press freedom in Dubai, although the fear of reprisals is very real. However, journalists are no longer sent to prison. Hours after two *Khaleej Times* reporters were sentenced to prison for libel in 2007, Sheikh Mohammed issued a pardon and declared that journalists should not be jailed for reasons relating to their work.

In an attempt to take further steps towards free speech, the Federal National Council is considering revisions to the media law. Issued in January 2009, the new draft law, the government says, would give journalists greater freedom of expression and protect them from having to reveal sources. But the country's journalists, as well as organisations such as Human Rights Watch (HRW), say that the new law does not go far enough and 'still suffers from unlawful content-based restrictions on speech, as well as unlawful and onerous government controls on licensing, registration, operation and management of the media'. So far, discussion about the provisions of the new law continue.

For the full ONI report, see http://opennet.net/research/profiles/uae. For HRW's assessment, go to www.hrw.org/node/82150.

ARCHITECTURE

Surprisingly, for a city with few buildings older than 100 years, the economic boom of the last 30 years has left it an architectural mishmash. But the incongruous blend of traditional Arabian architecture with futuristic structures make the city a remarkable sight. A boat ride along the Creek takes you from the wind tower houses in the Bastakia Quarter of Bur Dubai to the pointed dhowlike roof of the Dubai Creek Golf & Yacht Club, via the sail-like National Bank of Dubai. As you'll notice, these modern structures sit comfortably with the traditional architecture of the cosmopolitan city, its contrast representative of other juxtapositions in Dubai – East and West, old and new. Interestingly, much of the city's recent architecture, such as Madinat Jumeirah (but also private residences), sees a return to traditional Arabian forms, although projects such as Burj Khalifa show that the cloud-busting skyscraper isn't going anywhere in Dubai but up.

TRADITIONAL ARCHITECTURE

On your wanderings around the city, you'll notice that Dubai's traditional architecture consists of essentially four types of buildings – domestic (residential homes), religious (mosques), defensive (forts and watchtowers) and commercial (souqs). Readily available materials, such as gypsum and coral from offshore reefs and from the banks of the Creek, were put to use. The Sheikh Saeed Al-Maktoum House

---

DUBAI'S ICONIC BUILDINGS

Burj al-Arab (p79) The Burj was completed in 1999, and is set on an artificial island 300m from the shore. The 60-floor, sail-shaped structure is 321m high. A translucent fibreglass wall serves as a shield from the desert sun during the day and as a screen for an impressive light show each night. Until the Burj Khalifa arrived on the scene to steal its thunder, it was *the* iconic symbol of Dubai.

Burj Khalifa (p69) The world's tallest building clocks in at a cloud-tickling 828m. For the design, American architect Adrian Smith found inspiration in the desert flower Hymenocalis, whose patterning systems are embodied in Islamic architecture. The tower is designed as three petals arranged around a central core. As it rises from the flat base, the petals are set back in an upward-spiralling pattern.

Dubai Creek Golf & Yacht Club (p147) When you cross the bridges over the Creek, you'll notice the pointed white roof of the clubhouse set amid artificial, undulating hillocks. The idea behind this 1993 design was to incorporate a traditional element – the white sails of a dhow – into the form and style of the building, and while this motif is becoming overused now, the building is ageing well.

Dubai International Financial Centre (Map pp70–71) Dubai's stock exchange and leading international financial institutions are housed in a complex of six buildings surrounding a central 80m-high triumphal arch called The Gate. Designed by the American firm Gensler Associates, it sits on an axis with the Jumeirah Emirates Towers and the World Trade Centre, effectively framing these two landmarks.

Dusit Dubai (Map pp70–71; Sheikh Zayed Rd, next to Interchange No 1, Downtown Dubai) Sheikh Zayed Rd features many modern skyscrapers, but few are as eye-catching as this one. The 153m-high building has an inverted 'Y' shape – two pillars that join to form a tapering tower. It's supposed to evoke the Thai joined-hands gesture of greeting, appropriate for this Thai hotel chain, but looks more like a giant tuning fork.

Jumeirah Emirates Towers (p160) Designed in an ultramodern internationalist style, the twin, triangular, gunmetal-grey towers on Sheikh Zayed Rd soar from an oval base and are among the world's tallest. The taller of the two (355m) houses offices, while the other (305m) is a hotel. Balanced by the curvilinear base structure, the curved motif is also repeated in the upper storeys of the buildings. Perhaps the best-loved building in the city.

Jumeirah Beach Hotel (p161) This long S-shaped construction represents a wave, with the Gulf as its backdrop. The glimmering facades of the hotel and its close neighbour, the Burj al-Arab, are achieved by the use of reflective glass and aluminium. The two structures combined – a huge sail hovering over a breaking wave – symbolise Dubai's maritime heritage.

National Bank of Dubai (Map pp52–3) This shimmering building off Baniyas Rd in Deira, overlooking the Creek, has become another quintessential symbol of Dubai. Designed by Carlos Ott and completed in 1997, it combines simple shapes to represent a dhow with a sail billowing. The bronze windows reflect the activity on the Creek and, at sunset, when the light is just right, it's a beautiful sight.

(p61) in Shindagha is a fine example of this kind of construction. Limestone building blocks were also used and mud cemented the stones together. However, mud constructions suffered badly in the heat and had a limited lifespan, sometimes only a few years. Interestingly, the dimensions of buildings were often governed by the length of timber, mainly from India or East Africa, that could be loaded onto a dhow. There were two types of traditional house – the *masayf*, a summer house incorporating a wind tower, and the *mashait*, a winter house with a courtyard. You'll see both of these in the Bastakia Quarter (p61).

When you explore the lanes surrounding Bur Dubai Souq and behind Al-Ahmadiya School in Deira, you'll see that the alleyways are narrow and the buildings close together. The lanes are narrow to increase the velocity of wind, keeping the neighbourhood cooler, while houses, souqs and mosques were built close together to provide maximum shade so that inhabitants could move around town in comfort, protected from the harsh sun.

For a thorough introduction to traditional Arab architecture, visit the exhibit at Sheikh Juma Al-Maktoum House (p66).

THE MAJLIS

Majlis translates as 'meeting place' or 'reception area'. The *majlis* was a forum or council where citizens could come and speak to their leaders and make requests and complaints or raise issues. In Dubai the *majlis* system was preserved until the 1960s. In its domestic sense, a *majlis* is a reception area found in all older buildings in Dubai (such as Al-Fahidi Fort, the Dubai Museum and the Heritage House in Al-Ahmadiya). Its Western cousin is probably the lounge room. The *majlis* is still an important room in an Arab household and is usually the domain of the male members of the family. It's a place where they can get together and talk without disturbing the women of the house, as most traditional houses still have a separate *majlis* for women.

Wind Towers

Wind towers, or *barjeel* in Arabic, are the Gulf's unique form of non-mechanical air-conditioning, and scores of original wind towers still exist in the Bastakia Quarter as well as in the Bur Dubai and Deira souq areas. Traditional wind towers, rising 5m or 6m above a house, are open on all four sides to catch the breezes, which are channelled down around a central shaft and into the room below. In the process, the air speeds up and is cooled. The cooler air already in the tower shaft pulls in and subsequently cools the hotter air outside through simple convection. It works amazingly well. Sitting beneath a wind tower when it's a humid 40°C, you'll notice a distinct drop in temperature and a consistent breeze even when the air outside feels heavy and still. Test out the one at the Dubai Museum.

The wealthy Persian merchants who settled in Dubai around the beginning of the 20th century were the first to build a large number of wind towers in Bastakia. In some houses the tallest wind tower was above the master bedroom, while smaller wind towers cooled the living rooms. The merchants brought red clay from Iran, which they mixed with manure to make saruj. This was baked in a kiln and used to build the foundations of the wind tower house. Other materials included coral rock and limestone for the walls and plaster for decorative work. The walls were built as thick as 60cm, so the house could be extended upwards if the family expanded. Chandel wood from East Africa, palm-frond matting, mud and straw were used to build the roofs.

Courtyard Houses

Houses in Dubai were traditionally built around a central courtyard, known as *al-housh* in Arabic. All rooms surrounded the courtyard and all doors and windows opened onto it, except those of the guestrooms, which opened to the outside of the house. A verandah provided shade, kept sun out of rooms at certain times of the day, and was usually the place where the women did weaving and sewing. For great examples of courtyard houses, visit the Heritage House (p56) in Deira or XVA Gallery (p61) in Bastakia.

Barasti

Barasti describes both the traditional Arabian method of building a palm-leaf house and the completed house itself. *Barasti* houses are made from a skeleton of wooden poles (date-palm trunks) onto which *areesh* (palm leaves) are woven to form a strong structure through which air can still circulate. They were extremely common throughout the Gulf in the centuries before the oil boom, though few examples of this type of house survive today. They were relatively easy to build and maintain since, unlike the mudbrick houses you find around Al-Ain, their construction didn't require water. The circulation of air through the palms also made *barasti* houses much cooler than mudbrick ones during summer. Look for examples of *barasti* houses in the courtyard of the Dubai Museum (p60) and in the Heritage Village (p66).

Mosques

Fundamentally simple structures, mosques are made up of a few basic elements which are easy to identify. The most visible of these is the minaret, the tower from which the call to prayer is broadcast five times a day. Virtually every mosque in the world has a minaret; many have several. The first minarets were not built until the early 8th century, some 70 years after the Prophet's death. The idea may have originated from the bell towers that Muslim armies found attached to some of the churches they converted into mosques during the early years of Islam. The more minarets on a mosque, the more important it is. No mosque has more than seven minarets, the number on the Grand Mosque in Mecca.

A mosque must also have a mihrab, a niche in the wall facing Mecca, indicating the qibla, the direction believers must face while praying. Mihrabs were thought to have been introduced into Islamic architecture around the beginning of the 8th century and, like minarets, they can be simple or elaborate. The use of the minbar, a pulpit chair traditionally reached by three steps, dates from the Prophet's lifetime.

Mosques need to have a water supply so that worshippers can perform the *wudu* (ritual washing) required before they begin praying. Neighbourhood mosques in Dubai are visited five times a day for prayers, with worshippers travelling further afield to larger mosques for Friday prayers.

The Jumeirah Mosque (p75) is based on the Anatolian style, identified by a massive central dome, while other mosques in Dubai are based on Iranian and Central Asian models, which

---

THE FIVE PILLARS OF ISLAM

Islam is the official religion of Dubai and the majority of Emiratis are Sunni Muslims. Many of Dubai's expatriates also practise Islam, and in some parts of town mosques have largely Pakistani congregations. The diversity of Dubai's large expatriate population means most other religions are also represented.

Shahadah The profession of faith: 'There is no god but God, and Mohammed is the messenger of God.'

Salat Muslims are required to pray five times every day: at dawn *(fajr)*, noon *(dhuhr)*, mid-afternoon *(asr)*, sunset *(maghrib)* and twilight *(isha'a)*. Loudspeakers on the minarets of mosques transmit the call to prayer *(adhan)* at these times, and you can expect to be woken up at dawn if your hotel is situated in the cluttered streets of Deira or Bur Dubai. During prayers a Muslim must perform a series of prostrations while facing the Kaaba, the ancient shrine at the centre of the Grand Mosque in Mecca. Before a Muslim can pray, however, he or she must perform a series of ritual ablutions; if water isn't available for this, sand or soil can be substituted.

Zakat Muslims must give a portion of their income to help the poor. How this has operated in practice has varied over the centuries: either it was seen as an individual duty (as is the case in Dubai) or the state collected it as a form of income tax to be redistributed through mosques or religious charities.

Sawm It was during the month of Ramadan that Mohammed received his first revelation, in AD 610. Muslims mark this event by fasting from sunrise until sunset throughout Ramadan. During the fast a Muslim may not take anything into his or her body. Food, drink, smoking and sex are forbidden. Young children, travellers and those whose health will not allow it are exempt from the fast, though those who are able to do so are supposed to make up the days they missed at a later time.

Hajj All able Muslims are required to make the pilgrimage to Mecca at least once, if possible during a specific few days in the first and second weeks of the Muslim month of Dhul Hijja, although visiting Mecca and performing the prescribed rituals at any other time of the year is also considered spiritually desirable. Such visits are referred to as *umrah*, or 'little pilgrimages'.

have more domes covering different areas of the mosque. Shiite mosques are identifiable by their exquisite green and blue faience tile work covering the facades and main dome. The multidomed Grand Mosque (p66) in Bur Dubai is another variation on the Anatolian style.

MODERN ARCHITECTURE
In contrast to the traditional architecture that was all about function over form, and was built with regard for the environment, modern architecture in Dubai (until recently) has embraced an 'anything goes' ethos with complete disregard to the climate. About 90% of Dubai's architecture can be described as international and is built using concrete, steel and glass. However, many architects have recently started to question the thinking behind building glass towers in a country with extreme heat. The huge cooling costs alone are reason to go for designs that better respond to and integrate with the weather and surroundings. Because these cosmopolitan materials absorb heat and transfer it to other parts of the construction, they also cause damage over time. As a result, hi-tech, state-of-the-art materials with greater heat resistance are now starting to be used. Designs that are ageing well – and plenty aren't – are usually the ones produced by established architects, such as Carlos Ott (National Bank of Dubai building), whose fame stems from designing the Opéra de la Bastille in Paris, France.

ARTS
British satirist Rory Bremner once said that going to Dubai for its culture was like going 'to Tibet in search of nightlife'. It's really not quite that bad. It will be many years before Dubai can compete with the major European cities when it comes to music, theatre, art, literature and film, but progress is being made.

VISUAL ARTS
At the turn of the millennium there were only a handful of galleries in Dubai, most of which offered little more than clichéd watercolours of Arabian horses, camels and the like. Within the space of a few years, the city has become a focal point for contemporary Arabic and Persian art. With customary foresight, Dubai's decision-makers have recognised the potential of the art market in the region and gone all out to make sure it doesn't miss a trick.

The inaugural Gulf Art Fair in 2007, retitled Art Dubai the following year, brought gallery owners, artists and dealers from around the world to the plush setting of Madinat Jumeirah to talk business. Dubai's location at the crossroads of the Middle East, the Indian subcontinent and Africa, has helped it become an art industry hub. But it's also Dubai's relative openness that makes it such an attractive location for artists hoping to show their work. All the usual taboos, including anything that could be construed as criticism of Dubai, remain off limits. Nudity is a no-no, but Dubai is still more open than cities such as Tehran and Damascus, where some of the artists come from. Major exhibitions at venues such as the British Museum have fuelled a keen interest in Middle Eastern contemporary art, and Dubai is a lot more accessible to Western dealers than other cities in the region.

Although Dubai's art boom is being propelled mainly by commerce, rather than creativity, there are signs that ordinary residents of the city are becoming more interested in the art world. Much of the credit for the invigoration of the art scene goes to Sheikha Hoor al-Qasimi, daughter of Sharjah's ruler and director of the Sharjah International Biennial, who excited art lovers once again with a vibrant 9th Biennial in 2009. The next one is scheduled to take place from March to May 2011.

Perhaps the most surprising thing about Dubai's sudden enthusiasm for art is the development of an art district, tucked away in the otherwise uninviting Al-Quoz area. This featureless congregation of industrial estates along the edge of Sheikh Zayed Rd is home to several cutting-edge galleries including Gallery Isabelle van den Eynd (p73), Third Line (p73) and Meem Gallery (p73). Art isn't part of the school curriculum in the Emirates and is rarely written about in the Arabic-language press, but it is hoped that these galleries, along with events such as Art Dubai, will inspire a new generation of home-grown artists.

For its fourth outing in 2010, Art Dubai hosted more than 70 galleries from Berlin to Beirut, London to Tehran. Although it's certainly put Dubai on the art map, it's been criticised for being too industry-focused and not doing enough to stimulate a grassroots art movement in the region. Several Dubai galleries (including some that don't participate in the main fair) take part in an annual fringe event, the Bastakiya Art Fair. Organised by the dedicated owners of XVA Gallery (p61), it pools together the city's independent galleries to give visitors a more representative taste of the local art scene.

Dubai isn't the only city in the Gulf experiencing an upsurge in art interest. In Doha, Qatar, the government-funded Museum of Islamic Art opened in December 2008 in a spectacular building by IM Pei, the US-based architect nicknamed the 'mandarin of modernism'. South of Dubai, in Abu Dhabi, an international cast of five Pritzker Prize winners (the 'Oscar' of architecture) has been tapped to build four museums and a performing arts centre on Saadinat Island. Including Middle Eastern branches of the Louvre (designed by Jean Nouvel) and the Guggenheim (by Frank Gehry), the cultural district is poised to become a major showcase of 21st-century architecture, arts and culture. Of course, such ambitious plans leave Abu Dhabi open to a charge you could also direct at Dubai: that it's spending millions of dollars on importing culture while home-grown artists receive practically no support. Only a tiny percentage of the artists who exhibit in Dubai were raised in the Emirates and there are no government-funded galleries in the country.

CINEMA

Every December, the Dubai International Film Festival (www.dubaifilmfest.com) delivers a megadose of culture to the city's blockbuster-weary cinema goers. Launched in 2004, the festival has two main aims: to create cultural bridges and promote understanding, tolerance and peace; and to develop Dubai as a regional film hub. While some residents have complained that the organisers have an unhealthy obsession with luring star names onto their red carpets (Morgan Freeman, Oliver Stone, Orlando Bloom and Sharon Stone have all visited), there's no questioning the quality of the programming. Major international movies such as *Avatar,* Chris Rock's *Good Hair* and the musical *Nine* all screened here several months before their release dates in Europe. The categories established to promote the region's filmmaking talents – Arabian Nights and Gulf Voices – increase in size and scope every year and give young regional directors an opportunity to show their talents off to a wider audience.

Another Dubai-sponsored festival, the Gulf Film Festival (www.gulffilmfest.com), held annually since 2008, is training the spotlight squarely on regionally produced features, shorts and documentaries. Down the road, Abu Dhabi inaugurated its own prestigious event, the Middle East International Film Festival (www.meiff.com) in 2007 and presents home-grown movies as part of its Emirates Film Competition.

Despite increasing support, state-of-the-art facilities and a growing league of eager and talented filmmakers, the Emirati film industry is still in its infancy. One of the first locally produced movies was Hani al-Shabani's 2005 *Al Hilm* (The Dream). A light-hearted drama about a young writer's struggle to produce a script and a film, it reflected the challenges many aspiring Emirati filmmakers face. In 2009, *City of Life* by Ali Mostafa, the first feature-length movie written, produced and directed by an Emirati and set entirely in Dubai, premiered at the Dubai International Film Festival. An urban drama about the complexities of multiculturalism, it tells the story of a privileged young male Emirati, a disillusioned Indian cab driver and a former Romanian flight attendant whose lives collide. Despite critical acclaim, as of this writing it had not found a distributor (you can see the trailer on YouTube or at www.cityoflifefilm.com).

Both Dubai and Abu Dhabi are keen on luring Hollywood studios to shoot more movies in the region. Dubai has already hosted the crew of *Syriana* (starring George Clooney), while Abu Dhabi provided the backdrop to Jamie Foxx in *The Kingdom*. Dubai Studio City offers world-class production facilities and it seems likely that more American crews will shoot in Dubai, especially since so many films about the recent Iraq war are in the pipeline. If Dubai Studio City does bring in the megabucks of the big studios, the hope is that some of the foreign expertise will trickle down to local filmmakers. Film schools in the Emirates have already been established: the Manhattan Film Academy (http://mfacademy.com) in Dubai and the New York Film Academy (www.nyfa.com) in Abu Dhabi.

One major hurdle filmmakers face is the country's unpredictable censorship policies. Scenes involving nudity, drug taking, homosexuality and references to Israel are likely to be chopped. Even though it was filmed in Dubai, *Syriana* was cut so that scenes depicting south Asian workers being mistreated didn't make it to Emirate screens. When Hollywood knocked to produce scenes for the sequel to *Sex and the City* in Dubai, they did not get permission (although they did in Abu Dhabi). Paris Hilton was told there could be no drinking, no cursing and no wearing skimpy bikinis if she wanted to film an episode of her reality show *My New BFF*. Scenes of violence, on the other hand, are very rarely banned.

One way Dubai residents sidestep censorship is by purchasing illegal DVDs, usually imported from Malaysia or China. Piles of counterfeit DVDs can easily be found in the alleyways and basements of Karama, although most people living in Dubai have a 'DVD woman' turn up to their front door twice a week with a bag of pirated goods. Although these discs only work half the time, many people are prepared to spend Dh10 and take the risk. Fighting on behalf of the film industry is the Arabian Anti-Piracy Alliance (www.aaa.co.ae), who work with the Dubai authorities to tackle the problem. They're becoming increasingly successful at seizing the discs, and have trained sniffer dogs to help snuff out the problem. Sellers of pirated discs can expect a prison sentence and deportation if caught, with harsher punishments if they're also caught selling pornography.

DANCE

Dubai's contact with East and North African cultures through trade, both seafaring and by camel caravan, has brought many musical and dance influences to the UAE shores. Thus, traditional songs and dances are inspired by the environment – the sea, desert and mountains.

One of the most popular dances is the *liwa,* performed to a rapid tempo and loud drumbeat. Most likely brought to the Gulf by East African slaves, it is traditionally sung in Swahili. Another dance, the *ayyalah,* is a typical Bedouin dance, celebrating the courage, strength and unity of the tribe. The *ayyalah* is performed throughout the Gulf, but the UAE has its own variation, performed to a simple drumbeat. Anywhere between 25 and 200 men stand with their arms linked in two rows facing each other. They wave walking-sticks or swords in front of themselves and sway back and forth, the two rows taking it in turn to sing. It's a war dance and the words expound the virtues of courage and bravery in battle. You can see the dance on video at Dubai Museum (p60).

ARAB POETRY

Just as in Western countries, talent shows draw huge viewing figures in the Middle East. But unlike, say, *American Idol*, the most widely watched program – *Millions' Poet* – doesn't feature skimpy skirts, temper tantrums or boorish judges. Instead it sees *nabati* poets from across the Arab World compete for a Dh1 million prize.

Nabati, or vernacular poetry, is especially popular in the Gulf. Many Arabic-language newspapers and magazines publish pages of *nabati* poetry. The late Sheikh Zayed, former President of the UAE, and Sheikh Mohammed bin Rashid al-Maktoum, Dubai's ruler, are noted writers in this tradition. A collection of Sheikh Mohammed's works, *Poems from the Desert*, was published in 2009. When completed, the Palm Jebel Ali is expected to feature islands spelling out a four-line poem by Dubai's ruler.

In Bedouin culture a facility with poetry and language has always been greatly prized. A poet who could eloquently praise his own people while pointing out the failures of other tribes was considered a great asset. Emiratis spontaneously recite poetry with their friends, during social occasions, public events and even in shopping centres. Young people publish their own poetry, particularly romantic poems, on websites and in student magazines, and produce documentaries about the Emirati passion for poetic works.

Classic Emirati poets of note include Sultan al-Owais (1925–2000), some of whose poems have been translated into English, and Dr Ahmed al-Madani (1931–95), who wrote in the romantic *baiti* style. Palestinian resistance poets such as Mahmood Darwish (1941–2008) and Samih al-Qasim (b 1939) are popular, though traditionalists complain that they have broken with the 16 classical metres of poetry developed by the 8th-century Gulf Arab scholar Al-Khalil bin Ahmed.

There are about 50 other male UAE poets who still use the forms of classical Arabic poetry, though they often experiment by combining it with other styles. Names to look out for include Mohammad Sharif Al Shaibani, Mohammad bin Hader, Salem Al Zamr, Saif Al Murri, Karim Matooq, Arif Al Sheikh, Arif Al Khajah, Ahmed Mohammed Obaid, Ibrahim Mohammed Ibrahim, Khalid Badr and Jaffer Al Jamri.

There are also some well-known female poets, most of whom write in *tafila* (prose) style. Important names include Salihah Dhaiban (pen name Rua Salem) and her sister Amina Dhaiban (pen name Sarah Hareb), Salihah Ghabesh, Dhabia Khamees, Sheikha Maisoon Al Qasimi, Nugoom Al Ghanem, Aisha Busumait, Kaltham Shaibani and Kaltham Abdulla.

The instruments used at traditional musical celebrations in Dubai are the same as those used in the rest of the Gulf. The *tamboura,* a harplike instrument, has five strings made of horse gut, which are stretched between a wooden base and a bow-shaped neck. The base is covered with camel skin and the strings are plucked with sheep horns. It has a deep and resonant sound, a little like a bass violin.

A much less sophisticated instrument is the *manior,* a percussion instrument that's played with the body. It's comprised of a belt made of cotton, decorated with dried goats' hooves, which is wrapped around the player who keeps time with the beat of the *tamboura* while dancing. The *mimzar* is a wooden instrument a little like a small oboe, but it delivers a higher-pitched sound, which is haunting and undeniably Middle Eastern.

An unusual instrument and one that you'll often see at song and dance performances is the *habban,* the Arabian bagpipes. Made from a goatskin sack, it has two pipes attached. The sack retains its goat shape and the pipes resemble its front legs. One pipe is used to blow air into the sack and the other produces the sound. The *habban* sounds much the same as the Scottish bagpipes, but is shriller in tone.

The tabla is a drum, and has a number of different shapes. It can resemble a bongo drum that is placed on the floor, or it can be a *jasr,* a drum with goatskin at both ends, which is slung around the neck and hit with sticks.

CONTEMPORARY MUSIC

Emiratis have always acknowledged the importance of music in daily life. Songs have been traditionally composed to accompany different tasks, from hauling water to diving for pearls. These days, popular Emirati musicians include Mohammed al-Mazem, Fayez al-Saeed, Ruwaida al-Mahrooqi, Aida al-Manhali, Mehad Hamad and Eda bin Tanaf al-Manhaly. The most popular of all is the female singer Ahlam: Emiratis pay up to US$50,000 to have her sing at their weddings.

The Arabic music you're most likely to hear on the radio is *khaleeji,* the traditional Gulf style, recognisable to those familiar with Arabic pop music. Popular singers include Mohammed Nasser, who had a major hit with 'Ya Bint', and Dubai-born Yaseer Habeeb, the first UAE national to have a hit in Europe and the Middle East.

Alongside, an underground music scene is also increasingly taking shape. Loosely formed around Phride (www.phride.com), a website that connects the Middle East's rock and metal fans, this budding scene has produced a few Dubai bands worth taking notice of. The political ska-punk of Gandhi's Cookbook won't be used in adverts by the Dubai tourist board anytime soon (their EP *In the Cesspool of Culture* wasn't very complimentary about their hometown), while Indiephone produce hyperactive rock. One Dubai band to break into the mainstream is Abri, a soulful funk outfit fronted by Dubai-born Hamdan Al-Abri. Since releasing their debut album, *Sunchild,* they've shared a stage at the Desert Rhythm festival with Kanye West and Joss Stone, and appeared on the cover of *Time Out Dubai.*

Metal is big in Dubai. Keep an ear out for death metal band Nervecell, which toured around Europe in 2009 and became the first Middle Eastern metal band to sign an international record deal with German label Lifeforce Records. Hard rock band Nikotin is also poised for the big stage, as they demonstrated when opening a concert for Nickelback in late 2009. Topping the list of up-and-comers is Crow, whose sound gets its edge from mixing all sorts of metal styles, from new metal to trash, with thoughtful lyrics.

Headbanging not your thing? Try the hip hop collective The Recipe, reggae rock by Sho?, modern rock by Juliana Down or acoustic ethnic rock with a '70s influence by the Arabic trio Dahab. There's also Sandwash, who started out as punk rockers but now produce 'groovecore', an intricate alchemy of sounds influenced by East African rhythms, rap, R&B and rock.

In recent years, many home-grown bands have been featured at local music festivals such as Liverpool import Dubai Sound City, Dubai Desert Rock and Desert Rhythm, but unfortunately, after several instalments, these were 'postponed until further notice' at the time of writing. The good news is that practically all local bands have MySpace and Facebook pages, so you can check out the Dubai sound before you even hop on that plane. Locally, radio station Dubai 92 FM gives plenty of air time to local bands and *Time Out* also keeps tabs on who deserves a closer listen. Websites worth looking into include www.phride.com and www.dubaibands.com.

For information on live music, see p134.

NEIGHBOURHOODS

top picks

What's your recommendation? www.lonelyplanet.com/dubai

NEIGHBOURHOODS

Let's make this absolutely clear. There is no excuse for spending your entire holiday lazing by the pool. It's essential you explore Dubai's sights – and no, a trip to Dubai Mall does not count as sightseeing.

Dubai may be vast and amorphous but the areas of interest to visitors are actually fairly well defined. Not far from Dubai International Airport, the neighbourhoods of Deira and Bur Dubai make up historic Dubai. A pastiche of mosques and souqs, they flank the Creek, a 15km inlet, and remain the city's heart and soul. They offer something the mega-resorts and gleaming skyscrapers of the new city simply can't provide – real life.

'Deira and Bur Dubai... offer something the mega-resorts and gleaming skyscrapers of the new city simply can't provide – real life'

The Creek is crossed by four bridges – Al-Garhoud, Al-Maktoum, Business Bay and the Floating Bridge – as well as Al-Shindagha Tunnel, open for vehicles and pedestrians. The new Dubai Metro also links the two banks. For all the billions spent on making Dubai the greatest show on earth, though, a five-minute, Dh1 ride on an *abra* (water taxi) is still the most atmospheric way to cross the Creek.

Dubai's main artery is Sheikh Zayed Rd, a super-busy highway that runs from the World Trade Centre Roundabout on the edge of Bur Dubai 55km south to Jebel Ali Port. In this chapter, the section called 'Sheikh Zayed Road' follows the highway as it cuts through the main business district around the World Trade Centre and Dubai International Financial Centre (DIFC); the vibrant new Downtown Dubai area, home of Burj Khalifa; and industrial, art-gallery-filled Al-Quoz as far as Interchange No 4 near the Mall of the Emirates.

The area north of Sheikh Zayed Rd – called 'Jumeirah' in this book – covers a variety of distinct neighbourhoods. In the north, bordering Bur Dubai, is ageing but vibrant Satwa, which has great ethnic eateries and one of the city's most walkable streets, Al-Dhiyafah Rd. Next up is Jumeirah proper, known for its public beaches, a couple of historical sites and hundreds of luxury villas. The spine of this sprawling area is Jumeirah Rd, which begins by the flagpole at the end of Al-Dhiyafah Rd and runs a couple of blocks inland from the sea for about 16km past the iconic Burj al-Arab hotel as far as the sprawling Madinat Jumeirah development. Along the way, it takes in several subdivisions, such as the three Jumeirah areas (logically named Jumeirah 1, Jumeirah 2, Jumeirah 3) and Umm Suqeim (also 1, 2, 3).

The rest of the city is also its newest part, and therefore referred to as 'New Dubai' in this book. With the exception of a few hotels, everything around here has been built in the last five to 10 years. New Dubai encompasses coastal Al-Sufouh 1 and 2, home to royal palaces and luxury beach resorts; and high-rise-studded Dubai Marina, which has more fancy hotels; the Jumeirah Beach Residences (JBR); and the popular The Walk at JBR outdoor eating and shopping promenade. Jutting into the water is the Palm Jumeirah, capped by the gigantic Atlantis – The Palm hotel. The 'New Dubai' section in this chapter also covers the inland neighbourhood of Al-Barsha, which is bisected by the remaining stretch of Sheikh Zayed Rd linking the Mall of the Emirates with Jebel Ali via the Ibn Battuta Mall.

While Deira and Bur Dubai are best explored by foot, Jumeirah, Sheikh Zayed Rd and New Dubai are not particularly pedestrian-friendly. Dubai Metro runs along Sheikh Zayed Rd, but otherwise you'll have to rely on taxis (unless, of course, you have your own wheels). For orientation purposes, a spin around town with the Big Bus Company (p192) is recommended.

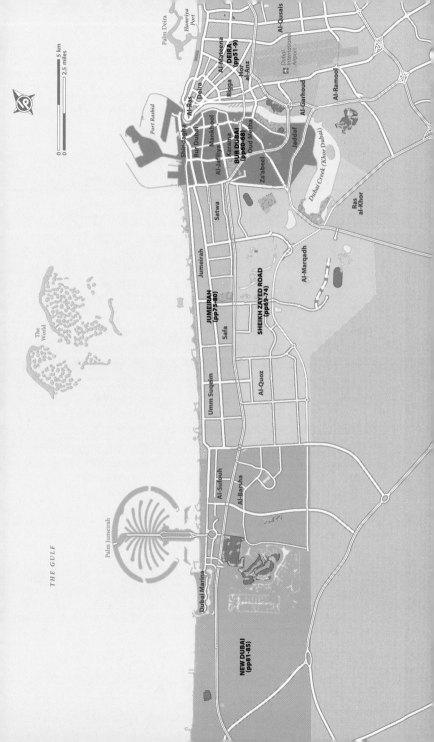

ITINERARY BUILDER

Two days is enough time to explore Bur Dubai and Deira. The area is relatively compact and can be covered by foot, with *abras* (water taxis) or water buses to cross the Creek. Jumeirah, Sheikh Zayed Rd and New Dubai are not so pedestrian-friendly and you'll either need to drive or take taxis. While it's fascinating to mix-and-match the old souqs of Deira with the beach resorts of New Dubai, the rush-hour traffic on the bridges can be horrendous, so it makes sense to stick to one side of the Creek at these times of day.

ACTIVITIES	Sights	Shopping
Deira	Al-Ahmadiya School (p56) Dhow Wharfage (p56) Heritage House (p56)	Deira Gold Souq (p51) Deira Spice Souq (p51) Pride of Kashmir (p93)
Bur Dubai	Bastakia Quarter (p61) Shindagha Heritage Area (p61) Dubai Museum (p60)	Amzaan (p94) Five Green (p94) Karama Shopping Centre (p96)
Sheikh Zayed Road	Burj Khalifa (p69) Dubai Fountain (p69) Third Line (p73)	Azza Fahmy Jewellery (p98) Dubai Mall (p99) Souk al-Bahar (p99)
Jumeirah	Burj al-Arab (p79) Jumeirah Mosque (p75) Madinat Jumeirah (p79)	Luxecouture (p100) Mercato Mall (p101) S*uce (p100)
New Dubai	Aquaventure (p81) Lost Chambers (p84) The Walk at JBR (p81)	Aizone (p102) Bauhaus (p102) Boutique 1 (p102)

AREA

HOW TO USE THIS TABLE

The table below allows you to plan a day's worth of activities in any area of the city. Simply select which area you wish to explore, and then mix and match from the corresponding listings to build your day. The first item in each cell represents a well-known highlight of the area, while the other items are more off-the-beaten-track gems.

Eating	Drinking	Sports, Spas & Outdoor Activities
Shabestan (p109)	Ku-Bu (p127)	Al-Mamzar Beach Park (p78)
Thai Kitchen (p110)	Irish Village (p127)	Amara (p142)
Verre by Gordon Ramsay (p108)		Dubai Creek Golf & Yacht Club (p147)
Bastakiah Nights (p111)	Chi@The Lodge (p133)	Creekside Park (p66)
Rajdhani (p113)	Ginseng (p128)	Pharaohs Club (p141)
Basta Art Cafe (p113)	New Asia Bar & Club (p128)	Za'abeel Park (p67)
Zuma (p116)	Calabar (p129)	Dubai Ice Rink (p144)
Spectrum on One (p116)	Neos (p129)	Ras al-Khor Wildlife Sanctuary (p72)
Karma Kafe (p115)	Hive (p129)	1847 (p142)
Lime Tree Café (p120)	360° (p130)	Jumeirah Beach Park (p78)
Pai Thai (p119)	Rooftop at Souq Madinat (p131)	Talise Spa (p143)
Ravi (p120)	Sho Cho (p131)	Wild Wadi Waterpark (p80)
Rhodes Mezzanine (p121)	Barasti Bar (p132)	Emirates Golf Club (p147)
Tagine (p123)	Maya (p132)	Oriental Hammam (p143)
Eauzone (p121)	Rooftop Bar (p132)	Ski Dubai (p144)

GREATER DUBAI

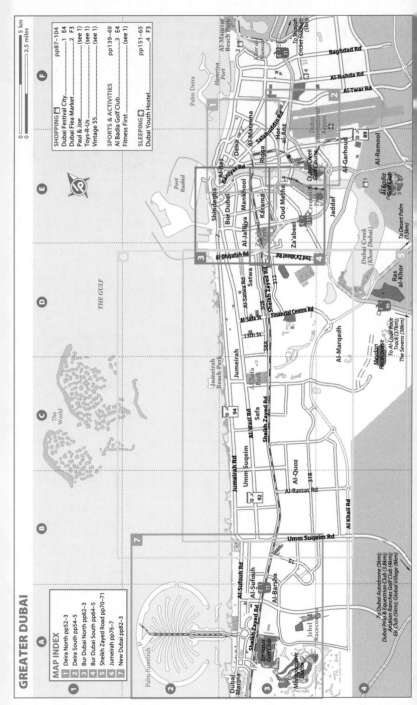

MAP INDEX

1	Deira North pp52–3
2	Deira South pp54–5
3	Bur Dubai North pp62–3
4	Bur Dubai South pp64–5
5	Sheikh Zayed Road pp70–71
6	Jumeirah pp76–7
7	New Dubai pp82–3

SHOPPING 🛍 pp87–104

Dubai Festival City...............	1 E4
Dubai Flea Market.................	2 F3
Paul & Joe..............................	(see 1)
Toys-R-Us..............................	(see 1)
Vintage 55.............................	(see 1)

SPORTS & ACTIVITIES pp139–49

Al Badia Golf Club..................	3 E4
Fitness First...........................	(see 1)

SLEEPING 🛏 pp151–65

Dubai Youth Hostel................	4 F3

Eating p108; Entertainment p127; Shopping p93; Sleeping p154

While the 'new' Dubai along Sheikh Zayed Rd feels like a blend of Singapore and Las Vegas, Deira feels more like a cross between Cairo and Karachi. Dusty, crowded and chaotic, it's a world away from the slick and sanitised city piercing the clouds at the other end of town. At the Dhow Wharfage, colourful wooden boats arrive from Iran with boxes of cuddly toys, televisions and batteries to be sold at the nearby souqs. At these atmospheric ancestors to today's malls, you can sip sugary tea and haggle for bargains with traders whose families have tended the same shop for generations.

Deira is fascinatingly multicultural. The language of the signs on shop windows changes every 50m, from Tamil to Sinhalese, Malayalam, Urdu, Pashto, Tagalog and Amharic. (Don't worry, everybody speaks a little English.) Adventurous foodies can lap up authentic fare in the Syrian, Ethiopian, Iraqi and Afghan sections of Deira. If you're there at night, you'll find Russian, Filipino, Lebanese, Indian and Pakistani nightclubs, often all on the same floor and typically featuring ear-rupturingly loud house bands, overpriced beers and, yes, plenty of illicit and seedy goings-on. Honestly, these dives are not without their charms; some of the best live music in the city is there for the taking if you keep your ears, eyes and mind open.

The most historic part of Deira is near the mouth of the Creek in an area called Al-Ras. This is where you'll find the souqs and markets. Baniyas Rd follows the Creek inland to an area called Rigga, which has a few hotels but is otherwise nondescript. South of Al-Maktoum Bridge, Port Saeed has pockets of interest, most notably the Deira City Centre mall, the Dubai Creek Golf & Yacht Club and the adjacent Park Hyatt hotel. Away from the Creek are Dubai International Airport and such exotic neighbourhoods as Al-Mateena and Naif.

The area is served by *abra* and water bus from Bur Dubai. The Dubai Metro Red Line stops at the airport, Deira City Centre, Rigga and Union Sq.

top picks

DEIRA

- Souqs Take in spicy aromas at the Spice Souq (below), glittering gold at the Gold Souq (below) and a glimpse of expat life at the Deira Covered Souq (p57) and the New Naif Market (p57).
- Al-Ahmadiya School (p56) and Heritage House (p56) Step back in time to discover the simpler life of old Dubai.
- Dhow Wharfage (p56) Marvel at how the dhows manage to stay afloat when there are several cars, a truck, and a warehouse's worth of electrical goods on deck.

DEIRA GOLD SOUQ Map pp52-3
On & around Sikkat al-Khail St, btwn Souq Deira & Old Baladiya Sts

All that glitters is gold (and occasionally silver) at this colourful market. At any given time over 25 tonnes of gold is on display in jewellery shop windows in Dubai. Even if you're not in the market for bling, a stroll through the covered arcades of the enormous Gold Souq is a must. Hundreds of stores overflow with every kind of jewellery imaginable – tasteful diamond earrings to over-the-top golden Indian wedding necklaces. It's the largest gold market in the region, and one of the largest in the world. Bonus: the people-watching. Settle down on a wooden bench beneath the wooden-latticed arcades of the main thoroughfare (Sikkat al-Khail St) and observe touts hawking knock-off watches, hard-working Afghan guys dragging heavy carts of goods and African women in colourful kaftans…it's all rather extraordinary.

DEIRA SPICE SOUQ Map pp52-3
Btwn Baniyas Rd, Al-Sabkha Rd & Al-Abra St

Just follow your nose to the best buys at this atmospheric souq. The guttural singsong of Arabic bounces around the lanes of this small covered market as stallholders work hard on you to unload aromatic frankincense, dried lemons, chillies or exotic herbs and spices. This ain't no Istanbul-like bazaar but it's still worth a half-hour of your time to take in

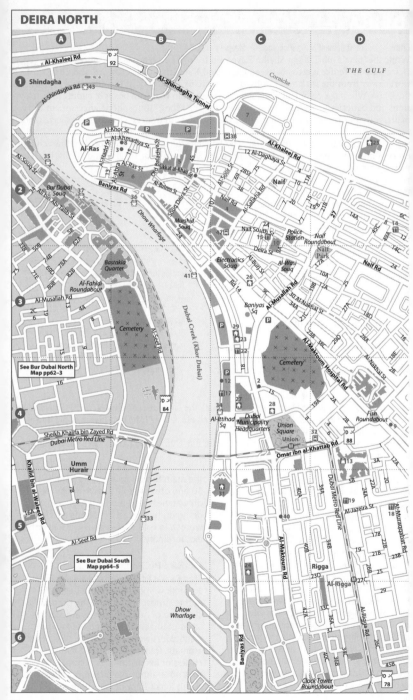

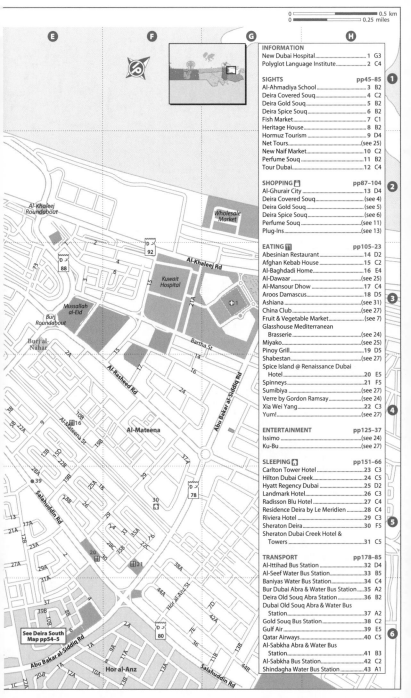

See Deira South Map pp54–5

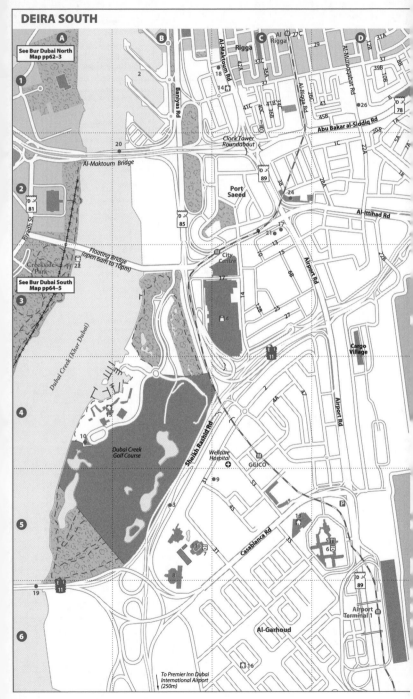

DEIRA SOUTH

See Bur Dubai North
Map pp62–3

See Bur Dubai South
Map pp64–5

Rigga

Al Rigga

Al-Maktoum Rd

Al-Muraqqabat Rd

Al-Rigga Rd

Abu Bakar al-Siddiq Rd

Baniyas Rd

Riyadh St

Clock Tower
Roundabout

Al-Maktoum Bridge

Port
Saeed

Al-Ittihad Rd

Floating Bridge
(open 6am to 70pm)

Creekside
Park

City
Centre

Dubai Creek (Khor Dubai)

Airport Rd

Cargo
Village

Dubai Creek
Golf Course

Wellcare
Hospital

GGICO

Airport Rd

Sheikh Rashid Rd

Casablanca Rd

Al-Garhoud

Airport
Terminal 1

To Premier Inn Dubai
International Airport
(250m)

54

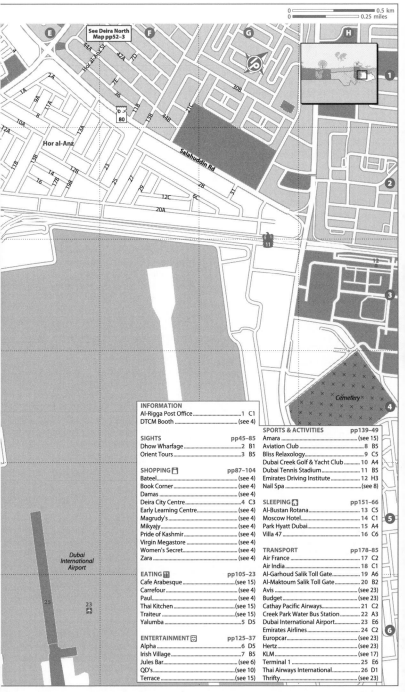

Hor al-Anz

Salahuddin Rd

Dubai International Airport

Cemetery

See Deira North Map pp52–3

the wonderfully restored wind towers and the pungent aromas from the jute sacks. Since this is a working souq, not a tourist attraction, the tiny shops also sell groceries, plastics and other household goods to locals and sailors from the dhows. Good buys include incense burners, saffron, rose water, henna kits and *sheesha* pipes.

HERITAGE HOUSE Map pp52-3
☎ 226 0286; Al-Ahmadiya St, north of Spice Souq; admission free; ◷ 8am-7.30pm Sat-Thu, 2.30-7.30pm Fri

This renovated 1890 courtyard house once belonged to Sheikh Ahmed bin Dalmouk, the founder of Al-Ahmadiya School (see below), and offers a rare opportunity to peek inside a wealthy pearl merchant's residence. Built from coral and gypsum, its rooms wrap around a central courtyard flanked by verandahs to keep direct sunlight out. Videos set up in several rooms highlight various aspects of daily life, including the types of traditional games children once played in the courtyard.

AL-AHMADIYA SCHOOL Map pp52-3
☎ 226 0286; Al-Ahmadiya St, north of Spice Souq; admission free; ◷ 8am-7.30pm Sat-Thu, 2.30-7.30pm Fri

Dubai's first school was founded by the pearl merchant Sheikh Ahmed bin Dalmouk and welcomed its first students, all boys, in 1912. You can see the original classroom where they squeezed behind wooden

desks to learn the Holy Quran, grammar, Arabic calligraphy, mathematics, literature and astronomy. Otherwise, exhibits are pretty basic but the building itself is not: note the exquisite detail, especially the intricate carving within the courtyard arches and the decorative gypsum panels outside the entrance. It remained in use as a school until the student body outgrew the premises in 1963.

DHOW WHARFAGE Map pp54-5
Along Baniyas Rd

Dhows are long, flat, wooden vessels used in the Indian Ocean and Arabian Sea, and they've docked at the Creek since the 1830s when the Maktoums established a free-trade port, luring merchants away from Persia. Today's dhows trade with Iran, Iraq, Pakistan, Oman, India, Yemen, Somalia and Sudan, and you'll see them precariously loaded with everything from air-conditioners to chewing gum to car tyres, almost all of it re-exported after arriving by air or container ship from countries like China, South Korea and Singapore. Try to chat to the sailors if you can – if you find one who speaks English, you may learn that it takes a day to get to Iran by sea and seven days to Somalia, or that dhow captains earn as little as Dh400 a month. If your sailor friend is in a chatty mood, he may even regale you with real-life pirate stories. The gangs of thieves that stalk the waters off Yemen and Somalia sometimes make life very tough for Dubai's hard-working dhow sailors.

GET LOST: DEIRA

Sometimes it pays to rip up the script and improvise. Some of the most fascinating parts of town aren't home to a single tourist attraction worth recommending, but are brimming with the soul the city is so frequently accused of lacking. Dubai is a safe city – there aren't any no-go areas and even the scariest-looking alleyways will be quite harmless. Be adventurous and spontaneous. Put away the maps and follow your instinct. But before you hurl this guidebook into the Creek, read our suggestions of the best areas in Deira in which to get hopelessly, joyously lost.

Naif (Map pp52-3) The area between Naif Rd and Al-Khaleej Rd is a labyrinthine muddle of slim, cluttered streets, and one of the best places in town for urban photography. It's not always pretty, but here you'll find old men smoking *sheesha* and playing backgammon on the pavements; pockets of Ethiopia and Somalia; hilariously awful fake Rolexes; games consoles; heady perfumes; blindingly bright neon shop facades; and the occasional goat, walking nonchalantly down the centre of the street. You just don't get this on The Palm Jumeirah...

Al-Mateena (Map pp52-3) Despite its out-of-the-way location, Al-Mateena St is one of the most enticing walk streets in town, with wide pavements, palm trees and a narrow park-like strip running along its centre. In the Iraqi restaurants and cafes you'll see *masgouf* – a whole fish sliced in half, spicily seasoned and barbecued over an open flame. And the *sheesha* cafes have to be seen to be believed: check out the rock gardens, dangling fronds and artificial lakes. Nearby Al-Muraqqabat Rd brims with superb Syrian and Palestinian eateries.

CREEK CROSSING

Dubai Creek (the Creek) meanders for some 15km from Shindagha to the Ras al-Khor Wildlife Refuge, dividing Deira from Bur Dubai. Its banks were where members of the Bani Yas tribe first settled when arriving in the area in 1833. Used for pearling and fishing expeditions in the early 20th century, the Creek was dredged in 1961 to allow larger commercial vessels to dock. The first bridge, Al-Maktoum Bridge, opened two years later.

To this day, many people have a mental barrier when it comes to crossing the Creek over to Deira. Think of it as Londoners' aversion to going 'south of the river' or Manhattanites' reticence to head across to Brooklyn. While it's true that traffic can be horrible during rush hour, congestion eased in 2007 with the opening of the 13-lane Business Bay Bridge near Festival City, and a six-lane Floating Bridge (open 6am to 10pm) near Creekside Park. A fourth bridge, Al-Garhoud Bridge, was widened to 13 lanes. There's also Al-Shindagha Tunnel near the mouth of the Creek, which is open for both vehicles and pedestrians.

Using public transport, you now have three options for crossing the Creek. The fastest and easiest is Dubai Metro's Red Line (p182), which runs below the Creek between Union and Khalid bin al-Waleed stations. The most atmospheric way to get across, though, is a Dh1 ride aboard a traditional abra (water taxi; p182) that links the Bur Dubai and Deira souqs in a quick five minutes. In summer, you might prefer the air-conditioned comfort of the new water buses (p183), which cost just a few dirham more.

FISH MARKET Map pp52-3
Al-Khaleej Rd, near Al-Shindagha Tunnel
Shrimp the size of bananas, metre-long kingfish and mountains of blue crabs are among the treasures of the sea being hawked at Dubai's largest and busiest fish market. The smell can be a bit overpowering but you'll get used to it after a while and it's great to watch not just the wiggling wares but the wild haggling between the blue-suited vendors and their customers. Come either early in the morning or in the evening, and wear sneakers or other waterproof shoes. If you're buying, ask to have the fish cleaned. The adjacent fruit and vegetable market isn't nearly as exciting but great for stocking up on anything fresh from pears to papayas, all neatly stacked and bargain-priced. Date lovers have a whole row of stands to peruse.

DEIRA COVERED SOUQ Map pp52-3
Btwn Al-Sabkha Rd, 107 St & Naif Rd
Despite the name, Deira Covered Souq is only partly covered and really more a warren of small shops on narrow lanes spread across a few square blocks. Even if you're not keen on cheap textiles, knock-off Dior scarves, kandouras (casual shirt-dresses worn by men and women) and kitchenware, you're sure to be wowed by the high-energy street scene.

NEW NAIF MARKET Map pp52-3
Btwn Naif South St, 9a St & Deira St
At the time of writing, shopkeepers were looking forward to moving into the New Naif Market, built on the same site as the historic Naif Souq that succumbed to a major blaze in 2008. Scheduled to open in May 2010, the new air-conditioned building is set to feature more than 200 shops spread over two floors.

DEIRA SOUQ STROLL
Walking Tour
1 Spice Souq As soon as you step off the *abra* at Deira Old Souq Abra Station, the heady scents of sumac, cinnamon, cloves and other spices will lure you across to the Spice Souq (p51). Take some time to explore and ask the shopkeepers what's in those sacks. Turn right as you exit on Al-Abra St, then left on Al-Ras St and right again on Al-Hadd St. The stores along here selling nuts, pulses and rice belong to wholesalers trading mainly with Iran and using the dhows to ply their goods.

top picks
HERITAGE SIGHTS
- Al-Ahmadiya School (opposite)
- Bastakia Quarter (p61)
- Dhow Wharfage (opposite)
- Dubai Museum (p60)
- Heritage & Diving Villages (p66)
- Heritage House (opposite)
- Jumeirah Archaeological Site (p78)
- Sheikh Saeed al-Maktoum House (p61)
- Shindagha Heritage Area (p61)

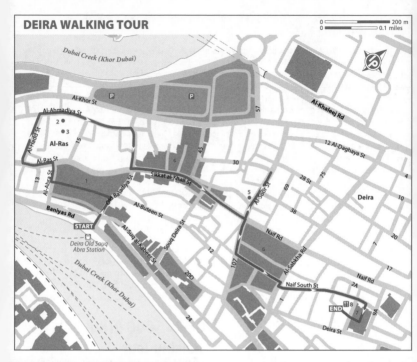

DEIRA WALKING TOUR

0 ——— 200 m
0 ——— 0.1 miles

2 Heritage House At the end of Al-Hadd St turn right and follow Al-Ahmadiya St to the beautifully restored Heritage House (p56) for intriguing insights into Dubai's history and culture and a closer look at the simple but splendid architecture of a historic courtyard house.

3 Al-Ahmadiya School Behind Heritage House is Dubai's first school, Al-Ahmadiya School (p56). Look around, then continue along Al-Ahmadiya St, turning right into Old Baladiya St, where you'll find more wholesalers, this time trading in *gutras* (men's white headcloths) and *agals* (black head ropes used to hold *gutras* in place), sandals and Chinese products. If you're in the market for an Emirati national dress as a souvenir, here's the place to shop.

4 Gold Souq Ahead, to the left, is the wooden latticed archway entrance to Dubai's famous Gold Souq (p51). Take time to pop into the small shops to look at over-the-top gold pieces created for brides' dowries and duck into the narrow lanes to suss out tiny teashops, simple cafeterias, busy tailors and barber shops.

5 Perfume Souq Exit the Gold Souq and follow Sikkat al-Khail St to Al-Soor St and turn left. This is the heart of the Perfume Souq, a string of shops selling heady Arabian *attars* (perfumes) and *oud* (fragrant wood), fake 'European' colognes with ridiculous labels, and pretty tinted perfume bottles. Backtrack and continue straight on what is now 107 St, where it can be bedlam some nights with hawkers competing to sell off their cut-price clothes, Chinese-made shoes and kitschy souvenirs.

6 Deira Covered Souq Tucked east of 107 St are the tiny alleys of the Deira Covered Souq (p57) which – natch! – isn't covered at all but a warren of little shops selling everything from textiles to luggage, groceries and *sheesha* pipes. Arriving near Al-Sabkha Rd bus station, cross the road and head into Naif South St.

7 New Naif Market Follow Naif South St, turn right into 9A St and keep going until you arrive at the New Naif Market (p57), which has risen from the ashes of the historic Naif Souq, which was devastated by fire in May 2008.

8 Afghan Kebab House If you've worked up an appetite rambling though Deira's souqs, a carnivorous feast at Afghan Kebab House (see boxed text, p110) will keep you sated for ages. Find it by turning right into a little alley about half a block past the Naif Mosque.

Eating p111; Entertainment p128; Shopping p94; Sleeping p156

Bur Dubai was the first part of the city to be settled and still serves up a slice of life from the emirate's early days. There are several distinct districts. The oldest areas are along the Creek. Near the mouth of the Creek, quiet Shindagha is filled with historic buildings and great for a waterfront stroll, especially at sunset. South of here, the Bur Dubai Souq district is almost as vibrant as its Deira counterpart, and is the place to catch *abras* and water buses to stops further along the Creek. Further on is Dubai Museum and the charming, car-free Bastakia Quarter with its restored courtyard houses and wind towers. From here, Al-Seef Rd leads south along the waterfront to Umm Hurair, home to most foreign consulates.

Away from the Creek, Bur Dubai becomes rather nondescript, if not without highlights. The Mankhool district is stacked with inexpensive hotel apartments, quirky nightlife, good restaurants and an upmarket mall called BurJuman Centre. South of the mall, across Sheikh Khalifa bin Zayed Rd, Karama is a hive of activity and has a real community feel to it thanks to its mostly Filipino and Indian population. It's well worth a wander for its excellent bargain shopping and ethnic eateries serving princely meals at paupers' prices. South of Za'abeel Rd, sprawling Oud Metha is easily recognised by the Egyptian-themed Wafi Mall and pyramid-shaped Raffles hotel.

Dubai Metro Red Line stops are Khalid bin al-Waleed (for BurJuman Centre), Al Karama and Al Jafiliya. Once the Green Line is operational, it will travel south to Oud Metha.

top picks

BUR DUBAI

- **Dubai Museum (below)** Visit the museum for a speedy and entertaining introduction to the city.
- **Sheikh Saeed al-Maktoum House (opposite)** Stroll through the elegantly restored house where there's a rare collection of amazing black-and-white photographs of early Dubai.
- **Bastakia Quarter (opposite)** Walk through Dubai's 'old town' and pop into XVA Gallery (opposite) for a salad, a fruit juice and a peek at the latest exhibition.

DUBAI MUSEUM Map pp62-3

☎ 353 1862; Al-Fahidi St, opp Grand Mosque; adult/child Dh3/1; ☗ 8.30am-8.30pm Sat-Thu, 2.30-8.30pm Fri; ⚹

Unless some mad scientist invents a magic time-travel machine, this nifty museum is your ticket to exploring Dubai's history, culture and traditions in an hour or so. Exhibits are housed in the 1799 Al-Fahidi Fort, considered the oldest building in Dubai and once the seat of government and residence of Dubai's rulers.

This low-key museum tells the Dubai story with minimal fuss and plenty of charm. Start with a quick spin around the courtyard with its old-time fishing boats and traditional dwellings, including a *barasti* house with wind tower. Pop behind the heavy carved wooden doors to check out modest displays of instruments and hand-crafted weapons before heading down a spiralling ramp to the main galleries. In the first room a slick multimedia presentation charts Dubai's exponential growth from tiny trading post to megalopolis, although the timeline on the opposite wall goes into greater depth. Beyond here, a series of cutesy dioramas recreate Old Dubai, complete with a souq, a school, a desert camp and other settings. Other displays focus on the Bedu and desert flora and fauna; traditional costumes and jewellery; and pearling, fishing and dhow boat building. Last up is the archaeology section with locally unearthed artefacts. A highlight is a recreated grave

ABRA CRUISING

Fifteen thousand people cross Dubai Creek (the Creek) each day on *abras*, traditional wooden water taxis, for just Dh1 a journey. You can hire an *abra* to do the same trip the cruise companies do, but you'll be at water level, with the wind in your hair and seagulls in your face. It's a more interesting experience, especially if the boat captain speaks a little English or you speak Urdu, Hindi or Arabic – you might learn a whole lot more about the Creek and those who work on it. *Abras* can be hired from *abra* stations along the Creek for Dh100 per hour.

from the Al-Qusais tombs. Explanatory panelling is in English and Arabic.

BASTAKIA QUARTER Map pp62-3

Traffic fades to a quiet hum in the labyrinthine lanes of the historic Bastakia Quarter teeming with restored wind tower houses built nearly a century ago by wealthy pearl and textile merchants from Persia. Typical houses are two storeys, with a central courtyard with rooms opening onto it, and decorative arches featuring intricate carvings. Quite plain from the outside, they feature wonderful carved wooden doors, crenulations, carved grilles and stucco panels. The Sheikh Mohammed Centre for Cultural Understanding (p66) operates guided Bastakia walking tours at 10am on Sunday and Thursday (Dh50, reservations advised), but the compact area is also easily explored on an aimless wander.

XVA GALLERY Map pp62-3

☎ 353 5383; www.xvagallery.com; behind Majlis Gallery & Orient Guest House, Al-Musallah Roundabout; ☯ 9am-7pm Sat-Thu
One of Dubai's best-loved and most reputable galleries, XVA occupies a warren of rooms in a beautifully restored Bastakia courtyard residence. Curators showcase contemporary paintings, sculptures and art installations from regional and international artists. They also organise the annual Bastakiya Art Fair (p16) and art-house movie screenings (November to April). The complex also houses the delightful XVA cafe (p113) and boutique hotel (p157).

MAJLIS GALLERY Map pp62-3

☎ 353 6233; www.majlisgallery.com; Al-Fahidi Roundabout; ☯ 9.30am-8pm Sat-Thu, closed Fri
In a fabulous old house in the Bastakia Quarter, Majlis Gallery is one of Dubai's oldest commercial galleries, established in 1989. Compared with the progressive galleries in Al-Quoz (p73), Majlis is much more traditional and gentle, focusing on paintings and sculpture created by international artists, many of them based in – and inspired by – the region.

AL SERKAL CULTURAL FOUNDATION Map pp62-3

☎ 358 7070; www.heritagehouse.ae; Heritage House 79, next to XVA, Al-Musallah Roundabout; ☯ 9.30am-8pm Sat-Thu, closed Fri

This rambling Bastakia Quarter courtyard building with its labyrinth of galleries provides a fitting setting for both traditional and cutting-edge works by local and international artists. In the courtyard are impressive relief portraits of Sheikh Zayed.

BUR DUBAI SOUQ Map pp62-3

Btwn Bur Dubai waterfront & Al-Fahidi St
The breezy renovated Bur Dubai Souq may not be old as the Deira souqs but it can be just as atmospheric. Friday evenings here are especially lively, as it turns into a virtual crawling carnival with expat workers loading up on socks, T-shirts and knock-off Calvins on their day off. Other stores specialise in colourful bales of fancy fabrics, most of them from India and other Asian countries. The surrounding streets – crammed with tailors, sari stores and jewellery shops – may not be as pleasing to the eye but are still intriguing and worth exploring.

SHINDAGHA HERITAGE AREA

Map pp62-3
The Shindagha waterfront near the mouth of the Creek is one of the most historical areas in Dubai, with origins in the 1860s. It significantly gained in importance in the late 19th century when the ruling family relocated here. The old district has been under restoration since 1996 and many of the gorgeous residences and mosques sparkle in renewed splendour. A paved walkway, dotted with a few restaurants, parallels the waterfront and is popular with strollers and joggers. The nicest time to visit is around sunset.

SHEIKH SAEED AL-MAKTOUM HOUSE Map pp62-3

☎ 393 7139; Shindagha Heritage Area; adult/child Dh2/1; ☯ 8am-8.30pm Sat-Thu, 3-9.30pm Fri
The grand courtyard house of Sheikh Saeed, the grandfather of current Dubai ruler Sheikh Mohammed, is the crown jewel of the restored Shindagha Heritage Area. Built in 1896, under Sheikh Maktoum bin Hasher al-Maktoum, the house was home to the ruling family until Sheikh Saeed's death in 1958. Aside from being an architectural marvel, the building now doubles as a museum of pre-oil times, with a neat collection of photographs of Dubai

BUR DUBAI NORTH

10A
24A
2A
3 Al-Wasl Rd
6A

See Jumeirah
Map pp76–7

8A
12A
16A 18A
Satwa
Roundabout

Al-Satwa Rd
6A
4

3A
12A
35
Satwa
18B
20A
22A

Al-Dhiyafah Rd

5

See Sheikh Zayed Road
Map pp70–71

Sheikh Zayed Rd

6

2nd Za'abeel Rd

Za'abeel Roundabout
(World Trade Centre
Roundabout)

36
2B
2A

DEC Gas
Power
Station

4B
6B
6B
8C
Al-Mankhool Rd
2B
4B

37
29
Kuwait St

4A
6A
3B

Al-Mankhool Rd

2A

43A
4E
35A
2A
4D
47A
39A

10D
12C
10C

Al-
Jafiliya

Al-Adhid Rd
Al-Jafiliya

Department of
Health & Medical
Services

Al Jafiliya

Sheikh Khalifa bin Zayed Rd

Al Karama

Al-Adhid Rd

Za'abeel Park

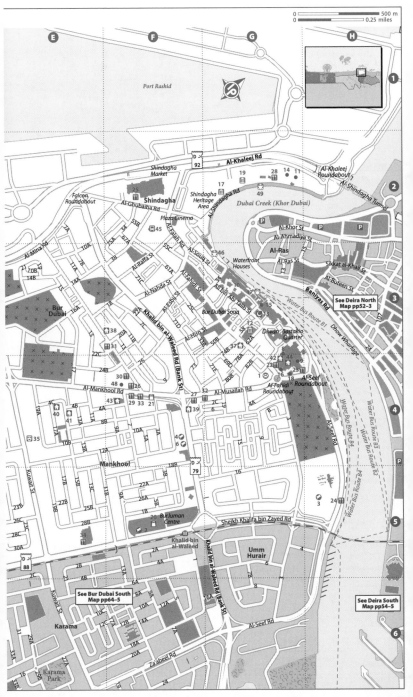

Port Rashid

Al-Khaleej Rd

Shindagha Market

Shindagha Heritage Area

Falcon Roundabout

Shindagha

Al-Ghubaiba Rd

Al-Shindagha Rd

Plaza Cinema

Al-Mina Rd

Al-Fahidi St

Al-Souq St

Al-Raffa St

Al-Nahda St

Al-Fahidi St

Al-Esbij St

Khalid bin al-Waleed Rd (Bank St)

Bur Dubai

Al-Hisn St

Bur Dubai Souq

Al-Jaa Abraham St

Al-Khaleej Roundabout

Al-Shindagha Tunnel

Dubai Creek (Khor Dubai)

Al-Khor St

Al-Ahmadiya St

Al-Ras

Al-Ras St

Sikkat al-Khail St

Al-Buteen St

Waterfront Houses

Baniyas Rd

See Deira North Map pp52–3

Water Bus Route B1

Dhow Wharfage

Diwan Bastakia Quarter

Al-Seef Roundabout

Al-Fahidi Roundabout

Al-Musallah Rd

Al-Mankhool Rd

Mankhool

Kuwait St

BurJuman Centre

Khalid bin al-Waleed Rd (Bank St)

Al-Seef Rd

Water Bus Route B4

Water Bus Route B3

Water Bus Route B2

Sheikh Khalifa bin Zayed Rd

Khalid bin al-Waleed

Umm Hurair

Al-Seef Rd

See Bur Dubai South Map pp64–5

See Deira South Map pp54–5

Karama

Kuwait St

Zabeel Rd

Karama Park

63

BUR DUBAI SOUTH

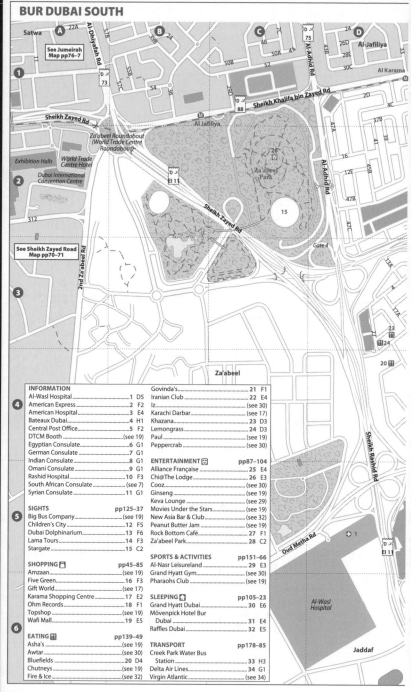

INFORMATION	
Al-Wasl Hospital	1 D5
American Express	2 F2
American Hospital	3 E4
Bateaux Dubai	4 H1
Central Post Office	5 F2
DTCM Booth	(see 19)
Egyptian Consulate	6 G1
German Consulate	7 G1
Indian Consulate	8 G1
Omani Consulate	9 G1
Rashid Hospital	10 F3
South African Consulate	(see 7)
Syrian Consulate	11 G1

SIGHTS	pp125–37
Big Bus Company	(see 19)
Children's City	12 F5
Dubai Dolphinarium	13 F6
Lama Tours	14 F3
Stargate	15 C2

SHOPPING	pp45–85
Amzaan	(see 19)
Five Green	16 F3
Gift World	(see 17)
Karama Shopping Centre	17 E2
Ohm Records	18 F1
Topshop	(see 19)
Wafi Mall	19 E5

EATING	pp139–49
Asha's	(see 19)
Awtar	(see 30)
Bluefields	20 D4
Chutneys	(see 19)
Fire & Ice	(see 32)

Govinda's	21 F1
Iranian Club	22 E4
Iz	(see 30)
Karachi Darbar	(see 17)
Khazana	23 D3
Lemongrass	24 D3
Paul	(see 19)
Peppercrab	(see 30)

ENTERTAINMENT	pp87–104
Alliance Française	25 E4
Chi@The Lodge	26 E3
Cooz	(see 30)
Ginseng	(see 19)
Keva Lounge	(see 29)
Movies Under the Stars	(see 19)
New Asia Bar & Club	(see 32)
Peanut Butter Jam	(see 19)
Rock Bottom Café	27 F1
Za'abeel Park	28 C2

SPORTS & ACTIVITIES	pp151–66
Al-Nasr Leisureland	29 E3
Grand Hyatt Gym	(see 30)
Pharaohs Club	(see 19)

SLEEPING	pp105–23
Grand Hyatt Dubai	30 E6
Mövenpick Hotel Bur Dubai	31 E4
Raffles Dubai	32 E5

TRANSPORT	pp178–85
Creek Park Water Bus Station	33 H3
Delta Air Lines	34 G1
Virgin Atlantic	(see 34)

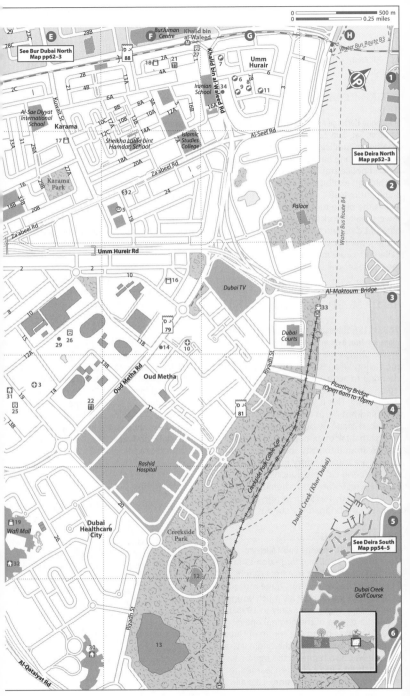

See Bur Dubai North
Map pp62–3

E   **28B**   **F** BurJuman Khalid bin
Centre al-Waleed

G   **H**

29   23C
28C

Water Bus Route B3

D 88   18 2A 21
4A 27   7

Umm
Hurair

4

2B
2C   4B   13A   Iranian
School   6
9   8
34   11

Kuwait St   6A
8B 8A 9A   12A 16B
Al-Sae Diyyat
International
School   10C 10B 13B 10A 12A 16A
17   12C
Karama   Sheikha Latifa bint
Hamdan School   Islamic
Studies
College

33A 31 29A   Za'abeel Rd
18A 20A   Al-Seef Rd

16   Karama
Park

See Deira North
Map pp52–3

18B 13B 20B   2
5 19   24

Za'abeel Rd

Umm Hureir Rd

2   2   10   16

Palace

Dubai TV   **Al-Maktoum Bridge**

D 79   33

Dubai
Courts

29 26   11B
14   10

3   13B   Riyadh St

22   **Oud Metha Rd**   **Oud Metha**   Floating Bridge
(Open 6am to 10pm)

31 19
25
13B   12   **D** 81

Rashid
Hospital

20   Creekside Park Cable Car

Dubai Creek (Khor Dubai)

See Deira South
Map pp54–5

19   **Dubai
Healthcare
City**
Wafi Mall
26   Creekside
Park
32
12
30
13   Dubai Creek
Golf Course

Al-Qatalyat Rd

0 ———————— 500 m
0 ———————— 0.25 miles

65

taken in the 1940s and '50s on the Creek, in the souqs and at traditional celebrations. Other rooms feature coins, stamps and documents dating back as far as 1791, as well as an interesting display on pearl diving.

SHEIKH JUMA AL-MAKTOUM HOUSE
Map pp62-3

Shindagha Heritage Area; admission free; 8am-8pm Mon-Sat, 8am-2.30pm Sun
Another magnificent Shindagha courtyard house, this one has seen stints as residence, jail and police station. Today it houses a thorough exhibit on traditional Arab architecture (see p38 for more information). This is the place to learn how those wind towers really work and why there are different dwelling types along the coast, in the mountains and in the desert. Some galleries feature informative videos, which the caretaker will be only too happy to start up.

HERITAGE & DIVING VILLAGES
Map pp62-3

393 7151; Shindagha Heritage Area; 8am-10pm Sat-Thu, 8-11am & 4-10pm Fri
On the Shindagha waterfront, the Heritage and Diving Villages are outdoor museums intended to acquaint tourists with the region's traditional arts, customs and architecture. This is where you can nibble on piping-hot *dosas* (paper-thin lentil-flour pancakes) made by burka-clad women, pose with a falconer, hop on a camel or browse around touristy souqs. Alas, the villages are usually pretty quiet year-round, except during Eid celebrations and the Dubai Shopping Festival (p15), when unusual traditional activities such as rifle-throwing competitions bring in the curious.

GRAND MOSQUE Map pp62-3
Ali bin Abi Talib St, opposite Dubai Museum
More than 50 small and large domes lorded over by Dubai's tallest minaret (70m high, if you must know) give this huge mosque its distinctive silhouette. It's much younger than it looks, dating back only to 1998, but is in fact a replica of the original one from 1900. As well as being the centre of Dubai's religious and cultural life, the original Grand Mosque was also home to the town's *kuttab* school, where children learned to recite the Quran from memory. Like all

Dubai mosques except Jumeirah Mosque (p75), it's off limits to non-Muslims.

'HINDI LANE' Map pp62-3
Behind Grand Mosque, off Ali bin Abi Talib St
Venturing behind the Grand Mosque you'll stumble upon two places of worship behind very modest exteriors – just keep an eye out for the piles of shoes at the bottom of stairways. One set of staircases leads to the Shri Nathje Jayate Temple, also known as the Krishna Mandir (*mandir* is Hindi for temple). Shri Nathje is the main deity of Pushtimarg, a Hindu devotional sect based near Udaipur in Rajasthan, India. Just beyond this temple (heading towards the Creek) is a colourful alleyway expats refer to as 'Hindi Lane', where vendors sell religious paraphernalia and offerings to take to the temples: baskets of fruit, garlands of flowers, gold-embossed holy images, sacred ash, sandalwood paste and packets of bindis (the little pendants Hindu women stick to their foreheads). Tucked amid the bustle is a series of staircases leading up to the other house of worship, the Sikh Gurudaba.

CREEKSIDE PARK Map pp64-5
336 7633; off Riyadh St, btwn Al-Garhoud & Al-Maktoum Bridges; admission Dh5; 8am-11pm Sat-Wed, 8am-11.30pm Thu-Fri & public holidays;
Large and lovely, this Creekside park has playgrounds for kids to romp around, gardens for relaxing, kiosks, restaurants and barbecue pits. It's hugely popular, especially on weekends. A 2.5km cable-car ride (tickets adult/child Dh25/15) delivers

OPEN DOORS, OPEN MINDS
Such is the enlightened motto of the Sheikh Mohammed Centre for Cultural Understanding (Map pp62-3; 353 6666; www.cultures.ae, near Al-Seef Roundabout, Bastakia), a unique institution founded by Sheikh Mohammed in 1995 to build bridges between the cultures and help visitors and expats understand the traditions and customs of the United Arab Emirates (UAE). In addition to conducting guided tours of the Bastakia Quarter and Jumeirah Mosque (p75), the centre also hosts a hugely popular Cultural Breakfast (Dh50; 10am Mon) and Cultural Lunch (Dh60; 1pm Sun) where you get a chance to meet, ask questions of and exchange ideas with nationals while tasting delicious home-made Emirati food. Make reservations as early as possible.

fabulous vistas of the park and waterfront from 30 metres in the air.

Kids naturally gravitate to Children's City (☎ 334 0808; www.childrencity.ae; enter through Gate 1; adult/child/family Dh15/10/40; ☽ 9am-8.30pm Sat-Thu, 3-8.30pm Fri; ♿), a learning centre jam-packed with interactive exhibits that playfully explain scientific concepts, the human body, space exploration and natural wonders. Since summer 2008, the resident bottlenose dolphins and fur seals of the Dubai Dolphinarium (☎ 336 9773; www.dubaidolphinarium.ae; enter through Gate 1; adult/child Dh100/50; ☽ shows 11am & 5pm Mon-Thu, 11am, 3pm & 6pm Fri & Sat) have delighted audiences with their tricks and stunts. Private swimming sessions with Flipper's cousins are also available (Dh1600 for up to three people). Although now quite popular, the facility's opening generated significant criticism from animal rights activists contending that these magnificent creatures should not be held in captivity.

ZA'ABEEL PARK Map pp64-5

☎ 800 900; cnr Sheikh Khalifa bin Zayed & Al-Qataiyat Rds; admission Dh5; ☽ 8am-11pm Sun-Wed, to 11.30pm Thu-Sat; ♿
This 51-hectare park has gorgeous lakes, ponds, a jogging track, a skateboard park, a BMX track and retail and food facilities – not to mention fabulous views of the Sheikh Zayed Rd skyline. The latest attraction to open here is Stargate (☎ 325 9988; www.stargatedubai.com; enter through Gate 4; admission Dh2, plus pay-as-you-go per attraction; ☽ 10am-10pm Sat-Wed, 10am-midnight Thu & Fri; ♿), a space-themed amusement park aimed at kids aged four to 14. It consists of five domed buildings (named Earth, Moon, Saturn, Mars and Ufo) where they can race go-karts, ride a roller coaster, take a spin on a small ice rink or watch 3D movies.

BUR DUBAI WATERSIDE WALK
Walking Tour
1 Bastakiah Nights This heritage walk of Dubai's oldest areas kicks off in the Bastakia Quarter, right at the romantic Bastakiah Nights (p111) restaurant, near Al-Seef Rd. Even if you're not eating, staff are usually happy for you to walk around this lavishly decorated courtyard house. Afterwards, spend some time wandering around the quarter's atmospheric narrow lanes and peeking into renovated wind tower houses.

2 XVA Savour the ambience of XVA (p61), an art gallery, cafe, gift shop and hotel in a superbly restored Bastakia courtyard residence.

3 Al Serkal Cultural Foundation Next door to XVA, check out the latest exhibits at the Al Serkal Cultural Foundation (p61), an art gallery and cultural centre inside yet another charming courtyard building.

4 Majlis Gallery Make three lefts as you exit Al Serkal to inspect the exquisite paintings and sculpture from regionally renowned artists at Majlis Gallery (p61).

5 Basta Art Cafe Grab a refreshing fruit cocktail or crisp salad at Basta Art Cafe (p113), a

WALK FACTS
Start **Bastakiah Nights**
End **Kan Zaman**
Distance **3km**
Duration **Three to four hours (including museum visit)**
Fuel Stop **Kan Zaman**

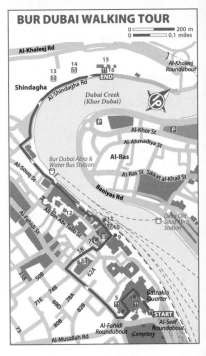

BUR DUBAI WALKING TOUR

charming walled garden where you can laze below drapes on turquoise benches or lounge on pillows in an outdoor *majlis* (sitting room) on a raised platform.

6 Dubai Museum Head north along Al-Fahidi St to the ancient fort converted into the delightful Dubai Museum (p60) for a relaxed hour soaking up the history, heritage and development of this burgeoning city.

7 Grand Mosque Turn right as you exit the museum and immediately make another right on 58A St for great views of the reserved architectural details of the multidomed Grand Mosque (p66). Make a mental note to look for old photos of the original Grand Mosque when visiting Sheikh Saeed al-Maktoum House later on this tour.

8 Shri Nathje Jayate Temple Take the lane to the mosque's right-hand side, passing the humble Hindu Shri Nathje Jayate Temple (p66), upstairs on your left.

9 Hindi Lane Continue straight ahead for a few steps to get to Hindi Lane (p66), a vibrant and colourful alley lined with tiny stores selling religious paraphernalia. Turn left into the alleyway.

10 Sikh Gurudaba Temple Walking along Hindi Lane, you'll notice rows of shoes at the bottom of stairs that lead up to the Sikh Gurudaba Temple (p66).

11 Creekside Plaza Follow Hindi Lane to the end, then turn right down a narrow walkway leading to an open plaza along the Creek, which gives you picture-perfect views of the *abra* and dhow traffic as well as the restored wind towers across the water in Deira. Looking back up the Creek on the Bur Dubai side you'll see some handsomely renovated traditional houses with wooden windows, decorative gypsum panels and screens. Backtrack up the walkway, then hook a right into…

12 Bur Dubai Souq Stroll beneath the wooden arcades of the Bur Dubai Souq (p61), plunging past colourful textile shops, perhaps pausing at a kiosk for freshly pressed orange juice or gazing at more revamped wind towers in the side lanes. The souq is generally hectic at night (chaotic on Friday evenings) but peaceful in the morning. When you get to the Bur Dubai Abra Station, walk past the boats along the waterfront to the Shindagha Heritage Area.

13 Sheikh Juma al-Maktoum House Fans of Arab architecture won't want to miss the in-depth exhibits inside the handsomely restored, if rambling, Sheikh Juma al-Maktoum House (p66).

14 Sheikh Saeed al-Maktoum House In a strategic location near the mouth of the Creek, the splendid Sheikh Saeed al-Maktoum House (p61) is the key building in the Shindagha Heritage Area. The former residence of Dubai's ruling Maktoum family, it now displays an intriguing collection of old photographs of Dubai.

15 Heritage & Diving Villages If you're visiting during Eid or the Dubai Shopping Festival, the Heritage & Diving Villages (p66) will be a hive of activity, providing a more authentic glimpse into Emirati traditions than on regular days. There are occasional traditional music or dance performances at other times of the year.

16 Kan Zaman Grab a waterfront table at Kan Zaman (p113) and relax, sit back and enjoy a fresh juice or tasty Arabic meal.

Dubai's main artery, Sheikh Zayed Rd is a super-busy highway that runs from the World Trade Centre Roundabout on the edge of Bur Dubai 55km south to Jebel Ali Port, halfway to Abu Dhabi. The road is flanked by a phalanx of skyscrapers, most famously of course the 828m-high Burj Khalifa. Overlooking a lake, the behemoth is the centrepiece of a new development called Downtown Dubai, which also includes the Dubai Mall, the Dubai Fountain, Souk al-Bahar and several five-star hotels.

North of here, the Financial District is anchored by the Dubai International Financial Centre (DIFC), home to the stock exchange, banks, other international institutions and Gate Village, with its art galleries. Other notable buildings include the World Trade Centre (a 1979 building that looks prehistoric alongside its futuristic cohorts) and the Jumeirah Emirates Towers, where Sheikh Mohammed has his offices.

South of Downtown Dubai, Sheikh Zayed Rd bisects gritty, industrial-flavoured Al-Quoz, which would be ignorable were it not for the fact that its warehouses are increasingly becoming bases of operation for many of the city's most exciting and cutting-edge galleries. This section of the chapter follows Sheikh Zayed Rd as far as Interchange No 4, near the Mall of the Emirates. For sights beyond here, see the 'New Dubai' section, p81.

top picks

FOR KIDS

- Al-Mamzar Beach Park (p78)
- Aquaventure (p81), Dolphin Bay (p84) & Lost Chambers (p84)
- Creekside Park (p66) & Children's City (p67)
- Dubai Aquarium & Underwater Zoo (p72)
- Dubai Museum (p60)
- Jumeirah Beach Park (p78)
- Sega Republic (p73)
- Ski Dubai (p144)
- Wild Wadi Waterpark (p80)
- Za'abeel Park (p67) & Stargate (p67)

The Dubai Metro Red Line conveniently runs along the entire length of Sheikh Zayed Rd. Major stations are Trade Centre, Financial Centre, Burj Khalifa/Dubai Mall, Al-Quoz and First Gulf Bank.

DOWNTOWN DUBAI

It's easy to spend an entire day taking in the sights of this brand-new development, which has positioned itself as the vibrant and urban centrepiece of Dubai. The nearest Dubai Metro station is Burj Khalifa/Dubai Mall.

BURJ KHALIFA Map pp70–71

☎ 888 8124, toll free 800 2884 3867; www .burjkhalifa.ae; enter on ground fl, Dubai Mall; reserved admission adult/child over 13yr Dh100/75, instant admission Dh400; ☉ 10am-10pm Sun-Wed, 10am-midnight Thu-Sat; ⑥
Call it impressive or preposterous, there's no denying that Burj Khalifa is a ground-breaking feat of architecture and engineering. The world's tallest building pierces the sky at 828m (seven times the height of Big Ben) and opened on 4 January 2010, only six years after excavations began. Up to 13,000 workers toiled day and night, at times putting up a new floor in as little

as three days. Inside Dubai's own 'Tower of Babel' is a mix of offices and apartments; at the time of writing, the sleek Armani Hotel was scheduled to open late in 2010. For visitors, the main attraction is the Observation Deck 'At the Top' on the 124th floor. From such lofty heights you can easily pinpoint The World, the three Palm developments and other landmarks. Getting there takes you past various multimedia exhibits to a double-deck lift that whisks you 10m per second for an entire minute to reach level 124 at a lofty 442m in the air. Reserved time-stamped tickets are available at the ticket office and online; ponying up Dh400 let's you go straight through. Apparently these prices are an 'introductory offer', so they may go up.

DUBAI FOUNTAIN Map pp70–71

Burj Khalifa Lake; admission free; ☉ shows every 20min 6-10pm Sun-Wed, 6-11pm Thu-Sat; ⑥
Against the backdrop of Burj Khalifa in the midst of a massive artificial lake, these

SHEIKH ZAYED ROAD

A

INFORMATION
Al-Zahra Medical Clinic..........................1 G3
Arabic Language Centre......................(see 3)
French Consulate......................................2 H3
Italian Consulate...................................(see 3)
Turkish Consulate....................................3 H3
United States Consulate.......................(see 3)

SIGHTS — pp45–85
Arabian Adventures..............................(see 49)
Art Space..(see 12)
Burj Khalifa..4 F3
Carbon 12...5 B3
Courtyard..6 B3
Cuadro..(see 12)
Dubai Aquarium & Underwater Zoo.....(see 9)
Dubai Fountain..7 F3

B

Dubai International Financial
   Centre..8 G3
Dubai Mall..9 G3
Emirates Towers.....................................10 H3
Empty Quarter......................................(see 12)
Gallery Isabelle van den Eynde...........11 B3
Gate Village...12 H3
KidZania...(see 9)
Knight Tours...13 F3
Meem Gallery...14 A3
Observation Deck 'At the Top'.............(see 4)
Ras al-Khor Wildlife Sanctuary.............15 H5
Sega Republic.......................................(see 9)
Souk al-Bahar...16 F3
The JamJar...17 A3
Third Line...18 B3
World Trade Centre...............................19 H3

C

D

SHOPPING — pp87–104
50 Degrees...(see 16)
Azza Fahmy Jewellery.........................(see 20)
Bateel...(see 9)
Bateel...(see 16)
Boulevard at Jumeirah
   Emirates Towers...............................20 H3
Candylicious..(see 9)
Dubai Mall...(see 9)
Gold & Diamond Park...........................21 A3
Marami...(see 9)
Margrudy's..(see 9)
Organic Foods & Cafe.........................(see 9)
Persian Carpet House &
   Antiques..(see 9)
Samsaara...(see 16)
Souk al-Bahar......................................(see 16)

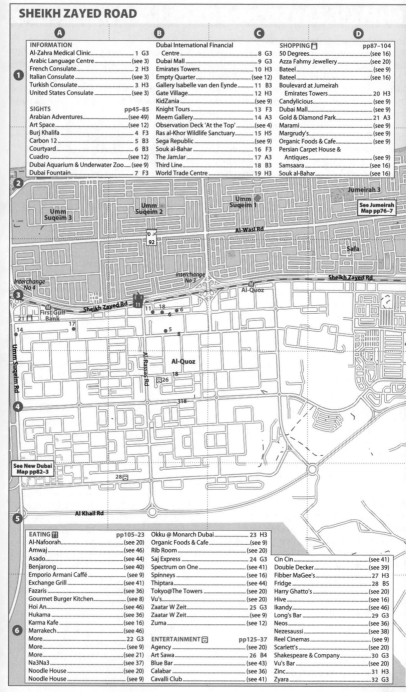

Map labels

Jumeirah 3

See Jumeirah Map pp76–7

Umm Suqeim 3
Umm Suqeim 2
Umm Suqeim 1

Al-Wasl Rd

Safa

Interchange No 4
Interchange No 3

Sheikh Zayed Rd
Al-Quoz

Interchange No 5

First Gulf Bank

Sheikh Zayed Rd

Umm Suqeim Rd

Al-Rasaa Rd

Al-Quoz

318

See New Dubai Map pp82–3

Al Khail Rd

A (bottom)

EATING — pp105–23
Al-Nafoorah..(see 20)
Amwaj..(see 46)
Asado..(see 44)
Benjarong..(see 40)
Emporio Armani Caffé.......................(see 9)
Exchange Grill.....................................(see 41)
Fazaris..(see 36)
Gourmet Burger Kitchen.....................(see 8)
Hoi An..(see 46)
Hukama...(see 36)
Karma Kafe...(see 16)
Marrakech..(see 46)
More...22 G3
More..(see 9)
More..(see 21)
Na3Na3...(see 37)
Noodle House......................................(see 20)
Noodle House......................................(see 9)

B (bottom)

Okku @ Monarch Dubai.......................23 H3
Organic Foods & Cafe.........................(see 9)
Rib Room..(see 20)
Saj Express...24 G3
Spectrum on One................................(see 41)
Spinneys..(see 16)
Thiptara...(see 44)
Tokyo@The Towers.............................(see 20)
Vu's...(see 20)
Zaatar W Zeit...25 G3
Zaatar W Zeit..(see 9)
Zuma...(see 12)

ENTERTAINMENT — pp125–37
Agency..(see 20)
Art Sawa...26 B4
Blue Bar..(see 43)
Calabar...(see 36)
Cavalli Club..(see 41)

C (bottom)

Cin Cin..(see 41)
Double Decker.....................................(see 39)
Fibber MaGee's.....................................27 H3
Fridge...28 B5
Harry Ghatto's.....................................(see 20)
Hive...(see 16)
Ikandy...(see 46)
Long's Bar..29 G3
Neos..(see 36)
Nezeaussi..(see 38)
Reel Cinemas.......................................(see 9)
Scarlett's..(see 20)
Shakespeare & Company.......................30 G3
Vu's Bar..(see 20)
Zinc..31 H3
Zyara..32 G3

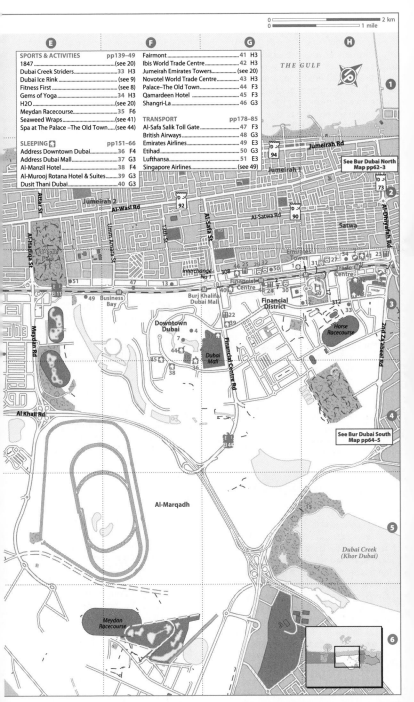

THE GULF

Jumeirah Rd

See Bur Dubai North
Map pp62–3

Jumeirah 1

Satwa

Al-Dhiyafah Rd

Jumeirah 2

Al-Wasl Rd

Al-Satwa Rd

Attar St

Al-Hadiqa St

Umm Amara St

13th St

Al-Safa St

Emirates
Tower

Trade Park
Centre

Interchange
No 1

Financial
Centre

Business
Bay

Burj Khalifa/
Dubai Mall

Financial
District

Downtown
Dubai

Horse
Racecourse

Dubai
Mall

Financial Centre Rd

Meydan Rd

2nd Zabeel Rd

Al Khail Rd

See Bur Dubai South
Map pp64–5

Al-Marqadh

Dubai Creek
(Khor Dubai)

Meydan
Racecourse

choreographed dancing fountains are the antithesis of what you'd expect to find in the desert. Water undulates as gracefully as a belly dancer, arcs like a dolphin and surges as high as 150m to overwhelming soundtracks gathered from around the world. There are plenty of great vantage points, including some of the restaurants at Souk al-Bahar (right), the bridge linking Souk al-Bahar with Dubai Mall, and the Dubai Mall terrace.

DUBAI MALL Map pp70-71
☎ 362 7500; www.thedubaimall.com; Sheikh Zayed Rd; ⊗ 10am-10pm Sun-Wed, 10am-midnight Thu-Sat; ⚙
The world's largest shopping centre, Dubai Mall is much more than the sum of its 1200 stores: it's a veritable family entertainment centre. Check out the Dubai Aquarium & Underwater Zoo (right), the Sega Republic (opposite) indoor amusement park, and the Olympic-sized Dubai Ice Rink (p114). Another attraction, scheduled to open in 2010, is KidZania (www.kidszania.com), an interactive miniature city with offices, a school, a racetrack, a fire station, a hospital and bank, and other real-world places. Kids dress up and slip into adult roles to playfully explore what it's like to be a doctor, mechanic, pilot or other professional. They even earn a salary (in a currency called Kidzos, no less) with which they buy goods and services, thus learning the value of money.

Dubai Mall has free wi-fi access but you need a UAE mobile number to register

---

FLIGHTFUL ENCOUNTERS OF THE BIRDING KIND

Right in the heart of the city, Ras al-Khor Wildlife Sanctuary (Map pp70-71; ☎ 206 4240; www .wildlife.ae; off Oud Metha & Ras al-Khor Rds; admission free; ⊗ 9am-4pm Sat-Thu; ⚙) is an amazing nature preserve. Pretty pink flamingos steal the show in winter, but in fact avid birdwatchers can spot more than 250 species in this pastiche of salt flats, intertidal mudflats, mangroves and lagoons. At the mouth of Dubai Creek, the sanctuary is also an important stop-over on the East African–West Asian Flyway. There are three hides (platforms) with fantastically sharp binoculars for close-ups of the birds without disturb-ing them. The flamingo roost is off the junction of Al-Wasl and Oud Metha Rds.

---

for the service (see p194 for details of how to obtain one), although this may soon change. For more on the mall, see p99.

SOUK AL-BAHAR Map pp70-71
☎ 362 7011; next to Dubai Mall; ⊗ 10am-10pm Sat-Thu, 2-10pm Fri
Designed in contemporary Arabic style, this attractive 100-store mall is Downtown Dubai's answer to Madinat Jumeirah. Meaning 'Market of the Sailor' it features natural stone walkways, high arches and front-row seats overlooking the Dubai Fountain from several of its restaurants and bars. Karma Kafe (p115) and Left Bank (p130), both licensed, are recommended. See also p99.

DUBAI AQUARIUM & UNDERWATER ZOO Map pp70-71
☎ 437 3155; www.thedubaiaquarium.com; aquarium tunnel & underwater zoo Dh50, aquarium tunnel only adult/child Dh25/20; ⊗ 10am-10pm Sun-Wed, 10am-midnight Thu-Sat; ⚙
Dubai Mall's most mesmerising sight is this gargantuan aquarium where 33,000 submarine beasties flit and dart amid artificial coral and behind the 'world's largest acrylic viewing panel', as recorded in the *Guinness Book of Records*. Sharks and rays are top attractions, but other crowd-pleasers include a Sumo-sized giant grouper and massive schools of pelagic fish. You can view quite a lot for free from the outside or pay for access to the walk-through tunnel. A highlight here is a darkened cave where you can go nose-to-nose with dozens of toothy sharks. If that's not close enough, don a wetsuit and join a dive instructor on a shark dive (Dh625 if PADI-certified, Dh825 if uncertified). Don't worry, all sharks are kept on a closely monitored feeding schedule to keep their predatory behaviour in check. If that's too thrilling, hop on a glass-bottomed boat for a glacial float (Dh25).

Upstairs, the very worthwhile Underwater Zoo journeys through three eco-zones: rainforest, rocky shore and living ocean. There are lots of rare and interesting deni-zens here, including air-breathing African lungfish, cheeky archerfish that catch insects by shooting water, spooky giant spider crabs and otherworldly sea dragons.

Budget at least half an hour for both the tunnel and the zoo.

SEGA REPUBLIC Map pp70-71

☎ 448 8484; www.segarepublic.com; 2nd fl, Dubai Mall; Pay & Play Pass Dh10 plus pay-as-you-go; ⏰ 10am-10pm Sun-Wed, 10am-midnight Thu-Sat; 👶

Dubai Mall's indoor amusement park is packed with thrills. Must-rides include Spin Gear, a rotating roller coaster that shoots you through complete darkness; the Wild Wing and Wild Jungle motion-simulators that take you on an Indiana Jones–style adventure; and Storm G, a high-speed bobsled ride that twists and turns 360°. Some rides have height restrictions. Pay either per ride (Dh15 to Dh30) or get a Power Pass (Dh140) for unlimited trips. The Platinum Power Pass (Dh220) includes unlimited rides plus Dh200 credit for arcade games.

AL-QUOZ

The most cutting-edge galleries within Dubai's growing art scene are in this industrial area south of Sheikh Zayed Rd between Downtown Dubai and the Mall of the Emirates. Don't picture yourself strolling from gallery to gallery as though you were in Soho though: most are tucked away in nondescript buildings or anonymous warehouses and hard to find. And don't count on your cabbie knowing the way. Most galleries have location maps on their websites; if lost call them from the road for directions. Also call to make sure they're open. The closest Dubai Metro station is Al-Quoz.

THIRD LINE Map pp70-71

☎ 341 1367; www.thethirdline.com; off Sheikh Zayed Rd, btwn Interchanges No 3 & No 4; ⏰ 11am-8pm Sat-Thu

Third Line is the 'baby' of a couple of talented young curators, Sunny Rahbar and Claudia Cellini, and is one of the city's more exciting art spaces. Artists represented often transcend the rules of traditional styles to create fresh new forms. Recent exhibitions have included the arresting op art of Rana Begum and the elaborate paintings of Iranian artist Farhad Moshiri, as well as group exhibits of emerging Emirati artists.

THE JAMJAR Map pp70-71

☎ 341 7303; www.thejamjardubai.com; 17A St, off Sheikh Zayed Rd exit 39, behind Dubai Garden Centre; ☎ 10am-8pm Mon-Thu & Sat, 2-8pm Fri

The JamJar is more than just another gallery exhibiting contemporary art by emerging

local and international talent. It's a DIY painting studio too, so if you're feeling the creative urge, you can hire an easel, a canvas and all the paint and paper you require to create your own masterpiece. Twice a year the space also hosts the independent film series Mahmovies! (p136).

MEEM GALLERY Map pp70-71

☎ 347 7883; www.meem.ae; Umm Suqeim Rd, off Interchange No 4; ⏰ 10am-7pm Sat-Thu

An ambitious co-venture by two Emirati business tycoons and British art dealer Charlie Pocock, this blue-chip gallery is dedicated to presenting the masters of modern Arab art. As such, it usually exhibits some pretty big names, such as Libyan calligrapher Ali Omar Ermes, the pop art of Jordan's Jamal Abdul Rahim or paintings by modern Arab art pioneer Dia Al-Azzawi from Iraq.

CARBON 12 Map pp70-71

☎ 050 464 4392; www.carbon12dubai.com; St 8, Al-Serkal Ave, Warehouse D37; ⏰ 11.30am-7pm Sat-Thu

This edgy gallery represents paintings, sculpture, photographs and media created by newly discovered as well as internationally established artists, all of them hand-picked. The clear lines and minimalist vibe of the white-cube space offers a perfect setting for both large-scale and smaller pieces.

GALLERY ISABELLE VAN DEN EYND Map pp70-71

☎ 340 3965; www.ivde.net; off Sheikh Zayed Rd, btwn Interchanges No 3 & No 4; ⏰ 10am-7pm Sat-Thu

Previously known as B21, this innovative gallery has lifted some of the most promising talent from around the Middle East from obscurity into the spotlight. The mythology-laced installations, videos and collages of Cairo-based Lara Baladi and the distorted photography of Iranian-born Ramin Haerizadeh are among the works that have attracted collectors and the curious since the space's opening in 2005.

COURTYARD Map pp70-71

☎ 347 5050; www.courtyard-uae.com; off Sheikh Zayed Rd, btwn Interchanges No 3 & No 4; ☎ 10am-6pm Sat-Thu

This cultural complex wraps around the eponymous courtyard flanked by an eccentric hodgepodge of buildings that makes it look like a miniature movie studio backlot: here an Arab fort, there a Moorish facade or an Egyptian tomb. It's the brainchild of Iranian expat artist Dariush Zandi, who also runs the bi-level gallery Total Arts at The Courtyard, specialising in Middle Eastern art. Other spaces are occupied by a cafe, artist studios and various creative businesses.

FINANCIAL DISTRICT

Anchored by the iconic twin Jumeirah Emirates Towers, the Financial District is largely the domain of the business brigade. If you're into art, however, there are several important galleries you need to check out in the Gate Village, a modernist cluster of 10 mid-rise stone-clad towers built around walkways and small piazzas and linked to the Dubai International Finance Centre (DIFC) by two wooden bridges. If you're riding the Dubai Metro, get off at Emirates Towers.

ART SPACE Map pp70-71

☎ 323 0820; www.artspace-dubai.com; Gate Village, Bldg 3; ☉ 10am-8pm Sun-Thu
Hobnob with collectors in this prestigious space, where owner Maliha Al Tabari puts on different shows every few weeks; recent ones featured Iraq-born Ayad Alkalhi and Kamal Boullata from Palestine.

CUADRO Map pp70-71

☎ 425 0400; www.cuadroart.com; Gate Village, Bldg 10; ☉ noon-6pm Sat, 10am-9pm Sun-Thu
In an enormous space taking up the entire ground floor of Gate Village's Bldg 10, this highly regarded gallery presents top-flight artists from both the West and Middle East.

EMPTY QUARTER Map pp70-71

☎ 323 1210; www.theemptyquarter.com; Gate Village, Bldg 2; ☉ 9am-10pm Sat-Thu, 3-10pm Fri
This sleek gallery is devoted exclusively to fine art photography.

ating p118; Entertainment p130; Shopping p99; Sleeping p161

Before there was the Dubai Marina and Palm Jumeirah, Jumeirah was the place where everybody went to realise their Dubai dreams. It's the emirate's answer to Bondi or Malibu, with excellent public beaches, boutique shopping, copious spas and health clubs, and a mix of Mercedes and expensive 4WDs in villa driveways.

On its northern edge, Jumeirah rubs up against Satwa, a colourful, densely populated district that's home to 100,000 or so low-income immigrants, mainly from southern and central Asia. The ageing neighbourhood with its candy-coloured houses was scheduled to be razed and redeveloped into something called Jumeirah Garden City. Fortunately, the economic crisis saved it from the wrecking ball, meaning you can still come here for great people-watching on Al-Dhiyafah Rd, superb *shwarma* at Al-Mallah or shirts tailored on the cheap on Al-Huidaba Rd. The souq-like main thoroughfare, Al-Satwa Rd, comes alive at night in a riotous blaze of neon.

top picks

JUMEIRAH

- Jumeirah Mosque (below) A perfect blend of spirituality and architecture.
- Burj al-Arab (p79) A perfect blend of hospitality and architecture.
- Madinat Jumeirah (p79) A perfect blend of commerce and architecture.

Al-Wasl Rd and Jumeirah Rd (sometimes referred to as Beach Rd) are Jumeirah's most important thoroughfares. Of the two, only the latter is of interest to visitors. A little bit further south, Jumeirah segues imperceptibly into residential Umm Suqeim, which also has lovely free beaches (including Kite Beach) but is best known for the Burj al-Arab and the Wild Wadi Waterpark. The road culminates at the sprawling Madinat Jumeirah hotel, shopping and entertainment complex.

There is no major public transport to this area, so you'll have to take a taxi.

JUMEIRAH

The most interesting stretch of Jumeirah is along Jumeirah Rd, just south of Jumeirah Mosque. This is where you'll find indie boutiques like S*uce (p100), fancy spas like Sensasia (p143), expat cafes such as Lime Tree Café (p120) and handsome shopping centres like Mercato Mall (p101). Further on, Jumeirah Beach Park (p78) is the most popular public beach in town. Because it stretches for many kilometres, the area has been officially subdivided into sections 1, 2 and 3.

JUMEIRAH MOSQUE Map pp76-7
☎ 353 6666; www.cultures.ae/jumeirah.htm; Jumeirah Rd, Jumeirah 1; tours free; ☽ tours 10am Sat, Sun, Tue & Thu

If you want to learn about Islamic religion and culture, beat a fast track to this splendid, intricately detailed mosque (stunningly lit at night). It's the only one in Dubai that's open to non-Muslims, but only during guided tours operated by the Sheikh Mohammed Centre for Cultural Understanding (see boxed text, p66), which wrap up with a

Q&A session. There's no need to pre-book; just register at the mosque before the tour. Show up dressed modestly (no shorts, back and arms should be covered and women need to wear a headscarf) and remove your shoes before entering. Cameras are allowed.

MAJLIS GHORFAT UM-AL-SHEEF
Map pp76-7
☎ 852 1374, 17 St, south of Jumeirah Rd (behind Citibank), Jumeirah 3; admission Dh1; ☽ 8.30am-8.30pm Sat-Thu, 3.30-8.30pm Fri

It is unusual to find a traditional building still standing so far from the Creek, but this one has been well restored and is worth a quick stop. The two-storey structure was built in 1955 as a summer residence of the late Sheikh Rashid bin Saeed al-Maktoum. Made of gypsum and coral rock with a palm frond roof and a wind tower, it provided a cool retreat from the heat. The palm tree garden features a traditional *falaj* irrigation system. The actual *majlis* (meeting room) upstairs is decorated with cushions, rugs, a coffee pot, pottery and food platters,

JUMEIRAH

THE GULF

33 🏛 Madinat Jumeirah
9
40 Umm Suqeim Beach
19 🏖
Kite Beach 15
Jumeirah Rd
94
43 ●
16
44 🏠 49
Al-Sufouh Rd
Wild Wadi Waterpark
Umm Suqeim Rd
Umm Suqeim 3
Umm Suqeim 2
Umm Suqeim 1
24
Al-Wasl Rd
31 🏛
Jumeirah 3
37 🏛
46
92
Safa
8
48
Interchange No 4
Mall of the Emirates
First Gulf Bank
Sheikh Zayed Rd
Interchange No 3
Al-Quoz
See Sheikh Zayed Rd Map pp70-71
See New Dubai Map pp82-3
Al-Quoz

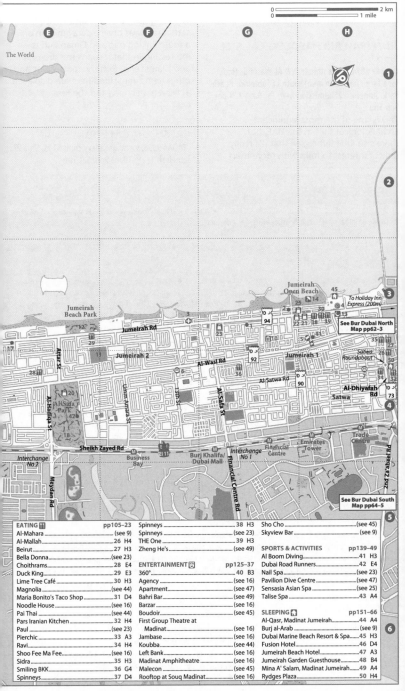

The World

Jumeirah
Open Beach

Jumeirah
Beach Park

Jumeirah Rd

Jumeirah 2

Attar St

Al-Wasl Rd

Al-Satwa Rd

Al-Hadiqa St

Al Safa Park

Al-Safa St

Al-Manara St

Umm Amara St

13th St

Jumeirah 1

Satwa
Roundabout

Al-Dhiyafah
Satwa Rd

See Bur Dubai North
Map pp62–3

Sheikh Zayed Rd

Interchange
No 2

Meydan Rd

Business
Bay

Burj Khalifa/
Dubai Mall

Interchange
No 1

Financial
Centre

Financial Centre Rd

Emirates
Tower

Trade
Centre

2nd Zaabeel Rd

To Holiday Inn
Express (200m)

See Bur Dubai South
Map pp64–5

and is pretty close to the way it would have looked in Sheikh Rashid's day.

JUMEIRAH ARCHAEOLOGICAL SITE
Map pp76-7

☎ 349 6874; btwn Jumeirah & Al-Wasl Rds (look for a large fenced-in area) south of Jumeirah Beach Park, Jumeirah 2; admission free; ✆ 9am-2.30pm Sun-Thu

This is one of the most significant archaeological sites in the UAE, but there's so little left to see that it's really only of interest to folks with more than a passing interest in the remote past. With origins in the 6th century AD, the settlement was once a caravan stop on a route linking Iraq and Oman and is interesting in that it spans the pre-Islamic and Islamic eras. Pottery, tools, coins and other items unearthed here are displayed at Dubai Museum (p60) and the Heritage Village (p66).

GREEN ART GALLERY Map pp76-7

☎ 344 9888; www.gagallery.com; 51 St, Villa 23, Jumeirah 1; ✆ 10am-9pm Sat-Thu

---

PUBLIC EXPOSURE

If you're not staying at a beachfront five-star place but want to swim in the Gulf, you've got two options: either head to one of Dubai's free public beaches or pay for a day at a beach club.

Dipping without Dirhams

Dubai's free beaches...

Jumeirah Open Beach (Map pp76-7; next to Dubai Marine Beach Resort & Spa, Jumeirah 1) Also known as Russian Beach because of its popularity with Russian tourists, this stretch of white sand is paralleled by a paved path popular with strollers, joggers, inline skaters and cyclists. Alas, on Fridays it teems with off-duty male guest workers keen on ogling bikini beauties. Although you probably won't get physically accosted, women may feel more comfortable further south at Jumeirah Beach Park (see below). Showers, toilets and kiosks are available.

Kite Beach (Map pp76-7; about 3km north of the Burj al-Arab, past Umm Suqeim Hospital, Umm Suqeim 1) Also known as Wollongong Beach, this long pristine stretch of sand is quiet and a great place for relaxed sunbathing but, alas, it has zero facilities.

Umm Suqeim Beach (Map pp76-7; btwn Jumeirah Beach Hotel & Kite Beach) This white sandy beach, with fabulous views of the Burj al-Arab, has showers and shelter and is popular with Jumeirah families and Western expatriates.

Jumeirah Beach Residence Open Beach (Map pp82-3; Jumeirah Beach Residence, Dubai Marina) This is a lovely wide beach paralleling The Walk at JBR. There are no facilities here.

Beaches for Bucks

The ones that cost...

Jumeirah Beach Park (Map pp76-7; per person/car Dh5/20; ✆ 7am-10.30pm Sun-Wed, 7am-11pm Thu-Sat, women & children only Mon) It's a real treat to take a walk on the grass at this verdant park, as it's a couple of degrees cooler than the beach. Fronting onto a long stretch of sand, the park has lifeguards on duty, a children's play area, barbecues, picnic tables, walkways and kiosks.

Al-Mamzar Beach Park (Map p50; ☎ 296 6201; Al-Mamzar Creek, Deira; per person/car Dh5/30; ✆ 8am-11pm, women & children only Wed) One of Dubai's hidden gems, this large, landscaped park on a small headland in Deira has lovely white sandy beaches, barbecues and kiosks. Kids have plenty of open space and play areas for romping around, plus three pools with waterslides for cooling off. Friday is busy, but during the week you can have the place to yourself.

Hilton Dubai Jumeirah (p163) Parents love the non-stop organised kids' activities, watersports and comparatively low prices (adult/child weekdays Dh180/95, weekends Dh250/95).

Le Meridien Mina Seyahi (p164) The calm beach, wonderful pools including a 150m-long winding lagoon, and a watersports centre offering everything from banana boat rides to windsurfing make this resort a family favourite (adult/child Dh150/75 Sunday to Thursday, Dh250/125 Friday and Saturday).

Mina A' Salam & Al-Qsar (p162) The Dh495 tab is exorbitant, even if it gives you access to a dreamy beach and fabulous pools and even if the price includes a food voucher. Buy tickets at the Health Club.

With regular temporary exhibitions and a growing permanent collection concentrating on the work of artists living in the UAE, this small commercial gallery is committed to nurturing local talent and developing the art scene. It also helps educate artists about international art distribution and promotion.

AL-SAFA PARK Map pp76-7

☎ 349 2111; bordered by Sheikh Zayed & Al-Wasl Rds & Al-Hadiqa & 55 Sts, Jumeirah 2; admission Dh3; ☺ 8am-11pm, women & children only Tue
Pretty and popular, this park is a pastiche of patches of lawn, gardens and waterfalls, a ladies' garden, children's playgrounds and even a lake where you can feed the ducks or take your sweetie for a spin in a row boat or paddle boat. Sporty types can get their heart pumping on the jogging track or over a game of volleyball, basketball, football or tennis. After dark the rides (near Al-Wasl Rd) get busy. Dubai Flea Market is held here once a month (p100).

UMM SUQEIM

Popular with families, residential Umm Suqeim (also divided into sections 1, 2 and 3) is flanked by fabulous beaches and a clutch of high-end resorts, including Jumeirah Beach Hotel and the Burj al-Arab. It is punctuated by Disneyesque but still evocative and romantic Madinat Jumeirah, with its souq, high-end hotels and fancy nosh and party spots.

BURJ AL-ARAB Map pp76-7

☎ 301 7777; www.burj-al-arab.com; Jumeirah Rd, Umm Suqeim 3
We're suckers for trivia, so let's kick off by telling you that the lobby of the Burj al-Arab is so high, the Statue of Liberty would fit quite nicely into it. Or that the sail-shaped building tops out at 321m, just a few metres shorter than the Eiffel Tower. And here's one more: 1600 sq metres in the hotel are sheathed in gold leaf. OK, that's enough. In its first decade since opening, the Burj al-Arab has been more than just the iconic symbol of a booming city in the sand; it has challenged preconceived ideas of what an Arab country in the Middle East can achieve. It's built on an artificial island 280m offshore from the Jumeirah Beach Hotel, to which it is linked by a causeway. This five-star hotel (it's best to

ignore the nonsense about seven stars) is worth visiting, if only to gawk at an interior that's every bit as gaudy as the exterior is gorgeous. If you're not staying, you need a restaurant reservation to get past lobby security. Don't expect any bargains: breakfast is Dh250 and afternoon tea will set you back Dh395. The latter is served from 1pm to 5.30pm Saturday to Thursday and consists of seven courses and unlimited champagne, so you probably won't be needing dinner. Best of all, it's served in the Skyview Bar (p130), some 200m above the waves. If you don't want tea, you can also book a drinks package for Dh275 (available between 7pm and 11pm).

MADINAT JUMEIRAH Map pp76-7
Al-Sufouh Rd, Umm Suqeim 3
A city within a city, the Madinat Jumeirah is a Dubai must-see. There's plenty to do at this fanciful hotel, shopping and entertainment complex with the Burj al-Arab in the background. Explore the Arabian-style architecture, snoop around the splendid Al-Qsar and Mina A' Salam hotels (p162), or get lost in the labyrinth of the souvenir-saturated souq. There are some exquisite details throughout, so if you see some stairs, take them – they might lead you to a secreted terrace with a mesmerising vista of the sprawling complex. If you're a hotel guest, or have a restaurant reservation, you can catch the silent *abras* cruising along the 4km-long network of Venetian-style canals for free. Otherwise, the cost is Dh50 for a guest tour. Billowing bougainvillea, bushy banana trees and soaring palms characterise the enchanting grounds, which are scrupulously maintained by a small army of gardeners. Sure, there's an undeniable

'Disney does Arabia' artifice about the whole place, but it's all done tastefully and, not surprisingly, it's one of Dubai's most popular spots.

WILD WADI WATERPARK Map pp76-7

☎ 348 4444; www.wildwadi.com; Jumeirah Rd, Umm Suqeim 3; admission over/under 110cm Dh195/165; ⊙ 10am-6pm Nov-Feb, 10am-7pm Mar-May & Sep-Oct, 10am-8pm Jun-Aug; ⑤ When the kids grow weary of the beach and hotel pool, you'll score big time by bringing them to Wild Wadi. Over a dozen ingeniously interconnected rides follow a vague theme about an Arabian adventurer named Juha and his friend Sinbad the sailor, who get shipwrecked together. There are plenty of gentle rides for kids and nervous nellies, a big-wave pool, a white-water rapids 'river' and a 33m-high Jumeirah Sceirah slide that drops you at a speed of 80km/h (hold on to your trunks, guys!). Thrill-seekers can also test their bodyboarding mettle on Wipeout, a permanent wave. Kids must be at least 110cm tall for some of the scarier rides. Check the website for discounts. From April to October Wild Wadi is open for women and children only on Thursday evenings (over/under 110cm Dh165/135; 8pm to midnight April, May, September and October, 9pm to 1am June to August).

1X1 ART SPACE Map pp76-7

☎ 348 3873; www.1x1artspace.com; Villa 1023, Al-Wasl Rd, opposite Choithram, Umm Suqeim 2; ⊙ 11am-8pm Sat-Thu
Dubai has of late been emerging as a key place for sourcing Indian art, in part because of the efforts of Malini Gulrajani, whose mission is to showcase the best in contemporary works from the subcontinent. With shows by such painters as Jatin Das and TV Santosh, this grand and elegant gallery has a fixed spot on the radar of avid collectors.

As you travel towards the dense forest of high-rises south of Jumeirah, imagine that until only a few years ago there was nothing here except desert and a few hotels fronting a pristine beach. Then the construction boom arrived with a vengeance, giving birth to hundreds of apartment buildings, office towers and even more hotels. There's no sightseeing in the traditional sense here, and much of the architecture is, well, uninspired, but the plethora of upmarket restaurants, bars and clubs, plus the lovely beach, will probably bring you here at some point in your trip.

New Dubai consists of several different areas. In Dubai Marina you not only find bobbing yachts but also the phalanx of buttercream-yellow towers known as the Jumeirah Beach Residence (aka JBR). Put up in a mere five years, the 40 towers flank 1.7km of beach as well as one of Dubai's most popular walking areas, The Walk at JBR. Fortunately, plans to turn the beach into an exclusive club for residents were nixed, meaning you're free to frolic as you please.

North of here, Al-Sufouh encompasses some of the most upmarket hotels in town, as well as the free zones of Dubai Internet City, an information technology park where such major companies as Microsoft, IBM and Nokia are based; and Dubai Media City, home to CNN, BBC World, Bloomberg and other outlets.

top picks

NEW DUBAI

- **The Walk at JBR** (below) A rare opportunity for al fresco strolling, people-watching and shopping.
- **Ibn Battuta Mall** (p85) A mall whose architecture (almost) outshines the shopping.
- **Ski Dubai** (p144) An alpine wonderland smack dab in the desert.

Jutting into the Gulf is the Palm Jumeirah, the smallest of three artificial palm-shaped islands off the coast of Dubai. It's punctuated by the massive playground that is the Atlantis – The Palm hotel. Construction of the much larger Palm Jebel Ali and Palm Deira was frozen in late 2009 because of the severe financial troubles of state-owned developer Nakheel.

This section of the chapter also covers the inland neighbourhood of Al-Barsha, which is bisected by the remaining stretch of Sheikh Zayed Rd linking the Mall of the Emirates with Jebel Ali via the Ibn Battuta Mall. Dubai Metro Red Line stops include Mall of the Emirates, Dubai Marina and Ibn Battuta.

THE WALK AT JBR Map pp82-3

In front of Jumeirah Beach Residence, Dubai Marina; most outlets 10am-10pm Sat-Thu, 3.30-10pm Fri;

'Nobody walks in LA', as that old Missing Persons song goes, and the same could be said about Dubai. At least, until the summer of 2008, when The Walk at JBR opened. The city's first outdoor shopping and dining promenade was built to meet the needs of the 20,000 people living in the Jumeirah Beach Residence development, a cluster of 40 yellow towers wedged between the beach and Dubai Marina. But right from the start, The Walk's attractive mix of over 300 largely family-friendly restaurants, cafes, shops, supermarkets and boutiques has also drawn scores of tourists and residents from other neighbourhoods. They come to stroll down the 1.7km stretch, watch the world on parade from a pavement cafe or to browse for knick-knacks at the Covent Garden Market (p103). On Thursday and Friday nights, traffic slows to a crawl, letting you get a good look at all those shiny Ferraris, Maseratis and other fancy cars ploughing along here.

AQUAVENTURE Map pp82-3

426 0000; www.atlantisthepalm.com; Atlantis – The Palm, Palm Jumeirah; over/under 1.2m Dh200/165, combo ticket incl Lost Chambers Dh250/200; 10am-sunset;
Adrenaline rushes are guaranteed at this water park at the Atlantis hotel. The centrepiece is the 27.5m-high Ziggurat (great views!), the launch pad for seven slides, including the most wicked of them all: Leap of Faith, a near-vertical plunge into a shark-infested lagoon, albeit protected by

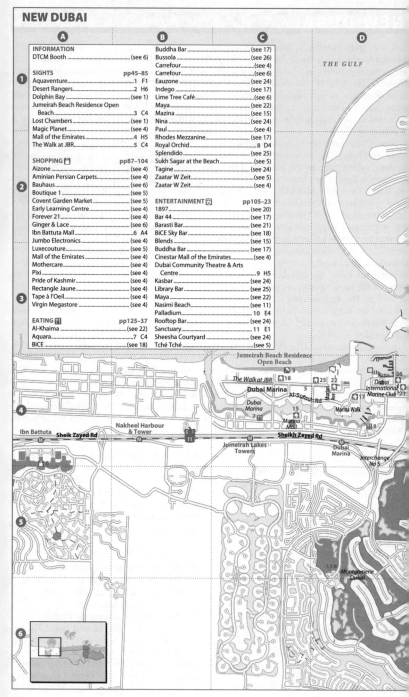

THE GULF

Jumeirah Beach Residence Open Beach

The Walk at JBR

Dubai Marina

Al-Sufouh Rd

Dubai Marina

Marina Mall

Marina Walk

Dubai International Marine Club

Ibn Battuta   Sheik Zayed Rd

Nakheel Harbour & Tower

Sheikh Zayed Rd

Jumeirah Lakes Towers

Dubai Marina

Interchange No 5

Montgomerie Dubai

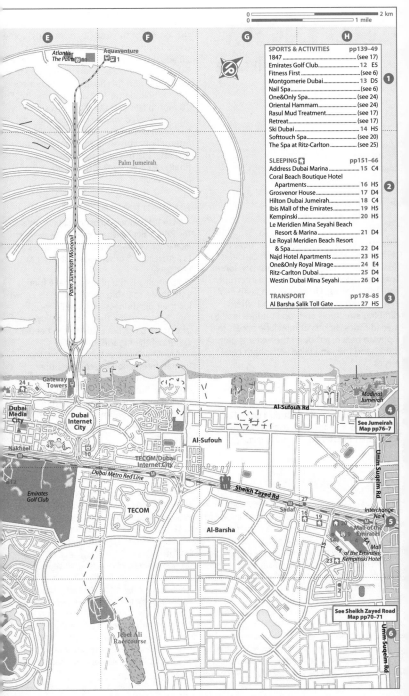

top picks

This fantastical labyrinth of underwater halls, passageways and fish tanks recreates the legend of the lost city of Atlantis. Some 65,000 exotic marine creatures inhabit 20 aquariums, where rays flutter and jelly fish dance, moray eels lurk, and pretty but poisonous lion fish float. The centrepiece is the 11 million-litre Ambassador Lagoon. For 18 months its 'star attraction' was Sammy, an endangered whale shark captured off the coast of Dubai in 2008. Bowing to international pressure from animal rights activists, the magnificent creature was finally released back into the open sea in March 2009.

a transparent tunnel. There's also more than 2km of nonstop river action with cascades, tidal waves and rapids. Unfortunately, long lines between attractions tend to interrupt your momentum. Little ones can keep cool in a ginormous water playground where climbing structures and rope bridges lead to myriad slides. Tickets also include access to a private beach, although the water is quite murky and the sand filled with sharp coral pieces.

LOST CHAMBERS Map pp82-3

☎ 426 0000; www.atlantisthepalm.com; Atlantis – The Palm, Palm Jumeirah; adult/child under 12yr Dh100/70, ray feeding Dh175, combo ticket incl Aquaventure Dh250/200; ☉ 10am-11pm; ♿

DOLPHIN BAY Map pp82-3

☎ 426 1030; www.atlantisthepalm.com, Atlantis – The Palm, Palm Jumeirah; shallow-/deep-water interaction Dh790/975, incl same day access to Aquaventure & private beach, observer pass Dh300; ♿
Dolphin Bay is the place to make friends with those sociable finny mammals known for their playfulness and intelligence. Touch, hug or kiss them in a shallow pool or catch a piggyback ride to the deeper waters of the lagoon.

Animal welfare activists believe that human interaction exacerbates the dolphins' stress already wrought by captivity, but people sure seem to be thrilled by the experience. Learn more about this contentious subject from the Whale and Dolphin Conservation Society (WDCS; www.wwdcs.com).

PALM JUMEIRAH: PITFALLS IN PARADISE

Even in a city known for its outlandish megaprojects, the Palm Jumeirah stands out: an artificial island in the shape of a palm tree made from 1 billion cubic metres of dredged sand and stone. Built to increase Dubai's beachfront, it consists of a 2km trunk and 16-frond crown, which are kept in place by an 11km-long crescent-shaped breakwater. An elevated, driverless monorail whisks passengers from the Gateway Towers station at the bottom of the trunk to the Atlantis – The Palm hotel. Eventually, it may be linked to the Dubai Metro's Red Line.

'May' seems to be the operative word when it comes to the Palm Jumeirah. When construction began in 2001, developers envisioned the island to be a mix of five-star hotels, luxurious beachfront villas, high-rise apartment buildings, marinas and malls. But it soon became clear that not all was going according to plan. The completion date kept getting pushed back, construction density was higher and building quality lower than advertised and, well, of all those luxury hotels only the Atlantis ever got built (thus far).

The environmental impact was significant as well. Dredging had an adverse effect on local marine life and the breakwater inhibited tidal movement, leading to stagnant water, excessive algae growth and smelly beaches. The problem has since been somewhat alleviated by cutting gaps into the breakwater. However, the bad news kept coming in December 2009, when reports surfaced that the island may be sinking at a clip of 5mm per year, although this may actually be due to natural settling of the artificially created landmasses.

MALL OF THE EMIRATES Map pp82-3

☎ 409 9000; Sheikh Zayed Rd, Interchange No 4, Al-Barsha; ☉ 10am-10pm Sun-Wed, 10am-midnight Thu-Sat

The most popular mall in Dubai – and the second biggest after Dubai Mall – sprawls with acres of polished white marble. The curiosity of Ski Dubai (p144) is a major draw, as are the remarkably good food court and comfortable multiplex with its Gold Class screening room. The downside is that relatively narrow walkways and lack of daylight make it feel a tad claustrophobic at peak periods. Also see p104.

IBN BATTUTA MALL Map pp82-3

☎ 362 1902; Sheikh Zayed Rd, btwn Interchanges No 5 & No 6; ☉ 10am-10pm Sun-Wed, 10am-midnight Thu-Sat

The shopping here is only so-so (see p103) but this mall is still worth a visit for its stunning architecture and design tracing the waystations of 14th-century Arab scholar and traveller Ibn Battuta. It's divided into six sections, each reflecting a region he visited, including Tunisia, Andalusia and Egypt. The most stunning is the Persia Court, which is crowned by an amazing handpainted dome. The centrepiece of the China Court is a full-size Chinese junk, while in the India Court you can pose with an 8m-high elephant. Surprisingly, there's nothing kitsch or 'Disney' about this place – the craftsmanship and attention to detail are simply stunning. There's also an exhibit about Ibn Battuta and his accomplishments.

SHOPPING

top picks

- Amzaan (p94)
- Azza Fahmy Jewellery (p98)
- Candylicious (p98)
- Dubai Mall (p99)
- Magrudy's (p93)
- Pride of Kashmir (p93)
- Five Green (p94)
- S*uce (p100) & S*uce Light (p100)
- Souq Madinat Jumeirah (p101)

What's your recommendation? www.lonelyplanet.com/dubai

SHOPPING

Dubai loves to shop. The city has just about perfected the art of the mall, which is the de facto air-conditioned 'town commons', the place to go with the family, hang out with friends and take in some entertainment. Dubai malls have ski slopes, ice rinks and aquariums. They look like ancient Persia or futuristic movie sets. The range of stores – high-street to designer, electronics to carpets – is amazing, but true bargains are as rare as tulips in Tonga, except possibly during the Dubai Shopping Festival (p95).

The explosion in themed mall architecture took off in 2002 with the opening of Mercato Mall and its Tuscany-meets-Venice architecture. Souq Madinat Jumeirah reinterprets the classic covered Arabian bazaars of old, with gracefully arching wooden ceilings above a maze of corridors designed to get you lost. Anchoring the complex at either end are two palatial, seaside hotels connected by a series of canals, with the iconic Burj al-Arab hotel looming in the background: think Disney does Arabia. Nearly 1.5km long, Ibn Battuta Mall is comprised of six interconnected shopping centres, each one styled after a country visited by the eponymous explorer, who travelled from Andalusia to China in the 14th century. Amble beneath faux starry skies, past towering live palms, and into a giant tiled Persian dome. The China section is the stunner: a life-size junk lies on its side – someone is always posing for pictures in front of it.

Mall of the Emirates is best known for its indoor ski slope, Ski Dubai, where fresh snow is generated overnight. The massive Dubai Festival City opened in 2007, with a red-carpet-lined VIP entrance (essentially valet parking). The back of the mall is most impressive: a three-storey-high, origami-inspired marble sculpture, with water running down its faces, doubles as a staircase for shoppers. *Abras* (water taxis) float past on outdoor canals, setting a picturesque if ersatz backdrop for alfresco performances.

Open since November 2008, Dubai Mall is the world's largest retail mall; it packs an Olympic-size ice rink, a huge aquarium and underwater zoo, several indoor amusement parks and 1200 stores into its massive frame. It's smack-dab in Downtown Dubai, at the foot of Burj Khalifa, the world's tallest tower. Opposite, reached via a bridge spanning Downtown Dubai Lake, is Souk al-Bahar, a diminutive version of Souq Madinat Jumeirah.

Looked down upon in other parts of the world, air-conditioned malls make sense in Dubai, their trickling fountains and cool marble floors a welcome respite from the oppressive heat. The problem is that every new mall offers more of the same corporate chain stores, repackaged in glitzier format. We've included some of these major style franchises, such as Zara and Topshop, but have endeavoured to suss out the independent shops: stores like the exotic Samsaara in Souk al-Bahar, whimsical Ginger & Lace in Ibn Battuta Mall, and the funky Lebanese fashion shop Aizone in Mall of the Emirates.

The Dubai shopping scene lacks the dynamism and breadth of major Western cities, such as London and New York, primarily because the city has no significant underground art scene to fuel new ideas. Everything in Dubai is imported, including creativity. That's why you'll be especially happy about two independent boutiques, S*uce and Five Green. While they won't bowl you over if you shop the world, you'll find brands and designs you otherwise wouldn't.

Scouring the souqs (covered outdoor markets) remains the city's quintessential shopping experience and the fastest way to get to the heart of the culture. Nothing compares with the atmosphere and chaos of the souqs – the colours and textures, the cacophony of sounds, the street hawkers barking for customers, and the call to prayer booming down narrow lanes. There's a souq for everything: fish, fruit and vegetables, Bedouin jewellery, Palestinian embroidery, curly-toed Aladdin slippers, Oriental perfumes, frankincense and myrrh, cheap headphones, and mosque-shaped clock radios to take home to friends.

Souqs are on either side of Dubai Creek and in the backstreets of Karama; malls are scattered about town. Hailing a taxi can take a long time (see p102). Malls have dedicated taxi lines (though they may be over an hour's wait in length). At the souqs you'll simply have to stand in the street; alternatively, head to the nearest main drag, or take a bus or *abra*. All malls have food courts, some remarkably good, especially Mall of the Emirates and Dubai Mall; they also boast full-service restaurants, some licensed, and ATMs and foreign-exchange offices. Whether they actually have any bargains is another story. Though there are no duties and taxes (see boxed text, p93), unless you're buying expensive luxury items such as a Rolex, you'll find prices only a bit cheaper than overseas, depending on your home currency. For the best deals, come during one of the shopping festivals (p95).

OPENING HOURS

Malls in Dubai open from 10am to 10pm Sunday to Wednesday, from 10am to midnight Thursday to Saturday (weekends), and later during the Dubai Shopping Festival and Ramadan (often until 1am). Traditionally, souqs and non-mall stores close a few hours during the afternoon for prayer, lunch and rest, and don't open on Fridays until late afternoon, but that's changing. These days many remain open all day. Malls get packed Friday nights: if you hate crowds, stay away. Otherwise, the people-watching is great.

BARGAINING

Bargaining is an obsession for some; others do anything to avoid it, immediately accepting the first offer. If you fall into the latter category, bear in mind that the first price suggested by spruikers in souqs is unrealistic; if you accept, you're overpaying and sending a signal to locals that out-of-towners are easy marks. Here's how to handle it. A counter-offer of half is made. The final figure will usually be somewhere about 20% to 50% lower than the shopkeeper's initial offer. Go for additional discounts if you're buying more than one piece from a vendor. Once the vendor agrees to your figure, you're expected to pay. Continuing to haggle once you've agreed is an insult. Leaving the store empty-handed after you've bargained is impolite. Remember, you may want to return; leaving on good terms will score you bigger discounts next time.

Confidence comes with practice; having a friend with you helps. Some like to play 'good cop, bad cop', with one feigning disinterest, trying to drag the other away. The shopkeeper will reduce the price rather than lose a sale. You don't typically bargain at chain stores in shopping malls, but at independent stores inside the malls, ask for the 'best price', especially on carpets, perfumes and electronics.

BEST BUYS
Gold & Gems

The City of Gold's glistening reputation grows from low prices and the sheer breadth of selection. There are a whopping 700 jewellery stores in Dubai, with nearly 300 at the Gold Souq and about 90 at the Gold & Diamond Park. Low import duties and no tax mean it's one of the cheapest places in the world in which to buy jewellery. Tradition keeps business booming: in India and the Gulf countries, when you provide gold for a dowry, it must be brand new – and over-the-top, apparently. Windows in the Gold Souq display the ornate necklaces, earrings and headpieces worn by Indian and Arabian brides. This is the jaw-dropping jewellery that you see in tourist-brochure photographs. But the selection inside the stores is significantly more diverse, ranging from intricately patterned pieces to sleek contemporary designs.

Dubai's jewellery shops also carry an impressive array of silver, diamonds, pearls and precious gems. And if you don't find anything you love, have something made. Either way, fear not: what you're buying is authentic. Local laws are very strict. Dubai Municipality carries out regular quality checks. Gold traders wouldn't dare risk their reputations in such a competitive environment. Look for the gold-purity hallmark, get a detailed invoice and ask for a Certificate of Authenticity for diamonds and gems. While gold is sold by weight and prices fluctuate, the rate is fixed twice daily, according to international rates, by the Gold and Jewellery Group; check www.dubaicityofgold.com for the current numbers. Prices for fashion jewellery vary depending on several factors, including the intricacy of the design, and whether the piece was made by machine or hand. Regardless, prepare to bargain.

BEST BOOKS FOR BUYING CARPETS

- *Oriental Rugs Today*, 2nd edition, by Emmett Eiland
- *Persian Rugs and Carpets: The Fabric of Life* by Essie Sakhai
- *Oriental Rugs, A Complete Guide* by Murray L Eiland
- *The Carpet: Origins, Art and History* by Enza Milanesi
- *Kilims: a Buyer's Guide* by Lee Allane
- *Tribal Rugs* by James Opie

Carpets

Dubai is a carpet lover's paradise. Fine Persian carpets, colourful Turkish and Kurdish kilims, and rough-knotted Bedouin rugs are all widely available. Dubai has a reputation in the region for having the highest-quality carpets at the best prices. Bargaining is the norm. If you can't secure the price you want, head to another store – there are hundreds of 'em. Dubai's malls have the greatest number of carpet shops; the streets around Baniyas Sq (Map pp52-3) and Sharjah souqs (p173) also have good selections. When you buy a carpet, ask for a certificate of authentication guaranteed by the Dubai Chamber of Commerce & Industry, so you can be sure that the carpet actually comes from where the vendor says it does. For more information and what to look for when shopping for rugs, see below and p89.

Arabian Handicrafts & Souvenirs

Arabian handicrafts are as popular with Dubai visitors as carpets, gold and perfume. The Oriental decor of the city's top-end hotels and restaurants seems to inspire travellers to pack away little pieces of exotica to recreate their own little genie bottles back home. Head to the souqs for Moroccan coloured lanterns, Syrian rosewood furniture inlaid with mother-of-pearl, Arabian brass coffee pots, Turkish miniature paintings, and embroidered Indian wall hangings and cushion covers dotted with tiny mirrors. If you're on a budget, use your imagination to create fab home furnishings. Colourful Indian saris make sexy curtains, and Kashmiri shawls look great atop tables and sideboards. Add foldable wooden legs to a decorative metal

CARPET BUYING 101

Due diligence is essential for prospective carpet buyers. Though you may only want a piece to match your curtains, you'll save a lot of time and money if you do a little homework. Your first order of business: read *Oriental Rugs Today* by Emmett Eiland, an excellent primer on buying new Oriental rugs.

In the early 1900s, rug makers started using fast-acting chemicals and machines to streamline the arduous processes of carding, washing, dying and spinning wool into thread, leaving only the actual weaving to be done by hand. One hundred years later, traditional cultures have been decimated, and the market flooded with bad rugs destined to depreciate in value.

A rug's quality depends entirely on how the wool was processed. It doesn't matter if the rug was hand-knotted if the wool is lousy. The best comes from sheep at high altitudes, which produce impenetrably thick, long-staple fleece, heavy with lanolin. No acids should ever be applied; otherwise the lanolin washes away. Lanolin yields naturally stain-resistant, lustrous fibre that doesn't shed. The dye should be vegetal-based pigment. This guarantees saturated, rich colour tones with a depth and vibrancy unattainable with chemicals.

The dyed wool is hand-spun into thread, which by nature has occasional lumps and challenges the craftsmanship of the weavers, forcing them to compensate for the lumps by occasionally changing the shape, size or position of a knot. These subtle variations in a finished carpet's pattern – visible only upon close inspection – give the carpet its character, and actually make the rug more valuable.

Dealers will hype knot density, weave quality and country of origin, but really, they don't matter. The crucial thing to find out is how the wool was treated. A rug made with acid-treated wool will never look as good as it did the day you bought it. Conversely, a properly made rug will grow more lustrous in colour over time and will last centuries.

Here's a quick test. Stand atop the rug with rubber-soled shoes and do the twist. Grind the fibres underfoot. If they shed, it's lousy wool. You can also spill water onto the rug. See how fast it absorbs. Ideally it should puddle for an instant, indicating a high presence of lanolin. Best of all, red wine will not stain lanolin-rich wool.

We've endeavoured to list good dealers, but you'll be taking your chances in Dubai if you're looking for an investment piece. However, if you just want a gorgeous pattern that will look great in your living room, pack a few fabric swatches from your sofa and curtains, and go for it. Patterns range from simple four-colour tribal designs in wool to wildly ornate, lustrous, multicoloured silk carpets that shimmer under the light. Look through books before you leave home to get a sense of what you like. Once in the stores, plan to linger long with dealers, slowly sipping tea while they unfurl dozens of carpets. The process is great fun. Just don't get too enthusiastic or the dealer won't as readily bargain.

If you're serious about becoming a collector, hold off. Read Emmett Eiland's book; Google 'DOBAG', a Turkish-rug-making cultural-survival project; and check out www.yayla.com for other reliable background info. Follow links to nonprofit organisations (such as DOBAG) that not only help reconstruct rug-making cultures decimated by modernisation, but also help to educate, house and feed the people of these cultures, giving them a voice in an age of industrial domination. And you'll get a fantastic carpet to boot.

serving platter for a cool coffee table, or stretch a camel bag over cube-shaped ottomans.

Sheesha pipes (aka hubbly bubblies or nargilehs) make memorable souvenirs. Note: the smaller pipes are decorative and don't work. If you intend to use your pipe, buy a complete *sheesha* kit in an easy-to-carry hard case, which includes all the little accessories you'll need. *Sheesha* pipes and the flavoured tobacco are available from souqs, specialist stores, tobacconists, supermarkets and souvenir shops. (See p136 for a lesson in how to use your new pipe.)

If you're shopping for family and friends, look for silver prayer holders, inlaid wooden boxes, tinted-glass perfume bottles and kitsch souvenirs (see below). Dad may appreciate a framed *khanjar* (traditional curved dagger) or silver gunpowder horn. Mum will definitely love a new pashmina (see p94). Kids will love a cuddly camel, some of which even play Arabian music when you squeeze them; Camel Company (p101) has the best selection of camel toys. For older kids, look for brightly painted pencil holders and boxes with Emirati scenes rendered in naïve style, from Gifts and Souvenirs in Karama Shopping Centre (p96). Sabine Moser's illustrated story books *Camel-O-Shy* make great gifts; find them at Magrudy's (p93).

For the best-quality souvenirs and handicrafts, head to Deira City Centre, Mall of the Emirates, Dubai Mall and Souq Madinat Jumeirah. For the best prices, head to Karama Shopping Centre and the souqs in Bur Dubai and Deira.

Kitsch Souvenirs

The ultimate kitsch souvenir used to be a colourful mosque clock with an irritating call-to-prayer alarm. Now the souqs and souvenir shops overflow with wacky, kitsch gifts – glass Burj al-Arab paperweights, wooden Russian dolls painted as Emiratis, Barbie and Ken dolls in Emirati dress, key rings strung with miniature towers, camel-crossing-sign fridge

top picks

HANDICRAFTS & SOUVENIR SHOPS

- Pride of Kashmir (p93)
- Al-Orooba Oriental (p95)
- Gift World (p96)
- Lata's (p102)
- Showcase Antiques, Arts & Frames (p99)

magnets, and coffee mugs and baseball caps with Sheikh Zayed or Sheikh Mohammed waving to the crowd. Karama Shopping Centre (p96) is where you'll find the most bizarre stuff, but it's more fun to wander around the Deira Covered Souq, especially at night.

Bedouin Jewellery

Bedouin jewellery is brilliant in Dubai and with the steady popularity of bo-ho ethnic chic, it makes a great gift. Look for elaborate silver necklaces and pendants, chunky earrings and rings, and wedding belts, many of which incorporate coral, turquoise and semiprecious stones. Very little of the older Bedouin jewellery comes from the Emirates; most of it is from Oman, Yemen and Afghanistan. General guidelines are: Omani jewellery is produced with good-quality silver and is more intricate of detail and design; Yemeni jewellery is elaborate and chunkier; Afghani jewellery looks cheap, but is the most fun and often comes embellished with coloured beads, ribbon and tiny mirrors. Like gold, silver jewellery is sold by weight. You'll pay more for intricate workmanship and quality, but the shopkeeper usually sets a fixed price on these items. There's also a lot of 'Bedouin-inspired' and other ethnic beaded-silver jewellery made in India; you'll pay a lot less for

---

KHANJARS

Visit the Al-Ain camel market (see p175) or the bullfights at Fujairah (see p176) and you'll see old Emirati men wearing *khanjars* (traditional curved daggers) over their *dishdashas* (men's shirt-dresses). Traditionally, *khanjar* handles were made from rhino horn; today, they are often made of wood. Regular *khanjars* have two rings where the belt is attached, and their scabbards are decorated with thin silver wire. The intricacy of the wire-thread pattern and its workmanship determine value. Sayidi *khanjars* have five rings and are often covered entirely in silver sheet, with little or no wire, and their quality is assessed by weight and craftsmanship. A *khanjar* ought to feel heavy when you pick it up. Don't believe anyone who tells you a specific *khanjar* is 'very old' – few will be more than 30 to 40 years old. If you're in the market for one, there's an especially good selection at Lata's (p102), Showcase Antiques (p99) and at Global Village (p95).

this stuff in Dubai than you will at boutiques in London or New York. Keep an eye out for necklaces, bracelets and earrings embellished with beads, charms and trinkets. You can also buy Bedouin jewellery displayed (à la *khanjars*) in glass-covered picture frames, or frame it yourself when you get home.

Perfume & Incense

Attars (Arabian perfumes) are spicy and strong. Historically, this was a necessity: with precious little water, washing was a sometimes-thing, so women smothered themselves in *attars* and incense. As you walk past Emirati women, catch a whiff of their exotic perfume. You can find Arabian-perfume shops in all Dubai's malls, but we highly recommend you visit the Perfume Souq (p58), a small stretch lined with perfume stores along Sikkat al-Khail and Al-Soor Sts in Deira, just east of the Gold Souq. Shopkeepers will daub you senseless with myriad scents, and if you buy a few (remember to bargain), you'll also receive a bag of tiny samples. Perfume is sold by the *tolah* (12mL or 12g) and prices vary, depending on the perfume. The expensive concentrated scents are made from agar wood from Malaysia. Perfume shops also sell a range of incense in the form of *oud* (fragrant wood), rock, crystals or compressed powder. Frankincense (*luban* in Arabic) is the most common form. Quality varies; the best comes from the Dhofar region of southern Oman.

To burn incense, you have three options: an electric incense burner; heat beads; or a traditional burner and a box of Magic Coal charcoal, a long-lasting Japanese coal sold in a black box. Set charcoal or heat beads over a gas burner or hotplate until they glow red, then put a piece of frankincense on top.

PERFUME SHOPPING: CLEARING YOUR PALATE

Shopping for perfume can wear out your sense of smell. If you're in the market for Arabian scents, do what top perfumiers do to neutralise their olfactory palate: close your mouth and make three forceful exhalations through your nose. Blast the air hard, in short bursts, using your diaphragm. But be careful, lest bogies come flying out (blow your nose first, if you're worried). Some people incorrectly say to smell coffee grounds, but all this practice does is numb your sense of smell.

Frankincense burned alone may remind you of church, but add *oud* for a sweet, rich, log-fire smell. The colourful burners themselves make great souvenirs, and many shops sell all-inclusive gift sets.

Textiles

Vendors at Bur Dubai Souq and along nearby Al-Fahidi St carry vibrant, colourful textiles from the Indian subcontinent and Southeast Asia. They're remarkably cheap, but quality varies. Silk, cotton and linen represent the best value. Dubai's tailors work quickly, and their rates are very reasonable. Prices start at around Dh35 for a shirt or skirt. Draperies may cost as little as Dh10 apiece.

Exotic Delicacies

Fragrant Iranian and Spanish saffron costs far less here than it does back home. Buy it in the Spice Souq or in supermarkets. Honey from Saudi Arabia and Oman is scrumptious. Look for it in speciality shops in Satwa, in the Spice Souq and in supermarkets. Its colour ranges from light gold to almost black. The most expensive varieties are collected by hand from remote areas in the mountains and deserts of Oman. As much as we love good caviar, because of over-fishing and pollution in the Caspian Sea, we cannot advocate the purchase of Iranian roe.

Electronics

If it plugs into a wall you can buy it in Dubai. Because of minimal duties, Dubai is the cheapest place in the region to buy electronics and digital technology. The selection is huge. Research products of interest before hitting the stores though; sales staff don't always know enough. For the lowest prices and no-name brands, head to Al-Fahidi St in Bur Dubai and the area around Al-Sabkha and Al-Maktoum Hospital Rds, near Baniyas Sq, known as the Electronics Souq (Map pp52-3; test items before you buy). If you want an international warranty, shell out the extra money and head to a mall, Carrefour or Plug-Ins. Prices on multiregion DVD players, digital cameras, PDAs and mobile phones vary hugely but may be cheaper than they are back home. For software and hardware, head to Khalid bin al-Waleed Rd (Bank St; aka Computer St) in Bur Dubai between Al-Mankhool Rd and the Falcon Roundabout. For iPods and other Apple products, try Virgin. Compare prices before you buy.

TAX-FREE DUBAI: WHAT IT MEANS

When people talk about Dubai being tax-free, they're referring to personal income tax on wages. There are, however, import duties. There's been talk of creating a consumer tax, but as of this writing there was still none. Does this mean that a new Donna Karan suit will cost less here than in Milan, New York or London? Not necessarily. If you're shopping for mid- and low-cost goods, depending on your home currency, you may not see much difference. But you will notice the difference on luxury goods and cars. If you're in the market for, say, a new Rolex, you'll save a bundle in Dubai. Otherwise don't be lulled by the tax-free promise. Find what you want at home, then price it in Dubai. You may pay more in overweight-luggage charges than you wind up saving in the first place. Caveat emptor.

DEIRA

BOOK CORNER Map pp54-5 — Books
☎ 295 3266; Deira City Centre, Baniyas Rd;
🕑 10am-10pm Sun-Wed, 10am-midnight Thu-Sat
The number of English and Arabic titles is astounding, but the best reason to come here is for travel-related and children's products. Look for the 'Quran Challenge Game', a wacky souvenir. NB: If you're buying travel books, check the publication dates (the store stocks out-of-date titles as well as new ones).

MAGRUDY'S Map pp54-5 — Books
☎ 295 7744; www.magrudy.com; Deira City Centre, Baniyas Rd; 🕑 10am-10pm Sun-Wed, 10am-midnight Thu-Sat
Magrudy's stocks a wide selection of English-language books, with a standout collection of travel, language and children's titles. There are also intriguing books on Middle East history and politics, and a full complement of coffee-table books on Dubai. Only the magazine selection is weak. Check the website for additional branches.

PRIDE OF KASHMIR
Map pp54-5 — Carpets & Handicrafts
☎ 295 0655; Deira City Centre, Baniyas Rd;
🕑 10am-10pm Sun-Wed, 10am-midnight Thu-Sat
The high-knot-density Kashmiri and Persian silk carpets are lovely, but you'll especially enjoy the selection of silky pashmina shawls and home furnishings such as velvet patchwork bedspreads, embroidered throws and sequined cushion covers. Look for branches in Souq Madinat Jumeirah, Mall of the Emirates and Mercato Mall.

ZARA Map pp54-5 — Clothing
☎ 295 3377; Deira City Centre, Baniyas Rd;
🕑 10am-10pm Sun-Wed, 10am-midnight Thu-Sat
Stylish Spain-based Zara has stores all over Dubai, but this is the original branch, with a fabulous selection of smart-looking affordable clothes and accessories. It rarely strays from its black, white, beige and grey colour palette, but the cuts and styling feel very now and look expensive.

MIKYAJY Map pp54-5 — Cosmetics
☎ 295 7844; Deira City Centre; Baniyas Rd;
🕑 10am-10pm Sun-Wed, 10am-midnight Thu-Sat
You feel like you're walking into a candy gift-box at tiny Mikyajy, the Gulf's home-grown make-up brand. Developed to suit the colouring of Middle Eastern women, it's now also popular with foreigners who appreciate vibrant colours like turquoise and tangerine.

DAMAS Map pp54-5 — Jewellery
☎ 295 3848; Deira City Centre, Baniyas Rd;
🕑 10am-10pm Sun-Wed, 10am-midnight Thu-Sat
Damas may not be the most innovative jeweller in Dubai, but with over 50 stores, it's the most trusted. Among the diamonds and gold, look for classic pieces and big-designer names like Fabergé and Tiffany.

VIRGIN MEGASTORE Map pp54-5 — Music
☎ 295 8599; Deira City Centre, Baniyas Rd;
🕑 10am-10pm Sun-Wed, 10am-midnight Thu-Sat
The enthusiastic sales staff are great at suggesting Middle Eastern music to take back home, from traditional oud music to Oriental chill-out. The selection is huge. Also

top picks

MALLS

- BurJuman Centre (p96)
- Dubai Mall (p99)
- Ibn Battuta Mall (p103)
- Mall of the Emirates (p104)
- Souq Madinat Jumeirah (p101)

PASHMINA: TELLING REAL FROM FAKE

Women around the world adore pashminas, those feather-light cashmere shawls worn by the Middle East's best-dressed ladies. If you're shopping for a girlfriend or your mother, you can never go wrong with a pashmina. They come in hundreds of colours and styles, some beaded and embroidered, others with pompom edging – you'll have no trouble finding one you like. But aside from setting it alight to make sure it doesn't melt (as polyester does), how can you be sure it's real? Here's the trick. Hold the fabric at its corner. Loop your index finger around it and squeeze hard. Now pull the fabric through. If it's polyester, it won't budge. If it's cashmere, it'll pull through – though the friction may give you a mild case of rope burn. Try it at home with a thin piece of polyester before you hit the shops; then try it with cashmere. You'll never be fooled again.

check out the Arabian and Iranian DVDs. The store in the Mall of the Emirates is bigger, but for Middle Eastern tunes, this one's best.

AL-GHURAIR CITY
Map pp52-3   Shopping Centre

☎ 295 5309; cnr Al-Rigga & Omar ibn al-Khattab Rds; ⏰ 10am-10pm Sat-Thu, 2-10pm Fri
If seeing all those flowing robes has made you want your own checked *gutra* (white head cloth worn by men in the Gulf States), grab yours at this ageing mall. The place to shop for national dress, it offers stylish *abbeyas* (full-length black robes worn by women) and *shaylas* (headscarves), quality leather sandals, and *dishdashas* (men's shirt-dresses) in chocolate and slate (popular for winter). There are also a couple of dozen fabric stores and a Spinneys supermarket.

DEIRA CITY CENTRE
Map pp54-5   Shopping Centre

☎ 295 1010; Baniyas Rd; ⏰ 10am-10pm Sun-Wed, 10am-midnight Thu-Sat
Though other malls are bigger and flashier, Deira City Centre remains a stalwart for its logical layout and wide selection of shops, from big-name chain stores like H&M and Zara to independent shops carrying good quality carpets, souvenirs and handicrafts. There's also a huge branch of the Carrefour supermarket, food courts and a multiplex.

CARREFOUR Map pp54-5   Supermarket

☎ 295 1600; Deira City Centre, Baniyas Rd; ⏰ 9am-midnight Sat-Wed, 9am-1am Thu & Fri
This enormous French hypermarket draws big crowds of Emiratis and European ex-pats for its off-the-jet-fresh seafood, foie gras, stinky cheeses, freshly baked bread and plump Arabian olives. It also stocks an excellent selection of well-priced mobile phones, digital cameras and electronics. Also in the Mall of the Emirates.

EARLY LEARNING CENTRE
Map pp54-5   Toys

☎ 295 1548; Deira City Centre, Baniyas Rd; ⏰ 10am-10pm Sun-Wed, 10am-midnight Thu-Sat
Parents: if you failed to pack enough toys to keep your little ones entertained, fret not. Early Learning Centre stocks great games designed to get kids thinking and develop key learning skills. And because they're not always easy to figure out, they'll keep children busy for hours. There are additional branches around town, including in the Mall of the Emirates and Souq Madinat Jumeirah.

WOMEN'S SECRET
Map pp54-5   Women's Clothing

☎ 295 9665; Deira City Centre, Baniyas Rd; ⏰ 10am-10pm Sun-Wed, 10am-midnight Thu-Sat
This sassy Spanish label thrills girls with its global-pop-art-inspired underwear, swimwear and nightwear. Expect anything from cute Mexican cross-stitched bra and pants sets to Moroccan-style kaftan-like nightdresses.

BUR DUBAI

AMZAAN Map pp64-5   Boutique

☎ 324 6754; Wafi Mall; Sheikh Rashid Rd, near Oud Metha Rd; ⏰ 10am-10pm Sat-Thu, 4-10pm Fri
Sharjah princess Sheikha Maisa al-Qassimi's funky little boutique specialises in local and out-of-town designers, with an ever-changing line-up of labels. Emirati labels to look for include Sweet Lolly, Crazy Daisy and Pink Sushi. These are complemented by international names such as Von Dutch and Antik Batik.

FIVE GREEN Map pp64-5   Boutique

☎ 336 4100; Garden Home, Oud Metha; ⏰ 10am-11pm Sat-Thu, 4-11pm Fri

DUBAI'S SHOPPING FESTIVALS

Every year from mid-January to mid-February, the month-long Dubai Shopping Festival (www.mydsf.com) draws hoards of bargain-hunting tourists from around the world. This is a good time to visit Dubai: in addition to the huge discounts in the souqs and malls, the weather is usually gorgeous and the city abuzz. Outdoor souqs, amusement rides and food stalls set up in many neighbourhoods, with the best on the Bur Dubai waterfront across from the British Embassy. There are traditional performances and displays at the Heritage and Diving Villages, family entertainment across the city, concerts and events in the parks, and nightly fireworks, best viewed from Creekside Park. Dubai Summer Surprises, a related event, is held during the unbearably hot months of July and August; it mainly attracts visitors from other Gulf countries. NB: For the best bargains at either festival, come during the last week, when retailers slash prices even further to clear out their inventory.

The carnival-like Global Village (off Map p50; ☎ 362 4114; www.globalvillage.ae; off Hwy E311; admission Dh10; ⏰ 4pm-midnight Sun-Wed, to 1am Thu & Fri) runs from late November to late February about 13km south of Sheikh Zayed Rd. Think of it as a sort of World Fair for shoppers. Each of the 30-something pavilions showcases a specific nation's culture and – of course – products. Some favourites: the Afghanistan pavilion for fretwork-bordered stone pendants and beaded-silver earrings; Palestine for traditional cross-stitch *kandouras* (casual shirt-dresses worn by men and women) and ever-popular cushion covers; Yemen for its authentic *khanjars* (traditional curved daggers); India for spangly fabrics and slippers; and Kenya for its kitsch bottle-top handbags. Dig the earnest entertainment, from Chinese opera to Turkish whirling dervishes.

You may get lost trying to find one of the city's leading indie boutiques and concept stores, but it's worth it to meet the cool kids of Dubai's retail scene. In addition to its art installations, kick-ass international magazines and music by Jazzanova and Soot, Five Green carries cool unisex labels such as Teenage Millionaire, Paul Frank, ENC, Xlarge and Upper Playground. It also stocks Pink Sushi, our fave local designer because of its fantastic bags and skirts made from checked *gutras*.

AL-OROOBA ORIENTAL
Map pp62-3 Carpets
☎ 351 0919; BurJuman Centre, cnr Khalid bin al-Waleed & Sheikh Khalifa bin Zayed Rds; ⏰ 10am-10pm Sat-Wed, 10am-11pm Thu & Fri
You'll have to decide whether to enjoy the ritual of unfurling fine carpets or combing over the cool collection of Bedouin jewellery, prayer beads, ceramics and *khanjars* – you won't have time for both: this is high-quality stuff that merits careful attention.

ETRO Map pp62-3 Clothing
☎ 351 3737; BurJuman Centre, cnr Khalid bin al-Waleed & Sheikh Khalifa bin Zayed Rds; ⏰ 10am-10pm Sat-Wed, 10am-11pm Thu & Fri
Jacopo Etro's exuberant paisley designs are inspired by his travels. Borrowing ideas from around the globe, his exotic collections have featured richly coloured chiffon kaftans, Rasta shawls, textured ponchos and sari-style tops. Even men's suits get playful touches thanks to plaid and houndstooth fabrics.

FACES Map pp62-3 Cosmetics
☎ 352 1441; BurJuman Centre, cnr Khalid bin al-Waleed & Sheikh Khalifa bin Zayed Rds; ⏰ 10am-10pm Sat-Wed, 10am-11pm Thu & Fri
There's an entire global menu of make-up, fragrances and skincare potions here to help you get prettified and smelling good. As well as the usual glamour brands (Armani to Chanel), Faces also stocks products by Bourgois from France, Bloom from Australia, Dr Brandt from Florida and other harder-to-source beauty purveyors.

COMPUTER PLAZA @ AL-AIN CENTRE
Map pp62-3 Electronics
☎ 351 6914; Al-Mankhool Rd; ⏰ 10am-10pm
Jam-packed with small shops selling every kind of software, hardware and accessory for PCs, this computer and electronics mall also has a good range of digital cameras. The ground floor has an internet cafe and fast-food outlets.

PLUG-INS Map pp62-3 Electronics
☎ 351 3919; BurJuman Centre, cnr Khalid bin al-Waleed & Sheikh Khalifa bin Zayed Rds; ⏰ 10am-10pm Sat-Wed, 10am-11pm Thu & Fri
If you left your digital camera on the back seat of a taxi, Plug-Ins carries a big selection of tiny digital cameras, as well as MP3 players, hand-held organisers and home-theatre systems. Prices are competitive, but you may do better at Carrefour. Also in Al-Ghurair City.

BATEEL Map pp62-3   Food

☎ 355 2853; BurJuman Centre, cnr Khalid bin al-Waleed & Sheikh Khalifa bin Zayed Rds; ☽ 10am-10pm Sat-Wed, 10am-11pm Thu & Fri

Old-style traditional Arabian hospitality meant dates and camel milk. Now Emiratis offer their guests Bateel's scrumptious date chocolates and truffles, made from 120 varieties using European chocolate-making techniques. Bateel's sales staff are always happy to give you a sample before you buy. For more on Bateel, see below. Other locations include Deira City Centre, Dubai Mall and Souk al-Bahar.

GIFT WORLD

Map pp64-5   Handicrafts & Souvenirs

☎ 335 8097; Block T, Karama Shopping Centre; ☽ 9am-10.30pm Sat-Thu, 4-10.30pm Fri

Imagine yourself in Aladdin's Cave as you bump your head on the hanging Moroccan and Syrian lamps while rummaging through Oriental bric-a-brac, ranging from Bedouin jewellery and beads to sequined bedspreads and dizzyingly patterned camel cushion covers.

OHM RECORDS Map pp64-5   Music

☎ 397 3728; half block south of Sheikh Khalifa bin Zayed Rd, opposite BurJuman Centre; ☽ noon-9pm

DJs dig Ohm, the first Dubai shop to carry vinyl. There's a discerning selection of house, trance, progressive, trip-hop and drum 'n' bass, as well as DJ equipment and accessories. Jason and the crew also bring some of the hottest international DJs to such venues as Chi @ The Lodge (p133) and Rooftop at Souq Madinat (p131).

AJMAL Map pp62-3   Perfume

☎ 351 5505; BurJuman Centre, cnr Khalid bin al-Waleed & Sheikh Khalifa bin Zayed Rds; ☽ 10am-10pm Sat-Wed, 10am-11pm Thu & Fri

The place for traditional Arabian *attars* (perfumes and essential oils), Ajmal custom blends its earthy scents and pours them into fancy gold or jewel-encrusted bottles. These aren't fancy French colognes – they're woody and pungent perfumes. Ask for 'Rageeb', a sandalwood-based scent (Dh200). Other branches are in Deira City Centre, Mall of the Emirates and Dubai Mall.

BURJUMAN CENTRE

Map pp62-3   Shopping Centre

☎ 352 0222; cnr Khalid bin al-Waleed & Sheikh Khalifa bin Zayed Rds; ☽ 10am-10pm Sat-Wed, 10am-11pm Thu & Fri; 🛜

BurJuman has one of the highest concentrations of high-end labels and an easy-to-navigate floor plan with wide expanses of shiny marble. Max out your credit card at over 320 top purveyors, including Saks Fifth Avenue, Dolce&Gabbana, Donna Karan, Kenzo, Calvin Klein, Etro, Christian Lacroix, Cartier and Tiffany. There's a neat food court on the 3rd floor and a tourist office desk on Level 1 in the North Village. The mall is also a stop on the Big Bus Company (p192) route. Bonus: free wi-fi.

KARAMA SHOPPING CENTRE

Map pp64-5   Shopping Centre

Karama, Bur Dubai; ☽ 9am-10.30pm Sat-Thu, 9-11am & 4-10.30pm Fri

A visually unappealing concrete souq, Karama's bustling backstreet shopping area is

---

BATEEL DATES

The de rigeur gift for any proper gourmet, Bateel dates are the ultimate luxury food of Arabia. At first glance, Bateel looks like a jewellery store, with polished-glass display cases and halogen pin spots illuminating the goods. A closer look reveals perfectly aligned pyramids of dates – thousands of them. Bateel plays to its audience with gorgeous packaging that might leave the recipient of your gift expecting gold or silver within: the fancy boxes of lacquered hardwood are worth far more than their contents. Alas, they're manufactured in China, but not the dates. These come from Saudi Arabia, which has the ideal growing conditions: sandy, alkaline soil and extreme heat. Quality control is tight: Bateel has its own farms and production equipment. The dates sold here are big and fat, with gooey-moist centers. Because they have a 70% sugar content, dates technically have unlimited shelf life, but you'll find they taste best around the autumn harvest.

If agwa dates are available during your visit, buy them – you may not have another opportunity. Agwa trees only yield every few years, so they're considered a delicacy. Look for them in September; other varieties arrive in November. The stuffed dates make a great gift – we love the candied orange peel and caramelised almonds. If you miss your chance in town, you can stock up at the airport as you leave Dubai. A cardboard box will set you back Dh120 per kilo, a fancy box Dh200, and a little beribboned sampler of five or seven perfect dates around Dh30.

TOP SHOPPING & EATS STREETS

When it's cool enough to be outdoors, escape the monotony of the shopping malls and hit the street. Though generally grimy, Dubai's commercial streets are chock-a-block with stores and restaurants, and each has its own flavour. Some are specific to particular types of consumer goods, others to a particular culture and its food. Since shopping and eating go hand-in-hand, we've crafted a shortlist of our favourite areas to do a bit of both. For the best people-watching and liveliest atmosphere, come in the evening. Note that many shops close between 1pm and 4pm.

Khalid bin al-Waleed Rd (Bank St), Bur Dubai (Map pp62-3) Nicknamed Computer St, Bank St's crowded pavements are lined with shops selling software, hardware, laptops, personal organisers and computer accessories. (Never mind the occasional hooker.) Go for inexpensive Sri Lankan food at Curry Leaf (p113), inside the computer-mall Al-Mussalla Tower.

Al-Fahidi St, Bur Dubai (Map pp62-3) This bustling Indian 'hood is great for textiles, saris, digital cameras and electronics, with myriad tailor shops and luggage dealers; it's also good for snacks at hole-in-the-wall Indian joints that serve strong black tea cut with milk.

Al-Hisn St and 73 St, Bur Dubai (Map pp62-3) Another predominantly Indian area with impossibly narrow pavements and buzzing neon. Here you'll find sari shops, sequined slippers, and Bollywood music and movies. Head to Rangoli (Map pp62-3; ☎ 351 5873; Meena Bazaar; mains Dh10-20; ⏰ 8.30am-3pm & 5pm-midnight), which makes great all-veg curries and gooey-delicious sweets.

Al-Rigga Rd, Rigga (Map pp62-3) A wide boulevard with broad pavements, Al-Rigga is good for specialist *sheesha* shops, discount gifts, internet cafes and traditional Emirati dress (head to Al-Ghurair City). Stop for Syrian and Iranian sweets along the way, but for a meal walk around the corner to Aroos Damascus (see boxed text, p110).

Al-Dhiyafha Rd, Satwa, between Al-Satwa Rd and Al-Mina Rd (Map pp76-7) A favourite walking street for its wide pavements, cultural diversity, and mix of day-to-day and speciality shops, Al-Dhiyafha is good for books, *sheesha*-pipe stores and Syrian handicrafts. But the standout attraction here is the bevy of great Lebanese food. For mezze, visit Sidra (p120); for *shwarma*, try Al-Mallah (see boxed text, p120) or Beirut (see boxed text, p120).

Al-Satwa Rd, Satwa, between Al-Dhiyafha Rd and Al-Hudheiba Rd (Map pp76-7) This thoroughfare feels anonymous but it is the place to buy low-cost luggage, cheap *kandouras* (robes) and textiles. Munch on Indian sweets at little cafes, or follow the Pakistani workers and five-star chefs to Ravi (p120).

crammed with stores selling handicrafts and souvenirs, 'genuine fake' watches and knock-off designer clothing. Since much of the latter is produced in Asian countries, sizes are likely to run small. In other words, if you normally wear a size S and now XL, it's probably not because you overindulged at those brunches. Prices are low, but bargaining lowers them further – be adamant. Listen for the cries of hucksters hawking pirated copies: 'Dee-vee-dees! Bloo moovees!' The municipality seems to look the other way.

WAFI MALL Map pp64-5   Shopping Centre
☎ 324 4555; Sheikh Rashid Rd, near Oud Metha Rd; ⏰ 10am-10pm Sat-Wed, 10am-midnight Thu & Fri
Westerners mistakenly bypass palatial Wafi in favour of the behemoth shopping malls, which explains why it's so quiet. Their loss. It may have once resembled a third-rate airport terminal, but the new wing's stained-glass pyramids are stunning (come before sunset). Emirati women love Wafi's fancy French stores like Chanel and Givenchy, but you may well prefer sussing out lesser-

known regional boutiques. Also duck into the basement to browse around Souk Khan Murjan, which has stunning decor (check out the stained-glass ceiling and carved pillars) and a good if pricey selection of crafts and goods from around the Arabian world. Alas, it too is practically deserted. Refuelling stops include Asha's (p111) and New Asia Bar & Club (p128) at the adjacent Raffles hotel.

PRAIAS Map pp62-3   Women's Clothing
☎ 351 1338; 1st fl, BurJuman Centre, cnr Khalid bin al-Waleed & Sheikh Khalifa bin Zayed Rds; ⏰ 10am-10pm Sat-Wed, 10am-11pm Thu & Fri
Emirati women wouldn't be caught dead wearing Praias' skimpy candy-coloured bikinis and swirly-patterned beach dresses in public. Perhaps you shouldn't either, unless you've first had a Brazilian wax job.

WHISTLES Map pp62-3   Women's Clothing
☎ 351 5070; BurJuman Centre, cnr Khalid bin al-Waleed & Sheikh Khalifa bin Zayed Rds; ⏰ 10am-10pm Sat-Wed, 10am-11pm Thu & Fri

An antidote to Dubai's overly glam-focused shopping scene, Whistles carries smart, well-tailored and understatedly sexy women's wear – think girls' night on the town.

SHEIKH ZAYED ROAD

MARAMI Map pp70-71 Accessories
☎ 434 3536; Dubai Mall, Downtown Dubai; ⏱ 10am-10pm Sun-Wed, 10am-midnight Thu-Sat
Every girl knows that you can pep up any bland outfit with the right accessory. And so does Salama Alabbar, who stocks ultra-chic jewellery, handbags, scarves and hair accessories in her elegant store near the aquarium in Dubai Mall. Look for brands like Lara Bohinc and Zufi Alexander, as well as a line custom designed by local creatives.

SAMSAARA Map pp70-71 Boutique
☎ 420 0122; Souk al-Bahar, Old Town Island; ⏱ 10am-10pm Sat-Thu, 2-10pm Fri
If you ever get a chance to walk down the red carpet for a Bollywood movie premiere, swing by this luxe boutique to pick out a pretty gown designed by the biggest names in Indian fashions – Vikram Phadnis to Manish Arora or Deepika Gehani.

PERSIAN CARPET HOUSE & ANTIQUES Map pp70-71 Carpets
☎ 434 3152; Dubai Mall, Downtown Dubai; ⏱ 10am-10pm Sun-Wed, 10am-midnight Thu-Sat
One of the country's largest carpet retailers carries a big selection of handmade Persian carpets and Oriental rugs from Turkey, Afghanistan, Pakistan, India and Kashmir. The antiques selection, though small, includes some cool old gramophones, radios and telephones. There are other branches around town, for instance in the Mall of the Emirates and the Boulevard at Jumeirah Emirates Towers.

CANDYLICIOUS Map pp70-71 Food
☎ 330 8700; ground fl, Dubai Mall, next to Dubai Aquarium; ⏱ 10am-10pm Sun-Wed, 10am-midnight Thu-Sat
Stand under the lollipop tree, guzzle a root beer float at the soda fountain or soak up the tempting aroma of Garretts' gourmet popcorn at this colourful candy emporium. The 1000th store to open in Dubai Mall, it's stocked to the rafters with everything from humble jelly beans to gourmet chocolate

HOW TO 'DO' DUBAI MALL

Dubai Mall is a shopper's Shangri La but it's so huge that it's all rather bewildering. Don't be intimidated: make your first order of business to pick up a map from one of 18 information desks strategically positioned near entrances and throughout the four floors. These are also staffed with friendly, English-speaking folk happy to point you in the right direction. Alternatively, you can use the interactive electronic store finders to show you the way to a particular store. Like all malls, Dubai Mall is busiest on Thursday night and Friday after 4pm, so avoid these times if you don't like crowds. There's a free shuttle service to select area hotels – pick up a timetable at an information desk. Wi-fi is free as well, but for now you need a United Arab Emirates (UAE) mobile number to register for the service.

from France and Switzerland. Pure bliss. Just don't tell your dentist.

ORGANIC FOODS & CAFE Map pp70-71 Food
☎ 3434 0577; ground fl, Dubai Mall; ⏱ 9am-10pm Sun-Wed, 9am-midnight Thu-Sat
Despite the massive amounts of jet fuel required to ship them in, the fruits and veggies are 100% organic at Dubai's first natural supermarket, providing a refreshing, much-needed alternative to the flavourless produce sold elsewhere. Also look for freshly baked bread, fresh-roasted fair-trade coffee and an extensive selection of gluten-free products.

50 DEGREES Map pp70-71 Gifts & Homewares
☎ 420 0414; Souk al-Bahar; ⏱ 10am-10pm Sun-Thu, 2-10pm Fri
The New York loft-style space is the vision of Japanese designer Manabu Ozawa and the quirky tchotchkes on sale reflect the taste of Dubai-born owners Shahi Hamad and Saadia Zahid. Forget about mass brands: 50 degrees is all about hand-picked jewellery, tableware, scarves, vinyl toys and other inspired lifestyle enhancers. Look for products by Blue Q, Nooka and Pink Sushi, along with Mona Ibrahim's handmade letter earrings and necklaces.

AZZA FAHMY JEWELLERY Map pp70-71 Jewellery
☎ 330 0346; Blvd at Jumeirah Emirates Towers, Sheikh Zayed Rd; ⏱ 10am-10pm Sat-Thu, 2-10pm Fri

Queens, supermodels and celebrities adore Egyptian Azza Fahmy's beautifully crafted jewellery. Inlaid with precious gemstones and fine calligraphy of classical Arabic poetry and spiritual sayings, the pieces express core values of Islam. Even if you're not a believer, there's no disputing the elegant simplicity of this 'wearable art'.

GOLD & DIAMOND PARK
Map pp70-71   Jewellery
☎ 347 7788; Sheikh Zayed Rd, near Interchange No 4; ☺ 10am-10pm Sat-Thu, 4-10pm Fri
A cooler alternative to the Gold Souq in the summer months, the air-conditioned Gold & Diamond Park houses some 90 retailers in an Arabian-style building. Don't forget to bargain.

BOULEVARD AT JUMEIRAH EMIRATES TOWERS Map pp70-71   Shopping Centre
☎ 330 0000; Sheikh Zayed Rd; ☺ 10am-10pm Sat-Thu, 2-10pm Fri
If you feel like you're being watched, you are. Emirates Towers is the location of Sheikh Mohammed's offices, and the secret police are everywhere. Dress appropriately and keep your voice down as you nose around exclusive designer boutiques like Bulgari, Cartier, Zegna, Armani, Gucci, Jimmy Choo and Pucci. Don't miss the wearable art of Azza Fahmy Jewellery (opposite). At day's end, sip chardonnay at Agency (p128), sing karaoke at Harry Ghatto's (p128) or refuel at the ever-popular Noodle House (p117).

DUBAI MALL Map pp70-71   Shopping Centre
☎ 362 7500; Sheikh Zayed Rd, Downtown Dubai; ☺ 10am-10pm Sun-Wed, 10am-midnight Thu-Sat; ☺
With around 1200 stores, this is not merely a mall but a small city unto itself, with an Olympic-size ice rink, a huge aquarium, indoor theme parks and 160 food outlets. There's a strong European label presence here, alongside Galeries Lafayette department store from France, Hamley's toy store from the UK and the first Bloomingdale's outside the United States. It's a ginormous, daylit mall with wide aisles and lots of open spaces, atriums and even a fashion catwalk. The four floors are divided into 'precincts' with clusters of product categories: search for high-end designers on Fashion Ave (which has marble floors and silver resting divans), high-street fashions on the ground

floor and activewear next to the ice rink. There's also a four-storey waterfall that's gorgeously lit at night. The Gold Souk at the centre of the mall is dominated by the beautiful Treasury Dome, but pathetically undervisited. Also see p72.

SOUK AL-BAHAR
Map pp70-71   Shopping Centre
☎ 362 7011; Old Town Island, next to Dubai Mall; ☺ 10am-10pm Sun-Thu, 2-10pm Fri
Much smaller and less flashy, Souk al-Bahar is Downtown Dubai's answer to Souq Madinat Jumeirah. As such, shops are primarily geared to the tourist market but there are also some gems, such as Indian couture at Samsaara (opposite) and stylish gifts at 50 Degrees (opposite). Spinneys supermarket in the basement has all the basics.

JUMEIRAH
GALLERY ONE Map pp76-7   Art
☎ 368 6055; Souq Madinat Jumeirah, Al-Sufouh Rd, Al-Sufouh 2; ☺ 10am-11pm
For an arty souvenir, consider a colourful Arabian abstract image, pop-art screen print or a black-and-white photograph of Dubai's bustling Creek scene or famous wind towers. Prices are very reasonable. The problem will be choosing which you like best.

SHOWCASE ANTIQUES, ART & FRAMES Map pp76-7   Art & Antiques
☎ 348 8797; Villa 679, Jumeirah Rd, Umm Suqeim; ☺ 9am-6pm Sat-Thu
Browse this three-storey Jumeirah villa for antique *khanjars*, firearms, Arabian coffee pots, Bedouin jewellery and costumes. It's one of few places in Dubai to carry quality collectables and antiques, with certificates of authenticity to back them up. It's across from Dubai Municipality Building, near the corner of Al-Manara St.

HOUSE OF PROSE Map pp76-7   Books
☎ 344 9021; Jumeirah Plaza, Jumeirah Rd, Jumeirah 1; ☺ 9am-8pm Sat-Thu, 5-8pm Fri
Presided over by a convivial American named Mike, this comfortably worn-round-the-edges bookstore overflows with second-hand English-language books, from classic lit to obscure biographies and travel guides. After you've read your book, you can bring it back for 50% credit towards

your next purchase. There's another branch in Ibn Battuta Mall.

BLUE CACTUS Map pp76-7   Boutique
☎ 344 7734; Jumeirah Centre, Jumeirah Rd, Jumeirah 1; ⏲ 10am-9pm Sat-Thu, 4.30-9pm Fri
The buyer at this upstairs boutique is from Mexico, and boy, does she have an eye for brilliant colour and sexy lines. The va-va-voom fashions are mostly American, and range from sleek long dresses with gorgeous drapings to sassy separates that look hot on a dance floor. NB: The downstairs shop carries cool Mexican silver jewellery.

FLEURT Map pp76-7   Boutique
☎ 342 0906; Mercato Mall, Jumeirah Rd, Jumeirah 1; ⏲ 10am-10pm Thu-Sat, 2-10pm Fri
This small boutique keeps trend-hungry stylistas looking good in funky-smart fashions by Betsey Johnson and Soul Revival, among other progressives. The collection is refreshingly offbeat, with spangles and sequins, curve-hugging lines, and cheeky party frocks. If you're into classic design, go elsewhere.

LUXECOUTURE Map pp76-7   Boutique
☎ 344 7933; Village Mall, Jumeirah Rd, Jumeirah 1; ⏲ 10am-10pm Thu-Sat, 4.30-10pm Fri
Alejandra Tokoph-Cox is a Dubai style-maker who often travels to New York to ferret out the latest design trends and import them to Dubai. Her sleek boutiques stock all the hot labels you see on Lindsay, Cameron and Paris, including NYC, Yumi Kim, Shoshana and Tracy Watts, plus jewellery by Dogeared and Nadri. Alejandra's growing emporium now also includes branches on The Walk at JBR and in Souq Madinat Jumeirah.

S*UCE Map pp76-7   Boutique
☎ 344 7270; Village Mall, Jumeirah Rd, Jumeirah 1; ⏲ 10am-10pm Thu-Sat, 4.30-10pm Fri
This is the original store of women-owned S*uce (pronounced 'sauce'), a pioneer on Dubai's growing indie fashion boutique scene. Join the style brigade searching for top-tier denim, flirty frocks, sassy accessories, sexy sandals and deluxe tees. Look for such key contemporary designers as Karta, Tsumori Chisato, Vanessa Bruno, Isabella Cappeto, Alice McCall and Philip Lim, as well as local labels such as Essa, Bil Arabi and Sugar Vintage. There's another branch in Dubai Mall.

CLOTHING SIZES

Women's clothing

Aus/UK	8	10	12	14	16	18
Europe	36	38	40	42	44	46
Japan	5	7	9	11	13	15
USA	6	8	10	12	14	16

Women's shoes

Aus/USA	5	6	7	8	9	10
Europe	35	36	37	38	39	40
France only	35	36	38	39	40	42
Japan	22	23	24	25	26	27
UK	3½	4½	5½	6½	7½	8½

Men's clothing

Aus	92	96	100	104	108	112
Europe	46	48	50	52	54	56
Japan	S		M	M		L
UK/USA	35	36	37	38	39	40

Men's shirts (collar sizes)

Aus/Japan	38	39	40	41	42	43
Europe	38	39	40	41	42	43
UK/USA	15	15½	16	16½	17	17½

Men's shoes

Aus/UK	7	8	9	10	11	12
Europe	41	42	43	44½	46	47
Japan	26	27	27½	28	29	30
USA	7½	8½	9½	10½	11½	12½

Measurements approximate only; try before you buy

S*UCE LIGHT Map pp76-7   Boutique
☎ 344 4391; 1st fl, Jumeirah Centre, Jumeirah Rd, Jumeirah 1; ⏲ 10am-9pm Sat-Thu, 4.30-9pm Fri
Not flush enough to drop Dh1500 for a pair of jeans at S*uce? Just pop across the street to its outlet, where a limited selection and a less glam ambience translate into items at 50% to 70% off.

TOPSHOP Map pp76-7   Clothing
☎ 344 2677; Mercato Mall, Jumeirah Rd, Jumeirah 1; ⏲ 10am-10pm
The jewel in the crown of British high-street fashion, Topshop's diverse selection runs from denim and jumpers to handbags and jazzy earrings. Also in Deira City Centre, Ibn Battuta Shopping Mall and Wafi Mall.

DUBAI FLEA MARKET
Map pp76-7   Flea Market
www.dubai-fleamarket.com; Gate 5 (Al-Wasl Rd), Al-Safa Park; admission Dh3; ⏲ 8am-3pm every 1st Sat Oct-May

CAMEL CRAZY

Our top five camel gifts:
- Stuffed camels that play Arabic music when cuddled
- *Camelspotting* CD – cool Middle Eastern music
- Sabine Moser's *Camel-O-Shy* kids books
- A camel road-crossing-sign fridge magnet
- Eye-poppingly intricate camel-patterned cushion covers

Flea markets are like urban archaeology: you'll need plenty of patience and luck when sifting through other people's trash and detritus, but oh the thrill when finally unearthing a piece of treasure! So trade malls for stalls and look for bargains amid the piles of pre-loved clothing, furniture, toys, home appliances, electronics, art, books and other stuff that's spilled out of local closets.

CAMEL COMPANY
Map pp76-7   Handicrafts & Souvenirs
☎ 368 6048; Souq Madinat Jumeirah, Al-Sufouh Rd, Al-Sufouh 2; ☾ 10am-11pm
If you can slap a camel on it, Camel Company has it. This hands-down best spot for camel souvenirs carries plush stuffed camels

that sing when you squeeze them, camels in Hawaiian shirts, on T-shirts, coffee cups, mouse-pads, notebooks, greeting cards and of course fridge magnets. The store is owned by the Austrian Sabine Moser, author of the book series *Camel-O-Shy*.

MERCATO MALL Map pp76-7   Shopping Centre
☎ 344 4161; Jumeirah Rd, Jumeirah 1; ☾ 10am-10pm
One of the most attractive malls in Dubai, Mercato blends the grandeur of a European train station with the playfulness of an Italian palazzo. Think soaring murals and an arched glass ceiling. It's fun to wander among the brick colonnades and the compact size makes shopping here less overwhelming than at other malls. There are a few stylish boutiques like Fleurt (opposite), a small Topshop, a Virgin Megastore, and some interesting carpet and curio shops.

SOUQ MADINAT JUMEIRAH
Map pp76-7   Shopping Centre
☎ 348 8797; Madinat Jumeirah, Al-Sufouh 2; ☾ 10am-11pm
More a themed shopping mall than a traditional Arabian market, the souq is

SOUVENIR SUGGESTIONS

Traditional Take-Homes

If you can't resist taking home gold, carpets, perfume and the like, here are some helpful hints:

Carpets Go for Persian; better value and finer quality than anywhere except Iran.

Gold Assuming you don't buy at its peak, you'll feel smug once it's valued back home.

Perfume No tax means French brands are cheaper than in Paris, but check the packaging to make sure they're authentic.

Pashminas Fakes are found all over the world, but in Dubai you'll find bargains on real, silky-soft 100% pashmina shawls. For tips on buying, see p94.

Oriental music Sure, you want to shimmy like a belly dancer on your desert safari, but listen before you buy – some of it is excruciating.

Cool Keepsakes

These Dubai-designed, home-grown and lesser-known regional products make more original mementos:

Colourful camel bags Make groovy ottoman covers.

Azza Fahmy jewellery Impress your friends by explaining the Arabic inscriptions and imagery.

Arabian *attars* (perfumes) You can be confident no other woman in the room will be wearing the same scent.

A Pink Sushi piece Funky feminine fashion made from the traditional *gutra* (white head-cloth) by an Emirati designer. They may be hard to find; call Five Green (p94), S*uce (opposite) and Amzaan (p94).

Lemonada or Blue Bedouin CDs Kick back to Arabian lounge and chill-out music made in Dubai.

a bit of a tourist trap, with prices that are considerably higher than they are in real souqs. Still, it's an attractive spot for a wander and worth visiting if only to see how the enormous Madinat Jumeirah complex (p79) fits together. Outside, *abras* float by on man-made canals, and dozens of alfresco bars and restaurants overlook the scene. The floor plan is intentionally confusing: officials say that it's meant to mimic a real souq but others think it's to keep you trapped and lull you into emptying your wallet.

LATA'S Map pp76-7   Souvenirs

☎ 368 6216; Souq Madinat Jumeirah, Al-Sufouh Rd, Al-Sufouh 2; ☺ 10am-11pm

This is our favourite one-stop shop for Arabian and Middle Eastern souvenirs, such as Moroccan lamps, brass coffee tables, *khanjars* and silver prayer holders. It also stocks some fabulous silver jewellery, and some not-so-fabulous costume pieces. Tell the staff what you're after, and they'll steer you right to it.

NEW DUBAI

AIZONE Map pp82-3   Boutique

☎ 347 9333; Mall of the Emirates, Sheikh Zayed Rd, Al-Barsha; ☺ 10am-10pm Sun-Wed, 10am-midnight Thu-Sat

Lose yourself for hours in this enormous Lebanese fashion emporium, with hard-to-find labels and snappy drag for twirling on the dance floor. Look for the latest from Bibelot, Juicy Couture, Spy, DSquared and Lotus. Prices skew high, but wow, what a collection.

BAUHAUS Map pp82-3   Boutique

☎ 368 5551; India Court, Ibn Battuta Mall, Sheikh Zayed Rd; ☺ 10am-10pm Sun-Wed, 10am-midnight Thu-Sat

High-energy tunes keep girls and boys flipping fast through Evisu denim, Bulzeye tees and Drifter hoodies at this hip lifestyle boutique specialising in nonmainstream fashion, art and music. The store design was inspired by the revolutionary 1920s Bauhaus design movement and mixes all sorts of materials, from acrylic to wood, leather to metal and bricks.

BOUTIQUE 1 Map pp70-71   Boutique

☎ 425 7888; The Walk at JBR, Dubai Marina; ☺ 10am-11pm

Ground zero for prêt-à-porter straight off the runways of Paris and Milan, Boutique 1 is the pinnacle of Dubai's fashion scene, with designers like Missoni and Yves St Laurent. Its gorgeous new three-storey store on The Walk stocks not only fashionable frocks but also home accessories, beauty products, furniture and even books.

GINGER & LACE Map pp82-3   Boutique

☎ 368 5109; Ibn Battuta Mall, Sheikh Zayed Rd; ☺ 10am-10pm Sun-Wed, 10am-midnight Thu-Sat

Ginger & Lace stocks an eclectic selection of colourful, whimsical fashion by high-spirited New York designers Anna Sui and Betsey Johnson, London-based bag maven Zufi Alexander and Spanish illustrator-turned-fashion designer Jordi Labanda. There's another store in Wafi Mall.

JUMPING THE TAXI QUEUE

Hailing a taxi at a mall on a weekend afternoon or evening can take well over an hour. Different malls have different systems. At some, you've no choice but to queue up, as at Deira City Centre – the worst of the lot – where the snaking line of people can easily exceed 200 tired shoppers. To avoid it, wander around the corner to the adjacent Sofitel and tip the doorman Dh5. (Consolidate or hide your shopping bags; the hotel's doormen aren't supposed to hail taxis for shoppers.) At Dubai Festival City, the system is more civilised: the doorman hands you a number telling you where you are in the queue (don't be surprised to learn that 100 people are ahead of you). The upside of this system is that you can plan your shopping around the wait: once you're nearly done, pick up your number, then head back inside and hit the stores near the taxi door. Alternatively, head to the adjacent InterContinental Hotel, at the far end of the mall, where you'll have to pony up extra for a hotel taxi, but will rarely wait. (Again, tip the doorman.) At Mall of the Emirates, avoid the long queue by heading to the front door of the Kempinski Hotel, adjoining Ski Dubai, where there's always a line of non-hotel taxis waiting. If there's a queue at Wafi Mall, head to Raffles Dubai and pony up the extra cash for a hotel taxi. At other malls, you'll just have to brave the wait. If you're shameless and really pressed, you can cheat and catch an arriving taxi before he pulls into the lot, but the taxi attendant will make a fuss. Be discreet.

AMINIAN PERSIAN CARPETS

Map pp54-5   Carpets

☎ 341 0402; Mall of the Emirates, Sheikh Zayed Rd, Al-Barsha; ☺ 10am-10pm Sun-Wed, 10am-midnight Thu-Sat

This trusted rug trader offers great service and stocks a wide selection of classic Persian carpets and colourful tribal kilims. Plan to linger long: the collection is far bigger than it first appears.

MOTHERCARE Map pp64-5   Children's Clothing

☎ 340 7575; Mall of the Emirates, Sheikh Zayed Rd, Al-Barsha; ☺ 10am-10pm Sun-Wed, 10am-midnight Thu-Sat

Mothercare is one of the most popular and affordable shops for kids' necessities, from cute clothes and cuddly toys to baby carriers and car seats. There are other branches in Al-Ghurair City, BurJuman and Ibn Battuta Mall, among others.

TAPE À L'OEIL

Map pp62-3   Children's Clothing

☎ 341 0480; Mall of the Emirates, Sheikh Zayed Rd, Al-Barsha; ☺ 10am-10pm Sun-Wed, 10am-midnight Thu-Sat

A refreshing alternative to Gap Kids, this French brand carries fun kids' clothes that look like miniature adult wear. Denim features prominently, as do skirts and sweaters that look best on kids who keep their hair combed.

FOREVER 21 Map pp82-3   Clothing

☎ 341 3412; Mall of the Emirates, Sheikh Zayed Rd, Al-Barsha; ☺ 10am-10pm Sun-Wed, 10am-midnight Thu-Sat

Cutting in on H&M for affordable style and selection, this is one of Dubai's largest stores, with a big range of youthful, affordable fashion and accessories.

PIXI Map pp82-3   Cosmetics

☎ 341 3833; Mall of the Emirates, Sheikh Zayed Rd, Al-Barsha; ☺ 10am-10pm Sun-Wed, 10am-midnight Thu-Sat

Sweden-born Petra Strand's fab make-up line will have you done up and ready for the red-carpet in no time – even after a night on the town. Try the eye zone brightener, the flawless beauty primer and the sheer cheek gel, all prettily packaged, making lovely gifts or satisfying your pampering needs.

JUMBO ELECTRONICS

Map pp82-3   Electronics

☎ 341 0101; Mall of the Emirates, Sheikh Zayed Rd, Al-Barsha; ☺ 10am-10pm Sun-Wed, 10am-midnight Thu-Sat

The mother of Dubai's electronics stores, this place is nirvana for geeks, with all the latest computers, cameras, mobile phones, games and gadgets under one giant roof. There are 15 more outlets sprinkled across town, including one in Deira City Centre and another in Wafi Mall.

COVENT GARDEN MARKET

Map pp82-3   Market

☎ 050 244 5795; www.coventgardenmarket.ae; The Walk at JBR, Rimal Sector (btwn Hilton & Sheraton); ☺ 5pm-midnight Wed & Thu, 10am-9pm Fri & Sat

If you're not into shopping, grab a latte and send the others out to peruse the lacy scarves, fancy necklaces, designer T-shirts and pretty purses at this bustling arts and crafts market. Bring the kids: clowns, bands and balloon-animal makers provide the entertainment.

RECTANGLE JAUNE

Map pp82-3   Men's Clothing

☎ 875 3225; Mall of the Emirates, Sheikh Zayed Rd, Al-Barsha; ☺ 10am-10pm Sun-Wed, 10am-midnight Thu-Sat

A great store for men, with a terrific selection of dress shirts in snappy stripes and bold patterns by a team of fashion-savvy Lebanese designers. There's another branch in Deira City Centre.

IBN BATTUTA MALL

Map pp82-3   Shopping Centre

☎ 362 1902; Sheikh Zayed Rd, btwn Interchanges No 5 & No 6; ☺ 10am-10pm Sun-Wed, 10am-midnight Thu-Sat

The 14th-century Arab scholar Ibn Battuta travelled 120,000km over 30 years. You'll have a better idea of how he felt after trekking from one end of this behemoth mall to the other. It's divided into six sections, each decorated in the style of a country he visited – Andalusia, Tunisia, Egypt, Persia, India and China. Alas, the shopping is not nearly as special, although worthwhile stops include Ginger & Lace (p102) and the Bauhaus (p102) lifestyle store. If you're too exhausted to walk back, hop on the golf-cart shuttle (Dh5).

SUPERMARKET SOUVENIRS

Happiness is shopping at Spinneys (p107), Carrefour (p107) and Choithram (p108) – the shelves are positively packed with international foodstuffs. Here are a few favourites.

Cardamon-flavoured condensed milk Worth weighing down the luggage for, this provides a taste of Arabia when you return home. Great in coffee.

Natco rose syrup Wow your dinner-party guests by pouring rose syrup over sorbet or vanilla ice cream.

Zaatar and sumac Add *zaatar* (a blend of thyme, sesame, marjoram and oregano) to your soups, salads or stews; add sumac (a spice with a lemony taste that's added to salads, hummus, kebabs and other Middle Eastern dishes) and lemon to a chopped salad to remind you of some of the fabulous Lebanese meals you ate in Dubai.

Saffron You won't find cheaper back home. Soak it in hot cooking water or broth to extract its aroma before adding it to the pot.

Indian tea Unlike in the West, Indian tea is powdered and instantly dissolves in hot water. Drink it with full-cream milk to evoke memories of Dubai's Indian-sweets pavement bakeries.

MALL OF THE EMIRATES
Map pp82-3   Shopping Centre

☎ 409 9000; Sheikh Zayed Rd, Interchange No 4, Al-Barsha; ☾ 10am-10pm Sun-Wed, 10am-midnight Thu-Sat

The second biggest after Dubai Mall, the Mall of the Emirates sprawls with acres of polished white marble. The curiosity of Ski Dubai (p144) is a major draw, as are the remarkably good food courts and comfortable multiplex with its Gold Class screening room. Relatively narrow walkways and lack of daylight make it feel a tad claustrophobic at peak periods. Along with the usual brands, there's a Harvey Nichols and a big Borders with an awesome selection of travel books (be nice and they may show you the banned-book list).

OTHER NEIGHBOURHOODS

PAUL & JOE Map p50   Boutique

☎ 804 5500; Dubai Festival City; ☾ 10am-10pm

Named for the proprietor's sons, Paul & Joe's French clothing is playfully postmodern – think coat dresses and flouncy peasant blouses – and a welcome change from standard mall fashions.

VINTAGE 55 Map p50   Boutique

☎ 232 6616; Dubai Festival City; ☾ 10am-10pm

Dress like dead celebrities in replicas of clothing they made famous. Vintage 55 creates limited-edition outfits worn by the likes of Marilyn Monroe and James Dean.

DUBAI FLEA MARKET
Map p50   Flea Market

www.dubai-fleamarket.com; Al-Mamzar Beach Park; admission Dh5; ☾ 8am-3pm every 3rd Sat Oct-May

The Deira offshoot of the Al-Safa Park Dubai Flea Market (p100) is in the main building of this popular beach park (the one with the food court), some 200m to the right of the main entrance.

DUBAI FESTIVAL CITY
Map p50   Shopping Centre

☎ 8003 3232; www.festivalcentre.com; Dubai Festival City; ☾ 10am-10pm

Billed as an 'urban retail resort', Festival City is so massive that you half expect to see a 787 parked outside. It encompasses a whopping 260,000 sq m and includes 600 stores – 25 of them 'anchor stores' – 100 restaurants and cafes, outdoor performance spaces, three enormous hotels and a golf resort. While the man-made canals and *abra* rides are cute, the real show-stopper is the origami-inspired cubist fountain that doubles as a grand staircase. Wear sensible shoes – you're gonna need 'em.

TOYS-R-US Map p50   Toys

☎ 206 6552; Dubai Festival City; ☾ 10am-10pm

You won't believe the size of this warehouse-like toy store. But the best reason to come is to see the Burj al-Arab built entirely of Lego.

EATING

top picks

- **Al-Mallah** (boxed text, p120)
- **Bastakiah Nights** (p111)
- **Eauzone** (p121)
- **Hoi An** (p114)
- **Noodle House** (p117)
- **Rajdhani** (p113)
- **Ravi** (p120)
- **Shabestan** (p109)
- **Thai Kitchen** (p110)
- **Verre by Gordon Ramsay** (p108)

What's your recommendation? www.lonelyplanet.com/dubai

EATING

Dubai's culinary landscape mirrors the imported expat population – Indian, Thai, Chinese, Lebanese – rather than local Emirati culture. In fact, you'll be hard-pressed to find anything indigenous. Unless you score an invitation to a wedding, you're unlikely ever to sample the local speciality, *khouzi*, a whole roasted lamb or baby camel stuffed with rice and spices. You might come across chicken, lamb or shrimp *mashbous* – spiced meat served with equally spicy rice – but they're nothing fabulous, mostly a mass of protein and starch. Blame it on tradition: the Bedouin diet once consisted only of fish, dates, camel meat and camel milk – tasty, yes, but even the Emiratis hardly eat it anymore. Now you spot them lining up at the fast-food chains with great frequency, indifferent to the major increase in Type 2 diabetes locally.

The best food is Middle Eastern, and includes Lebanese, Persian (Iranian) and Syrian. The cooking of the Indian subcontinent is also superb, with nearly 30 distinct subtypes available in Dubai. Asian cooking varies: you'll find good Thai and lots of Japanese (especially sushi), but Chinese is lacking. Likewise European: though Italian restaurants draw big crowds, few merit a critical look. Seafood is wildly popular and the favourite local fish is the tender and meaty *hammour*, a member of the grouper family, which you'll find on nearly every menu.

There are two types of restaurant in Dubai: the hotel restaurant and the independent. Only hotels are licensed to serve alcohol, which is why they house the city's top dining rooms. Alas, because they fall under the umbrellas of giant corporate hotel chains with strict S&P (standards-and-procedures) manuals that effectively flatten individuality, many of these top-end spots lack the individuality and eccentricity you'd find in a first-class Western restaurant. Creativity doesn't flourish in Dubai. Yes, there are standout exceptions, such as Gordon Ramsay's Verre, but even this is part of a small empire run from overseas. Head to the independent restaurants when you want ethnic authenticity and don't mind slumming it; head to the hotels when you want splash and panache – and a big glass of vino to wash it down.

OPENING HOURS & MEAL TIMES

Restaurants are generally open from noon to 3pm and from 7.30pm to midnight; inexpensive cafe-restaurants are generally open from 9am to midnight. *Shwarma* joints open in the late afternoon and stay open well past midnight. Most restaurants open seven days a week, with the exception of Friday lunch, when some smaller local eateries close. In top-end restaurants, most locals book an 8.30pm or 9pm table. For Arabic and Lebanese restaurants with live music, an 11pm booking is the norm, as entertainment usually starts at 10pm and continues until 3am; book earlier for quiet conversation.

HOW MUCH?

Street food, such as *shwarma*, costs around Dh4; an inexpensive curry at a cheap Indian restaurant runs to about Dh10. At midrange restaurants, mains run from Dh25 to Dh40, at top-end spots, Dh65 to Dh150. Alcohol will spike your cheque sky-high. Because booze is only sold in bars and restaurants attached to hotels (generally three-star or better), and a few stand-alone clubs, prices are outrageous (see p128). Expect to pay anything from Dh20 to Dh40 for a bottle of beer, or Dh25 to Dh100+ for a glass of wine, depending on quality and vintage; more at a club. Hotels add a 10% service charge to that amount.

BOOKING TABLES

Make reservations for hotel restaurants; at the indies, it's generally not necessary or possible. Be prepared to give your mobile number, and expect a call if you're late. Make weekend bookings – Thursday and Friday nights, and

PRICE GUIDE

Reviews in this chapter are listed under each neighbourhood in order of price for a main course, from the most expensive to the least expensive. Here's how we break it down:

$	under Dh50
$$	Dh50-100
$$$	over Dh100

Friday brunch – for top tables at least a week ahead. Some restaurants have one-off nights geared to foodies; check *Time Out* magazine to see what's doing during your visit.

TIPPING

Tipping is a tricky business in Dubai. Many restaurants, particularly in hotels, tack on a 10% service charge, but depending on the hotel, the employees may never see this money. Service is weak in Dubai, not because the servers are being obnoxious, but because employers in Dubai are cheap. They hire poor people from developing countries and don't spend the money to train them properly. Many workers will have never set foot in a five-star hotel before working in one. Don't hold their inexperience against them. The average hotel server works six days a week and makes Dh900 to Dh1000 per month, including housing. Those working at independent restaurants make a little more but must pay for their own housing; a studio apartment shared with several strangers eats up at least half of their wages. Frankly, we don't know how they remain so cheerful at all.

When it comes to the tip, leave an additional 10% to 15% in cash, under the ticket, particularly at low-end restaurants – some unethical bosses will take the money away from the waiter if they see it. If you must tip on your credit card, first ask the waiter if the manager will pay out the money that night or not. If not, then pony up cash. If service is perfunctory, it's okay to leave a mere 5%. But if you really feel pushed around by your server or otherwise badly treated, leave nothing.

SELF-CATERING

The small grocery stores around Dubai are good for a box of washing powder, but they're not much fun to browse if you're a foodie trying to suss out Dubai's culinary landscape. The closest thing you'll find to a farmers market is the Fruit and Vegetable Market (Map pp52-3) next to the Fish Market in Deira. There are several major supermarket chains with branches throughout town. Carrefour has probably the biggest selection but the quality tends to be better (and prices higher) at Spinneys. Both stock many products from the UK, North America and Australia and are predictably popular with Western expats; they even have separate 'pork rooms' that are off limits to Muslims. Choithram is cheaper and caters more to the Indian and Pakistani communities. The best selection of organic foods and products is at Organic Foods & Cafe (p98) in Dubai Mall. Many markets are open until midnight; some never close.

Supermarkets
SPINNEYS

Abu Bakar al-Siddiq Rd (Map pp52-3) In Deira.

Al-Mankhool Rd (Map pp62-3) Opposite Al-Rolla Rd.

Sheikh Khalifa bin Zayed Rd (Map pp62-3) Near Kuwait St.

Jumeirah Rd (Map pp76-7) Between Jumeirah Centre and Jumeirah Mosque.

Al-Wasl Rd (Map pp76-7) In Safa.

Mercato Mall (Map pp76-7) On Jumeirah Rd.

Souk al-Bahar (Map pp70-71) Next to Dubai Mall, Downtown Dubai.

CARREFOUR

Bur Dubai (Map pp62-3)

Deira City Centre (Map pp54-5)

Mall of the Emirates (Map pp82-3)

Ibn Battuta Mall (Map pp82-3)

BACCHANALIAN BOATING

A great way to experience the exotic magic of Old Dubai is during a dinner cruise along the Creek. Feed tummy and soul as you gently cruise past historic waterfront houses, sparkling high-rises, jutting wind towers and wooden dhows bound for India or Iran. Dining rooms are air-conditioned and alcohol is served.

- Al Mansour Dhow (Map pp52-3; ☎ 205 7333; www.radissonblu.com; outside Radisson Blu Hotel, Deira; 2hr dinner cruise Dh185) For a traditional experience, book a table on this old wooden dhow cheerfully decorated with bands of twinkling lights and operated by the Radisson Blu Hotel. The international buffet is heavy on Arabic and Indian choices and accompanied by an oud player. Afterwards, relax with a *sheesha* in the upper-deck lounge.
- Bateaux Dubai (Map pp64-5; ☎ 399 4994; www.bateauxdubai.com; Al-Seef Rd, opposite British Embassy, Bur Dubai Creek; 2½hr dinner cruise Dh195, Friday brunch cruise Dh350) If the food is more important to you than the ambience, indulge in a four-course à la carte feast aboard this stylish contemporary boat with floor-to-ceiling windows, linen-draped tables and a live DJ.

CHOITHRAM

Al-Rolla & Al-Mankhool Rds (Map pp62-3) Next to Al-Khaleej Shopping Centre.

Al-Wasl Rd (Map pp76-7) Jumeirah, near Al-Safa Park.

DEIRA

Deira has a great street scene: snag a pavement table beneath flickering neon and soak up the local colour. This is where many immigrants live, and here you eat their food – Chinese, Arabic, African and especially Indian. With several notable exceptions, most of them listed below, Deira lacks upmarket restaurants; for a white-tablecloth dinner with wine, head to Downtown Dubai or Dubai Marina. If you're on a budget, you can do well for under Dh20 (see boxed text, p110).

TRAITEUR Map pp54-5   French $$$

☎ 317 2222; Park Hyatt Dubai, next to Dubai Creek Golf & Yacht Club; mains Dh130-190; ⏰ 7pm-midnight

A meal at Traiteur is pure drama, both on the plate and in the striking 14m-high dining room with origami wall features and theatrical lighting. You can watch a small army of toqued cooks in the raised show

kitchen toil over classic French brasserie fare. The bouillabaisse is a virtual flavour bomb, while the chateaubriand (with foie gras and truffle sauce) is so tender it barely requires a knife. Ask the sommelier to help you choose from the 4200-bottle wine cellar, one of the largest in Dubai.

VERRE BY GORDON RAMSAY

Map pp52-3   Modern European $$$

☎ 212 7551; Hilton Dubai Creek, Baniyas Rd; mains Dh100-200; ⏰ 6-11pm

The eponymous British chef hardly ever comes by anymore, but fortunately executive chef Matt Pickop is competently helming the kitchen. Long one of the top eateries in town, Verre continues to stand out for embracing the gentle *art de la table* in all its sensuality – from your first sip of champagne to your last bite of chocolate, this is one meal you won't soon forget. The menu plays to sophisticates who recognise subtlety: there are no distracting gimmicks, no silly flourishes and no dumbing down of culinary traditions. Near-perfect executions of French-inspired classics are served with choreographed precision in an austere white-tablecloth dining room. If you're serious about eating, don't miss Verre.

FARSI FOOD *Matthew Lee*

Relations between the United Arab Emirates (UAE) and Iran haven't always been congenial – they're still disputing the ownership of three tiny islands in the Gulf. But the Iranian contribution to the success of the UAE shouldn't be understated. Large numbers of Iranian migrants moved to Dubai in the 1920s and 1930s and some of today's most influential and wealthy Emirati families have Iranian roots. There was another brief period of mass migration when thousands moved to Dubai to flee the Islamic Revolution of 1979. There are Persian buildings all over the city, such as the beautiful Iranian Hospital, and, of course, lots of fantastic restaurants. Dubai is a great place to sample this deeply underrated cuisine.

At most Persian restaurants in Dubai, your meal will begin with *noon-o-panir-o-sabzi* (bread, cheese and herbs). Roll the cheese and herbs together in the hot bread that waiting staff deliver – soft, puffy, warm-from-the-oven – to the table every few minutes. It's hard to resist filling up on it. Soup (*ash*) is also a staple of a traditional Persian meal, and at some restaurants a bowl of barley soup (*ash-e-jow*) comes with every order. It's also worth trying *kashk-e-bademjan*. *Bademjan* is aubergine in Farsi and *kashk* is a type of whey; the result is an alluringly creamy and smoky dip.

The preparation of rice becomes an art form in the Iranian kitchen, from the fluffy and light *chelo* rice to the herb-saturated *pollo* rice and the sticky *kateh* rice. Even the burned rice at the bottom of the pan is wondrous – it's called *tahdig* and is buttery, crunchy and zinging with saffron. The closest thing Iran has to a national dish is the *chelo kebab* (meaning 'kebab with rice'), a simple portion of grilled lamb or chicken usually marinated in lime and onion. There are also plenty of hearty lamb stews on the Persian menu; expect subtle spices and combinations of okra, aubergine and spinach. You can wash everything down with *dogh*, a yoghurt drink like the Indian lassi, and finish your meal with *falooda*, an icy dessert of frozen vermicelli noodles, rose water and cherry syrup.

For a Persian dining experience so authentic it's got the stamp of approval from Tehran, lunch at the Iranian Club (see boxed text, p122), where women have to cover their heads and a portrait of the Ayatollah greets you on arrival. If you're not in touch with your conservative side, you can't go wrong with a meal at Shabestan (opposite), Pars Iranian Kitchen (p119) or Special Ostadi (Map pp62-3; ☎ 397 1933; Al-Mussallah Rd, Bur Dubai; mains Dh30; ⏰ noon-4pm & 6.30pm-1am).

SHABESTAN Map pp52-3   Persian $$$

☎ 205 7333; Radisson Blu Hotel, Baniyas Rd; mains Dh90-155; ⏲ 12.30-3.15pm & 7.30-11.15pm

Shabestan is Dubai's top Persian restaurant. But don't take our word for it. Ask Sheikh Mohammed, who often pops in for lunch. At dinner time, the window-lined dining room reveals a panorama of glittering lights over the Creek. Hot fresh bread and home-made yoghurt hit the table shortly after you arrive. Start with a smoky *mizra ghasemi* (aubergine dip), move on to perfumed rice accompanying melt-off-the-bone braised lamb and do save room for vermicelli ice cream with saffron and rose water.

MIYAKO Map pp52-3   Japanese $$

☎ 317 2222; Hyatt Regency Dubai, off Al-Khaleej Rd; 3-course business lunches Dh75, mains from Dh90; ⏲ 12.30-3pm & 7pm-midnight

The coolly minimalist dining room of this excellent Japanese eatery feels very Tokyo, with sleek surfaces of stainless steel, *shoji* screens and an authentic tatami room. The sushi is stellar (as are its prices), but this is a place to branch out. *Shabu shabu* is superb, made with tender and tasty beef; the crumbed fried oysters and braised pork belly (*kakuni*) merit special attention. If you're not staying in the area, book for after 9pm or at the weekend to avoid the traffic.

ASHIANA Map pp52-3   Indian $$

☎ 207 1733; Sheraton Dubai Creek Hotel & Towers, Baniyas Rd; mains Dh80-120; ⏲ 7.30-11.30pm daily, noon-3pm Fri

This oldie but goodie is still one of the city's top Indian restaurants. Presentations of the northern Indian fare are brilliant: *dum biryani* is cooked in a pot sealed with bread, elegantly perfuming the meat. Sophisticated, complex curries justify the prices, as do the solicitous service, atmospheric dining room and live sitar music. Plan to linger long. Good vegetarian food, too.

SUMIBIYA Map pp52-3   Japanese Grill $$

☎ 205 7333; Radisson Blu Hotel, Baniyas Rd; mains Dh70-145; ⏲ 12.30-3pm & 7-11pm; ♿

At the first Japanese *yakiniku*-style restaurant in Dubai, every stone table has a recessed gas grill where you cook your own meat then pair it with a selection of sauces and condiments. Though the Wagyu beef and seafood run high (Dh100+), the set menus of various meat-and-veggie combos

are a relative bargain. There's nothing romantic about the narrow windowless room, but it's great interactive fun for families or groups of foodie friends.

CHINA CLUB Map pp52-3   Chinese $$

☎ 205 7333; Radisson Blu Hotel, Baniyas Rd; yum cha Dh95, mains Dh60-135; ⏲ 12.30-3.30pm & 7.30-11pm

Lunchtime yum cha – especially on Fridays – is a superb deal and big draw at this red-silk fancy dining room that comes across as an aesthetically smart but faded holdover from the *Dynasty* era. At dinner, the classics are spot-on, including a standout Szechuan-style boiled lamb and a crispy-delicious Peking duck carved and rolled tableside. Private dining rooms, with lazy Susans in the middle of the tables, are ideal for a group.

AL-DAWAAR Map pp52-3   International $$

☎ 317 2222; Hyatt Regency Dubai, off Al-Khaleej Rd; buffet lunches/dinners Dh165/230; ⏲ 12.30-3.30pm & 6.30pm-midnight

In a city that likes to teeter on the cutting edge, this revolving restaurant on the 25th floor is as delightfully old school as a bag of gummibears. Tacky you think? Not so. Actually, the decor is quite sophisticated, the buffet varied and bountiful, and the views of the city and half-finished Palm Deira quite nice, especially at night.

SPICE ISLAND Map pp52-3   International $$

☎ 262 5555; Renaissance Dubai Hotel, near Salahuddin Rd; buffets with soft/house/premium drinks Dh169/219/289; ⏲ 6.30-11.30pm; ♿

With dishes from China, Japan, India, Italy, Mexico and Mongolia, plus seafood and loads of desserts, Spice Island is not just a visual feast, it's one of the best all-round buffets in town. Its recession-friendly prices give it an edge with young expat families; the kiddie play area with supervised activities like face painting doesn't hurt either. Friday brunch is busiest; see p122 for details.

GLASSHOUSE MEDITERRANEAN BRASSERIE Map pp52-3   Mediterranean $$

☎ 212 7551; Hilton Dubai Creek, Baniyas Rd, Rigga; mains Dh60-95, brunches Dh220; ⏲ 7-10pm, brunch noon-3.30pm

Glasshouse is one of Dubai's most accomplished brasserie-style restaurants, overseen – as is its fine-dining neighbour Verre

– by Gordon Ramsay. The comfort-food menu offers fresh takes on such classics as pork belly, mushroom risotto and rib-eye steak with fries. Come on Monday and Wednesday and get drinks for just Dh1 when ordering two courses.

YUM! Map pp52-3 — Asian $$

☎ 222 7171; Radisson Blu Hotel, Baniyas Rd; mains Dh45-65; ☾ noon-1am; ♿

Though not as dynamic as Noodle House (p117), Yum! is a good pick for a quick bowl of noodles when you're wandering along the Creek – and you can be in and out in half an hour.

CAFE ARABESQUE Map pp54-5 — Cafe $$

☎ 317 2222; Park Hyatt Dubai, next to Dubai Creek Golf & Yacht Club; mezzes Dh35-70, kebabs Dh60-180, dinner buffets Dh129 Wed-Fri; ☾ 6.30am-midnight; ♿

Snag a table on the Creekside verandah, then dip into a pool of pleasurable dishes

from Jordan, Syria, Lebanon and Turkey at this classy yet low-key eatery at the Park Hyatt. A tantalising selection of mezzes and salads jostles for attention on the beautiful buffet, although it's just as tempting to have the chef prepare a juicy kebab in the wood-burning oven.

THAI KITCHEN Map pp54-5 — Thai $$

☎ 602 1234; Park Hyatt Dubai, next to Dubai Creek Golf & Yacht Club; small dishes Dh28-60, set menus Dh210; ☾ 7pm-midnight

The decor is decidedly un-Thai, with black-lacquer tables, a swooping wave-form ceiling and not a branch of bamboo. But the native chefs bustling in the open kitchens sure know their stuff: dishes are inspired by Bangkok street eats and served tapas-style, perfect for grazing and sharing. Standouts include chicken in pandanus leaves, minced beef with basil, and catfish in tamarind sauce. The Friday brunch here is one of the best in town (see p122).

DEIRA'S BEST CHEAP ETHNIC EATS

If you want to sample some of Dubai's best ethnic cooking, hit the backstreets of Deira, and eat beside the working-class expat workers who've imported their culinary traditions to Dubai. The following are for adventurous travellers, not the skirt-and-sweater crowd. At first glance, some might look scary – Westerners don't usually wander into these joints – but we've sampled all of them: they're the real deal. In a city that embraces artificiality, it's refreshing to find authenticity. Best of all, you'll probably get change on your Dh50 note. No credit cards.

Abesinian Restaurant (Map pp52-3; ☎ 273 7432; 10 St (Somali St), near 23 St junction; mains Dh12-35; ☾ 10am-midnight) The staff are welcoming and warm at this homey Ethiopian restaurant, where the big platters of curry and stews are best sopped up with *injera*, spongy flat bread of native grain. Tricky to find but worth it.

Afghan Kebab House (Map pp52-3; ☎ 222 3292; behind Naif Mosque, off Deira St; mains Dh15-35; ☾ 11am-1am) Big hunks of meat – lamb, beef, chicken – charred on foot-long skewers come served with rice and bread. That's it. Think caveman food. Eat with your hands. Tricky to find but locals can direct you.

Al-Baghdadi Home (Map pp52-3; ☎ 273 7064; Al-Mateena St, opposite Dubai Palm Hotel; mains Dh30-60; ☾ noon-3am) In Little Iraq, on one of Dubai's best, lesser-known walking streets, Al-Baghdadi spit-roasts whole fish beside an open fire (the traditional preparation) in the restaurant's window, and serves it with bread and lentil salad. (NB: Don't order randomly – *patchaa* is sheep's head.)

Aroos Damascus (Map pp52-3; ☎ 227 0202; Al-Muraqqabat Rd, at Al-Jazeira St; mains Dh10-30; ☾ 7am-3am; ♿) Syrian food is similar to Lebanese, but uses more cumin in the *fattoosh* and spice in the kebabs. Our favourite dish: *arayees* – Syrian bread stuffed with ground lamb and grilled. The sweetness of the bread plays off the gamey flavour of the meat. Great tabouli, fantastic fresh-from-the-oven bread, huge outdoor patio, cool flickering neon.

Pinoy Grill (Map pp52-3; ☎ 222 2225; Al-Rigga Rd at Al-Jazeira St; dishes Dh15-30; ☾ noon-2am Sat-Thu, 1pm-2am Fri; ♿) A friendly and welcoming intro to the weird, wonderful world of Filipino cuisine, which borrows from Spanish, Indonesian and French, mixing pungent ingredients, like garlic and chillies, in sweet and savoury combinations not always tastebud-friendly to foreigners. But the menu is in English, and the super-fun staff will guide you.

Xia Wei Yang (Map pp52-3; ☎ 221 7177; Baniyas Rd; hotpots Dh30-100; ☾ noon-2am; ♿) At this Chinese hotpot restaurant you order everything raw, then boil it at the table. Begin with veggies to enrich the broth, then add the meat – it has everything from fish- and meatballs to tendons, hearts and testicles (fear not: it also serves beef and chicken). Hardly anyone speaks English: plan to point.

BUR DUBAI

This is possibly the most eclectic eating area of Dubai: restaurants here run the gamut from dirt-cheap curry joints to white-tablecloth restaurants worthy of a Michelin star.

PEPPERCRAB Map pp64-5 — Asian $$$

☎ 317 2222; Grand Hyatt Dubai, Al-Qataiyat Rd, Oud Metha; mains Dh120-220; ☒ 7-11.30pm Sat-Wed, to 1am Thu & Fri

If you've never had Singaporean food, Peppercrab is perfect for surrendering your virginity. Prepare your palate with plump wonton and crunchy baby squid, then don an apron and get ready to do battle with the main event: the eponymous 'pepper-crab' – a succulent, flaky, tender crustacean paired with a feisty, pepper-laced sauce that's a virtual flavour bomb.

FIRE & ICE Map pp64-5 — Steakhouse $$$

☎ 341 9888; Raffles Dubai, Sheikh Rashid Rd, near Wafi Mall; mains Dh95-190, steaks Dh135-420; ☒ 7-11.30pm

With its floor-to-ceiling-brick walls, the Raffles steakhouse exudes a sleek, sophisticated New York vibe. Sip a martini while casually scanning the happy crowd and anticipating such menu stars as the boneless beef ribs, the veal chop and the 'Fire Burger'. And whatever you order, get a serving of fries – you'll thank us. Other assets: live jazz on Wednesday and Thursday and an award-winning wine list that's especially strong on New World varietals; over 60 are available by the glass.

ASHA'S Map pp64-5 — Contemporary Indian $$

☎ 324 4100; Pyramids, Sheikh Rashid Rd, Wafi Mall; mains around Dh70; ☒ 12.30-3pm & 7.30pm-midnight; ⓐ

Namesake of Bollywood singer Asha Bhosle, Asha's packs a see-and-be-seen crowd of rich Indian expats into its sexy, low-light, tandoori-orange dining room, with ethnic-fusion dance music playing in the background. The menu focuses on contemporary northwest Indian fare, which translates into such palate-teasers as spicy-ginger-garlic marinated prawns and *muscat gosht* (tomato-and-butter-braised spicy lamb) – both Asha's personal recipes. It's a fabulous place to party; if the tots are tagging along, they've even got their own play area.

PAUL Map pp62-3 — French Cafe $

☎ 351 7009; BurJuman Centre, cnr Khalid bin al-Waleed & Sheikh Khalifa bin Zayed Rds; sandwiches & salads Dh35-55, mains Dh70; ☒ 9am-midnight; ⓐ

This French cafe is an upscale mall staple packed with expats here for the scrumptious croissants, ample-sized breakfasts and solid salads and sandwiches. Browse through a selection of newspapers and magazines while nibbling beautiful pastries and cakes. It's a bit pricey but a reliable standby. There are additional branches in the Mall of the Emirates (Map pp82-3), Wafi Mall (Map pp64-5), Deira City Centre (Map pp52-3) and Mercato Mall (Map pp76-7).

AWTAR Map pp64-5 — Lebanese $$

☎ 317 2222; Grand Hyatt Dubai, Al-Qataiyat Rd; mains from Dh65; ☒ 7.30pm-3am Sun-Fri

Locals love the opulent Bedouin-tent-like atmosphere and warm welcome of this formal Lebanese restaurant, complete with a belly dancer and live band – it's not uncommon for women to stand up, clap and sway to the music. The menu lists the usual mezzes and kebabs, as well as a full page of raw-meat dishes, all served in mountainous portions. If you're loath to shout over the noise, book for 8pm. But for maximum fun, round up a posse and come at 10pm, when the scene gets rockin'. Request one of the swoop-backed booths for the best views.

BASTAKIAH NIGHTS Map pp62-3 — Arabic $$

☎ 353 7772; off Al-Fahidi St, Bastakia; mains Dh50-75, set menus Dh168; ☒ 12.30-11.30pm

One of the city's most romantic restaurants, Bastakiah Nights occupies a restored courtyard home with fabulous old Arabian-style atmosphere. The menu is mostly Lebanese but also includes a few Emirati dishes. Though you can order à la carte, we recommend the set menu, which includes soup, copious mezzes and a choice of mains, such as mixed grill or lamb stew. It's not the best food in town and service is sometimes weak, but on a balmy evening the candlelit courtyard, with the indigo night sky overhead, can't be beat. No alcohol.

CHUTNEYS Map pp64-5 — Indian $$

☎ 310 4340; Mövenpick Hotel Bur Dubai, 19 St; mains Dh40-80; ☒ noon-3pm & 7-11.30pm

The hotel lobby setting does not impress and neither does the decor, but the food, oh the food, is well worth the trip to Chutneys. It'll be a first-class culinary journey at economy prices to northern India, home of Hafeez and Hasib Qureshi, whose family traces its gastro lineage to the kitchens of the Moghul emperors. Tuck into toothsome kebabs and fluffy biryanis as Ghazal singers croon smoothly in the background.

IZ Map pp64-5 — Contemporary Indian $$
☎ 317 2222; Grand Hyatt Dubai, Al-Qataiyat Rd; dishes from Dh40, 3-course Thali lunches Dh85; ☯ 12.30-3pm & 7pm-1am, to 2am Thu & Fri
The modernist-feeling wood-and-stone dining room glows by candlelight at this tapas-style contemporary Indian eatery. The tandoori-oven specialities are perfectly executed (fantastic skewered roasted prawns), as are classics like *murgha tikka*, aka butter chicken in a creamy tomato sauce, perfect for sopping up with the fresh-from-the-oven bread. Sit at the open kitchen's counter and watch the chefs' theatrics. One drawback: all those little plates add up fast – plan for Dh300 a head.

KHAZANA Map pp64-5 — Indian $$
☎ 336 0061; off 10 St, near Lamcy Plaza; mains Dh40-80; ☯ noon-2.30pm & 7-11pm; ⚓
The steady stream of regulars seems to prove that Khazana is one of the best Indian restaurants in town. Curries are like poetry, thanks to personally calibrated spicing by chef Sanjeer Kapoor. Ample bamboo and rattan create a relaxed feel-good ambience, helped along by the friendly servers.

LEMONGRASS Map pp64-5 — Thai $
☎ 334 2325; 21 St, just south of Lamcy Plaza, Oud Metha; mains Dh32-62; ☯ noon-11pm; ⚓
If your belly's longing for the taste of Thailand, take it to Lemongrass' soothing lime-coloured dining room for brightly flavoured cooking and solicitous service. Pad Thai is presented in an omelette wrapper – a nice touch – and curries have marvellous depth of flavour. If you like spicy, say so; the kitchen is shy with the heat. Good for vegetarians.

LEBANESE FOOD LINGO 101

Break the hummus habit and try something new. Here's a primer to help you navigate some lesser-known dishes on Dubai's ubiquitous Lebanese menus. (Spellings may vary.)

Baklava The Lebanese use pistachios and almonds, not walnuts, in this classic honeyed pastry. Say bak-la-WAH or nobody will understand you.

Bastirma Air-cured beef (think pastrami).

Fattoosh Chopped salad topped with fried Arabic bread and a dressing of olive oil, lemon and sumac.

Felafel Deep-fried balls of seasoned, mashed chickpeas, best served with tahini sauce.

Kibbeh Balls of minced lamb and onion, rolled in cracked wheat and fried. These are the measure of a good Lebanese kitchen; they should be golden-brown and nongreasy outside, warm and juicy inside.

Kibbeh nayye Ground raw lamb served with egg and condiments.

Kofta Grilled skewers of spicy minced lamb.

Labneh Thick, strained yoghurt spreadable like cream cheese.

Muhammara Paste of red capsicum, ground nuts, breadcrumbs and pomegranate.

Mujadara Seasoned lentils and bulgur topped with caramelised onions.

Sambusak Pastries stuffed with ground lamb or cheese.

Shish tawooq Spiced chunks of chargrilled chicken.

Shwarma Rotisserie-cooked seasoned lamb or chicken, carved onto flatbread and rolled up with salad and sauce.

Soojuk Heavily spiced, air-dried beef sausage.

Tabouli Parsley salad with cracked wheat, tomato, mint, onion, lemon and olive oil.

Tahini Pulverised sesame seeds, often used to enhance dips or thinned into a sauce for felafel.

Waraq aynab Rice-stuffed grape leaves (dolmades in Greece).

BLUEFIELDS   Map pp64-5   Caribbean $

☎ 335 7377; Lamcy Plaza, across from Mövenpick Hotel, Oud Metha; mains Dh25-50; ☼ noon-2pm Sun-Thu, 6-11.30pm Sun-Fri

Dubai's first Caribbean restaurant is a tiny, exuberant space that feels as warm and welcoming as a hug from an old friend, thanks to affable owner Alison. Even though she's not from the Caribbean, the cooking (most of it made with a spice rub called jerk) is very authentic and homemade.

KAN ZAMAN   Map pp62-3   Arabic $

☎ 393 9913; Shindagha Heritage Area, near Heritage Village; mezzes Dh12-20, mains Dh30-70; ☼ 4.30pm-2.30am

While on a trip to Heritage Village, stop by this Creekside favourite to munch on mezzes and grills (the tangy lamb shwarma is delish) or fresh saj manakish (pastry topped with cheese, thyme, meat or other ingredients). During the cooler months, sit on the big outdoor patio and watch the passing parade of boats against the backdrop of historic Deira and Bur Dubai.

BASTA ART CAFE   Map pp62-3   Cafe $

☎ 353 5071; Al-Fahidi St, Bastakia Quarter; mains Dh30-45; ☼ 8am-10pm; ⓖ

A cool respite while exploring the Bastakia Quarter, this charmer takes over the backyard of an old Dubai house. The food is respectable cafe fare – the crunchy salads are refreshing on a hot day – but it's the sun-dappled garden that makes this place special. Good breakfasts. No credit cards.

RAJDHANI   Map pp62-3   Indian Vegetarian $

☎ 393 4433, 050 930 1138; Rolla St, near Choithram supermarket; mains Dh25-50; ☼ 11am-11pm; ⓖ

With a pedigree going back to 1947, it's no surprise this Mumbai-based chain has a huge fan base among Indian expats, visiting Bollywood stars and other clued-in foodies. The speciality here is vegetarian Thali, a selection of small dishes (curries, dhal, rice) served on a stainless steel platter. Everything's made from scratch using authentic recipes that have stood the test of time.

XVA CAFÉ   Map pp62-3   Vegetarian cafe $

☎ 353 5383; off Al-Fahidi St, Bastakia Quarter; dishes Dh20-35; ☼ 9am-7pm Sat-Thu year-round, 9am-5pm Fri Nov-Apr; ⓐ

WHINING & DINING

Emiratis prize the family. While you can take kids to most restaurants in Dubai, we've indicated with the ⓖ icon restaurants especially good for families. What this means is that your kids can 1) safely scream without freaking anyone out; 2) have fun; 3) possibly meet other children; and 4) find something on the menu to please them, if only a plate of noodles, that longstanding favourite of kids everywhere. If you're not sure where to eat, malls are a sure bet; most listed in this book have surprisingly good food courts. All hotels have at least one restaurant suitable for families, usually the 24-hour cafe or the buffet restaurant. In short, fear not. Your hardest task will be strapping the kids into the taxi, not finding something to eat.

Escape Dubai's bustle at this artsy courtyard cafe in the historic Bastakia Quarter. The menu eschews meat in favour of such offerings as aubergine burger, tuna salad and morjardara (rice topped with sautéed veggies and yoghurt). Wash it down with intensely green mint-lemonade – a must-order!

CURRY LEAF   Map pp62-3   Sri Lankan $

☎ 397 8940; Al-Mussalla Tower, Bank St; mains Dh15-30; ☼ 11.30am-midnight; ⓖ

Hoppers (crispy rice-flour pancakes with fried egg) go well with the smoky-hot, spice-rich curries at this Sri Lankan place in an electronics mall food court. A few Dutch colonial dishes round out the menu; try the lumpries (spiced rice baked with meat, egg and aubergine). There's zero atmosphere, but kids love to play in the adjacent fountain.

GOVINDA'S   Map pp64-5   Indian Vegetarian $

☎ 396 0088; off Sheikh Khalifa bin Zayed Rd, 2 blocks south of Regent Palace Hotel, Karama; mains Dh15-26; ☼ noon-3.30pm & 7pm-1am Sat-Thu, 1.30-3.30pm & 7pm-1am Fri; ⓖ

Jains run this super-friendly all-vegan Indian restaurant where the cooking is rich in character even though the chefs shun onion and garlic. Dishes to try include the velvety paneer makhanwala and the rich dal makhani. Do save room for the homemade ice cream from the attached parlour.

KARACHI DARBAR   Map pp64-5   Pakistani $

☎ 334 7272; Karama Shopping Centre, Karama; mains Dh6-30; ☼ 4am-2am

A favourite of guest workers and expats with an eye for a biryani bargain, Karachi

Darbar keeps 'em well fed with a huge menu of Pakistani, Indian and Chinese specialities – but stick to the Pakistani. Fear not: it'll be good. No credit cards.

SHEIKH ZAYED ROAD

The tower hotels lining the Sheikh Zayed strip are the psychological centrepoint of Dubai. Dinner here positions you well to travel elsewhere afterwards, but with so many nearby hotels, bars and nightclubs, you may as well stick around. But good luck crossing the road: there's only one pedestrian overpass. Take a taxi instead.

DOWNTOWN DUBAI

ASADO Map pp70-71 Argentinian $$$
☎ 428 7971; Palace – The Old Town, Emaar Blvd; mains Dh110-290; ⏲ 7pm-midnight

Meat lovers will be in bovine heaven at this cheerful, lusty steakhouse. Choose your quality cut of tenderloin, veal chop, rib eye or sirloin from a tray brought to your table by servers clad gaucho-style. While it's being cooked to order, sit back and savour the delicious bread, the views of Burj Khalifa (sit on the terrace) and the sultry tunes from the live band. All meats are served with a selection of delicious sauces, salts and mustards. A sommelier stands by to help you pick the perfect bottle from what is purportedly the biggest selection of Argentine wines in the Middle East.

AMWAJ Map pp70-71 Contemporary European $$$
☎ 405 2703; Shangri-La hotel, Sheikh Zayed Rd; mains Dh100-180; ⏲ Sun-Fri 7pm-midnight

It's rare in Dubai to find adroit kitchen staff properly schooled in classic European cuisine, which is exactly why we love Amwaj, where seafood is the focus of the French-infused menu. Risk protein shock when ordering the extraordinary seafood platter for two (Dh650), or play it safe with a plate of juicy grilled salmon. Also look for special promotions like this one: for the price of one bottle of wine, you get to drink all you want and make repeated trips to the bountiful cheese buffet.

OKKU Map pp70-71 Japanese $$$
☎ 501 8777; Monarch Dubai, Sheikh Zayed Rd; small dishes Dh30-120; ⏲ 7pm-3am

A platinum card is a handy accessory at this 'look-at-me' temple where the pretty people nibble on sushi and tuck into their miso-blackened cod. If you can put up with the hype and the high prices, you should feel right at home in this beautiful space anchored by an aquarium where jellyfish do their ethereal dances.

HOI AN Map pp70-71 French-Vietnamese $$$
☎ 343 8888; Shangri-La hotel, Sheikh Zayed Rd; mains Dh100-140; ⏲ 7pm-midnight

Teak latticework, plantation shutters and spinning wooden ceiling fans evoke a très civilisé colonial-era Vietnam at this upmarket restaurant where the flavours are lively and bright. Start with the crispy crab rolls, then move on to the signatures: lotus-leaf-wrapped sea bass with ginger-lemon sauce or tamarind-spiced rack of lamb. Not a bad date spot, thanks to deliciously low lighting and genteel service.

THIPTARA Map pp70-71 Thai $$$
☎ 428 7961; Palace – The Old Town, Emaar Blvd; mains Dh90-190, set menus from Dh250; ⏲ 7pm-midnight

Thiptara wows with its romantic setting in a lakeside pagoda with front-row views of Burj Khalifa and the Dubai Fountain. The food's just as impressive, with elegant interpretations of classic Thai dishes, although portions are small and the final bill can be quite steep. The chef grows his own herbs, which perk up such dishes as green-papaya salad and beef in spicy brown sauce with on-the-vine peppercorns. Alas, the interior is too austere (sit on the deck), but the exceptional cooking and the solicitous service by the all-Thai staff make up for it.

HUKAMA Map pp70-71 Chinese $$$
☎ 436 8888; The Address Downtown Dubai, Emaar Blvd; mains Dh80-160; ⏲ 7-11pm

A dramatic high-ceilinged dining room, complexion-friendly lighting, sweeping views of Burj Khalifa and wonderful Chinese gourmet fare are all woven together like a fine tapestry at this elegant restaurant. The menu is loaded with such interesting items as wasabi-coated king prawns or foie gras terrine with hawthorne jelly and sugar-cured dates. Alas, the Chinese servers floating about in their silk dresses seem to have been selected primarily for their beauty and not their serving skills.

top picks

MEALS WITH A VIEW

- Aquara (p122) Sleek yachts bobbing against a backdrop of skyscrapers, in the Dubai Marina.
- Pierchic (p118) Offshore views of the dramatic Burj al-Arab and the sultrily illuminated Madinat Jumeirah.
- Shabestan (p109) Gaze at the ballet of dhows on the Creek.
- Thiptara (opposite) Dine on a lakeview deck beneath the world's tallest tower.
- Vu's (p116) Top-of-the-world vistas from Jumeirah Emirates Towers.

NA3NA3 Map pp70-71   Arabic $$

☎ 438 8888; The Address Dubai Mall, Emaar Blvd; lunches/dinners Dh120/140; ☽ 6.30am-1am; ♿

If you're new to Arabic food, the bountiful and beautifully displayed buffet in this bright and airy restaurant would be a good place to start a culinary investigation. You'll probably be tempted to make an entire meal from the mezze (appetiser) selection alone, but that would mean missing the hot dishes and freshly baked breads streaming from the open kitchen. The curious name, by the way, means 'mint' in Arabic and is pronounced 'nana'.

FAZARIS Map pp70-71   International $$

☎ 436 8888; The Address Downtown Dubai, Emaar Blvd; mains Dh75-160; Fri brunches without/with alcohol Dh290/390; ☽ 6.30-11am, noon-3.30pm & 6.30-11pm

Named for an 8th-century Persian philosopher, this all-day restaurant lets you hopscotch from Japan (sushi) to India (chicken tikka) to Italy (penne arrabiata) without leaving your table. The white chocolate zabayon paired with marinated berries and pepper strawberry ice cream is the perfect coda.

KARMA KAFE Map pp70-71   Asian Fusion $$

☎ 423 0909; Souk al-Bahar; mains Dh75-150; ☽ 4pm-2am Sat-Wed, to 3am Thu & Fri

This gorgeous space is another Midas-touch venture by the people behind the Buddha Bar (p121). As in the mothership, a large Buddha oversees the dining room, which in this case is intimate and drenched in sensuous crimson. The food caters for adventurous palates: ahi pizza and sashimi tacos are typically experimental flavour combinations that work surprisingly well.

MARRAKECH Map pp70-71   Moroccan $$

☎ 405 2703; Shangri-La Hotel, Sheikh Zayed Rd; mains Dh60-100; ☽ 7pm-midnight Mon-Sat

Keyhole doorways, North African wall tiles and flickering candle lanterns casting moody shadows: Marrakech hits all the classic Moroccan design buttons yet manages to feel light, elegant and contemporary. The kitchen embraces a similar approach by dishing up modern spins on such signature dishes as pastilla (pigeon pie), couscous royale and tagine without sacrificing the cuisine's traditional earthiness. The best tables are in view of the soulful musician or, for privacy, in an arched alcove.

EMPORIO ARMANI CAFFÉ
Map pp70-71   Cafe $$

☎ 339 8396; ground fl, Dubai Mall; mains Dh55-160; ☽ 10am-11pm

The revolution in Dubai's mall food offers no better example than this outpost of the Armani empire. The coffee is as smooth as an Italian server, the food is as stylishly presented as the staff, and the Italian flavours so good we wish it had a liquor licence.

MORE Map pp70-71   Cafe $

☎ 339 8934; ground fl, Dubai Mall; mains Dh30-70; ☽ 8am-11pm; 🛜 ♿

The latest outpost of this local mini-chain is a jazzy, industrial-flavoured space in Dubai Mall that draws a congenial mix of locals, expats and tourists. The menu hopscotches around the world – from Thai curries and Italian pastas to Dutch pancakes and fat burgers. The execution is okay, but if it sounds too experimental, skip it. Breakfast is served all day. There's another branch near the Al-Murooj Rotana Hotel and one at the Gold & Diamond Park; see Map pp70-71.

ORGANIC FOODS & CAFE
Map pp70-71   International $

☎ 434 0577; ground fl, Dubai Mall; mains Dh16-45; ☽ 9am-10pm Sun-Wed, 9am-midnight Thu-Sat; ♿

This simple cafe attached to the UAE's first certified organic supermarket (see p98) is a good spot for a healthy shopping break. Breakfast is served all day, although come

RELIGION ON THE PLATE

You may never realise just how much you like pork until you travel to Dubai and are rarely allowed any. As an alternative to pork bacon, some supermarkets sell beef bacon and turkey bacon, but hypermarkets like Carrefour have dedicated 'pork rooms' that sell the real thing but are off limits to Muslims. To serve pork in a restaurant, you must have a pork licence. Likewise alcohol, which is generally only served in hotels. If an item on a restaurant menu has been prepared with either alcohol or pork, it must be clearly marked.

Muslims never eat pork: it is haram, forbidden by Islam – purely for health reasons, as pigs were considered disease-carrying animals. Alcohol is forbidden, not for health, but because it makes followers forgetful of God and prayer. The other major dietary restriction applies to meat: it must be halal, meaning religiously suitable or permitted. The animal must be drained of its blood at the time of slaughter by having its throat cut. This is why much of the red meat slaughtered and sold locally is very pale in colour. In restaurants, you'll easily find non-halal beef – just don't expect your tenderloin to be wrapped in a fatty strip of bacon before it's grilled.

lunchtime you'll probably be more tempted by the hormone-free burger, tofu and vegetable stir-fry, or any of the daily changing specials. The budget-priced Friday brunch (Dh65) is a good alternative to the usual boozy gluttonous affair. Kids can make new friends in the play corner.

FINANCIAL DISTRICT

ZUMA Map pp70-71   Japanese $$$
☎ 425 5660; Bldg 6, Gate Village, Dubai International Financial Centre; set lunches Dh110, dinners from Dh200; ⏱ 12.30-3pm & 7pm-midnight, to 1am Thu & Fri
One of a new crop of contempo Japanese restaurants, this dramatic bi-level den draws go-go executives for power lunches and the sexy crowd for low-light dinners. Tables are in full view of a massive bamboo sculpture and the two kitchens; one a sushi counter, the other a *robata* grill. Choice picks include barley miso marinated baby chicken, marinated black cod and salmon teriyaki. Immensely popular Friday brunch, too; see p122 for details.

EXCHANGE GRILL
Map pp70-71   Steakhouse $$$
☎ 311 8316; Fairmont hotel, Sheikh Zayed Rd; steaks Dh185-245; ⏱ 12.30-3.30pm Sun-Thu & 7pm-midnight daily
One of Dubai's premier steakhouses, the Exchange Grill has a clubby feel, with oversized leather armchairs orbiting linen-draped tables and big picture windows overlooking the glittering strip. You'll have a fine time spiking your cholesterol level with trendy Wagyu beef or the less pricey but actually more-flavourful aged Angus

prime. Seafood rounds out the menu, but beef is definitely the big draw. Respectable wine list, too.

VU'S Map pp70-71   European-Fusion $$$
☎ 319 8088; 50th fl, Blvd at Jumeirah Emirates Towers, Sheikh Zayed Rd; 3-course business lunches Dh165, dinner mains Dh150-225, dinner; ⏱ 12.30-3pm Sun-Thu, 7.30pm-midnight Sat-Thu
As the name implies, the views are stellar from this formal white-tablecloth dining room popular with the Rolex crowd celebrating the inking of a deal. That said, given the state of the economy, this place has certainly seen buzzier times, especially at night when it's so quiet you'll want to speak in a hushed voice. The current chef is heavily into culinary alchemy, weaving dishes from seemingly incongruous ingredients. A recent menu featured slow-roasted pork belly paired with pan-fried scallops. Sometimes it works, sometimes not so much.

SPECTRUM ON ONE
Map pp70-71   International $$$
☎ 311 8316; Fairmont hotel, Sheikh Zayed Rd; mains Dh100-245, 3-course menus Dh190; ⏱ 6.30pm-1am; ♿
Spectrum competes for top honours for Dubai's best live-action buffet. The food is solidly good and a visual feast, with no disappointments from its eight kitchens cooking up six distinct cuisines from around the world: Arabian, Indian, Thai, European, Japanese and Chinese. It's also great for kids. Signature dishes include sliced mixed teppanyaki, black pepper beef, yoghurt-marinated chicken and warm molten chocolate cake. Fantastic Friday brunch, too (see p122).

RIB ROOM Map pp70-71   Steakhouse $$$

☎ 319 8088; Blvd at Jumeirah Emirates Towers, Sheikh Zayed Rd; mains Dh75-240; ⏲ 12.30-3pm Sat-Thu, 7pm-midnight daily

Surrender helplessly to your inner carnivore at this power-player hangout where the air is practically perfumed with testosterone. The yummy cuts of aged steaks, juicy prime rib and chateaubriand speak for themselves, but even more complicated dishes like braised Wagyu beef cheeks in port wine arrive without needless flights of fancy.

AL-NAFOORAH Map pp70-71   Lebanese $$

☎ 319 8088; Blvd at Jumeirah Emirates Towers, Sheikh Zayed Rd; mezzes Dh25-40, mains Dh60-75; ⏲ 12.30-3pm & 8pm-midnight

Tucked away in the base of Emirates Towers, Al-Nafoorah's clubby, wood-panelled dining room feels like a Wall St power-lunch spot. The mezzes stand out – try the *kibbeh* (raw lamb) – more than the kebabs on the classic Lebanese menu, but really, the kitchen does everything quite well, if not beautifully. It's quieter and more formal than most Lebanese restaurants, making this a great choice for a dressy-casual night out without the noisy fanfare of the big Lebanese party places.

NOODLE HOUSE Map pp70-71   Asian $

☎ 319 8088; lower level, Blvd at Jumeirah Emirates Towers, Sheikh Zayed Rd; mains Dh30-66; ⏲ noon-midnight; 🖪

The concept at this reliably good, always-packed pan-Asian joint is simple: sit down at long wooden communal tables and order by ticking dishes on a tear-off menu pad. There's great variety – curry laksa to pad Thai to roast duck – to please disparate tastes. Some dishes even come in small and large sizes to match hunger levels. Wines by the glass and several Asian beers, including Tiger on tap, are available. If there's a wait, leave your mobile number and head next door to Agency (p128) for pre-dinner drinks. There are now four other branches around town, including in Souq Madinat Jumeirah (Map pp76-7) and Dubai Mall (Map pp70-71).

GOURMET BURGER KITCHEN

Map pp70-71   Burgers $

☎ 425 0187; Level B1, Dubai International Financial Centre; burgers Dh28-34; ⏲ 9am-10pm Sat-Wed, 9am-11pm Thu & Fri; 🖪

This patty-and-bun UK import stacks its burgers so high you risk dislocating your jaw when actually trying to bite into one. Go classic or try one of the more adventurous

RAMADAN & IFTAR

Muslims are required to fast during Ramadan, and everyone, regardless of religion, is expected to observe the fast when in public. That means no eating, drinking or smoking during daylight hours. Some hotels still serve breakfast and lunch, but this is in specially designated rooms; most of the time eating during the day means room service or self-catering. Non-Muslims offered coffee or tea when meeting a Muslim during the fast should initially refuse politely. If your host insists, and repeats the offer several times, you should accept, so long as it doesn't look as though you're going to anger anyone else present who may be fasting.

Ramadan would seem to be the ideal time to lose weight, yet a lot of locals pile on the pounds. For many, avoiding food from dawn to dusk results in immense hunger come sunset, and with hundreds of restaurants putting on good-value *iftar* buffets, the temptation to overindulge is everywhere. *Iftar*, the meal that breaks the fast, is traditionally very light – just a couple of dates, some *jallab* (date drink) and a bowl of lentil soup. But Dubai's commercially savvy restaurants have turned *iftar* into an all-you-can-eat glutton-fest. From huge spreads at the Burj al-Arab to bottomless buckets at KFC, there are plenty of ways to catch up on missed meals.

Ironically, those with a passion for Middle Eastern cuisine will find Ramadan a great time to visit. Restaurants may be closed during the day, but in the evenings they're at their busiest, liveliest and cheapest: this is the chance for Muslims to socialise with family and friends. Many hotels set up Ramadan tents for the entire month. They're often superbly situated beachside and serve Lebanese mezzes and *sheesha* until the wee hours. Here are our favourite hotels to take in the action:

- Jumeirah Emirates Towers (p160)
- Le Royal Meridien Beach Resort & Spa (p163)
- One&Only Royal Mirage (p163)
- Park Hyatt Dubai (p154)
- Raffles Dubai (p156)

choices, like the Kiwi Burger with beetroot, egg, pineapple and cheddar, inspired by the founders' New Zealand origins.

ZAATAR W ZEIT Map pp70-71 — Lebanese $
☎ 800 922 827; near Shangri-La hotel, Sheikh Zayed Rd; dishes Dh7-33; ⊗ 24hr; ♿
In the wee hours, this Lebanese fast-food joint gets howling with night owls hoping to restore balance to the brain with *manaeesh* – flatbread topped with cheese, tomatoes, minced meats or, of course, *zaatar* (thyme, sesame, marjoram and oregano). Think Lebanese pizza. *Laban taza* (salted yoghurt drink) goes best with 'em, not cola. Other branches are in Dubai Mall (Map pp70-71), Mall of the Emirates (Map pp82-3) and on The Walk at JBR (Map pp83-2).

JUMEIRAH

The restaurants in Dubai's low-rise, high-rent district draw wealthy locals and tourists on holiday. Though the beach is never far away, it's barely visible from some of the following eateries: for ocean views, head to New Dubai or Madinat Jumeirah. The restaurants at Madinat Jumeirah are generally good, entirely touristy and overpriced, but they're some of the most scenic. Note: Al-Dhiyafah Rd in Satwa is the best walking street in the city and is tops for a late-night *shwarma*.

AL-MAHARA Map pp76-7 — Seafood $$$
☎ 301 7600; Burj al-Arab, Jumeirah Rd, Umm Suqeim 3; mains Dh250-300; ⊗ 12.30-3pm & 7-11.30pm
A lift posing as a submarine deposits you at a gold-leaf-clad tunnel leading you to Dubai's most unique restaurant. Diners sit around a huge circular aquarium where clownfish flit and baby sharks dart as their sea bass and halibut cousins are being… devoured. Surreal yes, but at least the quality measures up to the hype. Patrons seem to include a disproportionate number of sheikhs, oligarchs and lissome blondes. Bring that platinum card.

PIERCHIC Map pp76-7 — Seafood $$$
☎ 366 6730; Al-Qasr, Madinat Jumeirah, Al-Sufouh Rd, Umm Suqeim 3; mains Dh100-240; ⊗ noon-3pm & 7pm-midnight
Looking for a place to drop an engagement ring into a glass of champagne? Make reservations for this stunning seafood house

at the end of a long pier jutting out to sea. The best tables line the outdoor decks and provide drop-dead-gorgeous vistas of the Burj al-Arab and Madinat Jumeirah. The food is solidly good, but the overambitious menu gets a little heavy-handed with its ingredient combinations; order simple and you'll fare better. But with so much romance, you'll hardly notice what you're eating. Note: sitting inside defeats the purpose of coming here.

MAGNOLIA Map pp76-7 — Vegetarian $$
☎ 366 6730; Al-Qasr, Madinat Jumeirah, Al-Sufouh Rd, Umm Suqeim 3; mains Dh70-85, set menus Dh180-250; ⊗ 7-11.30pm
Dubai's only high-end vegetarian restaurant, Magnolia overlooks the canals at Madinat Jumeirah, and if you make reservations, you can arrive by *abra* (water taxi). The so-called 'well-being' cooking takes itself a bit too seriously in its emulation of haute cuisine and lacks resonance on the palate, but the elegant presentations, romantic setting and top-end ingredients (organic whenever possible) make up for the pretence and price.

SHOO FEE MA FEE Map pp76-7 — Moroccan $$
☎ 366 8888; Souq Madinat Jumeirah, Al-Sufouh Rd, Umm Suqeim 3; mains Dh65-210; ⊗ 6pm-1am
The name literally means 'what's up?', and what's up at Shoo Fee Ma Fee are three floors of Moroccan ambience overlooking the romantic waterways of Madinat Jumeirah. Pigeon pastilla and other Maghreb favourites offer flavour bombs, but the more inventive dishes don't always hit the right notes.

ZHENG HE'S
Map pp76-7 — Contemporary Chinese $$
☎ 366 6730; Mina A'Salam, Madinat Jumeirah, Al-Sufouh Rd, Umm Suqeim 3; mains Dh60-220; ⊗ noon-3pm & 6.30pm-midnight
An army of 20 clatters pans and fires woks behind the glass of the open kitchen at Zheng He's, the spectacular contemporary Chinese restaurant known for its fresh, light dim sum and stellar seafood specials (many diners go for the live tank, but others prefer the wasabi prawns with black pepper). The Sino-chic room is gorgeous, with a pagoda-style ceiling and good symmetry. Alas, the hard surfaces mean high decibels, and the location at Madinat Jumeirah means high

VEGETARIAN EATS

Good news: restaurants with poor vegetarian selections are the exception in Dubai. You can thank all the wonderful cooking from the Indian subcontinent, the Middle East and Thailand. The city's many Indian restaurants do fantastic things with spiced vegetables, potatoes and rice. At any Lebanese restaurant, you can fill the table with all-veg mezzes for a small feast. At Thai places, plan to eat rice dishes with vegetable coconut curries. Vegans may have to ask more questions, but will be surprised by the choices. Alas, Dubai has barely started to catch on to the idea of organic food; plan to eat conventional produce or shop for yourself at Organic Foods & Cafe (p98), which now also has an attached cafe (p115). Here's a selection of our top five all-vegetarian restaurants so you won't have to endure even a whiff of meat.

- Govinda's (p113)
- Magnolia (opposite)
- Rajdhani (p113)
- Sukh Sagar at the Beach (p123)
- XVA Café (p113)

prices. Score an outside table for romantic views of the water and Burj al-Arab. No children under four years old.

PAI THAI Map pp76-7 Thai $$

☎ 366 6730; Al-Qasr, Madinat Jumeirah, Al-Sufouh Rd, Umm Suqeim 3; mains Dh55-180; ☺ 6.30-11.30pm

A boat ride, a waterside table and candlelight are the hallmarks of a romantic night out and this enchanting spot at the Al-Qsar hits on all cylinders. If your date doesn't make you swoon, then the beautifully crafted Thai dishes should still ensure an unforgettable evening. Or come for Friday brunch (with/without alcohol Dh240/190).

DUCK KING Map pp76-7 Chinese $$

☎ 342 8041; Beach Park Plaza Centre, Jumeirah Rd, Jumeirah 2; dim sum Dh20-40, half/whole ducks Dh168/288; ☺ 9am-midnight Sun-Wed, 9am-2am Thu & Fri;

Cap off a couple of hours at Jumeirah Beach Park with a meal at this contempo-chic nosh spot popular with Sinophiles tired of the kung pao school of Chinese cooking. Build a meal from the copious dim sum choices or lock in on the Peking duck, served first in pancakes and then prepared in one of six other ways, all delicious.

PARS IRANIAN KITCHEN

Map pp76-7 Persian $

☎ 398 4000; next to Rydges Plaza hotel, Satwa Roundabout, Satwa; mezzes Dh15-20, mains Dh40-65; ☺ 6pm-1am;

This convivial alfresco dining room often fills with patrons lusting after bread, tickled crisply by flames in the brick oven, finger-lickin' *muttabal* (purée of aubergine mixed with tahini, yoghurt and olive oil) and hummus, and juicy kebabs paired with perfect piles of saffron rice. You'll feel like a pasha lounging amid the fat pillows on a carpeted platform surrounded by twinkle-lit hedges. Too authentic? Opt for a traditional table. Alas, the lack of indoor seating makes Pars a poor choice in summer.

BELLA DONNA Map pp76-7 Italian $

☎ 344 7710; Mercato Mall, Jumeirah Rd, Jumeirah 1; pizzas & pastas Dh35-55; ☺ 11am-11pm;

Ponder the beauty of Marilyn, Audrey and other classic Hollywood stars as you sit in this art-deco-inspired dining room and munch on tender-crusted thin pizzas and house-made pastas. The strong coffee will jack you up for shopping in the adjoining Mercato Mall. Sit on the terrace for glimpses of the azure Gulf.

SMILING BKK Map pp76-7 Thai $

☎ 349 6677; off Al-Wasl Rd, near Jumeirah Post Office, Jumeirah 1; mains Dh25-50; ☺ 11am-midnight;

Locals will kill us for including this indie hole-in-the-wall Thai gem, but it's too good not to share. The walls of the cheek-by-jowl space are covered with hipster mishmash (think Van Gogh paint-by-numbers postcards), and scratchy rock-and-roll blaring through big speakers (sit outside for quiet conversation). A Thai national cooks your dinner. The food is good, sometimes very good, but what's even better is the adventure of finding this underground bo-ho hangout. (Hint: look for the moustachioed neon Mona Lisa, just west of the Jumeirah Post Office.)

THE ONE Map pp76-7 Cafe $

☎ 345 6687; Jumeirah Rd, near Jumeirah Mosque, Jumeirah 1; dishes Dh20-45; ☺ 9am-9pm

Deli dabblers will be in salad and sandwich heaven at this stylish outpost upstairs at THE One home design store. All food is freshly prepared and calibrated to health-

and waist-watchers without sacrificing a lick to the taste gods. Reliable choices include the smoked salmon wrap and the Arabic chicken salad. A good alternative if Lime Tree Café (below) is full.

SIDRA Map pp76-7 Lebanese $
☎ 398 4723; Al-Diyafah Rd, Satwa; mains Dh20-40; ☺ 24hr

Of all the Beirut-style pavement cafes lining pedestrian-friendly Al-Diyafah Rd, our top pick for mezzes is Sidra. Fantastic *fattoosh*, zinging *muttabal*, creamy-rich hummus, tangy tabouli and fresh, hot bread. The kebabs are okay, but the dips are what's best. Inside is ugly; sit on the pavement and soak up the street scene. Ideal after a night out.

LIME TREE CAFÉ Map pp76-7 Cafe $
☎ 349 8498; Jumeirah Rd, near Jumeirah Mosque, Jumeirah 1; mains Dh20-40; ☺ 7.30am-6pm;

Herbivore or meathead, no matter your persuasion, your tastebuds will love the carefully composed salads, imaginative wraps and perky smoothies (try the blueberry) at this expat favourite on the Jumeirah strip. Other assets are its use of fresh ingredients, including some organic produce, and the wholesome cooking, just how the yoga mammas, power shoppers and health nuts like it. Portions are generous, prices good, and the carrot cake the best in town. Also in the China Court in Ibn Battuta Mall (Map pp82-3).

MARIA BONITA'S TACO SHOP
Map pp76-7 Mexican $
☎ 395 5576; Umm al-Sheif St, Umm Suqeim 1; mains Dh20-30; ☺ noon-11.30pm;

Location, location, location...is definitely not what lures people to Maria, Dubai's only authentic Mexican restaurant. It's the tacos, stupid! And the quesadillas, burritos and other faves brimming with spot-on flavour – spicy, smoky and deep. Okay, so the squawking parrots are a bit much without any *cerveza* to soften the edges, but it's fun coming to this neighbourhood-adored snack shack just the same.

RAVI Map pp76-7 Pakistani $
☎ 331 5353; Al-Satwa Rd, Satwa; mains Dh12-20; ☺ 24hr;

Cabbies to five-star chefs flock to this legendary Pakistani eatery where you eat like a prince and pay like a pauper. Loosen that belt for heaping helpings of kick-ass curries, succulent grilled meats, perky dal (lentils) and fresh, buttery naan. There's a family room and a cafeteria, but it's worth waiting for an outside table to watch Satwa on parade.

NEW DUBAI
The city's sprawling beach resorts, with their many top-end restaurants, happening bars and popular nightclubs, dominate New Dubai. If you're not staying at a resort, spend an evening at one. They're far from the chaos of inner Dubai, and you won't have to hail a

SHWARMA SHOOTOUT
Shwarma is the snack food of the Middle East and the de rigueur snack after a night of partying. Dubai is blessed with an enormous number of *shwarma* joints, so to help you enjoy this delicious snack we undertook a massive research project involving countless late-night tastings to present you with our favourite *shwarmas*.

Al-Mallah (Map pp76-7; ☎ 398 4723; Al-Diyafah Rd, Satwa; dishes Dh5-20; ☺ 6am-4am Sat-Thu, noon-4am Fri;) Dependably sublime chicken and lamb *shwarmas*. The juicy chicken is loaded with pungent garlic sauce and jammed with pickles; lamb is tender with tons of fresh tomato, parsley, pickles and hummus. Great felafel, too.

Beirut (Map pp76-7; ☎ 398 8881; Al-Diyafah Rd, Satwa; mains Dh5-25; ☺ noon-2am) Beirut is one of the major *shwarma* joints on Al-Diyafah Rd and battles with Al-Mallah for the title of best lamb *shwarma*. Available in two sizes.

Lebanese Village (Map pp62-3; ☎ 352 2522; Al-Mankhool Rd; mains Dh22; ☺ noon-1am) The lamb *shwarmas* are zesty with onion, parsley, pickles and tomato. The felafel is good, too, but skip everything else.

Saj Express (Map pp70-71; ☎ 321 1191; Sheikh Zayed Rd, Oasis Tower, next to 21st Century Tower; mains Dh7-40; ☺ 8am-4am;) Saj Express is one of Sheikh Zayed Rd's top fast-food joints – the fresh bread (cooked on the *saj*, a curved, iron-dome-topped oven) is what makes the *shwarmas* here so special. Pair your shwarma with one of the fresh juices and you can't go wrong.

taxi until it's time to go home. This section also includes several restaurants in Mall of the Emirates.

RHODES MEZZANINE
Map pp82-3   Modern British $$$
☎ 317 6000; Grosvenor House, Al-Sufouh Rd, Dubai Marina; mains Dh180-240; ⏰ 7.30-11.30pm Mon-Sat
Celebrity chef Gary Rhodes is famous for bringing British cuisine into the 21st century and has a Michelin star to prove it. At his Dubai outpost, the emphasis is squarely on quality ingredients prepared in fresh, surprising ways. There's fish on the menu but it's meat lovers who will discover culinary nirvana in such dishes as rack of lamb or slow-roasted pork belly. Unlike the food, the modern baroque setting is anything but understated, with its candy-coloured Lucite room and shimmering chandeliers. But do leave room for the divine bread-and-butter pudding.

BUDDHA BAR Map pp82-3   Asian $$$
☎ 317 6000; Grosvenor House, Al-Sufouh Rd, Dubai Marina; mains Dh155-295; ⏰ 8pm-2am Sat-Wed, 8pm-3am Thu & Fri
At last a restaurant that knows the power of good lighting. So what if the bmm-bmm music requires you to shout over the table? You're in the shadow of a giant Buddha, rubbing shoulders with Dubai's beautiful crowd, and you look fabulous in that new outfit. Oh, the food? It (nearly) measures up to the room – a mishmash of Thai and Japanese with a dash of Chinese – but really, who cares? Like we said, you look a-m-a-z-i-n-g. Uh, you didn't forget your platinum card, did you? Make reservations several days ahead, even for during the week.

BICE Map pp82-3   Italian $$$
☎ 399 1111; Hilton Dubai Jumeirah, The Walk at JBR, Dubai Marina; pastas Dh80-210, mains Dh150-220; ⏰ noon-3pm & 7pm-midnight; ♿
With a reputation for being one of the best Italian restaurants in town, BiCE is often fully packed, which can prove challenging for the servers. Still, the food is solid, prepared in an unfussy, classic way using just a few top-quality ingredients and letting them shine. The recipes are traditional – beef carpaccio, veal Milanese, house-made pasta, wild-mushroom risotto – but presented with a contemporary style that matches the elegant, continental dining

room. This being an Italian eatery, there's even a play area and games room for the kids. Great tiramisu. Reservations essential.

INDEGO Map pp82-3   Contemporary Indian $$$
☎ 317 6000; Grosvenor House, Al-Sufouh Rd, Dubai Marina; mains Dh140-280; ⏰ 7.30pm-midnight Sun-Fri, to 1am Thu
Michelin-starred Vineet Bhatia is the consulting chef at this gracious Indian restaurant with a spacious and open dining room, lorded over by big brass Natraj sculptures. Recommended dishes include the house-smoked tandoori salmon, prawns poached in coconut and chilli masala, and the chocolate samosas. Note: unlike most Indian cooking, plates here are delicately composed and not designed for sharing.

SPLENDIDO Map pp82-3   Italian $$$
☎ 399 4000; Ritz-Carlton Hotel, The Walk at JBR, Dubai Marina; pastas Dh80-120, mains Dh140-220, Fri brunches Dh375; ⏰ 7-11am, 12.30-5pm & 7pm-12.30am daily, brunch 12.30-3.30pm Fri
Tall palms sway in the breeze around the outdoor patio at the Ritz-Carlton's northern Italian restaurant, an ideal spot to hold hands by candlelight. It's not as formal as you'd expect, given the setting and pricing. In fact, the cooking is more upmarket trattoria style: earthy and rich as in the *ravioli alle noci* (walnut-and-mascarpone ravioli) and *agnello arrosto* (pan-roasted lamb loin). The Friday champagne brunch has a constant league of fans.

EAUZONE Map pp82-3   Fine Dining $$$
☎ 399 9999; Arabian Court, One&Only Royal Mirage, Al-Sufouh Rd, Al-Sufouh; mains Dh115-225; ⏰ noon-3.30pm & 7.30-11.30pm
This jewel of a restaurant is an inspired port of call drawing friends, lovebirds and trendy families. The poolside setting is sublime, with decks jutting out over illuminated blue water like little islands, while the menu is a winning fusion of European cooking techniques and Pacific Rim flavours. This is smart cooking, some of the best in Dubai. Reservations essential.

MAYA Map pp82-3   Mexican $$$
☎ 316 5550; Le Royal Meridien Beach Resort & Spa, Al-Sufouh Rd, Al-Sufouh; mains Dh110-235; ⏰ 7.30am-midnight Mon-Sat
Richard Sandoval, the man who introduced modern Mexican food to America,

is behind the menu at this sophisticated restaurant where you'll be treated to a piñata of flavours. Start out with creamy guacamole, prepared tableside of course, before moving on to such authentic mains as *mole poblano,* salmon azteca or finger-lickin *costillas ahumadas* (smokey short ribs, that is). If you want Tex-Mex, go elsewhere. Great rooftop bar, too (see p132).

AQUARA Map pp82-3   Seafood $$$
☎ 362 7900; Dubai Marina Yacht Club, Marina Walk, Dubai Marina; mains Dh100-190; ☺ 7.30-10.30pm

The views of fancy yachts and a forest of sleek high-rises impress almost as much as the Asian-infused fare at this chic seafood shrine that's always packed to the gills thanks to dock-fresh ingredients and flaw-lessly crafted plates. The Friday brunch is hugely popular.

MAZINA Map pp82-3   International $$$
☎ 436 7777; The Address Dubai Marina, Dubai Marina; buffets with alcohol Dh250; ☺ 6.30am-10.30am, noon-3pm & 6.30-11pm; ♿

Like Las Vegas, Dubai is buffet city, so it's hard to stand out from the pack. But Mazina does get a few things right: the sushi, for instance, and the Chinese dishes. The clincher, though, is what's called the Teppanyaki Ice Cream station, where premium ice cream gets mixed up with your choice of ingredients: nuts to M&Ms and gummibears. Not just for kids! Ask about the Saturday family brunch.

AL-KHAIMA Map pp82-3   Arabic $$
☎ 316 5550; Le Royal Meridien Beach Resort & Spa; Al-Sufouh Rd, Al-Sufouh; mains Dh85-200; ☺ 7pm-midnight

In the cooler months there are few places more romantic than the *majlis*-style tents

LET'S DO BRUNCH...

The working week in Dubai runs from Sunday through Thursday, which means (nearly) everyone is off on Friday. An expat institution, Friday brunch is a major element of the Dubai social scene – particularly among Bacchanalian revellers – and every hotel-restaurant in town sets up an all-you-can-eat buffet with an option for unlimited champagne or wine. Some smaller, independent restaurants also serve brunch, but without alcohol, making them popular with local families. Here's our shortlist for top brunches in town.

Al-Qasr (Map pp82-3; ☎ 366 6730; Al-Qsar, Madinat Jumeirah; with drinks Dh495; ☺ 12.30-4pm) Prepare to loosen your belt when tucking into this unbelievable cornucopia of delectables – meats, sushi, seafood, foie gras, beautiful salads, mezzes, all sorts of hot dishes, etc. It's one of the most expensive brunch feasts in town but the quality and range justify the price tag.

Aquara (above; without/with house drinks Dh180/250; ☺ 12.30-3.30pm Fri) Seafood lovers rejoice over this fishy bonanza of sushi, sashimi, crabs, oysters, clams and cooked-to-order lobster, all artistically presented. Don't forget to hit the dessert room. It's extremely good value.

Iranian Club (Map pp64-5; ☎ 336 7700; Oud Metha Rd; brunches Dh70; ☺ 1-4pm) Feast at this Persian-cuisine showcase owned by the Iranian government. Start by rolling cheese and mint in hot bread, then sample soups and marinated salads, followed by tender kebabs and stews from an enormous buffet. Pace yourself. Women must wear headscarves, men long trousers, and there's no alcohol, but it's worth altering your habits for a culturally rich afternoon.

Spectrum on One (p116; without/with alcohol Dh295/550; ☺ noon-3pm) This top brunch pick features free-flowing champagne, eight buffets with six different cuisines and an entire room full of port and cheeses.

Spice Island (p109; with soft/house/premium drinks Dh149/199/269; ☺ noon-3pm Fri) The oldest brunch buffet in town, Spice Island offers seven cuisines and six live cooking stations. Great value and especially popular with families.

Thai Kitchen (p110; soft drinks/beer & wine Dh195/240; ☺ noon-4pm) Sample an enormous repertoire of Thai cooking, served tapas-style. Mellow scene, good for nondrinkers.

Yalumba (Map pp54-5; ☎ 217 0000; Le Meridien Dubai, Airport Rd; champagne brunches Dh429; ☺ 12.30-3.30pm) One of the few to offer an à la carte menu so you won't have to schlep plates. Great roasts. Go whole-hog with vintage Bollinger champagne. The raucous atmosphere gives it an edge with party people.

Zuma (p116; without/with alcohol Dh325/495; ☺ 12.30-3pm Fri) Uberhip Zuma also pulls in the punters for its pricey but top-notch brunch. Gorge on plump sushi, sashimi and oysters, nibble on juicy kebabs straight off the robata grill, and try such signature dishes as crispy fried squid and blackened cod.

in the garden of the relaxed Meridien resort. Classic mezzes like *baba ghanooj*, hummus and *fattoosh* are orchestrated into culinary symphonies, although the enormous platters of charcoal-grilled kebabs being rushed to your table are just as sterling. Wind down the evening pasha-style while languidly puffing on the *sheesha*.

TAGINE Map pp82-3 Moroccan $$
☎ 399 9999; The Palace, One&Only Royal Mirage, Al-Sufouh Rd, Al-Sufouh; mains Dh75-170; ⏲ 7-11.30pm Tue-Sun
Cosy up between throw pillows at a low-slung table in the shadowy-dim dining room, then take your tastebuds on a magic carpet ride while tapping your toes to the live Moroccan band. Fez-capped waiters jump in and dance between dashes to the kitchen for big platters of tagine and couscous. This is the real deal. Book ahead and request a table near the band. Reservations essential.

BUSSOLA Map pp82-3 Italian $$
☎ 451 7391; Westin Dubai Mina Seyahi Beach Resort, Al-Sufouh Rd, Al-Sufouh; pizza Dh55-85, mains Dh110-200; ⏲ 7-11.45pm daily year-round, lunch only Fri & Sat Oct-late June; ⑤
Skip the more formal downstairs dining room and report straight to the rooftop pizzeria to pick your favourite from the habit-forming pizzas. The ambience is relaxed and casual, making it suitable for families and groups. Bonus: stellar views of the Gulf and the Palm Jumeirah.

NINA Map pp82-3 Contemporary Indian $$
☎ 399 9999; Arabian Court, One&Only Royal Mirage, Al-Sufouh Rd, Al-Sufouh; mains Dh50-145; ⏲ 7-11.30pm Mon-Sat
Follow the locals to this lush den whose floor-to-ceiling purple fabric, red-orange

light and beaded curtains set a seductive backdrop for the dynamic cooking on offer. The chef combines Indian with a touch of Thai and tempers it with European techniques. The results will perk up even the most passive proboscis: rich spicing means flavours develop slowly on the palate with an elegant complexity that demands savouring. Choose the chef's selection of starters and curries for a sense of his broad repertoire. Reservations essential.

ROYAL ORCHID Map pp82-3 Chinese/Thai $$
☎ 367 4040; Marina Walk, Dubai Marina; mains Dh40-80; ⏲ 10am-midnight; ⑤
Never mind the mall setting, the terrace with a view of the bobbing boats is a delight on a balmy evening. Though the Peking duck is a standout, it's probably a good idea to stick to Thai here, including the fun build-your-own curry. The food, while tasty, won't win any awards, but the fall-over-backwards staff and gut-busting portions give this place an edge nonetheless.

SUKH SAGAR AT THE BEACH
Map pp82-3 Indian Vegetarian $
☎ 396 7222; Rimal 1, The Walk at JBR, Dubai Marina; mains Dh20-30, ⏲ 11am-12.30pm Sat-Wed, to 1.30am Thu, 1.30pm-1.30am Fri; ⑤
This buzzy Indian vegetarian chain has been in business since 1962 but has kept pace with current food trends by offering light, fresh and healthy cuisine. Sidle up to the counter for *dosa teppanyaki*: as many freshly prepared mini-dosas (a type of crêpe) with different fillings as you can manage (Dh39). Alternatively, the flaky samosas, creative curries and saffron-scented biryani will make your tummy just as happy.

ENTERTAINMENT

top picks

ENTERTAINMENT

A night on the town is a big deal in Dubai, and despite the municipality's ban on outdoor music and dancing in late 2007, every night of the week you'll find a place to whoop it up. The big nights are Thursday and Friday – Dubai's weekend nights – when expats burn off steam from their 12-hour-a-day working week. And boy, do they like to drink! Plan to head to hotels, which along with major sporting venues are the only places licensed to serve alcohol. In Dubai, there's no such thing as an independent, out-of-the-way neighbourhood pub that nobody knows about.

Finding the right bar can be tricky. Dubai is the playground of the parvenu as much as it's a city of expat workers trying to advance their careers and save some tax-free cash. You're in Dubai either to dump your wallet or fill it. Choosing an appropriate bar depends on the people with whom you want to rub shoulders. Wanna get a sense of the social lives of resident workers? Follow the expats. Wanna show off that new Marc Jacobs outfit you just bought? Follow the glam crowd. And then there are the niche bars, places frequented by, say, Russian oligarchs or British footballers. Wherever you wander, don't expect to strike up many conversations; most people in Dubai stick to their cliques. Occasionally, you'll spot a random *dishdasha*-clad local breaking ranks with his countrymen (and the law) by drinking alcohol alongside Westerners, but this is an anomaly.

DJs spin nearly every night of the week (except during Ramadan), with regular one-off dance events. The repertoire is global – funk, soul, house (lots of house), trip-hop, hip hop, R&B, African, Arabic and Latino. Some hotels engage full-time live bands but they're almost all cover bands: there's a lack of innovative local musical talent.

Clubs and bars close by 3am, smaller venues at 1am. Start early with sunset cocktails, head to dinner, then follow up with post-dinner drinks before hitting a dance club. Afterwards soak up the booze with a late-night *shwarma*. The fancy-pants bars are concentrated around Downtown Dubai and Dubai Marina. The seedy places are at cheap hotels in Bur Dubai and Deira; working girls are common – too common – but there are also some gritty-fun ethnic bars here worth a visit.

Alcohol is expensive (see p128), but that doesn't stop rowdy Westerners from downing pint after shot after pint. Nurse your drinks or you'll shell out a lot of dirhams. The irony is, it can be hard – really hard – to catch the eye of a bartender. Long waits at the bar are common at crowded venues. Conversely, waiters are trained to upsell guests (though not usually trained in the fine art of service). If you hear 'Would you like another round?', make clear exactly who at the table wants one or you may wind up with a full table of glasses – and a hefty bill. Likewise if you order a bottle of wine; waiters often empty a bottle into one person's glass rather than divvy the last of it up between everyone's, then look at those whose glasses are empty and ask, 'Another bottle?' Don't be duped. When there's not much left in the bottle, keep it out of the waiter's hand.

If you're not up for drinking, plan to hit the mellow *sheesha* cafes and play a game of backgammon. This is where you'll spot locals. Emiratis don't like to be around alcohol, but they sure love coffee.

There's not yet much going on in terms of high-brow entertainment since the first financial crisis of late 2008 put an end to ambitious plans for an opera house. Live performances tend to be light fare – musicals, cabaret or touring shows – that appeal to Western sensibilities. The Dubai Community Theatre and Arts Centre (DUCTAC, p137) is one of the few spaces that also trains the spotlight on local talent. If you want to catch a movie, you've got plenty of hi-tech multiplexes to take in the blockbusters; almost all are in shopping centres. Alternative and art house cinemas are practically nonexistent (there's one screen now at Reel Cinemas in Dubai Mall that screens nonmainstream fare), although galleries and alternative venues, such as the JamJar (p73) and XVA Café (p113), occasionally run one-off series.

It's best not to criss-cross the city on a weekend; traffic is abominable on Thursday and Friday nights and taxis can be hard to come by. Stick to a particular area or two, such as Dubai Marina, Jumeirah, Downtown Dubai, Deira or Bur Dubai. And under no circumstances should you *ever* get behind the wheel of a car if you've had even one sip of alcohol (see boxed text, p182).

DRINKING

From gritty to glam, multicultural Dubai has plenty of bars and pubs to match your mood. Plan to visit a beach bar in Jumeirah or Dubai Marina to see the sun set over the Gulf, a quintessential Dubai experience; a fancy spot, whether it be a dance club or a lounge, to giggle at arrivistes in impossibly high heels; and an expat bar to catch a buzz with overworked Westerners laughing too loudly. If you like to make your own discoveries, put down your guidebook and wander the ethnic backstreets of Deira, find a bar in a no-star hotel, maybe an Iranian or Filipino club, and soak up the colour (for a headstart, check out some of the lower-end listings in the Sleeping chapter, p154). Alas, this method cannot be recommended for women, single or in groups. There's much prostitution going on in these places and unless you're dressed with nun-like modesty, boozed-up patrons may mistake you for an easy girl.

Bars are open until 2am or 3am; alcohol service is illegal between 4pm and 6pm on Friday and Saturday. Drink prices are ridiculous (see boxed text, p128): you could pay anything from Dh20 to Dh40 for a pint of beer or Dh25 to Dh100+ for a glass of wine, depending on quality and vintage. Hotels add a 10% service charge. Tip a few dirhams per round. Take heart: nearly all bars in Dubai offer drinks specials at nonpeak times, happy hours and ladies' nights, when women drink free. (Dubai's population is 75% male; bars are desperate to pad the room with gals.) For current specials, check www .mumtazz.com. Some bars accept reservations for tables; call ahead.

DEIRA

ISSIMO Map pp52-3   Bar
☎ 212 7570; Hilton Dubai Creek, Baniyas Rd;
☉ 11am-2am

Illuminated blue flooring, black-leather sofas and sleek chrome finishing lend a James Bond look to this sports-and-martini bar. If you're not into sports – or TV – you may find the giant screens distracting. Good for drinks before dining at Verre by Gordon Ramsay (p108) or the Glasshouse Mediterranean Brasserie (p109).

KU-BU Map pp52-3   Bar
☎ 222 7171; Radisson Blu Hotel, Baniyas Rd;
☉ 6.30pm-2am

A DJ spins funky tunes at this window-less, tattoo-themed bar with stools draped in cowhide and secluded nooks that are made even more private with plush draperies. A good choice for drinks before or after dinner at the Radisson Blu's terrific restaurants.

TERRACE Map pp54-5   Outdoor Lounge
☎ 602 1234; Park Hyatt Dubai, next to Dubai Creek Golf & Yacht Club; ☉ noon-1.30am

Specialising in French oysters, caviar, champagne and vodka, the Terrace is one of Dubai's smartest waterside lounge bars. A DJ sets just the right mood with sensual chill-out beats. The dramatically lit interior is stylin', but it doesn't compare with sitting on the outdoor deck and watching the moored boats bobbing in the marina. Sunday is ladies' night and on Mondays there are drinks specials for all.

IRISH VILLAGE Map pp54-5   Pub
☎ 282 4750; Aviation Club, Al-Garhoud Rd;
☉ 11am-1.30am

Better known as 'the IV', this always-buzzy pub with its faux Irish main street facade is popular with expats for its pondside 'beer garden'. No happy hour, but there's Guinness and Kilkenny on tap.

HITTING THE TOWN

For entertainment listings, your safest bet is the weekly *Time Out* magazine, although the freebie *7 Days* is also worth a glance. Look for free guides and leaflets promoting clubs, dance parties and gigs; find them at bars, cafes, Virgin Megastore (p93) and Ohm Records (p96). The same places should also have copies of *Infusion*, an excellent free biweekly pocket-sized mag covering clubs, bars, movies, music, fashion and other lifestyle topics.

As usual, the most current information is on the web. *Infusion*'s website (www.infusion.ae) has an up-to-the-minute party schedule. Same goes for the online club guide on www.mumtazz.com (click on the United Arab Emirates flag for Dubai) and www.platinumlist.ae, which also let you book tickets to the major events.

Otherwise, for tickets to concerts and other shows, phone the *Time Out* ticketline on ☎ 800 4669 (☎ +971 4 210 8567 from overseas). Or buy online at either www.timeouttickets.com or www.boxofficeme.com.

BUR DUBAI

COOZ Map pp64-5 — Bar

☎ 317 1234; Grand Hyatt, Al-Qataiyat Rd;
🕑 6pm-3am

Sip a martini at this dimly lit, super-stylish cocktail bar and enjoy some smooth live jazz – some of the most authentic sounds in Dubai in fact – by the resident singer and pianist.

GINSENG Map pp64-5 — Bar

☎ 324 8200; Wafi Mall, Al-Qataiyat Rd;
🕑 7pm-2am Tue-Fri, 7pm-1am Sat-Mon

A fashionable spot to start the evening, Ginseng makes brilliant cocktails with everything from champagne to espresso. The faux-Asian decor needs a fluff job, and too many hard surfaces mean high decibel levels when it fills up.

KEVA LOUNGE Map pp64-5 — Bar

☎ 334 4159; Al-Nasr Leisureland, Oud Metha;
🕑 8pm-3am

This snazzy cocktail lounge welcomes you with low-slung seating, moody lighting and sensuous red, brown and golden decor. A live DJ and a respectable menu of tasty bar nibbles make it an ideal drinking hole before hitting the dance floor of the adjoining Chi@The Lodge (p133).

NEW ASIA BAR & CLUB Map pp64-5 — Bar

☎ 324 8888; Raffles Dubai, Sheikh Rashid Rd, near Wafi Mall; 🕑 7pm-3am

A huge Egyptian head welcomes you to the circular bar where mixologists whip up over 100 cocktails, including the home-grown invention called Dubai Sling. A sophisticated crowd makes it up here to the top of the pyramid of the ultra-plush Raffles hotel,

where the views are stunning and the eye-candy factor high. If you like it quieter, whisk yourself upstairs to the never-never land of the China Moon Champagne Bar.

SHEIKH ZAYED ROAD

AGENCY Map pp70-71 — Bar

☎ 319 8088; Blvd at Jumeirah Emirates Towers, Sheikh Zayed Rd, Financial District; 🕑 noon-midnight Sun-Thu

This is a decent spot for pre-dinner unwinding, even though it's in the basement of an office tower and feels like it. If you're a woman, the first two drinks are free on Tuesdays. Also in Souq Madinat Jumeirah (see p130).

CIN CIN Map pp70-71 — Bar

☎ 311 8316; Fairmont hotel, Sheikh Zayed Rd, Financial District; 🕑 6pm-2am

You'd be hard-pressed to find a more impressive wine-and-spirits list than the one at this sleek bar, styled out with blue light, deep leather club chairs and changing-colour ice buckets. The list is dizzying, with over 400 wines – 55 by the glass – 50 vodkas and 26 Scotches. Prices skew high, but you'll find good French vintages in the Dh300 range. Shine your shoes.

HARRY GHATTO'S Map pp70-71 — Bar

☎ 319 8088; Blvd at Jumeirah Emirates Towers, Sheikh Zayed Rd, Financial District; 🕑 8pm-3am

Knock back a couple of drinks if you need to loosen your nerves before belting out your best J Lo or Justin at this beloved karaoke bar in the same tower where Sheikh Mohammed has his office. Drinks are expensive and service only so-so, but we love the odd mix of people drawn here, including the occasional dishdasha-clad local.

WHY ALCOHOL COSTS SO MUCH: THE TAX FORMULA

Alcohol costs a small fortune in Dubai because it's forbidden by Islam. Understanding the importance of booze to tourism, the municipality allows it, but slaps on a hefty haram (literally, 'forbidden') tax – in short, a sin tax. Here's the formula.

A bottle of Californian plonk that costs US$10 wholesale automatically incurs a 50% import tax, upping the importer's price to $15. Add a 33% profit for the importer, and now it costs $20. The Dubai-based purchaser (ie the hotel that sells it to the consumer) pays a 30% tax. Now it costs US$26 – at wholesale. The hotel then marks up the price 200% to make its profit and pay its employees. Now it costs about $75. At the moment of sale, the public pays an additional 20%, jacking up the final retail price to a whopping $90.

Prices aren't going to come down any time soon: a duopoly controls all the alcohol sales in Dubai. If drinking is important to you, buy your alcohol at Dubai Duty Free before leaving the airport. Otherwise, you may get the jitters when you see your bar bill.

LONG'S BAR Map pp70-71   Bar

☎ 312 2202; Tower Rotana Hotel, Sheikh Zayed Rd, Financial District; ☽ noon-3am
The longest bar in the Middle East, live bands, cheap drinks and a late closure keep this American-style bar-and-grill hoppin'. Happy hour runs from noon to 8pm.

NEOS Map pp70-71   Bar

☎ 436 8927; Address Downtown Dubai, Emaar Blvd, Downtown Dubai; ☽ 6pm-2am
At this glamour vixen, you can swirl your cosmo with the posh set 63 floors above the Dubai Fountain. It takes two lifts to get to what is currently the highest bar in town, an urban den of shiny metal, carpeted floors and killer views. The dress code has relaxed a lot since opening: we even spotted sneaker-wearers – yikes!

SCARLETT'S Map pp70-71   Bar

☎ 319 8088; Jumeirah Emirates Towers hotel, Sheikh Zayed Rd, Financial District; ☽ noon-3am
The fact that the number of free drinks women can score on ladies' night is determined by the height of their heels should tell you something about this raucous American-style booze joint. High flirt factor, cheap bar food and loud DJ music fuel the fun.

VU'S BAR Map pp70-71   Bar

☎ 319 8088; Jumeirah Emirates Towers hotel, Sheikh Zayed Rd, Financial District; ☽ 6pm-3am
Until Neos opened, Vu's was *the* Dubai bar with a view. The panorama from the 51st floor is still breathtaking, but the soft red-and-black-leather chairs feel dated and are now filled largely with a moneyed salt-and-pepper crowd grateful for the dim lighting. Still, not a bad spot for cocktails and quiet conversation. Look sharp.

CALABAR Map pp70-71   Bar & Outdoor Lounge

☎ 436 8888; ground fl, Address Downtown Dubai, Emaar Blvd, Downtown Dubai; ☽ 6pm-2am
You'll have plenty of time to study the space-age Burj Khalifa, the eye-candy crowd and the sexy outdoor lounge setting while you're waiting…and waiting… for your pricey but potent cocktail at this Latino-themed bar. A winner the moment it opened, it's the kind of place that may very well stay cool long after it's done being hot.

HIVE Map pp70-71   Bar & Outdoor Lounge

☎ 425 2296; Souk al-Bahar, Downtown Dubai; ☽ 10am-late
Beyond the snooty door-staff awaits this good-looking party den where local and visiting lovelies heat up the dance floor or drape themselves into brown leather sofas on the terrace. Alas, there's no view of the Dubai Fountain. Special deals – ladies' night Tuesday, two-for-one-pizza Sunday – help draw in the punters nightly.

IKANDY Map pp70-71   Outdoor Lounge

☎ 343 8888; Shangri-La hotel, Sheikh Zayed Rd, Downtown Dubai; ☽ 6pm-2am Oct-Mar
Wear white to Ikandy and your clothes will glow in the diffuse hot-pink light reflecting off the diaphanous fabric hanging from the palm trees. The vibe is chill, almost mellow, helped along by the rooftop poolside setting, the ambient sounds and the inventive cocktails (try the Thai martini made with lemongrass and basil). Stellar views of the Burj Khalifa.

DOUBLE DECKER Map pp70-71   Pub

☎ 321 1111; Al-Murooj Rotana Hotel, Al-Saffa St, Downtown Dubai; ☽ noon-3am
You'll feel quite Piccadilly at this boozy, boisterous bi-level pub decked out in a London transport theme. Drinks promotions, quiz nights, English premiership football and better-than-average (by far) pub grub bring in the expat brat pack.

FIBBER MAGEE'S Map pp70-71   Pub

☎ 332 2400; behind Crowne Plaza Hotel, Sheikh Zayed Rd, Financial District; ☽ 7pm-3am
This scruffy boozer isn't about seeing and being seen – quite frankly, it's a bit too dark for that. It's Dubai's most authentic Irish pub, with great ales, stouts and fat fish and chips to sop it all up. Tuesday is quiz night (arrive by 8pm). Great fun on match nights.

NEZESAUSSI Map pp70-71   Pub

☎ 428 5888; Al-Manzil Hotel, Burj Khalifa Blvd, Downtown Dubai; ☽ 6pm-2am Sun-Thu, noon-2am Fri & Sat
Throw back pints with your mates at this high-end sports bar with wall-to-wall TVs and great food. The name is an amalgam of New Zealand, South Africa and Australia, and the bar snacks selection plays on those countries' classics. Standouts include

top picks

VIEW BARS

- Bar 44 (opposite)
- BiCE Sky Bar (opposite)
- Koubba (p135)
- Neos (p129)
- New Asia Bar & Club (p128)
- Skyview Bar (below)
- Vu's Bar (p129)

ostrich meatballs, *boerewors* (spicy sausage) and grilled New Zealand lamb. The rugby-ball-shaped bar is surrounded by sports paraphernalia donated by famous players. No smoking.

JUMEIRAH

AGENCY Map pp76-7   Bar
☎ 366 6320; Souq Madinat Jumeirah, Al-Sufouh Rd, Umm Suqeim 3; ☺ noon-1am

A convivial wine bar frequented by khaki-clad tourists and expats, Agency is a civilised spot for a predinner drink. As at its sister branch at Jumeirah Emirates Towers (p128), the wine list includes unusual varietals (skip the New World wines in favour of better French labels), but here there's a terrace overlooking the Madinat canals and with glimpses of the Burj al-Arab. Satisfying bar snacks include cheese fondue with truffle oil, and finger foods such as fried calamari. Good luck snagging a table at peak times.

BAHRI BAR Map pp76-7   Bar
☎ 366 6730; Mina A'Salam, Madinat Jumeirah, Umm Suqeim 3; ☺ 4pm-2am Sat-Wed, to 3am Thu & Fri

A great choice in winter, Bahri has a fabulous verandah laid with Persian carpets and big cane sofas where you can take in gorgeous views of the Burj al-Arab. The vibe is very grown-up – just the kind of place you take your parents for sunset drinks. For a fun treat, order the camel-milk mocktail. Live music after 9.30pm.

LEFT BANK Map pp76-7   Bar
☎ 368 6171; Souq Madinat Jumeirah, Al-Sufouh Rd, Umm Suqeim 3; ☺ noon-2am

We love the waterside tables, with *abras* (water taxis) floating past, but the real party is inside the dark bar, where moody lighting, giant mirrors, leather club chairs and chill beats create a dynamic lounge scene. Put your name on the list for a table; expect to wait. The food's all right but the mini-portions and high prices are not. Also in Souk al-Bahar (p72).

MALECON Map pp76-7   Bar
☎ 346 1111; Dubai Marine Beach Resort & Spa, Jumeirah Rd, Jumeirah 1; ☺ 7pm-3am

Tequila is the essential drink at Malecon, an important stopover for the party crowd. Tipping its hat to Havana's graffiti-walled Bodeguita del Medio, this Latino-inspired bar is the place to hit late, do shots and twirl with a Cuban heel. Look sharp; though unpretentious, the crowd appreciates nice gear.

SKYVIEW BAR Map pp76-7   Bar
☎ 301 7600; Burj al-Arab, off Jumeirah Rd, Umm Suqeim 3; ☺ noon-2am

Despite the stratospheric tab, cocktails (Dh275 minimum) or afternoon tea (Dh395) on the 27th floor of the Burj al-Arab ranks high on tourists' must-do lists. And with good reason: the views are simply breathtaking – you can even make out the islands of The World in the hazy distance. Do arrive before sunset or don't bother. And *do* book ahead. As for the Liberace-meets-*Star Trek* interiors, all we can say is, welcome to the Burj. Also see p79 and p161.

BARZAR Map pp76-7   Bar & Outdoor Lounge
☎ 366 6730; Souq Madinat Jumeirah, Al-Sufouh Rd, Umm Suqeim 3; ☺ 5pm-2am Sat-Wed, 5pm-3am Thu, 4pm-3am Fri

Barzar is a bit of a pick-up joint, but it's good for preclub cocktails. Skip the glorified sports bar upstairs and report straight to the waterfront terrace to sip cold beers and killer cosmos while lolling in a bean-bag chair. There are different promotions nightly and sometimes you can eavesdrop on entertainment in the adjacent Madinat Amphitheatre (p135).

360° Map pp76-7   Outdoor Lounge
☎ 406 8769; Jumeirah Beach Hotel, Jumeirah Rd, Umm Suqeim 3; ☺ 5pm-2am Sun-Thu, 4pm-2am Fri & Sat

Capping a long, curved pier, 360° delivers magical views of the Burj al-Arab, especially when the sun slips seaward. At weekends there's a guest list, burly bouncers, top-notch DJs and lots of shiny happy souls. Expect s-l-o-w bar service – don't come thirsty. Other nights are more mellow.

ROOFTOP AT SOUQ MADINAT
Map pp76-7   Outdoor Lounge

☎ 366 6730; Souq Madinat Jumeirah, Al-Sufouh Rd, Umm Suqeim 3; ⏰ 7pm-2am Tue, Wed & Sat, 7pm-3am Thu & Fri

Not to be confused with the Rooftop Bar at the One&Only Royal Mirage (p132), this alfresco party pen has killer views of the Burj al-Arab, and canopied day beds for lounging. On Thursday nights, the guys of Ohm Records (see p96) bring in top international DJs (cover Dh100, women free before 11pm).

SHO CHO Map pp76-7   Outdoor Lounge

☎ 346 1111; Dubai Marine Beach Resort & Spa, Jumeirah Rd, Jumeirah 1; ⏰ 7pm-3am

The cool minimalist interior, with its blue lights and wall-mounted fish tanks, may draw you in, but the beachside deck is the place to be. Take in the laid-back vibe as the cool ocean breezes blow and the DJ's soundtrack competes with the crashing waves.

NEW DUBAI

1897 Map pp82-3   Bar

☎ 341 0000; Kempinski Hotel, Mall of the Emirates, Al-Barsha; ⏰ 2pm-2am

Channel your inner Cary Grant and belly up to the bar at this grown-up, mood-lit thirst parlour at the Kempinksi. Don't bother if you're the beery type – you'd be wasting the bar staff's considerable talents. Decorated in plush purple and polished wood, this place lures chatty sophisticates huddled in intense tête-à-têtes and grateful for the low sound levels. Smoking, including cigars, is OK.

BAR 44 Map pp82-3   Bar

☎ 399 8888; Grosvenor House, Al-Sufouh Rd, Dubai Marina; ⏰ 6pm-2am

Service is slow, cocktails are wimpy and prices are high, but the views – oh, the views – really are worth the trip up to this swank bar on the 44th floor of the Grosvenor House hotel. Done in a retro-1970s chic, with high-backed tufted-velvet banquettes and buttery-soft leather tub chairs, this is the spot to kick up your (high) heels

and take in the sweeping panorama of the marina and Palm Jumeirah. Good backup if Buddha Bar is full. Live blues and jazz.

BLENDS Map pp82-3   Bar

☎ 436 7777; Address Dubai Marina Mall, Dubai Marina; ⏰ 5pm-2am Sat-Wed, 5pm-3am Thu, 3pm-3am Fri

The name is very apropos because Blends indeed folds three distinct libation stations into its 4th-floor space. Channel Ernest Hemingway in the clubby cigar room, complete with requisite leather sofa, dark woods and a coffered ceiling. For date night, the sultry, candlelit champagne bar with its floor-to-ceiling windows provides a suitable setting for quiet conversation. And finally, there's the trendy cocktail lounge for socialising with your best buddies over beers and mojitos.

BICE SKY BAR Map pp82-3   Bar

☎ 399 1111; Hilton Dubai Jumeirah, The Walk at JBR, Dubai Marina; ⏰ 6.15pm-2.30am

It may not be as much on the hipster radar as Neos or Bar 44, but when it comes to glorious views this quiet, chic lounge on the 10th floor of the ho-hum beachfront Hilton can definitely compete. In this case, it's the sparkling Palm Jumeirah and glistening Gulf waters that will make you want to order that second cocktail. Soft piano music and comfy leather chairs help create a relaxed, romantic mood.

BUDDHA BAR Map pp82-3   Bar

☎ 399 8888; Grosvenor House, Al-Sufouh Rd, Dubai Marina; ⏰ 8pm-2am Sat-Wed, 8pm-3am Thu & Fri

If there are celebs in town, they'll show up at Buddha Bar, where the dramatic Asian-inspired interiors are decked out with gorgeous chandeliers, a wall of reflective sheer glass, and an enormous Buddha lording over the heathens. The bartenders put on quite a show with their impressive shakes (think Tom Cruise in Cocktail). Arrive early or prepare to queue; otherwise book dinner for guaranteed admission. Also see p121.

LIBRARY BAR Map pp82-3   Bar

☎ 399 4000; Ritz-Carlton Hotel, The Walk at JBR, Dubai Marina; ⏰ 3pm-1.30am

This hushed and elegant bar feels like a retreat from Dubai's in-your-face modernity. Polished wood, leather sofas and rich carpets combine to create an ambience of timeless sophistication. The bar menu has some interesting nibbles, but this is really more the kind of place to steer your luxury sedan for a postprandial Glenfiddich and Cuban cigar.

BARASTI BAR Map pp82-3   Outdoor Lounge
☎ 399 3333; Le Meridien Mina Seyahi Beach Resort & Marina, Al-Sufouh Rd, Al-Sufouh; ⏰ 11am-2am
Seaside Barasti is the locals' (especially expat Brits) fave for laid-back sundowners. No need to dress up – you can head straight here after a day at the beach – but don't come unless you like crowds: at weekends, 4000 or more shiny happy people invade. DJs play indoors, but it's generally better to sit outside within earshot of the sea. The pub-style food is pretty good and Friday brunch (Dh295, including alcohol) is popular.

MAYA Map pp82-3   Outdoor Lounge
☎ 316 5550; Le Royal Meridien Beach Resort & Spa, Murjan Ave & Dhow St, off Al-Sufouh Rd, Dubai Marina; ⏰ 6pm-2am Mon-Sat
Arrive an hour before sunset to snag one of the Gulf-view tables on the rooftop bar of this upmarket Mexican resto at the Royal Meridien and swill top-shelf margaritas as the sun slowly slips into the sea. A plate of succulent duck enchiladas is the perfect booze antidote.

NASIMI BEACH Map pp82-3   Outdoor Lounge
☎ 426 0000; Atlantis – The Palm, Palm Jumeirah; ⏰ 1pm-1am
The Atlantis' spin on Barasti draws a more upmarket crowd to its fantastic beachside setting. Plop down on a beach bag and chill to soulful house, funk, electro and Chicago house. Friday nights, when international DJs hit the decks, are buzziest. On occasion, Nasimi also functions as a satellite club for Hed Kandi or Defected in the House label parties.

ROOFTOP BAR Map pp82-3   Outdoor Lounge
☎ 399 9999; Arabian Court, One&Only Royal Mirage, Al-Sufouh Rd, Al-Sufouh; ⏰ 5pm-1am
The fabric-draped nooks, cushioned banquettes, Moroccan lanterns and Oriental carpets make this candlelit rooftop bar one of Dubai's most sublime spots. Come at sunset to watch the sky change colour – but not earlier; the bar doesn't pick up until evening. There's a good menu of

mezzes (appetisers), in case you're feeling peckish. Views of the Palm Jumeirah, and the romantic vibe, make this an ideal spot for couples.

NIGHTLIFE

Dubai locals sure know how to party and you better pack some stamina if you want to join them. Hit the dance floor any day of the week, groove to homegrown bands or go mellow in a *sheesha* cafe.

CLUBBING

Clubbers come out in force when big-name DJs like Pierre Ravan, Roger Sanchez and Joey Negro jet in for the weekend, but even on a regular old Tuesday, you can find ardent club kids grooving beneath disco balls to house music, the preferred sound in Dubai. Thursday and Friday are the big nights out, when marauding expats join gyrating tourists on the dance floor. The scene remains segregated: not only are Dubai's clubs rife with racism (see p31), but cliques of club-goers keep to themselves – so don't go out expecting to meet new friends at a Dubai club. The scene starts late – around 1am – just two hours before clubs are required to close, and queues are sometimes preposterous. It's best to arrive early to snag seats and load up on drinks before it gets busy, then hit the dance floor when others arrive.

Dubai's dance floors reveal engrossing sociological studies and vignettes. The city's population is made up of well over 100 different nationalities, and everyone grooves differently. The Lebanese are the reigning kings of the club world. Some Western expatriates look down on them, tackily whispering things like 'That guy is such a Lebanese poser'. But damn, do they dress sharp and dance hard! Others don't move at all, endlessly looking for something to look for, frozen at the edge of the parquet floor, mobile phone in hand, desperately texting potential partners. Most people meander on and off the floor, some featuring their outfits, others their moves.

Cover charges range from Dh50 to Dh300, depending on whether there's a big-name DJ spinning; call ahead. Groups of men aren't always allowed admission on busy nights. For up-to-date details on what's happening in the club world, check out www .mumtazz.com, www.platinumlist.ae, www .timeoutdubai.com and promoters' sites such as iLL Communication (www.ohmrecords.com). And not to be alarmist, but many clubs have terrible emergency-exit signage. Spot the ways out on your way in.

ALPHA Map pp54-5

☎ 702 2640; Le Meridien Dubai; Airport Rd, Al-Garhoud, near Deira; ☿ 6pm-3am Sat-Thu, 4pm-3am Fri

Rebooted from a restaurant, Alpha may be comparatively small but it looms large on the Dubai party circuit. There's a pleasant low-key vibe to the bi-level space, with a downstairs dance floor and a cushy upstairs lounge. The crowd defines the word 'eclectic' and so does the line-up, with everything from local bands to prominent DJs playing house and techno bringing in the punters.

APARTMENT Map pp76-7

☎ 406 8000; ground fl, Jumeirah Beach Hotel, Jumeirah Rd, Umm Suqeim 3; ☿ 9pm-3am Mon-Fri

Another entry in Dubai's growing cadre of club lounges, this one has a beautifully calibrated seductive feel with fiery mood lighting and low-slung couches with gold and copper accents. There's a lot of SM (standing and modelling, that is) going on, but once past the tough bouncer you too can be part of the beautiful crowd.

BOUDOIR Map pp76-7

☎ 345 5995; Dubai Marine Beach Resort & Spa, Jumeirah Rd, Jumeirah 1; ☿ 7.30pm-3am

Though snooty expats distance themselves from the Lebanese crowd at Boudoir, we love the look of the place. Tufted red-velvet booths, beaded curtains and tasselled draperies lend a super-model vibe – indeed, you may spot one among the wannabes – and the circular layout is perfect for twirling away from the occasional unwanted advance by a Lothario. High on the chic-o-meter. Look sharp or be ostracised.

CAVALLI CLUB Map pp70-71

☎ 332 9260 or 050 856 6044; Fairmont Hotel, Sheikh Zayed Rd; ☿ 7pm-2am

Recession? Did anybody say recession? Not Roberto Cavalli, Italian fashion designer of over-the-top glam, rock, animal print, uberbling fame. And now he's got his own nightclub where the rich and beautiful keep the Champagne flowing like it's still 1999 amid a virtual Aladdin's cave of black quartz and Swarovski crystals. Girls, wear your little black dress or risk feeling frumpy. Boys, shine your shoes. Enter from the back of the hotel.

CHI@THE LODGE Map pp64-5

☎ 337 9470; 2A St, next to Al-Nasr Leisureland, Oud Metha, Bur Dubai; ☿ 8pm-3am

The shiny-shiny fave of young expats, Chi sometimes hosts live music, but the big draws are its kick-ass DJs playing funk, house, disco, drum & bass and whatever else inspires. Four big spaces, including a Balinese-themed outdoor garden, mean that if your legs need a break, you can chill in a cushioned lounge or VIP cabana. Arrive early to beat the queue.

JULES BAR Map pp54-5

☎ 702 2332; Le Meridien Dubai, Al-Garhoud, near Deira; cover incl 1 drink Tue, Wed, Fri & Sat Dh50, incl 2 drinks Thu Dh100; ☿ 11am-3am

The six-piece Filipino house band kicks, twirls and belts out Top-40 hits, while an odd mix of oil workers, Southeast Asians and European flight crews (especially on Fridays) grind shoulder-to-shoulder on the floor. Beer's a bargain on Sunday's Corona Beach Party, and on Tuesdays women get admission and one drink for free. If you need nibbles, there's a decent Mexican menu. Dig those charcoal portraits of Whitney and Mariah.

KASBAR Map pp82-3

☎ 399 9999; One&Only Royal Mirage, Al-Sufouh Rd, Al-Sufouh; nonguests Dh60, hotel guests free; ☿ 9.30pm-3am Mon-Sat

Kasbar can be inconsistent – one night it's packed, the next it's dead – but we highly recommend you check out this sexy three-storey Moroccan-themed club with glittering crystal chandeliers, a coffered ceiling and big dance floor. Call ahead to reserve a table on the mezzanine where you can take in the scene from above. Or forego the thump-thump in favour of a game of billiards on the quiet lower floor – a godsend for non-dancers whose dates want to twirl. When there's Arabian-fusion playing on the decks, don't miss it. Cover includes one drink.

SANCTUARY Map pp82-3

☎ 426 0561; Atlantis – The Palm, Palm Jumeirah; ☿ 9pm-3am

At this mega-'meet'-market, some of the world's top DJs whip mostly wrinkle-free, hormone-happy dancers into a frenzy with electronica, house and dance music. Brought to you by the folks behind Buddha Bar (p131), the decor is suitably dramatic: a sunken dance floor, suspended circular catwalk and VIP retreats. Pack attitude and credit cards. Thursday is buzziest.

SUBMARINE Map pp62-3
☎ 359 9992; Dhow Palace Hotel, Mankhool Rd, Bur Dubai; ◷ 6pm-3am
Dive into the basement of this ho-hum hotel to arrive at a compact, industrial bar popular with a refreshingly unpretentious, omnisexual crowd. There's often a band to kick things into gear, along with DJs that shower beat junkies with a heady mix of deep house to trance, funk to R&B.

ZINC Map pp70-71
☎ 331 1111; Crowne Plaza Hotel, Sheikh Zayed Rd, Financial District; ◷ 10pm-3am
This reliable standby has a killer sound system and plays R&B, popular tunes and house for a crowd that likes to have fun without the pretence, including lots of cabin crew. Though some uppity expats call it trashy, Zinc is good because people don't seem to care who you are; they're here to dance and drink, not show off. Bar service is quick – well, for Dubai. Men pay cover, women don't.

LIVE MUSIC

Dubai's live-music scene is finally generating a buzz. Although cover bands still predominate, there's an increasing pool of local talent hitting the stages of such venues as Alpha, Chi@ The Lodge, Barasti and the Irish Village in addition to those listed below. Homegrown bands to keep an ear out for include metal band Nervecell, the hip hop collective The Recipe, the Arabic folk trio Dahab, hard rock band Nikotin, and reggae rock by Sho?.

International top talent also comes to town, although many bypass Dubai to give concerts at the ultra-swank Emirates Palace in Abu Dhabi. Still, it was Sting, Carlos Santana and Elton John who gave the inaugural concerts at the Meydan Racecourse (p148) in early 2010. Other venues that have hosted big stars like Robbie Williams and Kanye West include the Dubai Autodrome (p149) and Dubai Festival City (p104).

In recent years, music festivals such as Liverpool import Dubai Sound City, which came to town in late 2009, have energised the local scene by bringing in indie bands from the UK, Germany and other countries, as well as by offering a showcase for local musicians. It's anybody's guess if there'll be a repeat performance in coming years, especially now that other big festivals like Dubai Desert Rock Festival and Desert Rhythm have been 'postponed until further notice'.

Meanwhile, you might also want to keep an eye out for Middle Eastern and subcontinental stars. When you see big posters and hear multiple radio ads for acts you're unfamiliar with, do a quick Google search to find out where they're from. There's a reason they're so popular. You'd be amazed by some of the acts that draw big crowds of expat locals – Lebanese, Indian, Pakistani, Persian. This is the stuff you can't hear back home. Check *Time Out* and *7 Days* magazines, as well as the ticket hotlines (p127).

BLUE BAR Map pp70-71
☎ 332 0000; Novotel World Trade Centre, Sheikh Zayed Rd; ◷ 2pm-2am
Cool cats of all ages gather in this relaxed joint for some of the finest live jazz and blues in town. It's tucked away in a ho-hum business hotel but once inside, all is forgiven. The mostly local talent starts performing at 10pm (Wednesday to Friday only), so get there early to snag a table and quaff a cold one from the standout selection of Belgian draught beers. When there's no band, it's just another bar.

FRIDGE off Map pp82-3
☎ 347 7793; 26 St, near Al-Rasaas Rd, Umm Suqeim 3
Music promoter the Fridge also presents the occasional concert in its funky warehouse venue in the industrial Al-Quoz district. It's big on local talent who are still below the radar, and features a super-eclectic line-up that may include a Japanese shakuhachi flute player, a dancing harpist or a Brazilian guitarist. Check *Time Out* for upcoming performances.

JAMBASE Map pp76-7
☎ 366 6730; Souq Madinat Jumeirah, Al-Sufouh Rd, Umm Suqeim 3; ◷ 7pm-2am Mon-Sat
If you enjoy dining, drinking and dancing without changing location, this moody basement supper club should fit the bill.

The ambience gets increasingly lively as blood alcohol levels rise and the band moves on from mellow jazz to soul, R&B, Motown and other high-energy sounds. The food's continental (think prime rib, roast chicken, mains Dh90 to Dh160) and solid if nothing out of the ordinary.

MADINAT AMPHITHEATRE Map pp76-7
☎ 366 6380; Souq Madinat Jumeirah, Al-Sufouh Rd, Umm Suqeim 3
This lovely outdoor stage, backed by a lagoon with views of the Burj al-Arab, is a romantic spot for a variety of concerts, from smooth jazz to chill-out festivals and oud players.

PEANUT BUTTER JAM Map pp64-5
☎ 324 4100; Wafi Mall, Al-Qataiyat Rd, Bur Dubai; ☽ 8pm-midnight Fri Oct-May
You never know what you're going to hear at PBJ. Sink into a beanbag in the rooftop gardens of Wafi Mall and munch on barbecued goodies while you take in the night's acts. Much of it is amateurish – a couple of steps up from karaoke – but you may be surprised.

ROCK BOTTOM CAFÉ Map pp64-5
☎ 396 3888; Regent Palace Hotel, Sheikh Khalifa bin Zayed Rd, Bur Dubai; ☽ noon-3am
Bask in the vintage vibe of this '70s-era American roadhouse, while a cheesy cover band blares Top-40 hits. While it's a regular pub by day, no self-respecting woman would come here alone at night. But with a mob of friends and a bottle of tequila gone, it's the quintessential ending to a rollickin' night on the town.

SHEESHA CAFES

Dubai's *sheesha* cafes give great insight into local culture. Even if you don't smoke, it's worth reclining languorously and sampling a puff to better understand this traditional Middle Eastern pastime; for more details, see p136. *Sheesha* cafes are open till after midnight, later during winter months. The going rate is Dh20 to Dh60 for all you can inhale.

KOUBBA Map pp76-7
☎ 366 6730; Al-Qasr Hotel, Souq Madinat Jumeirah, Al-Sufouh Rd, Umm Suqeim 3; ☽ 6pm-2am
Score a candlelit table on the terrace overlooking the Madinat canals and illuminated

Burj, and you'll instantly know you've found one of the most tranquil and romantic spots in all Dubai. The interior is nearly as compelling, with plush red velvet and Oriental cushions for you to lie against as you chill out to live Arabian-lounge music. Too bad it's illegal to lock lips in public.

QD'S Map pp54-5
☎ 295 6000; Dubai Creek Golf & Yacht Club, Deira; ☽ 6pm-2am Sep-May
Watch the ballet of lighted dhows (traditional wooden boats) floating by while sipping cosmos at this always-fun outdoor Creekside lounge shaped like a giant circle. The main action is on the (very public) raised centre ring, where Oriental carpets and cushions set an inviting mood. For privacy, retreat to the vast wooden deck jutting over the water, or book a cabana. Great for *sheesha*, but skip the food.

SHEESHA COURTYARD Map pp82-3
☎ 399 9999; One&Only Royal Mirage, Al-Sufouh Rd, Al-Sufouh; ☽ 7pm-1am
The Royal Mirage sure gets it right. Reclining on beaded cushions and thick carpets in an Arabian palm courtyard is the ultimate way to enjoy a *sheesha*. Though it would take a connoisseur to appreciate the 20 different flavours on offer, you can't go wrong with the sweet aroma of apple. Highly recommended.

SHAKESPEARE & COMPANY
Map pp70-71
☎ 331 1757; opposite KFC, just behind Sheikh Zayed Rd in Al-Attar Tower; ☽ 7am-1am
Linger long and puff *sheesha* under a big outdoor tent at this woman- and child-friendly hangout with mismatched velvet sofas, wicker chairs and big wooden tables. Perfect for a game of backgammon. The Lebanese–French menu is good for a nosh between smokes – think *croque-monsieur*, crêpes and pizzas, all around Dh30. Good breakfasts, too.

TCHÉ TCHÉ Map pp82-3
☎ 437 6456; The Walk at JBR, plaza level, Sadaf Tower 4, opp Ritz-Carlton Hotel, Dubai Marina; ☽ 9am-midnight
This Jordanian import is a vaunted haunt of both locals and expats, who come to pick their favourite smoke from the long *sheesha* menu while Arabic music videos

SHEESHA: A PRIMER

Sheesha pipes are packed with flavoured tobacco, such as apple, anise, strawberry, vanilla and coffee – the range of flavours is endless. Good *sheesha* cafes, like good wine bars, pride themselves on the variety they offer.

The *sheesha* pipes used in Dubai are similar to those found in Lebanon and Egypt and are available in the souqs, speciality shops and even some supermarkets. If, like many visitors to Dubai, you decide to take one home as a souvenir and forget the instructions the shopkeeper gave you, here's a primer on how to use one:

- First, fill the glass bowl with water and fix the metal turret into it, ensuring that the tube is underwater with the rubber stopper holding it in position.
- Next, return the metal plate to the top of the turret and put your small ceramic or clay bowl on top of it.
- Fill the bowl with some loose *sheesha* tobacco and cover it tightly with a small piece of foil, before poking about five holes into it with a skewer or fork.
- Using tongs, heat up some Magic Coal on a stove or a hotplate or over a gas burner, then pop it on top of the foil. (Magic Coal is the preferred brand of charcoal because it burns the longest. It's from Japan and comes in a black box. Check the souqs.)
- Lastly, place the pipe into the hole on the side of the *sheesha* pipe, pop a disposable plastic mouthpiece on the end if you're planning to share, and take a long hard puff on the pipe. Recline on the Oriental cushions you bought at the souqs and remember your time in Dubai.

are blaring in the background. Also gets thumbs up for its delicious Arabic food.

ZYARA Map pp70-71

☎ 343 5454; Union Tower, behind National Bank of Abu Dhabi, Sheikh Zayed Rd, Financial District; ⏱ 8am-1am

Puff in the shadow of giant skyscrapers at this convivial bo-ho-cool Lebanese cafe. The colourful dollhouse-like interior is great for booze-free socialising over a game of cards or backgammon. The *sheesha* is presented outdoors, where you sit at living-room-like clusters of cushy sofas on a palm-lined patio while gazing up at the impossibly tall towers.

THE ARTS

Dubai's performing arts scene is still in its infancy, but there are some new venues that give hope for an increasingly bright future.

FILM

The first thing you need to know about movie-going in Dubai is that locals don't view the cinema as a cultural institution but as a social scene. At mainstream cinemas, kids run up and down the aisles while adults talk on their mobile phones. It's excruciating. In response, some of the multiplexes now have ultra-cushy small screening rooms for over 18s only.

The Dubai International Film Festival (p42), usually held in December, is arguably the cinegraphic highlight of the year. The other 51 weeks of the calendar can be disheartening The only independent cinemas are dedicate to Tamil, Hindi and Malayalam films, while English-language films are restricted to the unadventurous multiplexes. Occasionally, a good film manages to sneak its way onto the schedules alongside the endless action movies, horror flicks and romantic comedies, but most of the time it's all too predictable. The festival's success suggests there's a market for independent and world film, a gap that's only modestly filled by the Picturehouse at Ree Cinemas in Dubai Mall (see opposite), which calls itself the United Arab Emirates' (UAE's) first art-house cinema.

In the absence of quality programming at the multiplexes, art galleries such as Third Line (p73), XVA Gallery (p61) and Art Sawa (Map pp70-71; ☎ 340 8660; www.artsawa.com; Rd 323, Al-Quoz occasionally hold film screenings. There's also Mahmovies!, an eclectic public film series sponsored by local filmmaker Mahmoud Kaabour and held twice annually at the JamJar (p73), usually for five weeks in January and October. There's no website but if you Google 'Mahmovies!' you should find all the info you need. Also check out the Alliance Française (Map pp64-5; ☎ 335 8712), which shows weekly films in French and occasionally hosts festivals. Indie screenings are usually free and promoted in *Time Out*. Another good site to unearth upcoming screenings is www.artinthecity.com.

For pure fluff value and a glimpse of local culture, consider taking in a Bollywood film instead – really, how often do you get the chance? They're pure spectacle, packed with melodrama, romance and action, and punc tuated by song and dance numbers. Plots are hardly complicated, so you'll be able to get the gist if the films aren't subtitled. If you're not up for Hindi, look for free outdoor movie nights (right), a big draw for European expats.

CINESTAR MALL OF THE EMIRATES
Map pp82-3

☎ 341 4222; www.cinestarcinemas.com; Mall of the Emirates, Sheikh Zayed Rd, Al-Barsha; tickets Dh30, Gold Class Dh110

Cinestar would be just another multiplex were it not for its Gold Class screening rooms, where seats are enormous recliners and servers bring you blankets, popcorn in silver bowls and drinks in glass goblets. This is adult movie watching: no one under 18 years old is allowed and everyone actually pays attention to the film. Reservations essential.

REEL CINEMAS Map pp70-71

☎ 449 1988; www.reelcinemas.ae; 2nd fl, Dubai Mall, Downtown Dubai; tickets Dh30, 3D films Dh40

Pre-assigned seats, THX sound and a staggering 22 screens make Reel one of the top flick magnets in town. The fare is mostly Hollywood blockbusters, except in the Picturehouse, purportedly the UAE's first dedicated art-house cinema. If you don't want to sit with the hoi polloi, shell out Dh110 for a reclining leather chair in a 32-seat Platinum Movie Suite.

PERFORMING ARTS

DUBAI COMMUNITY THEATRE & ARTS CENTRE Map pp82-3

☎ 341 4777; www.ductac.org; 2nd fl, Mall of the Emirates, Sheikh Zayed Rd, Al-Barsha

DUCTAC, as it's known, is a thriving performance venue at the Mall of the Emirates that puts on all sorts of diversions, from classical concerts to Bollywood retrospectives, Arabic folklore to large-scale mural projects. Much support is given to Emirati talent, making this a good place to plug into the local scene. The entrance is in the Orange Car Park, between rows S and T.

ALFRESCO FLICKS

Dubaians love their movies and their fine weather, so it's only logical to combine the two. Screenings under the stars have become a popular tradition, with classic and contemporary flicks spooling off in various locations around town. Come early to stake out a good spot.

Movies Under the Stars (Map pp64-5; ☎ 324 4100; Rooftop Gardens, Wafi Mall, Al-Qataiyat Rd, Bur Dubai; admission free; ⏰ 8pm & 10pm Sun Oct-May) Settle into a beanbag on a balmy winter's night with a bucket of beers and watch a themed double feature of vintage-modern films. Even if you don't appreciate, say, Tom Cruise night, it's hard to argue when admission is free.

Cine-Splash! (Map p50; ☎ 361 8111; www .poloclubdubai.com; Dubai Polo & Equestrian Club; admission Dh35; ⏰ 7pm & 9.30pm Thu) Weekly outdoor movie screenings at the club's pool bar where you can watch the flick floating in an inflatable pool chair. A kiddie movie is followed by more grown-up fare. Snacks and drinks are available.

FIRST GROUP THEATRE AT MADINAT
Map pp76-7

☎ 366 6546; www.madinattheatre.com; Souq Madinat Jumeirah, Al-Sufouh Rd, Umm Suqeim 3

An eclectic program of crowd-pleasing entertainment ranging from the Russian State Ballet to Broadway musicals and comedy shows feeds the cravings of Dubai's culture-starved residents. Performances take place in a gorgeous 442-seat theatre.

PALLADIUM Map pp82-3

☎ tickets 367 6520; www.palladiumdubai.com, tickets through www.boxofficeme.com; Dubai Media City, Dubai Marina

Dubai's newest performance venue can seat up to 3000 people and comes with so many hi tech trappings it's capable of hosting all sorts of events, from musicals to concerts, operas to conferences. A recent line-up included the Twelve Tenors, the Backstreet Boys and a touring show called *Merchants of Bollywood*.

SPORTS & ACTIVITIES

top picks

SPORTS & ACTIVITIES

Before the boom, Emiratis spent their free time watching camel races, riding horses and boating. Now that expats have shown up, sports in Dubai have broadened to reflect the new population. Europeans brought golf, tennis and rugby. Cricket is huge, owing to the enormous subcontinental communities. Emiratis have a new-found fondness for the world's most popular game of football (aka soccer). Visitors generally take it easier, sticking to the Gulf's placid, bathtub-warm waters. You could spend an afternoon skittering across the surf on a kiteboard or diving in the shallow Gulf on a scuba expedition. If you can't stand the sweltering heat, there's always Ski Dubai, the ultimate expression of Dubai excess. Or you could stay indoors; as you might expect in such a land of tourism and luxury hotels, spas and fitness clubs are big business. Spectator sports provide an occasional glimpse into Emirati life or the lives of expat workers. From a lowly game of cricket played out on a sandy lot by Indian and Pakistani labourers to the grand display of sheikhs barracking for their prize thoroughbreds, sports in Dubai unite its various subcultures.

HEALTH & FITNESS

The health-and-fitness set is composed primarily of Western expats. While Emiratis grow large beneath their robes, Westerners shed the hummus at health clubs, yoga studios and fitness centres. With so many people working so hard to continue wearing their skinny jeans, there are lots of sore muscles in Dubai. Consequently, massage and beauty-treatment schedules at day spas fill up fast: book ahead. If you prefer swimming in salt water instead of chlorine, check out our listings of the city's best public and paid beaches; see boxed text, p78.

GYMS

Nearly every hotel in Dubai has a gym, but the equipment is often chosen by people who don't work out. The worst have only a few stationary bikes and a cumbersome all-in-one machine with too many cables and pulleys that constantly need adjusting. The best have a full complement of top-end circuit- and weight-training equipment, including Smith racks, cable-crossovers and Power Plates. If it really matters, call the hotel and ask to speak to the fitness-centre manager. Because labour is so cheap in Dubai, many hotels have on-site trainers to help you tighten up. Some hotels sell memberships to nonguests, effectively packing them in during after-work hours; if you don't like crowds when you work out, avoid hitting the gym in the early evening. Admission to gyms generally costs about Dh100 for a one-day pass, twice that at a top-end hotel, but you'll gain access to the resort's grounds, tennis courts and swimming pool. If

you're going to a hotel gym, get your money's worth by making a day of it.

AVIATION CLUB Map pp54-5
☎ 282 4122; www.aviationclub.ae; Dubai Tennis Stadium, Al-Garhoud Rd, Deira; day pass Dh250, not incl group fitness; ⏱ 6am-11pm
Packed after work and at weekends – and with good reason – the Aviation Club has killer body pump and spinning classes, and a big selection of weights and circuit training for a pre-cardio workout or before a lap-swim in the half-Olympic-size pool. This is where the Dubai Tennis Championships are held; the club's five tennis courts are available only by reservation.

FITNESS FIRST
☎ 800-348 6377; www.fitnessfirstme.com; day pass Dh100; ⏱ 6am-11pm
This huge global chain has eight massive branches in Dubai with state-of-the-art cardio equipment, a great line-up of classes from Body Pump and Spinning to Pilates and kick-boxing and a full complement of free weights. Some also have swimming pools and gender-segregated sauna and steam rooms. On-site trainers help you tone your muscles. Handy branches are at Dubai Festival City (Map p50), BurJuman Centre (Map pp62-3), Dubai International Financial Centre (Map pp70-71) and Ibn Battuta Mall (Map pp82-3).

GRAND HYATT GYM Map pp64-5
☎ 317 1234; www.hyatt.com; Grand Hyatt Dubai, Al-Qataiyat Rd, Oud Metha; day pass Sun-Thu Dh200, Fri & Sat Dh250; ⏱ 6am-11pm

top picks

HOTEL GYMS

- Dubai Marine Beach Resort & Spa (p162)
- Grand Hyatt Dubai (p157)
- Kempinski (p164)
- Le Meridien Mina Seyahi Beach Resort & Marina (p164)
- Le Royal Meridien Beach Resort & Spa (p163)
- Radisson Blu Hotel (p155)
- Ramada Hotel (p157)
- Address Downtown Dubai (p159)

The top-notch equipment includes Smith racks, cable-crossover racks, and full circuit-training equipment. The gym also offers aerobics, yoga and on-site trainers to guide your workout. Justify the expense by spending the afternoon inside with a treatment at the glittering spa or outside by Dubai's biggest swimming pool. Also outdoors you'll find a meandering 450m running track beneath tall palms, and four tennis courts. Kids have their own pool.

PHARAOHS CLUB Map pp64-5

☎ 324 0000; fax 324 4611; www.wafi.com; Wafi Mall, Sheikh Rashid Rd, near Oud Metha Rd; weekly membership incl pool use Dh 450, pool per day Dh100 Other than Fitness First (opposite), this is the closest you'll find to an LA-style club, with some serious weight-lifting equipment (including 100lb dumbbells) for juiced-up grunters, a climbing wall, squash courts and multiple fitness classes (some for women only) including body pump, yoga, aikido, mat Pilates and step. The best amenity is the enormous, free-form 'lazy-river' rooftop swimming pool; kids love it. One caveat: temporary memberships are a nuisance to acquire. You must set one up, via fax or in person, at least three days prior to your week's membership; passport required. Don't bother if you're not staying nearby. The pool (☽ 9am-10pm), by contrast, is open for one-day drop-ins.

YOGA & PILATES

CLUB STRETCH Map pp62-3

☎ 345 2131; www.clubstretch.ae; next to Capitol Hotel, Al-Mina Rd, Bur Dubai; Bikram yoga class Dh70, Pilates mat/equipment Dh65/100; ☽ 8.30am-8pm

Feel flexible and invigorated after a session or two in this dedicated stretching studio. If you like it hot, try Bikram, a rigorous 90-minute yoga workout in a heated studio. The one-week introductory offer with all-you-can-handle sessions for Dh100 is a bargain for hard-core yogis. Alternatively, flex, extend and twist your way to better posture on either mat or specialised equipment with Pilates taught in small groups. Reservations required for Pilates only.

GEMS OF YOGA Map pp70-71

☎ 331 5161/1328; www.gemsofyogadubai.com; 17th fl above KFC, btwn Fairmont & Crowne Plaza hotels, Sheikh Zayed Rd, Financial District; introductory class Dh75-100, unlimited weekly classes Dh350-450; ☽ 6.30am-10pm Sat-Thu, 10am-8pm Fri
These guys are serious about their yoga. There's lots of specialised programs, from Desktop Yoga for stress relief to Weight-watcher Hatha Yoga and Power Yoga (a combination of aerobics and yoga). Call ahead or check the website for schedules.

DAY SPAS & MASSAGE

Though you can get a good rub-down at most sports clubs, for the proper treatment book a dedicated spa. Dubai's spas like to incorporate food into their treatments – berries, chocolate, even gingerbread at Christmas. You may disagree with us, but we remain unconvinced of their merit; if you're dubious, stick to the tried-and-true, not the out-of-the-blue. Make reservations as far in advance as possible; for top spas such as Amara and the Oriental Hammam, book weeks ahead. Ask if a spa treatment includes use of the pool and grounds; if it does, make a day of it – arrive early and lollygag poolside. If you're considering a facial and you like to sun, book an afternoon appointment – say, 5pm – following your tanning session. If you receive the treatment in the morning, your skin will be too sensitive for sun exposure that afternoon. Note: facials look best the next day, so if you have a fancy dinner engagement and want to look great, get the treatment the day before. Most spas offer manicures and pedicures, but if you want a dedicated nail salon, try Nail Spa; there are branches at Mercato Mall (Map pp76-7; ☎ 349 7766; Jumeirah), Aviation Club (Map pp54-5; ☎ 282 1617; Al-Garhoud) and Ibn Battuta Mall (Map pp82-3; ☎ 368 5070). All three branches are open from 9am to 9pm Saturday to Thursday and 10am to 9pm Friday.

1847 Map pp70-71

☎ 330 1847; Blvd at Jumeirah Emirates Towers, Sheikh Zayed Rd, Financial District; ⏰ 9am-9pm Sat-Thu, 1-9pm Fri

Men: if you're lucky enough to be able to grow a good-looking beard, we highly recommend you do so while in Dubai. Locals will approve and be ever-so-slightly more accepting of you. However, many expats prefer to keep a hairless visage; the dandies among them indulge in an old-fashioned straight-razor shave – complete with hot towels beforehand – at the clubby men-only 'grooming salon' 1847. Ask about packages, including mani-pedis and massages. Good haircuts, too. There's another branch at the Grosvenor House hotel (p165) in Dubai Marina.

AMARA Map pp54-5

☎ 602 1234; www.dubai.park.hyatt.com; Park Hyatt Dubai, next to Dubai Creek Golf & Yacht Club, Deira

Dubai's top spa at the Park Hyatt has eight treatment suites, including three for couples, all with their own private walled gardens complete with outdoor rain showers. Choose your own background music, then lean back for a luxurious foot bath followed by your selected treatment. Tempting ones, especially if you just got off the plane, include the two-hour Diamond Ceremony (Dh750), where you'll be pummelled into Gumby-like bliss with a variety of steps, including an aromatherapy deep-pressure back massage, a mineral-rich body masque and a chilled-stone eye massage. Best of all, afterwards you're not shoved out the door but are free to enjoy the tranquil garden over tea and dates. Treatments also entitle you to use the gym and relax by the palm-tree-shaded pool, so make a day of it. Reserve well ahead.

BLISS RELAXOLOGY Map pp54-5

☎ 286 9444; Shop 11, Emirates Blvd, G Block, Al-Garhoud (next to Welcare Hospital); ⏰ 9am-midnight

It's not quite pampering fit for Queen Nefertiti, but if you're in bad need of working out the kinks without spending buckets of money, this relaxation station near the airport might just do the trick. Treatments range from a traditional Thai massage to foot reflexology, and start at Dh90 for 30 minutes.

SPA AT THE PALACE – THE OLD TOWN Map pp70-71

☎ 428 7888; www.thepalace-dubai.com; Palace – The Old Town, Emaar Blvd, Downtown Dubai; ⏰ 9am-10pm

Surrender to the magic of Arabia in this intimate, sensuously lit spa where treatments incorporate Oriental products and techniques. A favourite is the One Desert Journey (Dh685), where you choose from a selection of traditional essences, such as jasmine, amber and musk, orange blossom or verbena, depending on your mood. The 'trip' starts with a rose-petal foot bath, followed by a revitalising sand and salt scrub. At the next stop you'll get drenched in an oil masque before submitting to a restorative massage using an 'oussada' cushion filled with hot dry mint. Finally, drift into semi-conscious bliss with a cup of tea in the relaxation room. There are only four treatment rooms for women and two for men, each with their own private shower and toilet. As a hotel guest, you're free to wallow in the gorgeously appointed spa with Jacuzzi, sauna and steam, even without booking a treatment.

ONE&ONLY SPA Map pp82-3

☎ 399 9999; www.oneandonlyresorts.com; One&Only Royal Mirage, Al-Sufouh Rd, Al-Sufouh; ⏰ 9.30am-9pm

THE ROYAL TREATMENT

In a city built on facsimiles and gimmicks, the not-to-be-missed Oriental Hammam at the One&Only Spa (above) stands out as the hands-down best recreation of another country's cultural institution: a Moroccan bathhouse. Moroccan-born attendants walk you into a giant, echoey, steamy marble room lit by stained-glass lanterns, where they wrap you in muslin, bathe you on a marble bench from a running hot-water fountain, then lay you down on an enormous, heated marble cube – head-to-toe with three other men or women (depending on the day) – and scrub your entire body with exfoliating coarse gloves. Next, they bathe you again, then lead you to a steam room where you relax before receiving an invigorating mud body mask and honey facial, a brief massage and your final rinse. Afterwards, you're wrapped in dry muslin and escorted to a meditative relaxation room, where you drift to sleep beneath a blanket and awaken to hot mint tea and dates – just like in Morocco. Pure bliss!

DUBAI'S TOP SPA TREATMENTS

24 Carat Gold Massage (The Spa at Ritz-Carlton, p163) Feel like a queen when getting limbered up with a deep tissue and Balinese massage combo using oil infused with gold extract (100 minutes, Dh700).

Diamond Ceremony (Amara Spa, opposite) You'll feel on top of your game after going through this 'ceremony' that melts away knots, tension and stress (120 minutes, Dh750).

Maya's Secret (Sensasia, below) Indulge your olfactory senses with a sandalwood-and-myrrh body polish followed by a 20-minute massage (60 minutes, Dh325).

One Desert Journey (Spa at The Palace – The Old Town, opposite) Deeply relaxing or rejuvenating, this trip can be tailored to your needs (105 minutes, Dh685).

Oriental Hammam (One&Only Spa, opposite) Impeccable recreation of a Moroccan bathhouse (80 minutes, Dh450).

Pure Awakening Package (Talise Spa, below) Get over your jetlag in 50 minutes – or at least feel somewhat refreshed – with this body brush, full-body purifying mask and mint foot massage combination (60 minutes, Dh475).

Rasul Mud Treatment (Retreat Spa, Grosvenor House, Map pp82-3) Soak in a hydrotherapy tub before getting slathered in detoxifying natural mud (55 minutes, Dh350).

Seaweed Wraps (Willow Stream Spa, Fairmont hotel, Map pp70-71) Great for marine-inspired treatments and exfoliating rubs (60 minutes, Dh325). Two pools mean you can chase the sun from morning till evening.

Do you want to unwind, restore or elevate? These are the magic words at this exclusive spa with a dozen treatment rooms where massages, wraps, scrubs and facials are calibrated to achieve your chosen goal. Hot-stone massage is just the way to melt away the strains of the day, although for the most unique experience, sign up for a treatment in the Oriental Hammam (see boxed text, opposite).

H₂O Map pp70-71

☎ 319 8181; www.jumeirah.com; Jumeirah Emirates Tower, Sheikh Zayed Rd, Financial District; ◷ 9am-11pm

Finally a spa squarely aimed at metrosexual moguls: stressed and jetlagged executives badly in need of – but having little time for – revitalisation. There's the usual range of massages and spa treatments, plus a few esoteric ones. How about kick-starting your capillaries in the Oxygen Lounge (15/30/60 minutes Dh85/165/330) or tricking your body into believing it got eight hours of sleep by spending only one in a flotation pool (Dh330)?

SENSASIA URBAN SPA Map pp76-7

☎ 349 8850; www.sensasiaspas.com; Village Mall, Jumeirah Rd, Jumeirah 1; ◷ 10am-10pm

Detox treatments, facials and massage from Bali, Japan and Thailand are the specialities at this women's indie day spa done in sensuous Far East–meets–Middle East style. The menu includes such highly original options as warm cocoa butter stone therapy, chocolate body buff, fennel colon cleanse and pro-collagen quartz lift. For the ultimate indulgence, become 'Queen for a Day' (Dh1500). Afterwards, hit the Lime Tree Café (p120) for lunch.

SOFTTOUCH SPA Map pp82-3

☎ 341 0000; www.kempinski-dubai.com; Kempinski Hotel, Mall of the Emirates, Sheikh Zayed Rd, Al-Barsha

Conveniently located for a post–Ski Dubai rubdown, Softtouch specialises in Ayurvedic oil-drip treatments as well as massages. The sumptuous Asian look – slate floors, Thai-silk walls, orange hanging lamps – is conducive to relaxation. An initial consultation is followed by a tailored treatment performed with you lying down on a special teak table imported from India.

TALISE SPA Map pp76-7

☎ 366 6818; www.madinatjumeirah.com/spa; Madinat Jumeirah, Al-Sufouh Rd, Umm Suqeim 3; ◷ 9am-10pm

Arrive by *abra* (water taxi) at this Arabian-themed spa, which has 28 gorgeous free-standing templelike treatment rooms complete with altars laden with quartz crystal – they're like the inside of a genie's bottle. The only problem is, once your treatment is over, you can't enjoy the sumptuous surroundings because you're hustled out the door to make room for the next appointment. Still, the treatments are

SAVING FACE IN DUBAI

Dubai does a roaring trade in plastic surgery, rivalling surface-deep Los Angeles for rhinoplasty, liposuction and breast augmentation. Think about it. Geographically speaking, Dubai is in the middle of nowhere, halfway between London and Singapore, and most of the world's airlines fly here. Londoners and Russians can jet here in a few hours and remain totally anonymous while they get their faces done, a world away from their normal social circles. And all that high-end shopping means they can also build new wardrobes to match their new noses, with zero fear of running into anyone they know. After all, the point of plastic surgery is not to let anyone know you've had it done, isn't it? Keying in to a need for good care in a region that once had none, the American Academy for Cosmetic Surgery (☎ 423 7600; www.aacsh.com) has set up shop at the new Dubai Healthcare City. If you're staying at a five-star beach resort, one of the self-contained compounds that guests need never leave before flying back home, keep an eye out for folks hiding behind oversized black sunglasses. Chances are there are a couple of big, fat shiners turning purple beneath those Gucci frames.

top-notch – a blend of Eastern and Western, from Ayurvedic cupping to Swedish massage – and convenient if you're staying at the Madinat.

ACTIVITIES
RUNNING

The winter months are cool enough for running nearly anytime during the day; in summer you've got to get up with the sun to jog with no fear of heatstroke. There are excellent jogging tracks in Al-Safa Park (p79) and Za'abeel Park (p67), and along Jumeirah Beach (Map pp76-7). Prefer running with company? Check out the groups listed here or, if you're into the more social aspects of running (read: drinking afterwards), look into Dubai's 'hashing' clubs at www.creekhash.net. The Dubai Marathon takes over city streets in January (see boxed text, p149).

DUBAI CREEK STRIDERS Map pp70-71
☎ 321 1999; www.dubaicreekstriders.com; meet on the road opposite the Novotel, 319 St, Financial District

The Striders meet for weekly training runs on Friday mornings at 7am near the convention halls of the World Trade Centre. The run's length varies depending on the season, but it's generally at least 10km. Contact the club to register before turning up (free).

DUBAI ROAD RUNNERS Map pp76-7
☎ 050-624 3213; www.dubai-road-runners.com; Al-Safa Park, Jumeirah; per adult Dh5; 6.30pm Sat

The club welcomes runners of all ages and abilities to run one or two laps of the park (3.4km per lap). Runners predict how

long it will take them to run the course; the one closest wins a prize. Fun and communal. Just show up in the car park of Gate 4 (off 55 St).

'WINTER' SPORTS
Ice Skating
AL-NASR LEISURELAND Map pp64-5
☎ 337 1234; www.alnasrll.com; off Oud Metha Rd, Oud Metha; adult/child incl boot hire Dh10/5; 2hr sessions at 10am, 1pm, 4pm & 7.30pm

Open since 1979, Leisureland is definitely long in the tooth, but it's got a bit of character and lots of facilities under one roof, including a gym, tennis and squash courts, a bowling alley and an ice rink. Sure, it's not as snazzy as the Dubai Ice Rink (see below), but it's bigger than the one at the Hyatt Regency Dubai (p154). Of the several eateries, Viva Goa is the most interesting.

DUBAI ICE RINK Map pp70-71
☎ 437 3111; www.dubaiicerink.com; ground fl, Dubai Mall, Downtown Dubai; per session incl skates Dh50; 2hr sessions at 10am, 12.15pm, 2.30pm, 5.45pm & 8pm daily, 9.45pm Thu-Sat

This state-of-the-art Olympic-size ice rink is ringed with cafes and restaurants and can even be converted into a concert arena. Sign up for a private or group class if you're still a little wobbly in the knees. Hormone-crazed teens invade for the night-time 'Disco Sessions'.

Skiing & Snowboarding
SKI DUBAI Map pp82-3
☎ 409 4000; www.skidxb.com; Mall of the Emirates, Al-Barsha; Snow Park admission Dh100, Ski Slope per 2hr adult/child Dh180/150, all day

Dh300/240; ☺ 10am-11pm Sun-Wed, 10am-midnight Thu, 9am-midnight Fri, 9am-11pm Sat; ♿ Skiing in the desert? Puh-leeze! Where else but in Dubai? The city's most incongruous attraction, Ski Dubai is a faux winter wonderland built right into the gargantuan Mall of the Emirates. It comes complete with ice sculptures, a tiny sledding hill, five ski runs (the longest being 400m) and a Freestyle Zone with jumps and rails. Gulf Arabs especially are fascinated by this snowy display, but they typically restrict themselves to the walk-through Snow Park, passing through a colour-lit igloo filled with carved-ice penguins and dragons, then sledding down a little hill in plastic toboggans. Skiers and boarders are kept separate from the Snow Park and instead whiz down a forking slope – one side for beginners, one for intermediates. The 60m (196ft) vertical drop is an ant hill when compared with a real ski mountain, but if you've never skied or boarded before, it's a good place to learn the basics. Advanced skiers quickly weary of the too-short runs (think 30 seconds at a good clip) but generally everybody is pleasantly surprised by the velvety snow. Conditions are ideal: at night, the interior is chilled to -8°C, and snow guns blow feather-light powder. During opening hours it warms to a perfect -1°C. Though weekends are more crowded, Ski Dubai operates a faster-moving secondary lift, a rope tow, that significantly shortens the ride uphill, giving you more runs per hour than you can get riding the chair. Pretty much everything, including socks and skis are provided, although gloves and hats are not (for hygiene reasons). Bring your own or buy some in the adjoining ski shop; gloves start at around Dh10, hats at Dh30. If you bring your own equipment and/or clothing you'll get a 5% discount on each.

WATERSPORTS
Diving
Diving around Dubai means mostly nosing around shipwrecks submerged on the sandy seabed of the Gulf at a depth of between 10m and 35m. The better sites are generally a long way offshore and mostly for experienced divers. Finny creatures you might encounter include clownfish, sea snakes, Arabian angelfish and possibly even rays and barracuda.

For novices the sites off the United Arab Emirates (UAE) East Coast (Khor Fakkan and Dibba; see pp175-6) are most suitable. Also popular are dive spots still further north, off the rugged Musandam Peninsula, which is actually part of Oman. However, fast-flowing currents here require a higher level of experience. In recent times, the eastern shores have been beleaguered by the red tide (see boxed text, p146), so be sure to ask dive operators about conditions. A day's diving includes two dives and costs around Dh350 to Dh650, including the boat ride and equipment.

For details on the top dive and snorkelling sites in the UAE and the Musandam, consult the 180-page *UAE Underwater Explorer.*

AL BOOM DIVING Map pp76-7
☎ 342 2993; www.alboomdiving.com; cnr Al-Wasl Rd & 33 St, Jumeirah 1
Al Boom is the largest dive operation in the UAE and leads daily guided dive trips off Dubai and to the East Coast and the Musandam Peninsula. The experienced staff also offer the gamut of courses, from Discover Scuba Diving to Instructor level.

HENNA
Henna body tattooing is a long-standing tradition dating back 6000 years, when central-Turkish women began painting their hands in homage to the Mother Goddess. The practice spread throughout the eastern Mediterranean, where the henna shrub grows wild. Today, Emirati women continue the tradition by decorating their hands, nails and feet for special events, particularly weddings. A few nights before the nuptials, brides-to-be are honoured with *layyat al-henna* (henna night). This is a women-only affair, part of a week of festivities leading up to the big day. The bride is depilated, anointed head-to-toe with perfumes and oils, and shampooed with henna, jasmine or perfume. Her hands, wrists, ankles and feet are then tattooed with intricate floral designs, which typically last around six weeks. Lore has it, the duration of the tattoos is an indication to the mother-in-law of what kind of wife the bride will become. If she's a hard worker – and thus a more desirable daughter-in-law – the henna will penetrate deeper and remain longer.

Want to give it a try? Henna tents are all over the city. Look for signs depicting henna-painted hands in Deira City Centre (Map pp52-3), BurJuman Centre (Map pp62-3), Souq Madinat Jumeirah (Map pp76-7), Jumeirah Emirates Towers (Map pp70-71) and hotel lobbies. Just don't show your mother-in-law; she may disapprove.

ATTACK OF THE KILLER TIDE

The waters off the United Arab Emirates (UAE) East Coast used to be a snorkellers' and divers' paradise, teeming with turtles, barracuda, small sharks and tropical fish. Then disaster struck in 2008: the red tide came and stayed for nearly eight months.

Red tide, or as scientists prefer to call it, 'harmful algal bloom', is a naturally occurring, cyclical phenomenon caused by a build-up of microscopic algae called *Karenia brevis*. Colouring the water blood-red to cola-brown, it deprives it of oxygen and blocks sunlight, killing fish and coral. The tide usually disappears after a few weeks, but under the right (or rather, wrong) conditions, the organisms continue to multiply. Though not toxic to humans, allergic types may come away with stinging and blotched skin.

During the eight months that the red tide lingered along the coast, it damaged or destroyed 95% of the colourful coral and left hundreds of tons of fish floating belly up, according to Dubai-based Emirates Diving Association (EDA; ☎ 04-393 9390; www.emiratesdiving.com), the UAE's official diving agency.

Scientists are still baffled as to the exact causes of the prolonged tide, but likely culprits include discharge of raw or partially treated sewage, aquaculture farming, spillage from passing freighters and dredging from the construction of nearby artificial islands. Recovery is slow, but as of early 2010 corals are reportedly replenishing themselves and marine life is returning as well.

PAVILION DIVE CENTRE Map pp76-7

☎ 406 8827; www.thepaviliondivecentre.com; Jumeirah Beach Hotel, Jumeirah Rd, Umm Suqeim 3
Pavilion runs the entire program of classes for PADI certification, rents equipment to experienced divers, and leads two-dive trips off the Musandam Peninsula.

Other Water Sports

The hot sun, warm sea and high volume of tourists make water sports big business in Dubai. Most facilities are at major beach hotels and private clubs, meaning prices skew high.

Kitesurfers congregate at northwest-facing Kite Beach (Map pp76-7), aka Wollongong Beach, where there's a designated launch and recovery area. It's about 3km north of the Burj al-Arab, past Umm Suqeim Hospital in the district of Umm Suqeim 1. Novices should take a few lessons (about Dh300 per hour). Qualified instructors can be found at www.ad-kitesurfing.net, or call ☎ 050-562 6383.

Waterskiing in the polluted Dubai Creek is not recommended. Instead, head to Dubai Marina or Abu Dhabi. Waterskiing at a Gulf-front five-star hotel with its own beach club costs around Dh150 for 20 minutes – which, if you've never waterskied, is a long time. Non-guests must also pay a daily admission fee for access to the hotel grounds and beach club (usually about Dh75 to Dh250). Try Le Meridien Mina Seyahi (p164), where beach access costs Dh150 (Dh250 on Friday and Saturday) and waterskiing Dh150.

To get perspective on just how far the city now stretches, see it from the water. Dubai Creek Golf & Yacht Club (Map pp54-5; ☎ 205 4646; www.dubaigolf.com; near Deira side of Al-Garhoud Bridge) offer boat charters aboard skippered 33ft vessels. A one-hour Creek cruise costs Dh800, while three-hour trips taking in the Palm Deira are Dh2200. The six-hour trip (Dh3800) goes down the coast to Palm Jumeirah via the Burj al-Arab and approaches the perimeter of The World islands.

Dubai also has two waterparks: Wild Wadi Waterpark (p80) and Aquaventure (p81).

GOLF

Dubai has become a big golfing destination over the past few years and boasts several championship courses designed by big names. Clubs don't require memberships but cheap they ain't: at the top spots green fees soar to Dh850 for 18 holes. Rates quoted in this section apply during the peak winter season (roughly mid-November to late March) and drop the rest of the year, especially in summer. Proper attire is essential. If you're serious about golf, reserve your tee times as soon as you book your hotel and flight.

AL-BADIA GOLF CLUB Map p50

☎ 601 0101; www.albadiagolfclub.ae; Al-Rebat St, Al-Badia, at Festival City; Sun-Thu Dh695, Fri & Sat Dh850
Close to the airport, this stunning course was designed by Robert Trent Jones II and is a pleasure to play – impeccably manicured and well laid out, with 11 lakes and several streams feeding into Dubai Creek. The changing rooms are like a mini-spa, complete with sauna and Jacuzzi. Driving range access is Dh75 and includes unlimited balls.

ARABIAN RANCHES GOLF CLUB
off Map p50

☎ 366 3000; www.arabianranchesgolfdubai.com; Arabian Ranches, cnr Umm Suqeim & Emirates Ring Rds; 18 holes Thu-Sat Dh660, Sun-Wed Dh555; 9 holes Thu-Sat Dh385, Sun-Wed Dh345

If you've golfed in the American southwest (ie Palm Springs or Scottsdale) you'll feel right at home on this 18-hole desert-style course designed by former golf champion Ian Baker-Finch. Nine-hole play also available.

DUBAI CREEK GOLF & YACHT CLUB
Map pp54-5

☎ 295 6000; www.dubaigolf.com; near Deira side of Al-Garhoud Bridge; Sun-Wed Dh595, Thu-Sat Dh795

The one-time host course of the Dubai Desert Classic has been redesigned by a former winner of the tournament, Thomas Björn. The Creekside location is gorgeous, as is the landscaping, with meticulously groomed fairways lined by date and coconut palms and water hazards. The high-class Park Hyatt Dubai (p154) is within walking distance of the greens. Beginners can go wild on the par-three nine-hole course (Dh75).

ELS CLUB off Map p50

☎ 425 1010; www.elsclubdubai.com; Emirates Rd, Dubai Sports City; Sun-Wed Dh595, Thu-Sat Dh795

This one comes courtesy of US and British Open winner Ernie Els; it was the first venue to open (in 2008) at the ambitious Dubai Sports City. On the edge of town, for now, it's a challenging course built right into the dunes with four teeing areas and a links-style layout.

EMIRATES GOLF CLUB Map pp82-3

☎ 380 1555; www.dubaigolf.com; Interchange No 5, Sheikh Zayed Rd; Majlis course Dh825, Faldo course Dh695

The first grass championship course in the Middle East is home to the Dubai Desert Classic (www.dubaidesertclassic.com), a major tourney on the PGA European Tour circuit. There are two 18-hole courses: the Faldo course, designed by Nick Faldo, and the Majlis course which, in 2009, got the nod from *Golf Digest* as one of the best courses outside the USA.

MONTGOMERIE DUBAI Map pp82-3

☎ 390 5600; www.themontgomerie.com; Emirates Hills, off Interchange No 5; Dh795

Fans of Scottish links will enjoy this world-class course with 14 lakes and 81 bunkers designed by Colin Montgomerie. The par-three 13th hole is on an island shaped like the UAE and is purportedly the largest single green in the world: 58,000 sq ft, or the size of nine normal greens combined.

SPECTATOR SPORTS

The single biggest sport among elite Emiratis is horse racing, with races now held on the spanking-new Meydan Racecourse. Expats turn out in force for the Dubai Rugby Sevens, when you may spot more drunken Brits in one place since VE Day. And then there's cricket, the most important sport for Indians and akistanis. Emirates Airlines teamed up with the International Cricket Council, and after nearly a century at Lord's in London, the council is now based in the UAE, much to the delight of the city's cricket fans. During any of these events, there's palpable excitement in the air; when a favourite team wins, people drive around blowing their car horns and waving flags.

This isn't the case when Lee Westwood wins the Dubai Desert Classic golf tournament or when Roger Federer aces the Dubai Tennis Championships, but spectators still show up in droves to cheer them on. Also see the Competition Sports Calendar, p149.

lonelyplanet.com

SPORTS & ACTIVITIES SPECTATOR SPORTS

UAE FOOTBALL

On winter weeknights, neighbourhood stadiums in Dubai are packed with up to 10,000 spectators – mostly young Emirati men – passionately barracking for their favourite football teams. Surprisingly, most foreigners, be they expats or visitors, hardly attend the matches. And they're rarely covered by the local English-language press. If you're a football fan, attend a match once and you may be hooked – the carnival atmosphere is electric. Fans dress up in colour-coordinated outfits, and a singer and band of drummers lead song and dance routines to inspire their teams. Founded in 1973, the United Arab Emirates (UAE) football league was renamed UAE Premier Division for the 2009/10 season and consists of a dozen teams. Tempers may flare during matches between the old rivals: Al-Ahli, Sheikh Mohammed's red-and-white jersey team, and the purple-clad Al-Ain. Dubai-based Al-Ahli also represented the UAE in the 2009 FIFA Club World Cup, held in Abu Dhabi, losing 0–2 to Auckland City in their only game.

HORSE RACING

MEYDAN RACECOURSE Map pp70-71

☎ 327 0077; www.meydan.ae/racecourse; about 5km southwest of Sheikh Zayed Rd; general admission free

A passionate love of Arabian thoroughbreds courses through the blood of Emiratis, and the Dubai-based Godolphin (www.godolphin.com) stables are well known to horse racing enthusiasts worldwide. Racing season starts in November with the 10-week Winter Racing Challenge, but doesn't heat up until January, when the Dubai International Racing Carnival gets under way. It culminates in late March with the elite Dubai World Cup (see boxed text, opposite), the world's richest horse race, with prize money of a dizzying US$10 million.

Dubai racing's new home (from 2010) is the spectacular Meydan Racecourse, a futuristic stadium with a grandstand bigger than most airport terminals. Spanning 1.6km, it has a solar- and titanium-panelled roof, can accommodate up to 60,000 spectators and integrates a five-star hotel. A museum and IMAX theatre are in the works as well. There's a free-admission area where dress is casual. For the grandstand you'll need tickets and should dress to the nines. For the exact racing schedule and tickets, contact Dubai Racing Club (☎ 327 2110; www.dubairacingclub.com). Even if you don't like horse racing, attending a race presents great people-watching opportunities.

Meydan is about 5km southwest of central Dubai. To get there, take the 2nd interchange from Sheikh Zayed Rd, turn left onto Al-Meydan Rd and follow the signs.

CAMEL RACING

AL-LISAILI RACE TRACK off Map p50

☎ 338 8170; Lisail, Al-Ain Rd exit 37, approx 40km from Dubai

THE 'JOCKEY-ING' TRUTH

Traditionally, camels were raced by child jockeys, sometimes as young as six or seven and weighing less than 20kg. They were often 'bought' from impoverished families in Pakistan or Bangladesh, trained in miserable conditions and kept deliberately underweight. International human-rights groups decried the practice and in 2005 the UAE issued a ban on the use of children. Human jockeys have since been replaced with robotic ones operated remotely by their owners who race around the inside track in their SUVs, cheering on their camels. Trust us, it's a weird sight.

Camel racing is not only a popular spectator sport but deeply rooted in the Emirati soul and originally practised only at weddings and special events. These days it's big business, with races held between October and early April. There's no fixed schedule, although there usually seems to be a two- or three-hour session starting around 7am on Fridays. Check the newspapers or call ahead before you drive an hour out of town.

Watching these mighty animals race at speeds of up to 60km/h is an amazing sight. If you can't make it to a racing session, you can usually catch training sessions in the afternoon, and these are also a great experience. The sheer number of camels is shocking. Bring your camera.

MOTOR RACING
Desert Rallying

Motor sports are exceedingly popular with Emiratis. The Emirates Motor Sports Federation (EMSF; www.emsf.ae) holds events throughout the year, with the important ones scheduled

CRICKET CRAZY

The enormous Indian and Pakistani communities in Dubai l-o-v-e cricket. You'll see them playing on sandy lots between buildings during their lunch breaks, in parks on their days off, and late at night in empty car parks. By contrast, you won't see Emiratis playing: cricket in Dubai belongs to the Subcontinental nationalities. If you want to get under the skin of the game, talk to taxi drivers – you can be sure most of them have posters of their favourite players taped to their bedroom walls. But first ask where your driver is from – there's disdain between Pakistanis and Indians. Each will tell you that his country's team is the best, then explain at length why. (Some drivers need a bit of cajoling; show enthusiasm and you'll get the whole story.) When Pakistan plays India, the city lights up. Remember: these two nationalities account for about 45% of Dubai's population, far outnumbering Emiratis. Because most of them can't afford the price of satellite TV, they meet up outside their local eateries in Deira or Bur Dubai to watch the match. Throngs of riveted fans swarm the pavements beneath the crackling neon – it's a sight to behold.

COMPETITION SPORTS CALENDAR

- **Dubai Marathon** (www.dubaimarathon.org) Sweat it out in January with thousands of other runners or just cheer 'em on during this popular street race with a prize fund of a million dollars. In 2010, Haile Gebrselassie won the race for the third year in a row. Less-energetic types can enter a 10km run or a 3km 'fun run'.
- **Dubai Desert Classic** (www.dubaidesertclassic.com) The golfing elite, including Rory McIlroy and Henrik Stenson, comes to town for this fine February event, held at the Emirates Golf Club (p147). There have been some thrilling finishes over the past couple of years – the 18th hole has become legendary on the PGA circuit.
- **Dubai Tennis Championships** (www.dubaitennischampionships.com) Big-name players like Serena Williams and Novak Djokovic volley away at this two-week pro event in February at the Aviation Club (p140). The women play in the first week, men in the second. It's a great opportunity to see some great hitting in a relatively small stadium.
- **Dubai World Cup** (www.dubaiworldcup.com) Racing season culminates in March with the world's richest horse race, now held at the spanking-new Meydan Racecourse (opposite). Prize money rings up at a record-holding US$10 million. While there's no betting, this is the city's biggest social event, with local society women sporting the silliest hats this side of Ascot. Godolphin, the stable owned by Dubai's royal family, tends to dominate proceedings on the racetrack.
- **Dubai Rugby Sevens** (www.dubairugby7s.com) Held in November or December, this is the first round of the eight-leg International Rugby Board Sevens World Series. The three-day event features 16 international squads, various amateur teams and live entertainment. Up to 150,000 spectators make the pilgrimage to the spanking-new 'The Sevens' stadium, about 30 minutes south of Sheikh Zayed Rd on the Al-Ain Rd. Book well ahead.
- **Dubai World Championship** (www.dubaiworldchampionship.com) This major new golfing championship in November is the crowning tournament of the Race to Dubai. It pits the PGA European Tour's top players against each other in 49 tournaments in 26 destinations over the course of one year. Held since 2008/9, it replaced the European Tour Order of Merit and comes with a purse of US$7.5 million. It's played on the new Jumeirah Golf Estates, which consists of four courses designed by Greg Norman, Sergio Garcia, Vijay Singh and Pete Dye.

to take place during the cooler months. A round of the FIA Cross-Country Rally World Cup, the Abu Dhabi Desert Challenge (www.abudhabidesertchallenge.com) brings top rally drivers to the UAE from around the world in March. There are several smaller rallies in February and March, including the 1000 Dunes Rally and the Spring Desert Rally, which are both 4WD events. Visit EMSF's website for details.

DUBAI AUTODROME off Map p50
☎ 367 8700; www.dubaiautodrome.com; Dubai Motor City, near Arabian ranches off Emirates Rd (take Interchange No 4 on Sheikh Zayed Rd)
Unleash your inner Michael Schumacher while taking a spin around the 5.39km Dubai Autodrome track in a rented Audi TTS Turbo or a Subaru ST Impreza (from Dh750 for 1¾ hours). After a safety briefing, you'll be let loose on the asphalt with an instructor by your side to teach you the tricks of the trade. If you've got wannabe racing drivers in tow, there's also a 1.2km Kartdrome outdoor track with special sessions for kids aged seven to 12 years.

CRICKET

SHARJAH CRICKET STADIUM
off Map p50
☎ 06-532 2991; 2nd Industrial Rd, Industrial Area 5, Sharjah
Cricket lovers surely remember the surprising move of the International Cricket Council to Dubai after 96 years at Lord's, the home of cricket. However, at present, international cricket in the UAE is actually held in nearby Sharjah (and also in Abu Dhabi), where matches are hosted over the winter months.

RUGBY

DUBAI EXILES RUGBY CLUB
☎ 050-253 0787; www.dubaiexiles.com
Since 2008, Dubai's rugby club has been headquartered at a slick new stadium called The Sevens (off Map p50), located about 30 minutes outside Dubai on the Al-Ain Rd. The Exiles are a founding member of the Arabian Gulf Rugby Football Union and put on one of Dubai's biggest annual sporting events, the Dubai Rugby Sevens (www.dubairugby7s.com) (see boxed text, above).

SLEEPING

top picks

- Best B&B: Jumeirah Garden Guesthouse (p162)
- Best boutique hotel: XVA Art Hotel (p157)
- Best for beaching: One&Only Royal Mirage (p163)
- Best for bragging rights: Burj al-Arab (p161)
- Best for business: Jumeirah Emirates Towers (p160)
- Best for shopping: Address Dubai Mall (p159)
- Best modern Arabian: Al-Qasr, Madinat Jumeirah (p161)
- Best newcomer: Address Downtown Dubai (p159)
- Best 'Old World' opulence: Palace – The Old Town (p159)

What's your recommendation? www.lonelyplanet.com/dubai

SLEEPING

Dubai's steady stream of visitors have more than 50,000 beds to accommodate them, with more hotels scheduled to come online in the next few years. Overcapacity and the economic crisis have brought once-stratospheric room rates somewhat down to earth, although the city's in no danger of turning into a budget destination. Still, even five-star places offer the occasional bargain, and a recent crop of budget brands like Holiday Inn Express, Ibis and Premier Inn is also making the city more attractive for the slimmer-wallet crowd. Another way to economise is by checking into a furnished hotel apartment. Generally speaking, rates drop as temperatures soar, so if you can bear 50°C heat, come between June and September.

But make no mistake, Dubai is still primarily a luxury travel destination. There's definitely no shortage of stylish and ultra-posh lodging options catering for the cravings of the 'Rolls-Royce crowd'.

If you need a tourist visa (see p195), most hotels will arrange one for their guests, usually for a reasonable fee. Many also offer airport pick-ups and drop-offs. Check if these services are offered by the property of your choice.

Accommodation in this chapter is listed by neighbourhood, with listings sorted by the price of a double room, from highest to lowest.

ACCOMMODATION STYLES

Dubai runs the gamut of places to unpack your suitcase, from fleabag hotels in Deira to international chain hotels in the financial district and five-star beach resorts like the iconic Burj al-Arab. There are essentially two types of hotel in Dubai: the city hotel and the beach resort. City hotels range from one star to five, while the beach resorts are generally all five-stars. Though there are no official camping sites in Dubai, some residents spend weekends camping on beaches or in the desert, but given the temperatures and lack of facilities, camping is neither a reliable nor popular option for a Dubai holiday.

Before you choose a hotel, determine what you want from your holiday. If you like to drink, make sure your hotel isn't 'dry'. City hotels are ideal for jaunts to shopping malls, souqs and historic areas. Beach resorts tend to be more lavish, with expansive grounds, swim-up bars and sandy shores. Most resort guests do the sights in a day and spend the rest of their time soaking up the sun.

Top-end resorts are like villages unto themselves, with multiple restaurants, bars and nightclubs. Alcohol is generally only served in hotels, which means expats flock to them in droves. At a good hotel, the party comes to you. Conversely, if you're at a low-end hotel, you'll wind up travelling to the big hotels for fun.

Increasingly popular among short-term visitors, especially groups and families, are stays in furnished hotel apartments. These

PRICE GUIDE	
$$$	over Dh1000
$$	Dh500-1000
$	under Dh500

vary in size from one-room studios to multi-bedroom flats and usually come with a kitchenette and a washing machine. Rates include daily cleaning and access to the building's facilities (pool, gym, parking etc).

There's also a small but growing number of B&Bs, usually set up by expats in private homes in residential areas. Staying in one of these won't give you buckets of privacy or a wide range of top-end amenities but it will give you easy access to personal perspectives on life in Dubai.

CHECK-IN & CHECKOUT TIMES

Because flights arrive in Dubai at all hours, it's crucial to confirm your check-in time with the hotel prior to arrival. Get a confirmation number when you book and present it at check-in; it's shocking how many reservations get lost. If you're really worried, call the hotel a day before your departure to confirm. Check-in is generally at 2pm or 3pm, although it's sometimes possible to get into your room earlier. Checkout is 11am or noon, unless you arrange for a late checkout, which is often granted for free on a goodwill basis unless the hotel is at capacity. If you must keep the room until the evening, enquire about a day rate, which is usually half the overnight rate.

Expect to present your passport at check-in. Hotels are legally required to photocopy or scan them and file a copy with the CID (Criminal Investigation Division), Dubai's secret police, so they can track your movements if they want to (welcome to Dubai). Some hotels also require you to leave a credit-card authorisation for incidentals. If you don't have a credit card, you must leave a cash deposit.

In theory, unmarried men and women are not permitted to share a room, but we've never heard of anyone actually being asked for proof of marriage. Having two different last names is not a tip-off either, as it's customary for Arab women to keep their name when married. Similarly, two men sharing a room is fine too. Women checking into a hotel room alone, however, may sometimes raise eyebrows due to the large number of 'working girls' in town.

LONGER-TERM RENTALS

The Bur Dubai area is full of longer-term rentals; many hotels throughout the city also rent furnished apartments. The chief advantages are the kitchens and washing machines. Prices start at around Dh300 for a studio in one of the midrange hotel apartments in Bur Dubai and often drop for stays longer than a week. At top-end hotel apartments, rates are stratospheric.

RESERVATIONS

Most major hotel chains have online booking engines, saving you expensive telephone calls. Smaller hotels sometimes offer online booking, but they don't always use a secure server; verify the site's security certificate (use an up-to-date browser; Firefox has good security) before sending your credit card number. When reserving a hotel that you can't book online, expect miscommunications via email. Pick up the phone and expect to stumble through conversations with people who don't fully understand English. Once reserved, the reservation must be guaranteed with a faxed copy of your credit card, along with a signed guarantee. Upon sending the fax, verify receipt of it by telephone. Keep your fax-confirmation page, and get a reservation number: bring them both with you. This detail is crucial. You may need proof of your reservation on a sold-out night. You will seriously bum out

if you arrive at your hotel at 3am, following a too-long flight, only to learn you've nowhere to lay your head or have a shower.

Hunt for specials on hotels' proprietary websites (if none are available, it typically means occupancy is high). Quite a few hotels reviewed in this book can also be booked via Lonely Planet's own website (see above). Other online booking services include www .expedia.com, www.lastminute.com and www .hotel.de. Last-minute bargains can often be found at www.hrs.com and www.booking. com. It is also possible to make online reservations through the Dubai Department of Tourism & Commerce Marketing website (www.dubaitourism.ae), but rates tend not to be the most competitive.

ROOM RATES

Since rates fluctuate so enormously in Dubai, we've given you the standard, published, high-season, non-weekend 'starting from' rates. These are usually good for the cheapest double room category and go up according to room size and comfort level. During city-wide sell-outs, prices spike higher, sometimes as much as 50%, although these times have become rarer because the room inventory has grown considerably in recent years. Always ask for the 'best price' or whether there are any specials – generally the hotels won't say unless you ask. If you work for a big company, presenting a business card may qualify you as a corporate client and earn you a substantial discount.

Practically all hotels in Dubai have rooms with private bathroom and air-conditioning. Budget rooms are tiny, with closet-size bathrooms and basic amenities, although they're usually clean and comfortable enough, especially in the international budget-chain properties like Ibis and Holiday Inn Express.

Midrange hotel rooms are big enough to unpack two suitcases, and usually have tea- and coffee-making facilities, minibars and extras such as flatscreen TVs. Top-end hotels have enough space to throw a cocktail party and inevitably have huge marble bathrooms with amenities like rainfall showerheads and free-standing oversize bathtubs. Many also have 'executive floors' where rates include access to a lounge where complimentary breakfast, a light lunch, afternoon tea and dinner drinks are served. Despite the name, these rooms are actually an especially good choice for families, and rates are often only slightly higher than those for rooms on regular floors.

Hotels charge 20% tax: 10% municipal tax, plus 10% service charge.

DEIRA

Deira is the city's grittiest, most colourful area. Near the neon-lit chaos of the souqs, it's fun for getting lost in back alleys, but horrible for taxis. The best hotels front the Creek. Budget hotels are tucked inland along narrow streets. Many hotels provide airport, mall and beach shuttles; enquire when you book. You'll find great deals in Deira, but if you have business elsewhere, you'll be slowed (way) down by traffic; choose Bur Dubai instead.

PARK HYATT DUBAI Map pp54-5   Hotel $$$
☎ 602 1234; www.dubai.park.hyatt.com; next to Dubai Creek Golf & Yacht Club; r from Dh1275; ▢ ⊚ ⊠

The mile-long driveway through a lush date palm grove is only the first hint that the Park Hyatt is no ordinary hotel, an impression quickly confirmed the moment you step into the domed and pillared lobby. Tiptoeing between hip and haute, Park is Hyatt's luxury brand, and it's evident in the details: the light-flooded rooms are artfully styled in natural tones, tactile textiles and subdued Moroccan design flourishes. Count the dhows (traditional wooden boats) from your Creek-view balcony or rinse off the jetlag in the rain shower or huge oval tub. If you're staying, take advantage of the online e-concierge to score a coveted reservation at the hotel's top-flight spa, Amara (p142), or the attached Dubai Creek Golf & Yacht Club (p147).

HYATT REGENCY DUBAI
Map pp52-3   Hotel $$$
☎ 209 1234; www.dubai.regency.hyatt.com; off Al-Khaleej Rd; r from Dh1000; ▢ ⊚ ⊠

The granddaddy of Dubai's five-stars opened in 1980 but, thanks to multiple

top picks

VIEWS

- Al-Qasr, Madinat Jumeirah (p161)
- Burj al-Arab (p161)
- Hilton Dubai Creek (below)
- Jumeirah Beach Hotel (p161)
- Mina A' Salam, Madinat Jumeirah (p162)
- Park Hyatt Dubai (left)
- Shangri-La (p160)
- Address Downtown Dubai (p159)

facelifts, sparkles all the way from the grand, all-white lobby to the 414 spiffy guestrooms. Key features here are sumptuous beds and giant picture windows overlooking the Palm Deira. You can stroll to the souqs or grab a cab for a quick ride to Al-Mamzar beach. Restaurants include the stellar Miyako (p109), Dubai's only rotating dining room. Work off any overindulgence at the superb fitness club or take a spin on the ice rink (Dh25 per session, including skates) in the integrated shopping mall.

HILTON DUBAI CREEK
Map pp52-3   Hotel $$
☎ 227 1111; www.hilton.com; Baniyas Rd, Rigga; r from Dh850; ▢ ⊚ ⊠

In a building by Bastille Opera designer Carlos Ott, this sexy glass-and-chrome hotel offers a smart alternative to the in-your-face white-marble opulence of Dubai's other luxury hotels. After a day of turf-pounding you can retreat to rooms with wood-panelled walls, leather-padded headboards, grey-granite baths, and fabulous beds with feather-light duvets. Your flatscreen TV may have a gazillion channels, but you'll probably prefer the amazing Creek views. Great value overall. Also on site: Verre by Gordon Ramsay (p108), one of Dubai's top tables. Small rooftop pool with fabulous views.

SHERATON DUBAI CREEK HOTEL & TOWERS Map pp52-3   Hotel $$
☎ 228 1111; www.starwoodhotels.com; Baniyas Rd; r from Dh850; ▢ ⊠

Floor-to-ceiling windows provide mesmerising Creek vistas at this classic business-class chain property. Rooms don't get kudos for elbow room and creative design, but amenities such as flatscreen TVs, DVD players, cushy bed linens and marble baths provide extra comfort. Good gym and nice triangular pool.

AL-BUSTAN ROTANA Map pp54-5 Hotel $$
☎ 282 0000; www.rotana.com; Casablanca Rd, Al-Garhoud; r from Dh850; 💻 🛜 🖵
Everything works like a well-oiled machine at this venerable five-star that manages to be warm and welcoming despite being near the airport and catering largely for the business brigade. A recent major facelift has propelled it from dowdy to dashing, with rooms now dressed in tactile fabrics, thick carpets and colours ranging from vanilla to chocolate. Wall-mounted flatscreen TVs, big desks, spotless baths, good mattresses and an oversized pool are additional comfort factors.

RADISSON BLU HOTEL
Map pp52-3 Hotel $$
☎ 222 7171; www.radissonblu.com; Baniyas Rd; r from Dh750; 💻 🛜 🖵
This Creekside stalwart was the city's first five-star hotel when it opened in 1975. As such it's old-fashioned but fits as comfortably as your favourite jeans. Rooms are snug but have been fast-forwarded into the 21st century, boasting a good range of business-class amenities and small, furnished balconies. Other trump cards include a location close to the souqs and dhow wharves and, most of all, the restaurants: Sumibiya (p109) for Korean-Japanese, China Club (p109) for yum cha, Shabestan (p109) for Persian and Yum! (p110) for noodles. The 24-hour gym has a separate work-out area for women. Free wi-fi.

SHERATON DEIRA Map pp52-3 Hotel $$
☎ 268 8888; www.starwoodhotels.com; Al-Mateena St; r from Dh650; 💻 🛜 🖵
Rates are reasonable at this off-the-beaten-path five-star in Little Iraq. Standard rooms skimp on size if not on amenities, which include flatscreen TV and a coffeemaker. Alas, the VCR and CD player hint that the place hasn't yet arrived in the 2010s. Go for the junior suites, if you can score a good rate; they're extra-spacious, with big marble bathrooms and giant tubs.

MOSCOW HOTEL
Map pp54-5 Hotel $$
☎ 228 8222; www.moscowhoteldubai.com; Al-Maktoum Rd; r from Dh650; 💻 🛜 🖵

An eye-poppingly kitsch slice of Moscow, the lobby sports an over-the-top Bolshoi Theatre–styled dome. The Russia-by-the-Creek theme continues throughout, with the crowning touch being the Red Square nightclub (get a room far away if you need a good night's sleep). Rooms are big and colourful, but furnishings border on tacky (think French provincial chairs with vinyl seats).

LANDMARK HOTEL Map pp52-3 Hotel $$
☎ 228 6666; http://lmhotelgroup.com; just off Baniyas Sq; r from Dh600; 💻 🖵
Along with its sister, the nearby Landmark Plaza, this is one of the better hotels around Baniyas (or Al-Nasser) Sq, a hyperbusy Indian business district. Rooms are furnished in mass-market blonde wood, but they're clean and have satellite TV and enough room to unpack. The tiny rooftop pool reveals a delicious panorama of Deira, especially during the call to prayer, when mosques' loudspeakers compete in a blaring cacophony.

CARLTON TOWER HOTEL
Map pp52-3 Hotel $$
☎ 222 7111; www.carltontower.net; Baniyas Rd; r/ste from Dh550/1200, Creek view extra Dh100; 💻 🖵
Ageing but adequate, the Carlton is a fine base of operation if you want a flavour of Old Dubai. The Creekside location (definitely pony up the extra dirhams for a room with a view) is stellar and within earshot of the souqs. Rooms sport easy-on-the-eyes colours along with blonde wood and glass-topped furniture; bathrooms are spacious. Work out the kinks in the gym or the good-sized pool, but skip the on-site restaurants and clubs. Wi-fi works in the lobby only.

RIVIERA HOTEL Map pp52-3 Hotel $$
☎ 222 2131; www.rivierahotel-dubai.com; Baniyas Rd; r from Dh500; 💻
Next to the Carlton Tower Hotel, the Riviera's Indian-fanciful chintz decor may be long in the tooth, but the Creekside location can't be beaten. Bathrooms are immaculate, and beds even have down pillows. Aesthetes may bemoan the recessed fluorescent lighting, but splurge on a Creek view and you'll hardly notice. Great value, but no alcohol.

RESIDENCE DEIRA BY LE MERIDIEN

Map pp52-3   Hotel $

☎ 224 1777; www.starwood-hotels.com /lemeridien; cnr Al-Maktoum Rd & 15 St; r from Dh450; 🖳 🛜

If you're not a member of the FWS (Fat Wallet Society) but are still in need of good-sized, immaculate rooms (with full kitchens!) and attentive service, this property should hit the mark. Don't expect the same luxe touches as you usually find in Meridien properties. However, perks such as being a mere Frisbee toss from Union Metro station and access privileges at the nearby Meridien Dubai (gym, pools, tennis courts) are nothing to sneeze at.

PREMIER INN DUBAI INTERNATIONAL AIRPORT

off Map pp54-5   Hotel $

☎ 885 0999; www.premierinn.com; Airport Rd, outside Terminal 3; r from Dh375; 🖳 🛜 🏋

If your plane lands late or leaves early, this surprisingly stylish shut-eye zone is a convenient place to check in. The third Dubai property of this huge UK-based budget hotel chain delivers modern, if pocket-sized, digs appealingly accented with the company's trademark purple. Plane-spotters can indulge their obsession while floating in the rooftop pool.

VILLA 47 Map pp54-5   B&B $

☎ 268 8239, 050 634 1286; www.villa47.com; cnr 19 & 26 Sts, Al-Garhoud; r incl breakfast Dh350; 🖳 🛜

A superb find if you don't need buckets of privacy, this B&B is just two rooms in a bougainvillea-draped private home on a quiet street, yet close to the airport (no plane noise, though). Your outgoing hosts Ancy and Thomas make a mean breakfast and will happily help you plan your day. The Irish Village pub (p127) and restaurants are close by.

DUBAI YOUTH HOSTEL Map p50   Hostel $

☎ 298 8151/61; www.uaeyha.com; 39 Al-Nahda Rd, Al-Qusais, btwn Lulu Hypermarket & Al Bustan Centre; dm/s/d/tr HI members Dh90/170/200/270, nonmembers Dh100/190/220/300; 🖳 🏋

Dubai's only hostel has facilities more typical of a hotel, including a pool, gym, sauna, Jacuzzi, tennis court, coffee shop and laundry. However, being located north of the airport, towards Sharjah, makes it

top picks

ON A BUDGET

- Four Points by Sheraton Bur Dubai (opposite)
- Fusion Hotel (p162)
- Ibis World Trade Centre (p161)
- Jumeirah Garden Guesthouse (p162)
- Residence Deira by Le Meridien (left)

a less than convenient base for extensive city exploring. Private rooms in the new wing (Hostel A) come with TV, refrigerator and bathrooms, but the dorms in the older wings (Hostels B and C) are basic and exude that familiar institutional blah. To get to the hostel from the airport take bus 34 from the Terminal 1 departure level; it runs every 30 minutes between 7.45am and 10.15pm (15 minutes, Dh3). A taxi should cost about Dh35 to Dh40. Once the Metro Green Line is operational, the closest station will be Stadium, about 400m from the hostel.

BUR DUBAI

Bur Dubai's heritage sights – Bastakia and Bur Dubai Souq – should be on every traveller's list, and the closer you stay to them, the richer your experience of Dubai will be. Alas, with the exception of the dynamic Indian quarter between Khalid bin al-Waleed Rd and Al-Fahidi St, the rest of Bur Dubai feels soulless, full of low-rise concrete-block apartments. There are lots of apartment-hotels here, but few you'd get excited about recommending; Golden Sands (p158) dominates the market.

RAFFLES DUBAI Map pp64-5   Hotel $$$

☎ 324 8888; www.dubai.raffles.com; Sheikh Rashid Rd, near Wafi Mall, Oud Metha; r from Dh1275; 🖳 🛜 🏋

Here's a luxury hotel that lives up to the moniker. Built in the shape of a pyramid, Raffles is a high-octane hot spot with magnificent oversized rooms (with balconies) done in the colours of a Moroccan kilim – deep blue, burgundy red and sandy taupe. Bathrooms are of limestone and sandstone imported from Egypt, with giant sunken tubs and rainfall showerheads. Zeitgeist-capturing in-room touches include Lavazza espresso machines, lighting controlled from a bedside console, iPod docking stations and free wi-fi. Nice extras: the rooftop botanical garden and fantastic poolside water clock.

GRAND HYATT DUBAI
Map pp64-5   Hotel $$$

☎ 317 1234; www.dubai.grand.hyatt.com; Al-Qataiyat Rd, Oud Metha; r from Dh1160; 🖥 🛜 🕭
The vast white-marble lobby at this hulking resort recreates a tropical rainforest, with dhow hulls hanging from the ceiling. Rooms are sheathed in sophisticated shades of taupe, peach and auburn and exude a timeless elegance with their thick carpets, picture windows and tasselled draperies. Bathrooms have separate tub and shower combinations. Facilities are impressive and include Dubai's biggest swimming pool, extensive palm-tree-studded gardens, a kids' club, tennis courts, a fantastic gym, and several excellent restaurants. Bonus points for the solar-panelled roof that cools down the pools (or heats them up in winter).

MÖVENPICK HOTEL BUR DUBAI
Map pp64-5   Hotel $$

☎ 336 6000; www.moevenpick-hotels.com; 19 St, Oud Metha; r from Dh950; 🖥 🛜 🕭
The lobby looks like it was decorated by a court jester, with red-leather walls, faux gold-leaf ceilings and a sweeping staircase. The rooms' decor plays it safer in a midrange business kind of way, but crisp white duvets and feather pillows compensate for the buttermilk blandness; spacious bathrooms provide plenty of room. The rooftop pool is good for laps and the gym has extensive equipment. Note: choose a

city-view room or you'll overlook the sunless atrium.

RAMADA HOTEL
Map pp62-3   Hotel $$

☎ 351 9999; www.ramadadubai.com; Al-Mankhool Rd, Mankhool; r from Dh650; 🖥 🕭
The most attention-grabbing feature of this mid-budget hotel is its striking stained-glass feature stretching 10 storeys up the atrium. The 172 split-level rooms have been nicely made over and feature warm furnishings and 25" plasma TVs. Bonus points for the excellent gym, the selection of restaurants and bars and for being within walking distance of good ethnic eateries, BurJuman Centre and the Metro station.

FOUR POINTS BY SHERATON DOWNTOWN DUBAI
Map pp62-3   Hotel $$

☎ 354 3333; www.starwoodhotels.com; 4C St, off Al-Mankhool Rd, Mankhool; r from Dh600; 🖥 🕭
The stark-white chrome-and-marble lobby can't quite decide what it's trying to be – contemporary Italian, 1950s modern, or 1970s disco – but rooms at this midrange hotel are spacious enough for a small family. The location is a bit nondescript, but extras such as comfy mattresses, big flatscreen TVs, and rooftop gym and pool compensate. Good value.

XVA ART HOTEL
Map pp62-3   Boutique Hotel $$

☎ 353 5383; www.xvagallery.com; behind Basta Art Cafe, off Al-Fahidi St, Bastakia Quarter; r incl breakfast Dh600-750; 🛜
This hippie-chic boutique hotel occupies a century-old villa, complete with wind towers, in the heart of the historic Bastakia Quarter. Rooms open onto a courtyard doubling as a cafe and leading to a well-regarded gallery. Each one is different, but all are decked out with local artwork, arabesque flourishes and rich colours. Best of all, you get the feeling of staying in a real Arabian guest house. Put XVA at the top of your list. No TVs. No alcohol.

ORIENT GUEST HOUSE
Map pp62-3   Boutique Hotel $$

☎ 351 9111; www.orientguesthouse.com; off Al-Fahidi St, Bastakia Quarter; r Dh425-1200
Tucked into the historic Bastakia Quarter, this charismatic boutique hotel captures the feeling of old Dubai. Rooms in the former home surround a central courtyard;

TAXI SIR?

Many four- and five-star hotels in Dubai offer guests dedicated taxi service in chauffeur-driven sedans under contract with the hotel. These 'limos' have no signage, though they do have meters (if not, don't get in) and generally cost about Dh5 more than a regular taxi, provided there's no slowdown. But when you're stuck in heavy traffic, the meter ticks fast: expect to pay nearly double the fee of a regular cab. If you object to paying more, tell the bell captain you want a regular taxi (you might have to insist). But if you are pressed for time and there are no other cabs available, you'll be grateful for the wheels.

each is styled with carved wooden head-boards, delicate chandeliers and velvety-soft jewel-tone fabrics. Alas, the bathrooms are tiny and the pillows thin, but the charming service and romantic vibe more than compensate.

FOUR POINTS BY SHERATON BUR DUBAI Map pp62-3   Hotel $
☎ 397 7444; www.starwoodhotels.com; Khalid bin al-Waleed Rd, Mankhool; r from Dh425; 🖳 🖭
Despite the gritty pavement scene out front, this Four Points (one of three in Dubai) is a reliable business address. Rooms are bathed in cheerful golds and yellows and sport exceptionally good bedlinen – crisp white cotton duvet covers with plump feather pillows, a rarity in this price range. You'll find an adequate gym, a small pool, a hot tub and a British pub downstairs. The location is convenient for sightseeing, but taxis are hard to hail.

ARABIAN COURTYARD HOTEL & SPA
Map pp62-3   Hotel $
☎ 351 9111; www.arabiancourtyard.com; Al-Fahidi St; r from Dh400; 🖳 🖭
Being located opposite the Dubai Museum makes this hotel an excellent launch pad for city explorers. The decent-sized rooms are comfy, decked out in fresh, good-mood colours and exude a homey ambience thanks to Arabic design flourishes. Ask for one from which you can spy the Creek. Overall, a good-value pick in a central location.

GOLDEN SANDS HOTEL APARTMENTS Map pp62-3   Hotel Apartments $
☎ 355 5553; www.goldensandsdubai.com; multiple locations off Al-Mankhool Rd, Mankhool; studio apt from Dh325; 🖳 🛜 🖭
Golden Sands gets kudos for being a pioneer of the hotel apartment concept in Dubai but, on the downside, it shows. The 750 studios, one- and two-bedroom apartments spread over 12 stand-alone buildings, all boxy concrete structures, have seen a lot of wear and tear from travellers over the years. Furnishings are utilitarian and bland and the efficiency-style kitchens are tiny, but include a washing machine. Overall, though, still satisfactory crash pads.

DAR AL SONDOS HOTEL APARTMENTS BY LE MERIDIEN
Map pp62-3   Hotel Apartments $
☎ 393 8000; www.starwoodhotels.com; Rolla St; r from Dh300; 🖳 🖭

THE CALL TO PRAYER

If you're staying in the older areas of Deira or Bur Dubai, you may be awoken around 4.30am by the inimitable wailing of the azan, the Muslim call to prayer, through speakers positioned on the minaret of nearby mosques. It's jarring, to be sure, but there's a haunting beauty to the sound, one that you'll only hear in Islamic countries.

Muslims pray five times a day: at dawn; when the sun is directly overhead; when the sun is in the position that creates shadows the same length as the object shadowed; at the beginning of sunset; and at twilight, when the last light of the day disappears over the horizon. The exact times are printed in the daily newspapers and on websites. Once the call has been made, Muslims have half an hour to pray. An exception is made at dawn: after the call they have about 80 minutes in which to wake up, wash and pray, before the sun has risen.

Muslims needn't be near a mosque to pray; they need only face Mecca. If devotees cannot get to a mosque, they'll stop wherever they are and drop to their knees. If you see someone praying, be as unobtrusive as possible, and avoid walking in front of the person. All public buildings, including government departments, libraries, shopping centres and airports, have designated prayer rooms. In every hotel room arrows on the ceiling, desk or bedside table indicate the direction of Mecca. Better hotels provide prayer rugs, sometimes with a built-in compass.

When you hear the call to prayer, listen for the phrasing. First comes 'Allah-u-akbar', which means 'God is Great'. This is repeated four times. Next comes 'Ashhadu an la illallah ha-illaah' (I testify there is no god but God). This is repeated twice, as is the next line, 'Asshadu anna muhammadan rasuulu-ilaah' (I testify that Mohammed is His messenger). Then come two shorter lines, also sung twice: 'Hayya ala as-salaah' (Come to prayer) and 'Hayya ala al-falaah' (Come to salvation). 'Allah-u-akbar' is repeated twice more, before the closing line, 'Laa ilaah illa allah' (There is no god but God).

The only variation on this standard format is at the dawn call. In this azan, after the exhortation to come to salvation, comes the gently nudging, repeated line 'As-salaatu khayrun min al nawn', which translates to 'It is better to pray than to sleep'.

If you're not in a hotel where you can hear the call to prayer, stop by the souqs in Deira and pick up a mosque alarm clock – it's the perfect souvenir to take home to friends.

Smack-dab in the heart of historic Dubai, these roomy digs put you within walking distance of the Shindagha Waterfront, the Bur Dubai Souq, the Dubai Museum and the Bastakia Quarter. You could even catch an *abra* (water taxi) to Deira and pick up some goodies at the Spice Souq and the Fish and Vegetable markets, then whip up a delicious meal back in your kitchen. Afterwards you can wind down the day looking out over the sparkling city while splashing around in the rooftop pool.

SHEIKH ZAYED ROAD

Lined with giant towers, Sheikh Zayed Rd's biggest selling point is location: it's at the city's geographic centrepoint, making it great for exploring. Most of the luxury hotels are near the Dubai International Financial Centre (DIFC) and around Burj Khalifa in Downtown Dubai. Rates skew high, but fluctuate wildly with demand. Alas, rush-hour traffic is terrible.

ADDRESS DOWNTOWN DUBAI
Map pp70-71   Hotel $$$
☎ 436 8888; www.theaddress.com; Emaar Blvd, Downtown Dubai; r from Dh1400; 🖥 🛜 🏊
In a striking tower that's almost as much a lens magnet as the nearby Burj Khalifa, the flagship property of this small chain embodies everything Dubai has to offer: beauty, style, glamour, sexiness and ambition. Since its opening in late 2008, the Address has drawn the cognoscenti in droves, not only to its rooms but also to its edgy restaurants and buzzy bars. If you do stay, you'll find oversized rooms dressed in rich woods and tactile fabrics and endowed with killer views and the latest communication devices. And if that's not enough, the 24-hour gym and five-tiered infinity pool beckon. Wi-fi is free throughout and, if you're staying in a suite or club room, there's a '24-hour stay benefit' (meaning you get to stay 24 hours no matter when you check in).

FAIRMONT Map pp70-71   Hotel $$$
☎ 332 5555; www.fairmont.com; Sheikh Zayed Rd, Financial District; r from Dh1400; 🖥 🛜 🏊
The Fairmont is a distinctive sight at night, when its four-poster towers are illuminated by changing coloured lights. Beyond the flash entrance portals, it also packs plenty

top picks

HOTELS FOR SHOPPING

- Coral Boutique Hotel Apartments (p165)
- Hyatt Regency Dubai (p154)
- Kempinski (p164)
- Palace – The Old Town (below)
- Address Dubai Mall (below)

of design cachet in its public areas and rooms, whose perks include firm, extra-comfy mattresses and a big desk for writing those postcards. When you've got some downtime, the two rooftop pools prove to be solid kicking-back zones. The food outlets are exceptional, especially the Exchange Grill (p116) and Spectrum on One (p116).

PALACE – THE OLD TOWN
Map pp70-71   Hotel $$$
☎ 428 7888; www.thepalace-dubai.com; Emaar Blvd, The Old Town Island, Downtown Dubai; r from Dh1200; 🖥 🛜 🏊
City explorers with a romantic streak will be utterly enchanted by this luxe contender in the shadow of Burj Khalifa. A successful blend of Old World class and Arabic aesthetics, the Palace appeals to those with refined tastes. Rooms have all the careful placement of a still life and are no less arty. Chic and understated, they're styled in soothing earth tones and have balconies overlooking Dubai Fountain. Personal attention is key, from the personal check-in desk to the intimate spa and fab restaurants such as Thiptara (p114) and Asado (p114). Free wi-fi throughout and 24-hour stay benefit in suites and club rooms.

ADDRESS DUBAI MALL
Map pp70-71   Hotel $$$
☎ 438 8888; www.theaddress.com; Emaar Blvd, Downtown Dubai; r from Dh1200; 🖥 🛜 🏊
A modern interpretation of Arabic design traditions, this fashionable newcomer is directly connected to Dubai Mall and thus tailor-made for shopaholics. Lug your loot to spacious rooms where sensuous materials – leather, wood and velvet – provide a soothing antidote to shopping exhaustion, as do the ultracomfy beds draped in fluffy pillow tops and cloud-soft Egyptian cotton. Rooms are also jammed with such lifestyle

essentials as huge flatscreen TVs, an iPod docking station and an espresso machine. Wi-fi is free throughout and the gym and business lounge are both open around the clock. As at other Address hotels, there's a 24-hour 'stay benefit' if staying in a club room or suite.

SHANGRI-LA Map pp70-71 Hotel $$$

☎ 343 8888; www.shangri-la.com; Sheikh Zayed Rd, Downtown Dubai; r from Dh1200; 🖳 🛜 🕸
Shangri-La is the mythical paradise first described in James Hilton's 1933 novel *Lost Horizon*. In Dubai, it's a business hotel imbued with an understatedly sexy vibe. Rooms are a winner in the looks department, with their blonde woods, soft leather headboards and free-standing tubs. The range of first-rate restaurants is superb, as is the sizzling Ikandy rooftop bar (p129). Oh, and for all you trivia buffs: Clooney and Damon slept here while filming scenes from *Syriana* on site – natch!

JUMEIRAH EMIRATES TOWERS
Map pp70-71 Hotel $$

☎ 330 0000; www.jumeirah.com; Sheikh Zayed Rd, Financial District; d from Dh950; 🖳 🛜 🕸
A top business hotel in the Middle East, this high-profile property is one of Dubai's iconic hotels. The black-and-grey aesthetic is ultramasculine and heavy on angular lines; the room layout is sleek and functional with mega-plush gadgets, chief among them a Bang & Olufsen TV. Club-executive rooms even have a radio-frequency USB plug to broadcast tunes from your computer to the TV. Alas, lower-floor bathrooms are disappointingly cramped. Solo women travellers should book the Chopard ladies' floor, where pink replaces grey and in-bath fridges let you chill your caviar face creams. Service here is among Dubai's best.

AL-MUROOJ ROTANA HOTEL & SUITES Map pp70-71 Hotel $$

☎ 321 1111; www.rotana.com; Al-Saffa St, Downtown Dubai; r from 950; 🖳 🛜 🕸
Although catering largely for a business clientele, the Al-Murooj also has plenty in store for leisure travellers, including several pools, a resort-style layout and a fine fitness centre. Rooms can't quite decide whether they're formal-fancy or trendy, but such schizophrenia is easily overlooked in favour of location (next to Burj Khalifa and Dubai Mall) and

top picks

FOR ROMANCE

- Al-Qasr, Madinat Jumeirah (opposite)
- Desert Palm (boxed text, p164)
- One&Only Royal Mirage (p163)
- Park Hyatt Dubai (p154)
- Raffles Dubai (p156)

in-room comforts like oversized tubs and big desks. The Club Rotana rooms include free breakfast, afternoon tea, cocktails, internet access and L'Occitane toiletries.

AL-MANZIL HOTEL Map pp70-71 Hotel $$

☎ 428 5888; www.southernsun.com; Burj Khalifa Blvd, Downtown Dubai; r from Dh930; 🖳 🛜 🕸
Arabesque meets mid-century modern at Al-Manzil, where rooms whip vanilla, chocolate and orange hues into a sophisticated style sorbet. The open-floor-plan rooms (read: no walls, just blinds, between the bed and bath) may not be for the ultramodest, but the giant rainfall showerheads and free-standing tub are tempting nonetheless. Dubai Mall is next door, and if you're jetting in on a late flight, the 24-hour pool and business centre might come in handy. Guests also have free access to the nearby Hayya gym.

DUSIT THANI DUBAI Map pp70-71 Hotel $$

☎ 343 3333; www.dusit.com; Sheikh Zayed Rd, next to Interchange No 1; r from Dh900; 🖳 🛜 🕸
Shaped like an upside-down tuning fork, this is one of Dubai's most architecturally dramatic towers. It's a Thai chain and the name evocatively translates as 'Town in Heaven'. While this sounds romantic, the target market is the business traveller; rooms have big desks and oversized leather chairs, and the usual high-end amenities, like feather-light down pillows. Upper-floor views are stellar. The rooftop pool is good for laps (though overhead trusses partially block the sun).

QAMARDEEN HOTEL Map pp70-71 Hotel $$

☎ 428 6888; www.southernsun.com; Burj Khalifa Blvd, Downtown Dubai; r from Dh810; 🖳 🛜 🕸
Sister to the Al-Manzil (above), the Qamardeen manages to be hip but not overbearing,

with bold splashes of colour in its soaring lobby and big rooms. The look appeals to the lifestyle crowd, thanks at least in part to fresh, ultrasuede upholstery, bright-white linens and uncluttered rooms. The palm-lined, blue-tiled pool with waterfalls and fountains is pretty but small and doesn't get much sun. If you need to let off steam, head to the nearby Hayya gym.

IBIS WORLD TRADE CENTRE

Map pp70-71   Hotel $

☎ 332 4444, reservations 318 7000; www .ibishotel.com; behind World Trade Centre, Sheikh Zayed Rd, Financial District; r Dh225-550; 💻
Of several Dubai branches of this good-value chain, this one near the World Trade Centre is the most central. After the airy feel and mod design in the public areas, the ship's-cabin-sized rooms are a bit of a let-down, but at this price it's hard to find a hotel that's cleaner or more comfortable.

JUMEIRAH

The primary advantage of staying in Jumeirah is its oh-so-civilized and calm beachside location. This is where Emiratis live in big villas. The Creekside heritage sights are a good 20 minutes away. Further west, Umm Suqeim is home to several iconic beach resorts, including the Burj al-Arab. Inland Satwa is bustling, multi-ethnic flair and is considerably less chic, if more real-world.

BURJ AL-ARAB Map pp76-7   Hotel $$$

☎ 301 7777; www.burj-al-arab.com; Jumeirah Rd, Umm Suqeim 3; ste from Dh6500; 💻 📶 🎦
We adore the exterior of Dubai's iconic sail-shaped hotel, but when we first saw the interior, we laughed and nicknamed it the Bourgeois à l'Arabe. Decorated in Sheikh Mohammed's favourite colours – gold, royal blue and carmine red – it regularly beds pop stars, royalty, billionaire Russians

top picks

BOUTIQUE HOTELS

- Fusion Hotel (p162)
- Jumeirah Garden Guesthouse (p162)
- Orient Guest House (p157)
- XVA Art Hotel (p157)

and the merely moneyed. Beyond the striking lobby with its attention-grabbing fountain lie 202 suites with more trimmings than a Christmas turkey. Even the smallest measure 170 sq metres and spread over two floors, making them bigger than most apartments. The decor is l-u-s-h, with moiré silk walls, mirrored ceilings over the beds, curlicue high-backed velvet chairs, and inlaid bathroom tiles displaying scenes of Venice. Staying here means being whisked through customs at the airport and travelling to the hotel by Rolls Royce or helicopter.

AL-QASR, MADINAT JUMEIRAH

Map pp76-7   Resort $$$

☎ 366 8888; www.madinatjumeirah.com; Al-Sufouh Rd, Umm Suqeim 3; d from Dh2050; 💻 📶 🎦
If cookie-cutter hotels don't do it for you, this is your kind of place. Sister to Mina A' Salam (p162), the 292-room Al-Qasr was styled after an Arabian summer palace. Details are extraordinary, like the lobby's Austrian-crystal chandeliers reflecting rainbows onto mirror-polished inlaid-marble floors. Rooms sport heavy arabesque flourishes, rich colours, and cushy furnishings, including sumptuous beds and his-and-her bathroom amenities. The side-by-side balconies lack privacy but overlook the grand display of Madinat Jumeirah. Excellent service, great beach.

JUMEIRAH BEACH HOTEL

Map pp76-7   Resort $$$

☎ 348 0000; www.jumeirah. com; Jumeirah Rd, Umm Suqeim 3; r from Dh2000; 💻 📶 🎦
The most family-friendly Jumeirah Group hotel is shaped like a giant wave. The beach is huge (nearly 1km long), but the lobby is a bit garish and the rooms need help: the curly-wurly-patterned bedspreads badly clash with the multi-hued carpets and the red-blonde furniture looks mass-issue. Stellar Burj al-Arab views, often from your private balcony, somewhat make up for the retro look, and we've been told that a floor-by-floor update is forthcoming. It's a great resort for active types, with plenty of water sports, a superb health club, a climbing wall and tennis and squash courts. Little ones can make new friends in Sinbad's Kids Club; admission to the adjoining Wild Wadi Waterpark (p80) is free for guests.

MINA A' SALAM, MADINAT JUMEIRAH Map pp76-7 Resort $$$

☎ 366 8888; www.jumeirah.com; Al-Sufouh Rd, Umm Suqeim 3; r from Dh1550; 🖥 🛜 🛎

Meaning 'harbour of peace', the Mina A' Salam has few false notes. The striking lobby is a mere overture to the full symphony of luxury awaiting in huge, amenity-laden rooms with balconies overlooking the romantic jumble that is Madinat Jumeirah or the striking Burj al-Arab. Guests have the entire run of the place and adjacent sister property Al-Qasr (p161), including the pools, the private beach and the kids' club. Rates include free admission to Wild Wadi Waterpark (p80).

DUBAI MARINE BEACH RESORT & SPA Map pp76-7 Resort $$$

☎ 346 1111; www.dxbmarine.com; Jumeirah Rd, Jumeirah 1; r from Dh1200; 🖥 🛜 🛎

You'll forgive the vintage-1980s condo box architecture when you consider the convenience of staying a frisbee toss from the paved Jumeirah Beach path (great for jogging or cycling), within earshot of the Jumeirah Mosque and close to eclectic shopping on Jumeirah Rd. Dubai Marine is a compact beachside resort with meandering gardens, terrific restaurants and nightclubs, three pools, a well-equipped gym and a small sandy beach. Rooms are comfy enough but at no risk of being featured on the pages of *Architectural Digest* – it's the facilities that make it stand out.

FUSION HOTEL Map pp76-7 B&B $

☎ 050 478 7539; www.fusionhotels.com; Villa 14, 25 St, off Al-Wasl Rd, Jumeirah 3; r from Dh425; 🛜 🛎

This well-priced B&B, tucked away in a dreamy garden in residential Jumeirah, is a perfect hideaway for anyone tired of big, anonymous hotels. Rooms are rather minimalist, but rates are terrific for what you get – privacy, space, breakfast and, best of all, the sense that you're a guest in someone's home. There's a supermarket and a couple of eateries within walking distance.

JUMEIRAH GARDEN GUESTHOUSE Map pp76-7 B&B $

☎ 050 956 2854; www.thejumeirahgarden.com; 15 St, Al-Manara; r Dh350-400; 🖥 🛜 🛎

The convivial British expat owners have poured their hearts and cash into turning

top picks

HOTEL DINING

- Al-Qasr, Madinat Jumeirah (p161)
- One&Only Royal Mirage (opposite)
- Palace – The Old Town (p159)
- Park Hyatt Dubai (p154)
- Radisson Blu Hotel (p155)
- Shangri-La (p160)

this stately garden villa into an oasis of charm. All 10 rooms bulge with character and hand-picked furnishings; from some rooms you even spy the Burj al-Arab in the distance. The beach, malls and restaurants are a longish walk or short cab ride away. At night, chef Andy whips up gourmet dinners served family-style in the garden (optional, Dh170).

RYDGES PLAZA Map pp62-3 Hotel $

☎ 398 2222; www.rydges.com; Al-Dhiyafah Rd, near Satwa Roundabout, Satwa; r Dh300-700; 🖥 🛎

In the heart of polyethnic Satwa, one of Dubai's most dynamic walking areas, the Rydges has chintzy English-style dark-wood decor and big showers capable of pummelling you back from the bleary-eyed brink. Jumeirah Beach and Deira are just a quick hop away and taxis are plentiful. You'll be a hop, skip and jump from famous Ravi (p120) and Al-Mallah (see boxed text, p120) but the on-site restaurants also have their fans. The health club has great circuit-training machines; the pool is good for laps.

HOLIDAY INN EXPRESS off Map pp76-7 Hotel $

☎ 407 1777; www.ichotelsgroup.com; cnr Jumeirah Rd & 60 St; r from Dh270; 🖥 🛜

This contemporary property would be more attractive if it wasn't overlooking Port Rashid, but at least you'll be close to the beach and posh Jumeirah without eviscerating your wallet. Being quite new, this property has a clean contemporary feel, starting in the Bauhaus-meets-Arabia lobby and transitioning nicely to the rooms kitted out in ebony and apricot hues. There's no pool but a free beach shuttle.

NEW DUBAI

The ritziest of the beach hotels cluster in and around the Dubai Marina, a spanking-new high-rise development on the southern reaches of the city. Many offer views of the new Palm Jumeirah. Of late, a growing crop of hotel apartments and budget to midrange hotels has been sprouting inland, west of the humungous Mall of the Emirates. We've listed a few in this section, but also look for Centro Barsha, the promising new budget hotel by Rotana that had not yet opened during our research visit. Check www.rotana .com for updates.

ONE&ONLY ROYAL MIRAGE

Map pp82-3   Resort $$$

☎ 399 9999; www.oneandonlyresorts.com; Al-Sufouh Rd, Al-Sufouh; Palace/Arabian Court r Dh2240-3740, Residence & Spa r Dh3540-5320; 🖳 🛜 🖭

A class act all around, the Royal Mirage consists of three parts: the Moorish-style Palace, the romantic Arabian Court, and the Residence & Spa, with its majestic spa and hammam (bathhouse). All rooms face the sea, are tastefully furnished and shine with thoughtful feel-at-home touches such as supremely comfortable beds. Spend your days meandering the palm-lined gardens, lollygagging by the giant pools, or strolling along the 1km private beach. The bars and restaurants here are among Dubai's best.

LE ROYAL MERIDIEN BEACH RESORT & SPA Map pp82-3   Resort $$$

☎ 399 5555; www.leroyalmeridien-dubai.com; cnr Murjan Ave & Dhow St, off Al-Sufouh Rd, Al-Sufouh, Dubai Marina; r from Dh2050; 🖳 🛜 🖭

An urge to splurge would be well directed towards this 500-room resort flanking a gorgeous beach and extensive gardens. While rooms in the main building are the most family-friendly (some have connecting doors), discerning couples may be more charmed by the elegant, classically furnished retreats in the Tower Building. All have sea-view balconies. With three pools (one for kids only), a top-notch gym, a full menu of water sports and lots of activities for kids and teens, no one will get bored. Applause for such greening efforts as watering the gardens with grey water and using steam from the laundry to heat the swimming pool in winter.

RITZ-CARLTON DUBAI

Map pp82-3   Hotel $$$

☎ 399 4000; www.ritzcarlton.com; The Walk at JBR, Dubai Marina; r Dh2100; 🖳 🛜 🖭

In a city that likes to teeter on the cutting edge, the Ritz-Carlton exudes an aura of timeless elegance. When it first opened in 1998, Dubai Marina was still the middle of nowhere. Now high-rises loom above, but the mature gardens and tall palms create a visual berm. The Mediterranean villa–style resort is typical of the chain's restrained and elegant European style – conservative, but cushy – with plush fabrics, marble foyers and colonial-style hardwood furniture. All 138 rooms face the gardens and sea beyond. Spend the day by one of three pools or on the expansive beach.

HILTON DUBAI JUMEIRAH

Map pp82-3   Resort $$$

☎ 399 1111; www.hilton.com; The Walk at JBR; r from Dh1500; 🖳 🛜 🖭

Right on the popular The Walk at JBR (p81), the Hilton remains a solid choice for a family vacation. Rooms are nothing special – think pastel boxes – but most face the sea, and it has a generous stretch of beach, a playground, babysitting, casual eateries and kids' activities. Unless you can get a deal, you can probably do better elsewhere.

WESTIN DUBAI MINA SEYAHI

Map pp82-3   Resort $$$

☎ 399 4141; www.starwoodhotels.com; Al-Sufouh Rd, Al-Sufouh; r from Dh1450; 🖳 🛜 🖭

The top choice for water sports enthusiasts, this spiffy beach resort sits smack next to the yacht harbour and aesthetically appears like a cross between a sheikh's summer palace and an Italian palazzo. With their classic furniture and vanilla and chocolate hues, the oversized rooms look sharp yet

top picks

SWIMMING POOLS

- Grand Hyatt Dubai (p157)
- Le Royal Meridien Beach Resort & Spa (left)
- One&Only Royal Mirage (left)
- Ritz-Carlton Dubai (above)
- Address Downtown Dubai (p159)
- Westin Dubai Mina Seyahi (above)

homey. Just don't get stuck in one without a sea view! As at all Westins, the biggest selling point is the ultracush Heavenly Bed. And we love the three pools, especially the 150m-long lagoon-like winding pool for lazing (the others are for kiddies and for swimming laps). The hotel shares facilities, including a water sports centre, with the neighbouring Le Meridien Mina Seyahi (right).

KEMPINSKI Map pp82-3   Hotel $$$

☎ 341 0000; www.kempinski-dubai.com; Mall of the Emirates, Al-Barsha; r from Dh1375; 🖳 🛜 🖭
Adjoining the Mall of the Emirates, the Kempinski is tops for a shopping holiday. The monumental marble lobby contrasts with the rooms, which are warmly furnished in a silver, burgundy and white colour scheme and have polished wooden floors and subtle Arabic design accents. Some of the bathrooms sport enormous

tubs and travertine, sit-down shower stalls with rainfall showerheads. Spot the Burj al-Arab through floor-to-ceiling windows facing Sheikh Zayed Rd. The Kempinksi is also home to unique 'Ski Chalets', enormous Alpine-style apartments overlooking Ski Dubai; alas, they get no sun. Good gym. Great beds.

LE MERIDIEN MINA SEYAHI BEACH RESORT & MARINA Map pp82-3   Resort $$$

☎ 399 3333, www.lemeridien-minaseyahi.com; Al-Sufouh Rd, Al-Sufouh; r from Dh1350; 🖳 🖭
Twinned with the Westin (p163), this beachfront hotel is nirvana for active types, offering a plethora of water sports (from waterskiing to kayaking), tennis courts and an enormous gym with state-of-the-art equipment and courses from Thai boxing to Pilates. The giant freeform pool is as lovely as the meandering palm-tree-lined

DESERT DREAMS

Just a short drive from the traffic jams, construction sites and megamalls are three stellar desert resorts. If you're craving a little peace and quiet, and are prepared to spend some serious money, these hotels will show you a calmer, less-hurried side of Dubai.

Desert Palm (off Map p50; ☎ 323 8888; www.desertpalm.ae; Hatta/Oman Rd; ste incl breakfast Dh1850-2500, villa Dh4000-6250; 🛜 🖭) Feel the stresses nibbling at your psyche evaporate the moment you step inside this luxe boutique retreat a short drive south of town and set on a private polo estate. You can opt either for a tony suite with floor-to-ceiling windows overlooking the polo fields, or go for total privacy in one of the villas with private pool. Either way, you'll feel quite blissed out amid earth-toned decor, fancy linens and soft tunes emanating from a Bose surround-sound system. There's also an on-site spa for peaceful pummelling and a gourmet deli for picking up tasty treats to enjoy on the terrace or as a desert picnic.

Bab al-Shams Desert Resort & Spa (Map p169; ☎ 832 6699; near Endurance Villlage; r incl breakfast from Dh950; 🖳 🛜 🖭) Resembling an Arabian fort and effortlessly blending into the desertscape, Bab al-Shams is a tonic for tourists seeking to indulge their The Thousand and One Nights fantasies. While the Al-Hadheerah restaurant whirls dervishes, wiggles bellies and caravans camels in a dinner show of Disneyesque proportions (Dh395, including soft drinks), the hotel itself is more restrained. Its labyrinthine layout displays both Arabic and Moorish influences, while rooms are gorgeous, spacious and evocatively earthy, with pillars, lanterns, paintings of desert landscapes and prettily patterned Bedouin-style pillows. While this is the perfect place to curl up with a book or meditate in the dunes, the stimuli-deprived will find plenty to do. A wonderful infinity pool beckons, as do the luscious Satori Spa and an archery range. Kids under 12 years can let off steam in Sinbad's Club. Off-site activities include desert tours as well as horse and camel rides. Bab al-Shams is about 40 minutes south of Dubai.

Al Maha Desert Resort & Spa (Map p169; ☎ 303 4222; www.al-maha-com; off the Dubai to Al-Ain Rd; ste weekday/weekend incl all meals from Dh2750/5430; 🛜 🖭) It may only be 65km southeast of Dubai, but Al Maha feels like an entirely different universe. Gone are the traffic, gone the skyscrapers, gone the go-go attitude. At this remote desert eco-resort it's all about getting back to some elemental discoveries about yourself and where you fit into Nature's grand design. Part of the Dubai Desert Conservation Reserve (DDCR), Al Maha is one of the most exclusive hotels in the Emirates and named for the endangered Arabian oryx, which are bred as part of DDCR's conservation program. The resort's 42 luxurious suites are all stand-alone, canvas-roofed bungalows with private plunge pools. Each one has its own patio with stunning vistas of the beautiful desert landscape and peach-coloured dunes, punctuated by mountains and grazing white oryx and gazelles. Rates include two daily activities such as a desert wildlife drive or a camel trek. Private vehicles, visitors and children under 12 years are not allowed, and taking meals at your suite rather than in the dining room is a popular choice.

gardens and calm beach. The 210 rooms have all the expected amenities but are a bit dated; a renovation was slated for 2010.

GROSVENOR HOUSE Map pp82-3   Hotel $$$
☎ 399 8888; www.grosvenorhouse.lemeridien .com; Al-Sufouh Rd, Dubai Marina; r from Dh1150; 🖥 🛜 🖳

Grosvenor House was the first hotel to open among the jumble of the Marina's sky-punching towers. The public areas are sleek, grown-up and angular, but rooms feel warm and homey with their cream and brown hues brightened by red accents. Beds have gazillion-thread-count linens and even come with a 'pillow menu'. Downstairs is the famous Buddha Bar (p131). Staying at the Grosvenor entitles you to full access to pool and beach facilities at the nearby sister hotel, Le Royal Meridien (p163), which is served by a shuttle bus.

ADDRESS DUBAI MARINA
Map pp82-3   Hotel $$$
☎ 436 7777; www.theaddress.com; Dubai Marina; r from Dh1000; 🖥 🛜 🖳

This new contender in the Marina sports the sophistication of a city hotel yet gets leisure cred by being close to the beach and The Walk at JBR. It's also connected to the Dubai Marina Mall, which is not to be confused with the much bigger Dubai Mall (free shuttles to there run from the hotel). Rooms have lots of elbow room and a contemporary, fresh flair, as well as the gamut of amenities. The huge infinity pool on the 4th floor is the perfect unwinding station, with views of the Marina yachts and highrises. Free wi-fi.

NAJD HOTEL APARTMENTS
Map pp82-3   Hotel Apartments $$
☎ 361 9007; www.najdhotelapartments.com; btwn 6A & 15 Sts, Al-Barsha; 1-/2-bedroom apt Dh950/1450; 🖥 🛜 🖳

One of the nicer of the new crop of hotel apartments mushrooming around the Mall of the Emirates, Najd welcomes you with Arabic hospitality (love those dates and coffee in the lobby). The tiled-floor apartments make maximum use of space, packing a living room, bedroom, kitchen, full bathroom and guest bathroom into a relatively compact frame. Ask for a room overlooking Ski Dubai. Discounts are often available.

CORAL BOUTIQUE HOTEL
APARTMENTS Map pp82-3   Hotel Apartments $$
☎ 340 9040; cnr 21 & 2 Sts, Al-Barsha; 1-/2-/3-bedroom apt Dh650/1100/1200; 🛜 🖳

You'll have plenty of space to stretch out in these stylish apartments with flatscreen TVs, tiled floors and natural stone bathrooms, within walking distance of the Mall of the Emirates. We also like the range of freebies: breakfast buffet, internet and shuttle to the mall. The rooftop pool is great for post-shopping relaxation.

IBIS MALL OF THE EMIRATES
Map pp82-3   Hotel $
☎ 382 3000; www.ibis.com; 2A St, Al-Barsha; r from Dh270; 🖥 🛜

Open since June 2009, this is classic Ibis: a good deal with low frills. If you'd rather drop your cash in the adjacent mall than loll by the pool or nosh on pillow treats, this is not a bad place to hang your hat. Just remember that you can't hang much more than that in the ship's-cabin-sized – if sparkling – rooms.

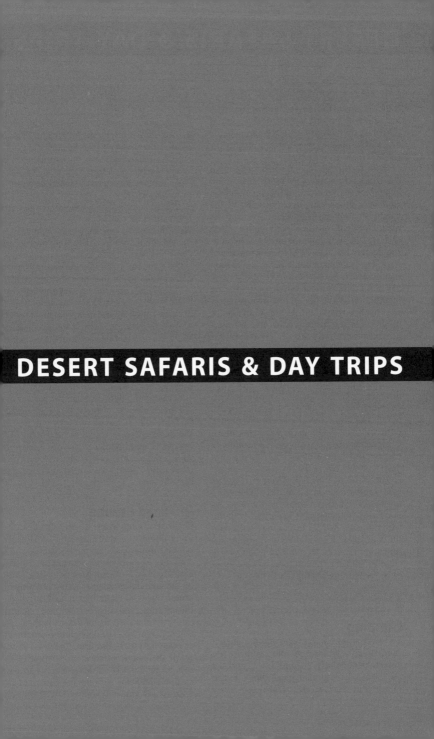

DESERT SAFARIS & DAY TRIPS

DESERT SAFARIS

It may be one of the most urbanised countries in the world, but the United Arab Emirates (UAE) is extremely proud of its Bedouin heritage, and its people retain a strong affinity for the desert.

In the pre-oil age, life was harsh for Bedouin tribes in what was then the Trucial States. Food and water were scarce and living conditions were very simple, and uncomfortable at the height of summer. Bedu would live in tents made from goat or camel hair, dig for water, and use falcons to hunt for birds and hares to supplement their basic diet of dates and camel milk. Those living on settlements had to pool their resources in order to survive, and a sense of community spirit imbued Bedu with the qualities of hospitality and generosity. Soon after the discovery of oil, the government built modern houses, roads, schools and hospitals for Dubai's desert dwellers, but the traditions and culture of life in the desert – from falconry to song and dance – remain intact.

A trip to the desert is an essential part of any Dubai holiday. If you can get some distance from the main road, the emptiness, enormity and tranquillity of the landscape can be breathtaking, with the ochre and orange dunes rippling gently in the wind and undulating as far as the eye can see. The country's biggest sand dune, Moreeb Hill, is in the Liwa desert, on the edge of the vast expanse known as Rub' al-Khali, the Empty Quarter. If you've read *Arabian Sands,* Sir Wilfred Thesiger's mesmerising account of his journeys across the Empty Quarter and experiences living with nomadic Bedu, a trip to Liwa will bring the book to life. That middle-of-nowhere satisfaction is harder to come by when you're close to Dubai, although there are plenty of quiet spots alongside the road to Hatta.

ACTIVITIES
Camping

The UAE does not yet have any designated campsites, but many people camp in the desert, particularly around Liwa, and on the East Coast, especially near Dibba. Beach camping at Jebel Ali near Dubai requires a camping permit from Dubai Municipality (☎ 221 5555) but is marred by the construction of the Palm Jebel Ali. Littering is a major problem: camels, gazelles, birds and other animals often die from ingesting plastic bags or bottles, so please be sensitive to this. To curb the problem, the UAE Ministry of Environment and Water recently announced the launch of several designated campgrounds, although no timeline was given.

If you've got a 4WD, the possibilities are fantastic. You can head to the windswept sand dunes of Liwa, the wadis near Hatta, the mountains of Ras al-Khaimah or the East Coast beaches around Dibba. If you don't have a 4WD, you can still find some beautiful spots within walking distance of well-paved roads.

A camping trip between May and September is likely to be extremely uncomfortable – days are scorching and nights hot and humid. Make sure you are adequately equipped. Carry a fully charged mobile phone, all the necessary maps (preferably a GPS), sunscreen, insect repellent and plenty of water. If you go camping in December or January, make sure you're prepared for cold night-time weather.

Some of the best destinations for camping are: Huwaylat, a tiny village surrounded by wadis; Qarn Nazwa, a rocky outcrop in the desert; Jebel Rawdah, a mountain just over the Omani border in an area known as 'Death Valley'; and Khor Khalba, renowned for its beautiful mangrove forests and excellent birdwatching.

Off-Road Driving

Off-road driving in the desert (also disturbingly known as 'dune-bashing') is hugely popular in the UAE. At weekends, the city's traffic-tired workers zip down the Dubai–Hatta road and unleash their pent-up energy on the sand dunes, such as a ruby-red heap of sand halfway to Hatta nicknamed 'Big Red'. Pitting your 2½ tonnes of machinery against this giant clenched fist of a dune is thrilling, although you won't be doing the environment any favours (see boxed text, p170).

All the major car-hire companies (p181) can provide 4WD vehicles. Expect to pay around Dh500 for 24 hours for a Toyota Fortuner or a Hummer H3, plus CDW (Collision

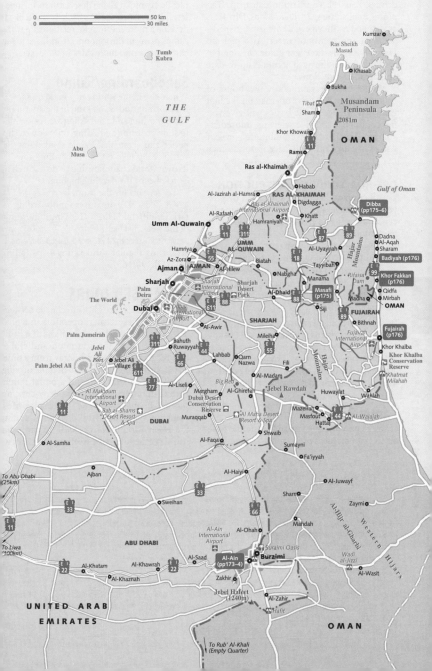

Damage Waiver) of Dh60 and an extra Dh12 for personal insurance.

If you're driving off-road for the first time, you should ideally travel with other cars and drivers. You'll also need up-to-date maps (Explorer Publishing's *Off-Road Maps*, Dh145, is as detailed as they get), a tow rope, a spade, a shovel and plenty of water. Also pick up Dariush Zandi's excellent guide *Off-Road in the Emirates* for the most accurate, up-to-date and detailed directions.

We strongly recommend a few hours of training before you drive off-road for the first time. Knowledge of the basics will give you the confidence to drive safely on unpredictable terrain. Don't be overambitious – even if you're an expert off-road driver, your car may not be able to handle the biggest bumps.

OFF-ROAD DRIVING INSTRUCTION

On all courses drivers must be aged over 25 years and have an international driving licence, as well as a home licence valid for at least another year.

Desert Rangers (Map pp82-3; ☎ 357 2233; www.desertrangers.com) From September to May, this company – located in the Pearl Coast Hotel, near the Mall of the Emirates – runs one-day desert driving courses costing Dh1800 (Dh1000 if you bring your own car). Prices cover two students per vehicle.

Emirates Driving Institute (Map pp54-5; ☎ 263 1100; www.edi-uae.com) Near the Al-Bustan Center in Al-Qusais (Deira), EDI runs desert driving courses that are very thorough and offer fantastic value for money. A full-day course in one of its vehicles costs Dh500 (Dh550 on Fridays) and includes lunch. There's a maximum of two students per vehicle.

Camel Riding

If you're on your first trip to the Middle East, a short camel ride is pretty much compulsory.

It's cheesy, clichéd and ever-so-slightly uncomfortable, but a souvenir shot of you and your humped pal will delight your family back home and do wonders for your Facebook profile. Pretty much all the desert safaris include a few minutes on a camel's back. If you'd like to develop a more meaningful relationship with a camel, many of the tour operators listed opposite can arrange one-hour rides in the desert.

Sandboarding/Skiing

Where else in the world can you ski on snow in the morning and ski on sand in the afternoon? Sandboarding and sand skiing are very similar to snowboarding and skiing, only slower, slipperier and scratchier. While sand skiing has yet to really take off, sandboarding now has its own world championships – do a search on YouTube for the dazzling highlights.

To get you on the sand, Desert Rangers (Map pp82-3; ☎ 357 2233) organises sandboarding safaris (adult/child Dh250/160) most mornings of the week. Net Tours (Map pp54-5; ☎ 266 6655; www.nettoursdubai.com; Hyatt Regency Dubai, off Al-Khaleej Rd, Deira) runs regular sand-skiing trips (adult/child Dh190/165).

ORGANISED TOURS

At first glance, there's little to choose between most of the desert safari operators in Dubai. They all offer daily half-day safaris that begin in the middle of the afternoon and end at around 10pm. These rarely stray from a time-tested formula: an hour or so of dune driving, a visit to a camel farm, and a buffet dinner with all the anticipated extras – belly-dancing, *sheesha*, henna tattoos and camel rides. Most companies also offer full-day tours, adding the Hajar Mountains or Hatta to the usual half-day schedule. If the weather's pleasant, w

THE FRAGILE DESERT

An unfortunate consequence of the rapid growth of Dubai's tourism industry is that the desert is being damaged. It is an extremely fragile ecosystem and home to hundreds of species. In the parts of the desert where topsoil has been damaged by 4WDs, very little lives or grows. The Bedouin people have always had a huge amount of respect for the desert, but the desert is getting more scarce as the development of Dubai continues apace. The biggest problem is pollution. Hundreds of camels die every year due to eating plastic bags carelessly dumped in the desert; lumps of calcified plastic frequently found in the stomachs of dead camels can weigh up to 60kg.

By supporting the Dubai Desert Conservation Reserve (see boxed text, opposite) and limiting the area that desert safari companies can operate in to the environs of Al-Awir, the government is taking important steps to protect the environment. To do your bit, stick to tracks wherever possible when driving off-road and avoid damaging vegetation. Don't drive in wadis: these are important sources of drinking water and can be polluted by oil and grease from cars. And take your rubbish home with you.

DUBAI DESERT CONSERVATION RESERVE

The largest project in Dubai to date, at least in terms of square kilometres, is one we hear practically nothing about. At 225 sq km, the Dubai Desert Conservation Reserve (www.ddcr.org) accounts for five per cent of the emirate's total land. It's a national park, where the primary goal is to protect the desert's biodiversity.

Dubai's approach to environmentalism is characteristically commercial. The DDCR is managed and funded by an airline – a major supplier of climate change – and its super-luxurious resort inside the reserve. But Emirates Airlines, who initiated the project, has done a good job on the DDCR and now other countries are studying Al Maha Desert Resort and Spa (p164) as a model for luxury-sector ecotourism. Since its establishment in 1999, the reserve has reintroduced mountain gazelles and sand gazelles to Dubai's desert, as well as the Arabian oryx, which had almost completely disappeared a few decades ago.

The DDCR is divided into four zones. In the first zone, all human intervention is prohibited, and in the second only very limited operations are allowed to take place. The third zone is only open to resort guests and the fourth is open to a small number of desert tour operators including Arabian Adventures (below), Alpha Tours (below) and Lama Tours (below). If you can't afford a villa at Al Maha – and very few people can – going on a tour with one of these companies is the only way you'll get in.

uggest you spend a little extra (but much less han the cost of a night in a hotel in Dubai) nd opt for an overnight safari – there's othing like sleeping under the stars. Some ompanies have access to the Dubai Desert Conservation Reserve.

Organised desert safaris can be a little disppointing. Tour operators usually hire drivrs rather than guides and they often know ext to nothing about Bedouin culture or he desert environment. It's dispiriting, but on't let this put you off. Even a personality-ree tour of the desert will show you what's nderneath all the new developments and mphasise just how remarkable Dubai's rapid rowth has been.

Most companies also offer an entire menu f other tours, from city tours of Dubai, Alin and Sharjah to active excursions such s fishing expeditions, trekking in the Hajar Mountains, crab hunting on the East Coast, vernight camel treks, and so on. Call or conult the websites of companies listed below or details.

The following companies are all well esablished and licensed by the Department of ourism and Commerce Marketing. Prices uoted are for adults; children's discounts re usually available. Note that some tours nly depart with a minimum number of assengers.

lpha Tours (☎ 294 9888; www.alphatoursdubai.com; HSBC Building, near Al-Maktoum Rd, off exit 61 Sheikh ashid Rd; half-day/overnight safari Dh260/350)

rabian Adventures (Map pp70-71; ☎ 303 4888; ww.arabian-adventures.com; Emirates Holidays Bldg, heikh Zayed Rd; half-day/full-day/overnight safari h330/345/450)

Desert Rangers (Map pp82-3; ☎ 357 2233; www .desertrangers.com; half-day/overnight safari Dh295/425)

Hormuz Tourism (Map pp52-3; ☎ 228 0668; www .hormuztourism.com; Bin Jarsh Bldg, Fish Roundabout, Deira; half-day/overnight safari Dh165/300)

Knight Tours (Map pp70-71; ☎ 343 7725; www .knight tours.co.ae; Al-Wadi Bldg, Sheikh Zayed Rd; half-/full-day safari Dh220/450)

Lama Tours (Map pp64-5; ☎ 334 4330; www.lama .ae; Al-Sayegh Bldg, Oud Metha Rd, Bur Dubai; half-day/ overnight safari Dh275/395)

Net Tours (Map pp54-5; ☎ 209 1234; www .nettoursdubai.com; Hyatt Regency Dubai; half-day/full-day/overnight Dh275/320/425)

Orient Tours (Map pp54-5; ☎ 282 8238; www .orienttours.ae; Al-Garhoud Rd, Deira; half-/full-day safari Dh290/310)

DAY TRIPS

Dubai's relentless drive to create the tallest, longest, biggest and best versions of just about everything has made it the pin-up boy of 21st-century urban development. But while the mad scientists of the city get ever closer to

BEATING THE DRUM

Here's an environmentally friendly, social and entertaining way of seeing the desert – join a drum circle. Dubai Drums (www.dubaidrums.com) hosts regular full-moon drum circles (adult/child Dh190/85) in desert camps. These sessions usually last several hours and occasionally until the early hours of the morning. Watch for the near-legendary all-nighter events. Drums and a barbecue dinner are provided.

complete domination of the *Guinness Book of Records,* some of the villages and towns a short drive away resemble the dioramas of yesteryear at the Dubai Museum. Get some distance from the city and pass tiny roadside mosques, date palms burdened with fruit, camels wandering down the middle of highways, and pristine white-sand beaches with barely a hotel in sight.

The following day trips are selected to add another dimension to your Dubai experience. To the north, Dubai blends imperceptibly into the northern emirate of Sharjah, which has plenty of cultural and artistic assets. To the southeast, Al-Ain is a temperate, convivial and verdantly green city, while the East Coast between Dibba and Fujairah boasts some of the most spectacular scenery in the Emirates. To find out more about what the UAE has to offer visitors, see Lonely Planet's *Oman, UAE & Arabian Peninsula* guide.

SHARJAH

Dubai's northern emirate neighbour, Sharjah, doesn't dazzle with glitz but with culture. Its restored central Arts and Heritage Areas are among the most interesting neighbourhoods in the UAE. Add to that some lively souqs where you can indulge your souvenir cravings and you've got a fascinating destination that's well worth braving the traffic for. The entire centre is fairly compact and best explored on foot to avoid having to deal with the manic traffic. Central Sharjah wraps around Khalid

TRANSPORT: SHARJAH

Distance from Dubai 15km

Direction north

Travel time 30 minutes to two hours, depending on traffic

Car From the World Trade Centre roundabout, take the E11 (Sheikh Zayed Rd) north to Sharjah where it's called Al-Ittihad Rd. Traffic can be horrible, especially during rush hours, so it's best to travel in the late morning and late evening.

Public transport Buses to Sharjah's Al-Jubail station near the Central Souq and Heritage Area depart every 10 minutes from Al-Ittihad station in Deira (Map pp52–3) and from Al-Ghubaiba station in Bur Dubai (Map pp62–3). The ride takes about 40 to 60 minutes and costs Dh5. A taxi to or from Dubai starts at about Dh30.

Lagoon. The historic old town, with the souqs, museums, and heritage and arts area, is to the north across Sharjah Bridge.

One caveat: Sharjah takes its decency laws very seriously, so do dress modestly. That means no exposed knees, backs or bellies – and that goes for both men and women. It's also the only emirate that is 'dry' (ie no alcohol is available anywhere).

Sights

Back in the 19th century, Sharjah's 'who's who' lived just inland from the Corniche between Burj Ave and Al-Maraija Rd, today's so-called Heritage Area. Many of the beautiful residences have been authentically restored using traditional materials such as sea rock, coral and gypsum. Just take an aimless wander through this labyrinthine quarter to come upon the 1845 Bait al-Naboodah (☎ 06-568 1738; adult/child/family Dh5/free/10; ☼ 8am-8pm Sat-Thu 4-8pm Fri), a former pearl trader's home, or the atmospheric Souq al-Arsa (☼ 9am-1pm & 4-9pm Sat-Thu, 4-9pm Fri), the oldest souq in the UAE. The traditional coffeehouse inside is a great stop for a reviving mint tea and plate of dates.

Anchoring the Arts Area, Sharjah Art Museum (☎ 06-568 8222; admission free; ☼ 8am-8pm Sat-Thu 4-8pm Fri) is one of the UAE's largest and most impressive galleries. Its permanent exhibition includes 18th- and 19th-century oil paintings, watercolours and lithographs from the ruling family's collection; curators also mount changing shows of local and international contemporary talent.

A short stroll north is the fantastic Sharjah Museum of Islamic Civilisation (☎ 06-565 5455; www .islamicmuseum.ae; cnr Corniche & Gulf Rd; adult/child/family Dh5/free/10; ☼ 8am-8pm Sat-Thu, 4-8pm Fri), which zeroes in on different aspects of the Islamic faith, scientific accomplishments in the Arab world and 1400 years of Islamic art. Don't miss taking a peek at the central dome with its striking deep-blue zodiac mosaic.

South of the Khalid Lagoon, popular Qanat al-Qasba (☎ 06-556 0777; www.qaq.ae) is a car-free, lively mix of restaurants, cafes and family-friendly entertainment venues along a canal. Diversions include a Ferris wheel and *abra* (water taxi) rides.

West of here, at the Sharjah Maritime Museum (☎ 06-522 2002; adult/child under 18yr/family Dh8/4/20; ☼ 8am-8pm Sat-Thu, 4-8pm Fri), wooden dhows, fishing tools, devices used in pearl diving and historic photographs of grizzled old sea captains pay tribute to the key role the sea

SHARJAH DESERT PARK

About 26km east of central Sharjah towards Al-Dhaid, Sharjah Desert Park (adult/child Dh15/free; 🕑 9am-5.30pm Sun-Mon, 2-5.30pm Fri, 11am-5.30pm Sat) packs four venues into a one-square-kilometre package. The main attraction is the Arabian Wildlife Centre (☎ 531 1999), a zoo and breeding centre showcasing the diversity of critters that call the region home. The indoor aviary is home to flamingos, Houbara bustards and Indian rollers, while the outdoor enclosures house hamadryas baboons, striped hyenas, Arabian wolves and the splendid Arabian leopard.

For a more hands-on experience take kids to the Children's Farm (☎ 531 1127; 🕑 closed noon-4pm), where they can meet, pat and maybe even feed goats, camels and ducks, or ride ponies or camels (Dh5, weekends only). From fossils to dinosaurs to desert plants, the Natural History Museum (☎ 531 1411) takes you through the region's ecosystems and back millions of years in time and is an excellent complement to the new Botanical Museum, which delves deeper into the mysteries of plant life (you get to see inside a plant cell) and the role plants have played in human evolution.

The park grounds also include a cafe and picnic facilities.

---

has played in the emirate's heritage. It's right next to the Sharjah Aquarium (☎ 06-528 5288; www sharjahaquarium.ae; adult/child under 5yr/family Dh20/ free/50; 🕑 8am-8pm Mon-Thu, 4-9pm Fri, 8am-9pm Sat), where ethereal sea horses, charming clown-fish, spooky moray eels, prowling reef sharks and 250 or so other underwater species never fail to amuse, enlighten and entertain.

Shopping

Also called the Blue Souq, the Central Souq (🕑 9am-1pm & 4-11pm Sat-Thu, 9am-noon & 4-11pm Fri) is a beautiful two-part building designed in an appealing, if flashy, Arabic style. The ground floor has mostly modern jewellery, watches and designer clothing, while the little stores upstairs sell pashminas, rugs and curios from such far-flung places as Afghanistan and Rajasthan. If possible, come in the evenings – only tourists shop here during the day.

Sleeping

Marbella Resort (☎ 06-574 1111; www.marbellaresort.net; Buheirah Corniche; 1-/2-bed ste Dh600/1000, villas Dh1500; 🖥 🖭) Looking like a village transplanted from southern Spain, this oldie but goodie has 50 private villas set in lush tropical gardens, making it perfect for families. Facilities include two pools, a gym and tennis and squash courts, to get you off that lounge chair, and a free daily shuttle to Dubai.

Millennium Hotel (☎ 06-555 6666; www.millennium hotels.com; Buheirah Corniche; d from Dh850; 🖥 🖭) A superb lagoon location, plush amenities and a splendid swimming pool are among the many assets that recommend a stay at this snazzy hotel, not far from Qanat al-Qasba. Ask at reception about the free shuttle to the beach and to Deira (in Dubai).

Eating

Sadaf (☎ 06-569 3344; Al-Mina Rd; mains Dh23-40; 🕑 lunch & dinner) Popular with Emirati families, who dine in private booths, Sadaf serves up excellent authentic Persian cuisine. The spicy, moist kebabs are particularly good and the 'Zereshk Polo Meat' (rice with Iranian red barberries and chicken or meat) is another star pick.

Lemongrass (☎ 06-556 5366; Qanat al-Qasba; mains Dh32-62; 🕑 noon-11.30pm) The soothing lime-coloured dining room, brightly flavoured cooking and solicitous service make Lemongrass one of Sharjah's top Thai parlours. If you like spicy, say so – the kitchen is shy with the heat.

Shababeek (☎ 06-554 0444; Block B, Qanat al-Qasba; mezze Dh12-18, mains Dh40-60; 🕑 noon-midnight Sat-Wed, to 1am Thu & Fri) With its deep-purple walls, black furniture and Arabic design flourishes, this upmarket Lebanese restaurant channels Dubai trendiness but without the attitude – or the alcohol.

AL-AIN

With markets, forts, museums and a famous date-palm oasis, Al-Ain is a breath of fresh air after the frantic pace of Dubai. On the border with Oman, about a two-hour drive out of town, the birthplace of Sheikh Zayed (see boxed text, p25) has greatly benefited from his patronage and passion for greening the desert; it's even nicknamed 'Garden City'. But the desert is never far away: simply driving the serpentine road up Jebel Hafeet will treat you to sweeping views of the arid splendour that is the Empty Quarter. Al-Ain itself is an increasingly dynamic place and undergoing all sorts of improvements, including upgraded roads and parks, a new mosque and a wildlife centre, and restored historical sites.

TRANSPORT: AL-AIN

Distance from Dubai 160km

Direction southeast

Travel time 90 minutes

Car From the World Trade Centre roundabout, head south on E11 (Sheikh Zayed Rd), then take exit 56 to Oud Metha Rd (E66) and follow it all the way to Al-Ain

Public transport Al-Ghazal runs minibuses between Al-Ain (Dh20, 1½ hours) and the Al-Ghubaiba bus station (Map pp62-3) in Dubai every hour from 6.30am to 11.30pm. Al-Ain's bus station is off the Al-Murabba (coffeepot) roundabout opposite the Lulu Centre. A taxi to or from Dubai will cost around Dh150.

Al-Ain is quite tough to navigate thanks to a bewildering abundance of roundabouts. To remedy the situation, the city government is converting the most confusing headspinners into signal-controlled intersections. Unfortunately, until the project's completion (target date unknown), this noble effort translates into lots of roadworks and snarled traffic. Brown signs directing visitors to the major tourist attractions are helpful, but a few more sure wouldn't hurt.

Sights

Sheikh Zayed's residence from 1937 to 1966 has been rebooted as the Sheikh Zayed Palace Museum (☎ 03-751 7755; cnr Al-Ain & Zayed ibn Sultan Sts; admission free; ☻ 8.30am-7.30pm Sat-Thu, 3-7.30pm Fri). You can step inside the *majlis* (meeting room) where the ruler received visitors, see the curtained canopied bed he shared with his wife, and snap a photo of the Land Rover he used to visit the desert Bedu. Walls of faded photographs of old Al-Ain show how far the town has come in just a few decades.

The charmingly old-fashioned Al-Ain National Museum (☎ 03-764 1595; www.aam.gov.ae; Zayed ibn Sultan St; admission Dh3; ☻ 8.30am-7.30pm Sat-Thu, 3-7.30pm Fri) is perfect for boning up on the ancient past of Al-Ain and indeed the entire region. Highlights include archaeological displays and artefacts from the 3rd millennium BC tombs at nearby Hili and Umm an-Nar. The ethnography galleries contain beautiful silver Bedouin jewellery, traditional costumes and a harrowing circumcision display.

Linking the museums is the atmospheric date palm Al-Ain Oasis. A marked route leads through this labyrinth of shaded cultivated plots irrigated by a traditional *falaj* (underground system of tunnels). There are nearly 150,000 date palms here, along with mango, orange, banana and fig trees.

In freshly restored glory, Al-Jahili (☎ 03-784 3996; Hazah St; admission free; ☻ 9am-5pm Sat, Sun & Tue-Thu, 3-5pm Fri) is one of the largest forts in the UAE, built in the 1890s as a royal summer residence. It now houses a visitor information centre and a permanent exhibit on British explorer, writer and photographer Sir Wilfred Thesiger.

Use the knowledge you've gained at Al-Ain National Museum to make better sense of the remains in the nicely landscaped Hili Archaeological Park (admission free; ☻ 10am-1pm, families only 4-11pm). Dating back to the Bronze Age (about 4000 years), these include foundations of a tower and mud-brick buildings as well as the restored circular Grand Tomb with its decorative carvings.

Al-Ain is also home of the region's largest and arguably best zoo (☎ 03-782 8188; adult/child Dh15/5; ☻ 10am-7pm Sat-Thu, 10am-8pm Fri Oct-May, 4-10pm Sat-Thu, 10am-10pm Fri Jun-Sep, last admission 1hr before closing), with spacious enclosures inhabited by grazing Arabian oryx, prancing gazelles, lazy crocodiles and hundreds of other species. The zoo runs a successful conservation and breeding program and is being transformed into the Al-Ain Wildlife Park & Resort; this will have a heavy emphasis on sustainability. For a preview, see www.awpr.ae.

Don't leave Al-Ain without driving up Jebel Hafeet. This majestic, jagged, 1240m limestone mountain rears out of the plain south of Al-Ain. A new and extremely curvy road snakes its way up to the top, past evocatively eroded formations and shrubs eking out a living between the rocks. Near the top of the mountain is the Mercure Grand Hotel (☎ 03-783 8888; www.mercure-alain.com; r Dh750; 🖳 🔊), where the views are great but the food is lousy.

The top of Jebel Hafeet is about 30km from central Al-Ain, including the 12km stretch of mountain road. From the town centre, head west on Khalifa bin Zayed St towards the airport, then follow the brown signs.

Sleeping

InterContinental Al-Ain Resort (☎ 03-768 6686; www.ichotelsgroup.com; cnr Khalid ibn Sultan & Al-Salam Sts; r Dh580-1275; 🖳 🔊) Plunged within lush gardens, the InterConti is a winning combination of plus-sized rooms outfitted with microwaves,

HOW MUCH FOR THAT CAMEL?

It's dusty, noisy, pungent and chaotic, but never mind: Al-Ain's famous camel market (Mezyad Rd, just before Bawadi Mall; admission free; ⏰ 7am–sunset) is a wonderful immersion in ancient Arabic culture that's so hard to find in the UAE today. All sorts of camels are holed up in pens, from babies that might grow up to be racers to studs kept for breeding. The intense haggling is fun to watch, but you'll also quickly realise that you're as much an attraction to the traders as they are to you (especially if you're a woman!). Some may try to make you pay for a tour but you're free to walk around on your own. If you take photos of the animals or their owners (always ask first, of course) it's nice to give a small tip. Note that the trading takes place in the morning, but it's usually possible to see the corralled animals all day long.

and refrigerators, interesting restaurants, and facilities such as a landscaped pool with rock formations and a waterfall.

Al-Ain Rotana Hotel (☎ 03-754 5111; www.rotana.com; Zayed bin Sultan St; d Dh1150-1250; 🖥 🛜 🍴) This central hotel with its soaring atrium lobby is a top choice and has plush, spacious rooms in various sizes, all sporting the full range of mod cons.

Eating

Al-Mallah Cafeteria (☎ 03-766 9655; Khalifa St; dishes from Dh5; ⏰ 11am-3pm & 5pm-midnight) This simple, spotless eatery serves reliable Lebanese staples, including tangy chicken *shwarmas* and a long list of mezze, including a kick-ass hummus with pine nuts.

Al-Diwan Restaurant (☎ 03-764 4445; Khalifa St; mains Dh30-80; ⏰ 8am-2am) Lebanese *shish tawooq* (marinated chicken grilled on skewers), pizza margarita, Mexican steak, Iranian yoghurt chicken – this big, bright eatery with floor-to-ceiling windows certainly covers all the bases. Judging by what's on the plates of diners, though, it's the grilled kebabs that give this place local-fave status.

Trader Vic's (☎ 03-754 5111; Al-Ain-Rotana Hotel, Zayed bin Sultan St; mains Dh50-100; ⏰ 12.30-3.30pm & 7.30-11.30pm) Sip exotic rum concoctions while taking in the trippy tiki decor and anticipating platters of crispy duck, jumbo prawns or sesame chicken, all prepared with the Trader's trademark Sino-Polynesian touch. A live Cuban band gets your toes tapping at dinnertime.

UAE EAST COAST

About 130km east of Dubai, the UAE East Coast is a popular and easy weekend getaway for harried city folk in need of some R&R. Plan an early start if you're going just for the day and want some time to relax on the beach. If you do this excursion on a Friday, you can catch the bull-butting (p176) in Fujairah on the way home, although downsides include traffic and more-crowded beaches.

The road from Dubai towards the coast is strangely desolate, a dune landscape punctuated only by power poles. A minor roadside attraction is Masafi's Friday Market. Contrary to its name, this strip of nearly identical stalls is actually open daily from 8am to 10pm. It's a good place to stock up on fresh fruit, but otherwise the quality of the rugs, souvenirs, pottery and household goods leaves much to be desired.

In Masafi, point the compass north and cut through the dramatically rugged Hajar Mountains to the sleepy fishing village of Dibba. This is the northernmost point of the 65km scenic East Coast highway to Fujairah, hemmed in by the Hajars, shimmering beaches and the turquoise expanse of the Gulf of Oman. The diving and snorkelling are still good here, despite the damaging effects of a prolonged red tide (see p146).

Dibba is unique in that its territory is shared by two emirates and the Sultanate of Oman. The most interesting section is the harbour in the Omani section – take your passport if you want to cross the border. Here you can watch grizzled fishermen haul in their catch, or take

TRANSPORT: EAST COAST

Distance from Dubai 130km
Direction east
Travel time 90 minutes

Car Take the E11 towards Sharjah and then head in the direction of Al-Dhaid, on the E88. At Masafi you can take the E89 road heading north to Dibba or south to Fujairah: we recommend going north first to Dibba and then driving south along the coast

Public transport Minibuses to Fujairah leave from Al-Ittihad station (Map pp52-3; cnr of Omar ibn al-Khattab & Al-Rigga Rds) in Deira every 45 minutes and cost Dh25. It will cost just over Dh200 if you go by taxi. A taxi from Fujairah to Al-Aqah beach costs around Dh75. Unfortunately there's no public transport from Fujairah to Dubai, so you will have to return by taxi.

A DATE WITH A DATE

If you visit Al-Ain in early summer, one of the things you will be struck by is the enormous number of date clusters hanging off the palms lining many streets and parks. The ubiquitous date palm has always held a vital place in the life of Emiratis. For centuries dates were one of the staple foods of the Bedouin, along with fish, camel meat and camel milk. 'Not a great deal of variety,' you might think, but consider the fact that there are over 80 different kinds of dates in the UAE. Dates are roughly 70% sugar, which prevents them from rotting, making them edible for longer than other fruits. Apart from providing a major foodstuff, the date palm was also used to make all kinds of useful items. Its trunk was used to make columns and ceilings for houses, its fronds (called *areesh*) for roofs and walls.

a dhow trip headed to unspoilt dive sites along the remote eastern coast of the Musandam Peninsula. Al-Marsa (☎ 968-26 836550; www.musandam diving.com), based at the Golden Tulip Hotel, is a reliable local operator. Dibba is also a launch pad for trekking and mountain-biking tours through the Hajar Mountains. Absolute Adventure (☎ 04-345 9900; www.adventure.ae), near the Golden Tulip, organises all sorts of outdoor adventures, including kayaking tours around the Musandam Peninsula.

The beautiful stretch of beach south of town is getting increasingly snapped up by hotels and resorts. About 8km down the road, Dibba Rock is a popular scuba-diving and snorkelling site. Freestyle Divers (☎ 244 5756; www .freestyledivers.com; ☼ 9am-5pm), based at the Royal Beach Hotel, rents gear and offers dive trips, PADI courses and Musandam excursions.

Next up, Badiyah (also spelt Bidyah and Bidiya) is known mainly for its mosque (☼ 7am-10pm). Thought to be the oldest in the UAE (possibly dating back to the early 15th century), it's a small and simple structure, adorned with four pointed domes and resting on an internal pillar. A sign says that non-Muslims are not allowed to enter, but the resident imam will not take offence if you do catch a peek as long as you are modestly dressed, take off your shoes and cover your head (women only). Behind the mosque, up on a hill, is a pair of ruined watchtowers; walk up for superb 360° views of the Hajar Mountains, the gloriously blue ocean and a lush date palm plantation.

Leagues of expats have a soft spot for the charmingly old-fashioned Sandy Beach Hotel &

Resort (☎ 244 5555; www.sandybm.com; d from Dh500 🛜 🖾), not far from the mosque opposite Snoopy Island, another popular snorkelling site. The onsite dive shop is a pro operation that rents equipment and organises a wide range of excursions. Beach access passes for nonguests cost Dh75.

Continuing south, you'll soon arrive in Khor Fakkan, home to a superbusy container port. Still, the town is not without its charms, especially along the nicely maintained corniche, whose palm trees, gardens, kiosks and playground are popular with families for picnics and waterfront strolls. Another reason to stop is for a meal at Taj Khorfakkan Restaurant (☎ 237 0040; off Corniche Rd, Al-Tufail bin Malik St; mains Dh18-30; ☼ noon-midnight). Although completely ambience-free, it serves possibly the best Indian food on the East Coast. Note that since Khor Fakkan is part of Sharjah emirate, it's 'dry' as a bone.

The biggest East Coast city, and its commercial hub, is Fujairah, also a port town. For a peek into its past, drop by the dusty Fujairah Museum (☎ 222 9085; cnr Al-Nakheel & Al-Salam Rds; adult/child Dh5/free; ☼ 8.30am-1.30pm & 4.30-6.30pm Sun-Thu, 2-6.30pm Fri) or the newly restored 16th-century fort, which is spectacularly floodlit at night. Nature lovers should shoot down to the idyllic mangrove lagoon at Khor Kalba, which is a paradise for birdwatchers. Explore on your own or book a guided canoe safari with Dubai-based Desert Rangers (☎ 04-357 2233; www.desertrangers.com, adult/child Dh300/210).

For sustenance, steer towards Al-Meshwar (☎ 222 1113; Hamad bin Abdullah Rd; mezze Dh6-45, mains Dh25-115; ☼ cafe 9am-midnight, dining rooms 11.30am-2.30pm & 7-10pm), which serves up the gamut of

BULLFIGHTING – FUJAIRAH-STYLE

If possible, visit Fujairah on a Friday when the ancient sport of bull-butting (☎ 783 8888; btwn Corniche & Coast Rd; ☼ 4-7pm Fri Oct-May) takes place in a dusty dirt patch on the southern outskirts of town (before Al-Rughailat Bridge). It was introduced centuries ago by the Portuguese, and today's contests see bulls brought here from all over the UAE to lock horns and test their strength against each other. The goal is to push the other out of a circle, which usually takes only a couple of minutes. Traditionally, the fighting took place in an open field, but since angry bulls would occasionally charge spectators, a new wire fence was recently built to protect them.

Lebanese tummy temptations in a *Flintstones*-inspired building. The downstairs *sheesha* cafe has free wi-fi.

Sleeping

If you decide that one day is not enough on the East Coast, consider staying overnight in these places.

Sandy Beach Hotel & Resort (☎ 244 5555; www.sandybm.com; d Dh500, ocean-view d Dh625, 1-/2-bedroom chalet Dh700/900, apt Dh1200; 🛜 🖳) At this expat favourite near the Badiyah Mosque, lodging ranges from basic ocean-view rooms to small cabins with private barbecues and a new wing with sparkling, modern apartments with balconies.

Hotel JAL Fujairah Resort & Spa (☎ 204 3111; www.jalfujairahresort.ae; 6km south of Dibba; d from Dh700; 🖳 🖳) Zen minimalism meets Arabian hospitality at this sprawling Japanese-owned outpost where you can open up the balcony door of your oversized room to let in the ocean breezes.

Le Meridien al-Aqah Beach Resort (☎ 244 9000; www.lemeridien-alaqah.com; d from Dh850; 🖳 🖳) Just north of the Sandy Beach Hotel, this upmarket resort does everything to put you in the mood for a beach vacation. The balconied rooms give you plenty of elbow space and overlook the lush gardens, private beach and ocean. Days pass languidly lazing poolside, diving, waterskiing or playing volleyball.

TRANSPORT

AIR

There are direct flights to Dubai from most European countries and hubs in Africa and Asia. The Americas are increasingly well connected, with Emirates and Etihad both flying from New York and Toronto, and Delta flying direct from Atlanta. Dubai is also increasingly a major stopover hub between Europe and Asia. For airport information and flight enquiries visit the website at www.dubai airport.com.

Emirates Airlines (www.emirates.com), which is owned by the Dubai government, remains the major player in the region, flying to more than 100 destinations globally. In recent years, it has faced serious competition from Abu Dhabi-based Etihad (www.etihad.com), the United Arab Emirates' (UAE's) national airline. The first Dubai-based budget carrier, FlyDubai (www.flydubai.com), an affiliate of Emirates, began operating in June 2009. At the time of writing it offers a limited flight schedule to such Middle Eastern destinations as Beirut, Amman and Doha, although more cities are expected to come online before too long.

A more established regional low-cost airline is Air Arabia (www.airarabia.com), which uses Sharjah's airport as its base and covers many destinations in the Middle East and the Indian Subcontinent, as well as a few European cities (including Amsterdam, Paris and Barcelona).

Dubai is also served by Kuwait-based Jazeera Airways (www.jazeeraairways.com), which operates flights mostly within the region and to Istanbul and Mumbai. Most trips from Dubai involve a change in Kuwait.

Airlines

The following is a selection of carriers that fly to and from Dubai:

Air France (AF; Map pp54-5; ☎ 602 5400; www.airfrance.com; ground fl, Al-Shoala Bldg, cnr Al-Maktoum Rd & 9 St, Deira)

Air India (AI; Map pp54-5; ☎ 227 6747; www.airindia.com; Sheikh Rashid Bldg, Al-Maktoum Rd, Deira)

British Airways (BA; Map pp70-71; ☎ 800 0441 3322; www.britishairways.com; 21st fl, Al-Attar Business Tower, Sheikh Zayed Rd)

Cathay Pacific Airways (CX; Map pp54-5; ☎ 204 2888; www.cathaypacific.com; Al-Naboodah Travel Agencies, Al-Shoala Bldg, cnr Al-Maktoum Rd & 9 St, Deira)

Delta Air Lines (DL; Map pp64-5; ☎ 397 0118; www.delta.com; Sharaf Travel, Sharaf Bldg; Khalid bin al-Waleed Rd, Bur Dubai)

Emirates Airlines (EK; ☎ 214 4444; www.emirates.com) Map pp54-5; DNATA Bldg, Al-Maktoum Rd, Deira; Map pp70-71; DNATA Travel Centre, Sheikh Zayed Rd, btwn Metropolitan Hotel & Business Bay Metro Station.

Gulf Air (GF; Map pp52-3; ☎ 271 6207, 651 6888; www.gulfair.com; Salahuddin Rd, Deira)

KLM (KL; Map pp52-3; ☎ 602 5444; www.klm.com; ground fl, Al-Shoala Bldg, cnr Al-Maktoum Rd & 9 St, Deira)

Lufthansa (Map pp70-71; ☎ 343 2121; www.lufthansa.com; 2nd fl, Hilal Salim Bin Taraff Blvd, Sheikh Zayed Rd)

Oman Air (WY; Map pp62-3; ☎ 351 8080; www.omanair.com; mezzanine fl, Al-Rais Shopping Centre, Al-Mankhool Rd, Bur Dubai)

Qatar Airways (QR; Map pp52-3; ☎ 221 4210; www.qatarairways.com; Doha Centre, Al-Maktoum Rd, Deira)

Singapore Airlines (SQ; Map pp70-71; ☎ 316 6888; www.singaporeair.com; ground fl, DNATA Travel Centre, Sheikh Zayed Rd)

Thai Airways International (TG; Map pp54-5; ☎ 268 1701; www.thaiair.com; Shop 1, Bu Haleeba Plaza, Al-Muraqqabat Rd, Deira)

Virgin Atlantic (VS; Map pp64-5; ☎ 406 0600; www.virgin-atlantic.com; 3rd fl, Sharaf Bldg; Khalid bin al-Waleed Rd, Bur Dubai)

Dubai International Airport

In the north of the city, on the border with the Sharjah emirate, Dubai International Airport (Map pp54-5; ☎ 224 5555, flight enquiries 224 5777 ww.dubaiairport.com) is the busiest in the Middle East, with over 40 million passengers passing through in 2009. The major international airlines use Terminal 1, the main terminal. Smaller airlines and charter flights, mostly en route to Iran, East Africa and the countries of the former Soviet Union, use the dismal Terminal 2. The snazzy new Terminal 3, which opened in 2008, is only used by Emirates. For now, facilities in Terminal 1 are being pushed to extremes by large crowds, especially at the beginning and end of the day, when the bulk of departures and arrivals are scheduled.

There are several places to eat in the departures lounge including a small food court, a seafood bar, the Irish Village pub and Starbucks, although finding a table at peak times can be a problem. Dubai Duty Free sprawls over an entire floor of the departures terminal, so there's no lack of shopping facilities. Here you can find travel essentials, books and magazines, electronics, perfumes, cigarettes, and food and alcohol at competitive, if not world-beating, prices. You'll also find credit card–powered internet terminals, banks, several currency-exchange outlets, a business centre, a prayer room, a health club, designated quiet lounges and free wi-fi throughout. There's also an on-site hotel, Dubai International Hotel (☎ 224 4000; www.dih-dca .com), with two locations – one on the Arrivals level in Terminal 1 and the other in Terminal 3, levels 5 and 6, above Dubai Duty Free. Upon request, rooms are available at hourly rates.

Sharjah International Airport

Sharjah is the emirate bordering Dubai to the north. Its airport (☎ 558 1111; www.shj-airport.gov.ae) is about 15km east of the Dubai–Sharjah border and has significantly increased its capacity since becoming the hub of Air Arabia, the region's first budget airline. The main problem, as ever, is the traffic on the roads. A journey to Dubai in the evening, when commuters are making their daily slog home, can take up to three hours. If possible, book flights that leave very late at night, early in the morning, or on a Friday.

To get to/from the airport you have to take taxis, since there's no public transport. Sharjah taxis are reliable, metered and comfortable. A trip to Dubai's Gold Souq from Sharjah airport costs approximately Dh60; a trip to Dubai Marina around Dh120.

Abu Dhabi International Airport

Abu Dhabi's airport (☎ 505 5555, flight information 575 7500; www.abudhabiairport.ae) is about 30km northeast of the city centre. It has three terminals, including Etihad's exclusive base, Terminal 3, which opened in early 2009 and raised the airport's capacity to 12 million passengers per year. Free wi-fi is available throughout the airport, which is compact and efficient, meaning

CLIMATE CHANGE & TRAVEL

Climate change is a serious threat to the ecosystems that humans rely upon, and air travel is the fastest-growing contributor to the problem. Lonely Planet regards travel, overall, as a global benefit, but believes we all have a responsibility to limit our personal impact on global warming.

Flying & Climate Change

Pretty much every form of motor transport generates carbon dioxide (the main cause of human-induced climate change) but planes are far and away the worst offenders, not just because of the sheer distances they allow us to travel but because they release greenhouse gases high into the atmosphere. The statistics are frightening: two people taking a return flight between Europe and the US will contribute as much to climate change as an average household's gas and electricity consumption over a whole year.

Carbon Offset Schemes

Climatecare.org and other websites use 'carbon calculators' that allow travellers to offset the greenhouse gases they are responsible for with contributions to energy-saving projects and other climate-friendly initiatives in the developing world – including projects in India, Honduras, Kazakhstan and Uganda.

Lonely Planet, together with Rough Guides and other concerned partners in the travel industry, supports the carbon offset scheme run by climatecare.org. Lonely Planet offsets all of its staff and author travel.

For more information check out our website: www.lonelyplanet.com

GETTING INTO TOWN

Ask about airport transfers to your hotel when making your reservation. If you're staying at one of the beach hotels along the Jumeirah strip, a transfer may save you some money. All transport leaves outside the arrivals halls, and the areas are well signposted (bus, limo, taxi etc).

Unlike other Middle East destinations, getting a taxi isn't at all intimidating in Dubai. Cabs line up patiently and the journey is metered. Rides cost about Dh30 to the Deira souq area, Dh45 to Bur Dubai, Dh60 to Downtown Dubai, Dh75 to Jumeirah and Dh90 to Dubai Marina. All rates include a Dh20 airport surcharge, meaning fares *to* the airport are about Dh20 less.

Dubai Metro Red Line (see p182) stops at Terminals 1 and 3 and is the most efficient way to get across town by public transport. Public buses leave from Terminal 1, but they're comparatively slow and cumbersome. The most useful lines are bus 401, which runs every 30 minutes to Al-Sabkha bus station (Map pp52-3) near the Deira souqs, and bus 402, which goes past Deira City Centre through Karama and the Golden Sands hotel apartment area to Al-Ghubaiba bus station (Map pp62-3) in Bur Dubai. Services stop running for about six hours around midnight; in the interim the N3 night bus travels every 30 minutes from Terminal 2 to Jebel Ali, with a stop near the World Trade Centre on Sheikh Zayed Rd.

that you can sometimes get from the plane to the street in under half an hour. It's situated 22km from Abu Dhabi in the direction of Dubai, which means Dubai Marina is only about an hour's drive away. Travelling to the same hotels from Dubai airport during rush-hour traffic can take considerably longer.

Etihad passengers can use free shuttle buses to and from the Etihad office in Dubai (Map pp70-71; Chelsea Tower, Sheikh Zayed Rd). Limo service operated by Fast Company or National Company charges Dh250 for the journey to Dubai. There is no direct public transport to Dubai from Abu Dhabi airport. If you've got more time than money, you could take local bus 901 from the airport to the Abu Dhabi city centre (Dh3) and then catch a bus to Dubai from the main bus station at the corner of East Rd and Haza'a bin Zayed St (Dh20, two hours).

THE WORLD'S BIGGEST AIRPORT

Dubai never shies away from superlatives, which is why it should be no surprise that it not only has the world's tallest tower but soon will also have the world's biggest airport. Upon completion, Al-Maktoum International Airport in Jebel Ali will boost the emirate's annual passenger potential to an estimated 120 million and be capable of handling over 12 million tonnes of cargo per year. It will be 10 times the size of Dubai International Airport and Dubai Cargo Village combined. Don't expect to land at this behemoth any time soon, though. Although freighter operations were scheduled to begin in June 2010, no target date has been set for passenger operations to commence.

BUS

Well-maintained minibuses or buses operated by the Dubai-based Roads & Transport Authority (RTA ☎ 800 9090; www.rta.ae) travel to all the emirates, but only services to Sharjah and Ajman return passengers to Dubai. From the other towns, you have to come back by local taxi or bus. Routes are generally served between 6am and 11pm. Buses are air-conditioned and dirt-cheap but can get rather overcrowded. Maps and timetables are available online and at the two main bus stations, which are Al-Ittihad in Deira and Al-Ghubaiba in Bur Dubai.

The following services depart from Al-Ittihad bus station (Map pp52-3; cnr of Omar ibn al-Khattab & Al-Rigga Rds) which is next to the Union Metro station.

Destination	Frequency	Cost	Duration
Ajman	every 20min	Dh7	1-1½hr
Fujairah	every 45min	Dh25	2-2½hr
Ras al-Khaimah	every 45min	Dh20	2hr
Sharjah	every 10min	Dh5	40-60min
Umm al-Quwain	every 45min	Dh10	1½hr

Buses to Abu Dhabi leave from the Al-Ghubaiba station (Map pp62-3; Al-Ghubaiba Rd, Bur Dubai), next to the Carrefour supermarket. A 24-hour service to Sharjah, with departures every 30 minutes between midnight and 6am, also departs from here.

Destination	Frequency	Cost	Duration
Abu Dhabi	every 40min	Dh20	2hr
Al-Ain	every hr	Dh20	1½hr
Sharjah	every 10min	Dh5	40-50min

CAR

If you are planning on taking a day or overnight excursion from Dubai, consider hiring your own wheels so you can get off the major highways and stop and explore as you please. Well-maintained multilane highways link the cities, often lit along their entire length.

If you decide to hire a car to get around the city, don't expect a very relaxing holiday… Traffic congestion in Dubai can be a nightmare at peak hours, ie between 7am and 9am, 1pm and 2pm and most of the evening from 5pm onwards. The worst congestion is around the approaches to Al-Maktoum and Al-Garhoud Bridges and along Al-Ittihad Rd towards Sharjah. Accidents are frequent, so it's a good idea to tune into the radio to get traffic updates. It is compulsory to wear seatbelts in the front, and it is illegal to use a hand-held mobile phone while driving, although many motorists seem to ignore this rule. Also read the section on road rules (p182) and the 'Motoring Mayhem' boxed text, p184, for some important safety messages.

If you have a breakdown call the Arabian Automobile Association (☎ 800 4900). As you would expect, Dubai is not short of petrol stations and fuel is cheap compared with the rest of the world. Petrol is sold by the imperial gallon (an imperial gallon is just over 4.5L) and costs around Dh7 per gallon.

Hire

To hire a car, you'll need a credit card and an international driver's licence in addition to your home licence. Some companies may be willing to take a cash deposit instead, but you'll probably have to leave your passport with them and may not receive full insurance. Some agencies insist on a credit card deposit as well as your passport. Find another agency if this is the case. You do not have to leave your passport with them. A photocopy of it is sufficient.

Daily rates start at about Dh175 for a small manual car such as a Toyota Echo, including comprehensive insurance and unlimited kilometres. Expect surcharges for airport rentals, additional drivers, one-way hire and drivers under 25 years. Most companies have child and infant safety seats for a fee, but these must be reserved well in advance. For longer rentals, prebooked and prepaid packages arranged in your home country may work out cheaper than on-the-spot rentals. Check for deals with the online travel agencies, travel agents or car-rental brokers such as the US company Auto Europe (www.autoeurope.com) or UK-based Holiday Autos (www.holidayautos.co.uk).

Dubai has scores of car-rental agencies, from major global players to no-name local companies. The former may charge more but you get peace of mind knowing that you can get full insurance and that they'll get you out of a fix if you need assistance.

The international agencies have offices in the airport arrivals hall, around town and in major hotels. Check the website or call the head office for the nearest location.

Avis (www.avis.com; ☎ airport 224 5219, head office 295 7121)

Budget (www.budget-uae.com; ☎ airport 224 5192, head office 282 2727)

Europcar (www.europcar-dubai.com; ☎ airport 224 5240, head office 339 4433)

Hertz (www.hertz-uae.com; ☎ 206 0206)

Thrifty (www.thrifty.com; airport arrivals hall; ☎ 224 5404; ☽ 24hr)

FOR WHOM THE ROAD TOLLS

A road toll, known as Salik (meaning 'clear and moving'), was introduced in 2007 to help combat congestion. There are four toll points:

- Al-Barsha Salik Toll Gate – Sheikh Zayed Rd, just north of Mall of the Emirates (Map pp82-3)
- Al-Garhoud Salik Toll Gate – south side of Al-Garhoud Bridge (Map pp54-5)
- Al-Maktoum Salik Toll Gate – north side of Al-Maktoum Bridge (Map pp54-5)
- Al-Safa Salik Toll Gate – Sheikh Zayed Rd, just north of Safa Park (Map pp70-71)

Each time you pass one of these points Dh4 is automatically deducted from the car's prepaid Salik account. If you buy or borrow a car you must make sure there is a Salik tag affixed to the windshield. These are available from EPPCO, ADNOC and Emarat petrol stations, as well as from post offices and branches of Dubai Islamic Bank and Emirates Bank. The fee is Dh100 and includes Dh50 of credit. Rental cars come with the Salik tag installed; however, citing a dubious Dh1 administrative fee, companies charge Dh5 for each toll point crossing. Taxis are exempt from this charge. For more information on anything Salik, call ☎ 800 725 45 or log on to www.salik.ae.

DRIVING TO OMAN

If you plan on taking the car to Oman, check with the rental agency that you're permitted to do so. If yes, bring written permission in case you're asked for it at the border as well as the car registration and proof of insurance valid in Oman. If your insurance doesn't cover Oman, you can obtain Omani insurance at most border crossings. A 20km section of the highway to Hatta passes through Oman, although there is no border checkpoint.

Local companies cluster in Deira on Abu Baker al-Siddiq Rd, just north of the Clock Tower Roundabout, and on Omar ibn al-Khattab Rd. They are also found on the Bur Dubai side of the Creek on Sheikh Khalifa bin Zayed Rd, just north of Al-Adhid Rd; and on Kuwait St in Karama.

Road Rules

Most people drive on the right in Dubai, which is the side you're supposed to drive on. The speed limit is 60km/h on city streets and 80km/h on major city roads. On Sheikh Zayed Rd and on other dual-lane highways around the UAE the official speed limit is 100km/h along some sections, but otherwise it's 120km/h. If you are caught speeding, you will be fined either on the spot or sent a bill by the police. For this reason, most car-rental companies require customers to sign a statement acknowledging that they are aware of this and authorising the rental company to charge their credit card for any tickets that turn up after they have left town. So if you see a flash of light while powering down Sheikh Zayed Rd, check your credit card statements when you get home. There are also speed cameras on the major highways around the UAE.

Parking

Increasingly, the busier city streets have a strictly enforced four-hour limit on parking. Tickets must be purchased from an orange machine and displayed on your dashboard. Rates start at Dh1 for the first hour, Dh5 for two hours, Dh8 for three and Dh11 for four hours. Parking rates apply from 8am to 1pm and from 4pm to 9pm Saturday to Thursday. Pay with cash or by credit card. Parking in the centre of Dubai is free on Friday and holidays. Fines for not buying a ticket start at Dh100.

LOCAL TRANSPORT

Dubai's local public transport is also operated by RTA and consists of the Dubai Metro, buses, water buses and *abras* (water taxis). For trip planning and general information, call the 24-hour hotline on ☎ 800 9090 or go online to www.rta.ae.

Abras

Abras are motorised traditional wooden boats linking Bur Dubai and Deira across the Creek on two routes:

Route 1 – Bur Dubai Abra Station (Map pp62-3) to Deira Old Souq Abra Station (Map pp52-3); daily between 5am and midnight.

Route 2 – Dubai Old Souq Abra Station (Map pp62-3) to Al-Sabkha Abra Station (Map pp52-3) around the clock.

Abras leave when full (around 20 passengers), which rarely takes more than a few minutes. The fare is Dh1 and you pay the driver halfway across the Creek. Chartering your own *abra* costs Dh100 per hour.

Dubai Metro

It took 30,000 workers just four years to build the hi-tech marvel that is Dubai's spanking-new Metro, a light-rail system that runs primarily on elevated tracks. The first 10 stations of the Red Line opened to great fanfare in September 2009, with the remaining 19 to follow in 2010. It runs for 52.1km from near Dubai International Airport to Jebel Ali past Dubai Marina, mostly paralleling Sheikh Zayed Rd.

At the time of writing, a second line, the 22.5km Green Line, linking the Dubai Airport Free Zone with Dubai Healthcare City, was expected to start operating in mid-2011.

JUST SAY NO! REALLY.

Drinking and driving are never a good idea but in Dubai you'd be outright crazy to do so. Let's make it absolutely clear – if you've had as much as one sip, you've had too much. Dubai has a zero-tolerance policy on drink-driving, and if your vehicle is stopped and you're found to have been driving under the influence of alcohol, you'll be a guest of Dubai Police for up to 30 days.

If you are involved in a traffic accident, it's a case of being guilty until proven innocent, which means you may be held by the police until an investigation determines whose fault the accident was.

NOL CARDS

Before you can hop aboard a local bus or the Metro, you must purchase a rechargeable Nol Card (*nol* is Arabic for fare) from ticket offices in any Metro and some bus stations. There are also ticket vending machines (with English instructions) in all Metro and bus stations, at some bus stops and other places such as malls and the airport.

There are four categories of Nol Card: red, silver, gold and blue. If you're only going to use public transport a few times, get a Red Card, which costs Dh2 and may be recharged for up to 10 journeys. Fares depend on distance and are divided into five zones. For Red Cards the cost is Dh2.50 for one zone, Dh4.50 for two zones and Dh6.50 for three to five zones. Short trips under 3km cost Dh2.

Those planning on travelling more frequently should get a Silver Card for Dh20 (including Dh14 of credit). These are equipped with an 'e-purse', meaning that the correct fare is deducted automatically every time you swipe the card at the station turnstiles, up to a daily maximum of Dh14. It can be topped up with more credit as needed. The fare is Dh1.80, Dh2.30, Dh4.10 and Dh5.80, for short trips, one, two and three to five zones, respectively.

The Gold Card has the same features as the Silver Card but gives you access to the Gold Class carriage. It comes with a price tag of Dh20 (including Dh14 credit) with individual rides being charged at Dh3.60, Dh4.60, Dh8.20 and Dh11.60.

Finally, the Blue Card costs Dh70 (including Dh20 of credit) and comes with your photograph, online services and loyalty programs – it's primarily geared towards residents. Fares are Dh1.80, Dh2.30, Dh4.10 and Dh5.80.

Day passes for unlimited travel in all zones are Dh14 (not available for Gold Class). Children under five years of age travel for free.

For full details, see www. nol.ae.

t intersects with the Red Line at Union and Khalid bin al-Waleed (next to BurJuman shopping mall) stations. At each station, cabs and feeder buses stand by to take you to your final destination.

Trains run roughly every 10 minutes from 6am to 11pm, Saturday to Thursday, and 2pm to midnight on Fridays, although this may increase during peak hours. Each train consists of four standard cars and one car that's divided into a women-only section and a 'Gold Class' section where a double fare buys carpets and leather seats. Women may of course travel in any of the other cars as well.

Mobile phone service is available throughout, as is wi-fi access for Dh10 per hour when paying with a credit card or Dh20 per hour when using prepaid scratch cards available at the ticket counter.

In the first months of operation, passengers were not allowed to bring suitcases on trains (hand luggage only), although this regulation was expected to be revisited.

Local Buses

RTA (☎ 800 9090; www.rta.ae) operates local buses on 79 routes primarily serving the needs of low-income commuters. Buses are clean, comfortable, air-conditioned and cheap (Dh2 per ride), but they're slow. So unless you have more time than money, a bus is not a very efficient way of getting across town. The first few rows of seats are generally reserved for women and children.

For information and trip planning call the RTA or check the website. Free route maps and timetables can be picked up from major bus stations, such as the Gold Souq Station (Map pp52-3; off Al-Khor St, near the Gold Souq) in Deira, Al-Sabkha Station (Map pp52-3; cnr Al-Sabkha Rd & Deira St) in Deira and Al-Ghubaiba Station (Map pp62-3; Al-Ghubaiba Rd, next to Carrefour) in Bur Dubai. Buses to most destinations in the city leave from these stations. From Saturday to Thursday, buses run every 15 to 20 minutes between 6am and 11.30pm. Friday service is less frequent and may start later and finish earlier. Night buses operate at 30-minute intervals in the interim along three routes.

Monorail

The elevated, driverless Palm Jumeirah Monorail connects the Palm Jumeirah with the Dubai Marina. There are only two stations: Gateway Towers near the bottom of the trunk and the Aquaventure Park at the Atlantis Hotel. The 5.45km trip takes about five minutes and costs Dh15 (Dh25 round trip). A planned link to the Metro Red Line has been put on indefinite hold, and as a result the monorail remains sadly underused.

Water Buses

Air-conditioned water buses travel along four Creek-crossing routes from 6am to 11pm daily. Routes B1 and B4 operate every 30 minutes, B2 and B3 at 15-minute intervals. Tickets are Dh4.

MOTORING MAYHEM

Driving in Dubai is not for the faint of heart. In fact, it can be terrifying. Although it's not as chaotic as in other parts of the Middle East, drivers tend to cut in front of you, turn without indicating and view roundabouts as a lane-less free for all. Out on the freeway, driving in the lane closest to the centre of the road at speeds of less than 160km/h will invoke some serious headlight flashing from the latest-model Mercedes trying to break the Dubai–Abu Dhabi land-speed record.

So it's no surprise that the United Arab Emirates (UAE) has one of the world's highest rates of road deaths per capita. In fact, Sheikh Zayed Rd is the deadliest road in the country. Inappropriate speed and reckless driving are the major causes, as well as pedestrians crossing against the lights or not at crossings. In 2008 an average of 13 people a month died on Dubai's roads.

The worst aspect of this is that there doesn't seem to be sufficient incentive not to drive badly. Although speeding fines are meted out, many people view speed cameras as toll booths you don't have to stop at. Causing a death through an accident requires the payment of blood money (dhiyya) to the victim's family. Although this is a large sum (up to Dh200,000), nationals are insured against it. This often means that the only punishment for causing death or injury through reckless driving is an increased insurance premium.

Route B1 – Bur Dubai Station (Map pp62–3) to Al-Sabkha Station (Map pp52–3)

Route B2 – Dubai Old Souq Station (Map pp62–3) to Baniyas Station (Map pp52–3)

Route B3 – Al-Seef Station (Map pp52–3) to Al-Sabkha via Baniyas

Route B4 – Bur Dubai Station to Creek Park Station (Map pp64–5) via Al-Seef Station

A fifth route, the tourist-geared B5, travels between Shindagha Station (Map pp62–3) near Heritage Village and Creek Park every 30 minutes, stopping at Bur Dubai Station, Deira Old Souq Station and Al-Seef Station. All-day tickets cost Dh50 (Dh25 for children under six years). The entire journey lasts 45 minutes but you're free to get on and off throughout the ticket's validity (9am to midnight).

TAXI

Taxis are operated by Dubai Taxi Corporation (DTC; ☎ 208 0808; www.dubaitaxi.ae) and are metered, quite inexpensive and the fastest and most comfortable way to get around, except during rush-hour traffic. Daytime flagfall is Dh3 (Dh6 with advance booking) plus Dh1.60 per kilometre. From 10pm to 6am the starting fare is Dh3.50 (Dh7 when reserved). Trips originating at the airport have a flagfall of Dh20. There's a minimum charge of Dh10 and fares include all tolls. Tips are not compulsory but drivers tend to round off the amount, meaning if your fare is Dh27 you won't get change from Dh30 unless you ask for it. Always carry small bills since most cabbies can't or won't make change.

It's perfectly fine for women to ride alone in a taxi, even at night, although you can also call DTC and request a woman driver (flagfall Dh7), who will arrive in a pink car, no less! If you call ahead, it can also provide eight-seater vehicles or wheelchair-accessible taxis at no additional cost.

If you ask for a taxi at a five-star hotel, you may be shown to an unmarked limo, which may well charge double. Confirm the fare and if you don't like it, ask the concierge to call you a regular cab. Also see the boxed text, p157.

Most taxi drivers speak at least some English and are good at their jobs, but some really don't have a clue. Since they receive no formal training, their knowledge of city roads may be sketchy, especially if they're new to the city. To avoid an expensive and frustrating journey, ask the driver to radio his office or flag down a colleague to get directions as soon as it's clear he's inexperienced. Rather than giving a street address, mention the nearest landmark (eg a hotel, mall, roundabout, major building). If you're going to a private residence, phone your host and ask them to give the cabbie directions.

ACCIDENT ALERT

If you are unfortunate enough to have an accident, no matter how small, you are required to wait at the scene and report it to the police (☎ 999). Unless your car is causing a major traffic jam, do NOT move it until the cops arrive. If there has been an injury, or it's not blindingly obvious who was at fault, don't move the vehicles at all. For insurance-claim purposes you must have a police report, and if you move your car, the police may not be able to issue a complete report. Outside Dubai you should leave your car exactly where it is, no matter how bad an obstruction it is causing, and call the police immediately.

It's usually fairly easy to catch a taxi, but there are a few trouble spots where hour-long waits are not unusual. Expect lengthy queues at the major shopping malls on weekday evenings (especially Thursday) and Friday afternoons. There's also a chronic taxi shortage near the *abra* stations in Deira, by the shopping district of Karama, in Bur Dubai by the bus station, and along The Walk at JBR in Dubai Marina. Finding a free taxi is especially tough between 4pm and 5.30pm when most drivers end their shifts and have to deliver their cars to their partners (usually two drivers share a car, working 12 hours each). Few drivers are willing to risk picking up customers who might extend their shift and delay their partner's start time.

Taxi companies include the following:

Cars Taxis (☎ 269 3344)

Dubai Transport Company (☎ 208 0808)

Metro Taxis (☎ 267 3222)

National Taxis (☎ 339 0002)

DIRECTORY

BUSINESS HOURS

The United Arab Emirates (UAE) weekend is on Friday and Saturday. The following information is a guide only. Hours are more limited during Ramadan.

Banks 8am to 1pm (some until 3pm) Sunday to Thursday, 8am to noon Saturday

Government offices 7.30am to 2pm (or 3pm) Sunday to Thursday

Private offices 8am to 5pm or 9am to 6pm, or split shifts 8am to 1pm and 3pm (or 4pm) to 7pm Sunday to Thursday

Restaurants noon to 3pm and 7.30pm to midnight

Shopping malls 10am to 10pm Sunday to Wednesday, 10am to midnight Thursday to Saturday

Souqs 9am to 1pm and 4pm to 9pm Saturday to Thursday, 4pm to 9pm Friday

Supermarkets 9am to midnight daily; some open 24 hours

CHILDREN

Travelling to Dubai with tots and teens can be child's play. Many top-end hotels and some midrange ones have kids clubs, pools and playgrounds. Formula is readily available in pharmacies, and disposable nappies at grocery stores and supermarkets. Restaurants almost always provide high chairs and special children's menus. We have highlighted the best family restaurants with the child-friendly icon ⊕ in the Eating chapter.

Even outside the hotel, there's certainly no shortage of fun things to do around town. Keep cool on the rides and slides at Wild Wadi Waterpark (p80) and Aquaventure Water Park (p81), or on the slopes or the snow park at Ski Dubai (p144). Most kids love animals, and they'll have plenty of opportunity to make finny friends at Dolphin Bay (p84) and the Lost Chambers underwater world (p84) at the Atlantis Hotel, The Palm, or at the Dubai Aquarium & Underwater Zoo (p72) in Dubai Mall. Just about any respectable mall also has an indoor amusement park, such as Magic Planet at Mall of the Emirates (Map pp82-3) and Deira City Centre (Map pp54-5), and Sega Republic (p73) at Dubai Mall. Little kids may enjoy playing grown-up at KidZania (p72), also at Dubai Mall.

The city also has quite a few parks with playgrounds and picnic areas. One of the largest is Creekside Park (p66), which has a cable-car ride and a dolphinarium. Then there's Za'abeel Park (p67) with its space-themed amusement park, and Al-Safa Park (p79), which is anchored by a lake.

For general advice, pick up Lonely Planet's *Travel with Children*, which prepares you for the joys and pitfalls of travelling with the little ones. The website Dubai Kidz (www.dubaikidz.biz) contains detailed and up-to-date listings specific to children.

Babysitting

Most of the large hotels offer babysitting services from Dh70 for three hours. These tend to be reliable, as hotels are used to large numbers of children visiting.

CLIMATE

We can't stress strongly enough that Dubai turns into a sauna in the summer months (May to September). In July and August average daytime temperatures are around 43°C with 85% humidity. Sometimes the heat reaches 48°C and the humidity 95% – and rumours always swirl around in the heat that it has reached 50°C somewhere in the UAE. The sea temperature in the height of summer (July and August) is about 37°C, which provides no relief, and hotel swimming pools have to be cooled during this time so the guests don't assume they're being parboiled for dinner. Don't expect to do any sightseeing beyond shopping malls and hotel lobbies during these months.

In March and April, and October and November, the weather is very pleasant, with temperatures in the low 30s. In winter (December to February), the weather is usually

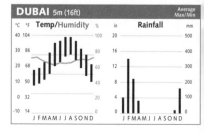

perfect, although there are the occasional cold patches around New Year. Unlike the desert area inland, Dubai doesn't get too cold on winter nights, with the lowest temperature hovering around 15°C, but bring a warm jacket if you're visiting at this time of year.

It doesn't rain often, or heavily, although when it does getting around can suddenly become difficult as streets turn into rivers and traffic becomes chaotic, with accidents everywhere. Drivers are not used to wet road conditions, and the city planners decided Dubai didn't need a drainage system, so there are no gutters or stormwater drains. The average annual rainfall is about 6.5cm per year (and it rains only five days a year on average), but rainfall varies widely from one year to the next. Sandstorms can occur during March and April, although Dubai is protected from the swirling dust and sand to some degree by its ever-increasing number of tall buildings.

COURSES
Cultural

Dubai International Art Centre (Map pp76-7; ☎ 344 4398; www.artdubai.com; Villa 27, Street 75B, near Mercato Mall, Jumeirah Rd, Jumeirah) Offers a plethora of art-related courses, but it's the Arabic calligraphy lessons that are most appealing. Classes cost Dh190 per three-hour session.

Language

Most language courses on offer are for English. There are only a few places where English-speakers can study Arabic. This is because of the great demand by UAE national students and expats from the Indian subcontinent who want to improve their employment opportunities in the world of business, which is dominated by the English language. The following centres offer Arabic courses:

Arabic Language Centre (Map pp70-71; ☎ 308 6036; www.dwtc.com; Dubai World Trade Centre, Sheikh Zayed Rd) Runs six courses a year in Arabic from beginner to advanced levels. Private tuition starts at Dh200 per hour and group classes cost Dh1950 for 30 hours.

Berlitz Language School (Map pp76-7; ☎ 344 0034; www.berlitz.ae; Jumeirah Rd) Offers courses in a number of languages, including Arabic and Urdu. The latter is useful to know to some extent, as this is the language of many of the Pakistani expats in the UAE.

Polyglot Language Institute (Map pp52-3; ☎ 222 3429; www.polyglot.ae; Al-Masaeed Bldg, Al-Maktoum Rd, Deira) Beginner courses and conversation classes in Arabic,

French, German and English. A 10-week Arabic course with three classes per week costs Dh2050 including materials. Private tuition costs around Dh8000 for 25 90-minute lessons.

CUSTOMS REGULATIONS

Anyone aged over 18 years is allowed to bring in duty-free: 400 cigarettes plus 50 cigars plus 500g of loose tobacco; 4L of alcohol or two cartons of beer, each consisting of up to 24 355ml cans (non-Muslims only); gifts not exceeding Dh3000 in value. You are generally not allowed to bring in alcohol if you cross into the UAE by land. No customs duties are applied to personal belongings. There's a long list of goods that are proscribed, including controlled substances (see boxed text, p190), materials that insult Islam, firearms, pork, pornography and Israeli products. For a full list see www.dubaicustoms.gov.ae.

ELECTRICITY

The electric voltage is 220V AC. British-style three-pin wall sockets are standard, although most appliances are sold with two-pin plugs. Adaptors are inexpensive and available in supermarkets. The two-pin plugs go into the three-pin sockets, but this does involve a technique that won't be seen in a workplace safety video anytime soon.

EMBASSIES

Generally speaking, the embassy will not be much help in emergencies if the trouble you're in is your own fault. Remember that you are bound by the laws of the UAE. Your embassy will not be very sympathetic if you end up in jail after committing a crime locally, even if such actions happen to be legal in your own country.

In genuine emergencies you might get some assistance, but only if other channels have been exhausted. For example, if you need to get home urgently a free flight is exceedingly unlikely – the embassy would expect you to have insurance. If you have all your money and documents stolen, it might assist with getting a new passport, but a loan for onward travel is out of the question.

Most countries have diplomatic representation in the UAE. Dubai is home to several consulates and one embassy, the British embassy; other embassies are in Abu Dhabi and are listed in the front pages of the Dubai phone book. Many consulates cluster in the Consulate Zone, an area north of Al-Maktoum Bridge between the Creek (Al-Seef Rd) and Khalid bin al-Waleed Rd. Several others are in the Dubai World Trade Centre and near the BurJuman Centre.

The telephone area code for Dubai is ☎ 04.

Australia (Map pp62-3; ☎ 508 7100; www.uae .embassy.gov.au; 25th fl, BurJuman Business Tower, Trade Centre Rd, Bur Dubai; ☺ 8am-1pm & 1.30-4.30pm Sun-Thu)

Canada (Map pp62-3; ☎ 314 5555; dubai@ international.gc.ca; 7th fl, Bank St Bldg, Khalid bin al-Waleed Rd, next to Citibank, Bur Dubai; ☺ 8am-4pm Sun-Thu)

Egypt (Map pp64-5; ☎ 397 1122; www.mfa.gov.eg; Consulate Zone, Khalid bin al-Waleed Rd, Umm Hurair; ☺ 9am-noon Sat-Wed)

France (Map pp70-71; ☎ 332 9040; http://consulfrance -dubai.org; 18th fl, API World Tower, Sheikh Zayed Rd, Trade Centre District; ☺ 8am-1pm Sat-Thu)

Germany (Map pp64-5; ☎ 397 2333; www.dubai .diplo.de; 1st fl, Sharaf Bldg, Khalid bin al-Waleed Rd, opp BurJuman Centre, Bur Dubai; ☺ 8-11am Sun-Thu)

India (Map pp64-5; ☎ 397 1222; www.cgidubai .com; Consulate Zone, near Khalid bin al-Waleed Rd, Umm Hurair; ☺ 8am-noon Sun-Thu)

Iran (Map pp76-7; ☎ 344 4717; www.iranconsul.ae; cnr Al-Wasl Rd & 33 St, Jumeirah; ☺ 8am-noon Sun-Thu)

Italy (Map pp70-71; ☎ 331 4167; www.consdubai .esteri.it; 17th fl, Dubai World Trade Centre, Sheikh Zayed Rd, Trade Centre District; ☺ 9am-noon Sun-Thu)

Netherlands (Map pp62-3; ☎ 352 8700; www .netherlands.ae; 5th fl, Royal Bank of Scotland Bldg, Khalid bin al-Waleed Rd, Mankhool, Bur Dubai; ☺ 9am-noon Sat-Thu)

Oman (Map pp64-5; ☎ 397 1000; www.ocodubai .com; Consulate Zone, near Khalid bin al-Waleed Rd, Umm Hurair; ☺ 7.30am-2.30pm Sun-Thu)

Qatar (Map pp62-3; ☎ 398 2888; dubai@mofa.gov.qa; cnr Al-Adhid Rd & 52 St, Al-Jafiliya; ☺ 9-11.30am Sun-Thu)

South Africa (Map pp64-5; ☎ 397 5222; www.south africadubai.com; 3rd fl, Sharaf Bldg, Khalid bin al-Waleed Rd, opp BurJuman Centre, Bur Dubai; ☺ 8.30am-12.30pm Sun-Thu)

Syria (Map pp64-5; ☎ 266 3354; Consulate Zone, near Khalid bin al-Waleed Rd, Umm Hurair; ☺ 8.30am-2.30pm Sat-Wed)

Turkey (Map pp70-71; ☎ 331 4788; tcdubkon@emirates. net.ae; 11th fl, Dubai World Trade Centre, Sheikh Zayed Rd, Trade Centre District; ☺ 10am-noon Sun, Mon, Wed & Thu)

UK (Map pp62-3; ☎ 309 4444; http://ukinuae.fco .gov.uk/en; Consulate Zone, Al-Seef Rd, Umm Hurair; ☺ 7.30am-2.30pm Sun-Thu)

USA (Map pp70-71; ☎ 311 6000; http://dubai.us consulate.gov; 21st fl, Dubai World Trade Centre, Sheikh Zayed Rd, Trade Centre District; ☺ 12.30-3pm Sun-Thu) Scheduled to move to the Consulate Zone in 2011.

EMERGENCY

Ambulance (☎ 998/999)

Fire department (☎ 997)

Police (emergency ☎ 999, headquarters ☎ 229 2222)

GAY & LESBIAN TRAVELLERS

While Dubai is certainly not a 'gay' destination along the lines of Berlin, Sitjes or Amsterdam, same-sex couples are unlikely to encounter problems as long as they respect local customs. Open displays of affection are likely to land you in trouble (same goes for heterosexuals, of course) but sharing a room will barely raise an eyebrow.

Homosexual acts are illegal under UAE law and can incur a jail term. You will see men walking hand in hand, but that's a sign of friendship and no indication of sexual orientation. Although no bars, clubs or cafes would dare identify themselves as gay-friendly for fear of being raided and shut down, there are venues in the city that attract a sizeable gay and lesbian crowd. It is sometimes possible to get info on these venues from websites, but you can't access gay and lesbian interest websites from inside the UAE.

For more on the subject, an interesting read is *Gay Travels in the Muslim World* by Michael Luongo.

HOLIDAYS

See the Islamic Holidays table (opposite) for the approximate dates of the religious holidays observed in Dubai. Hejira is the Islamic New Year. Eid al-Fitr marks the end of Ramadan fasting and is a three-day celebration spent feasting and visiting with friends and family. Eid al-Adha is a four-day celebration following the main pilgrimage to Mecca, the hajj.

Secular holidays are New Year's Day (1 January) and National Day (2 December). A three-day mourning period usually follows the death of a royal family member, a government minister or a head of a neighbouring state; government offices, some businesses

ISLAMIC HOLIDAYS

Islamic Year	Hejira	Prophet's Birthday	Ramadan	Eid al-Fitr	Eid al-Adha
1431	18 Dec 09	26 Feb 2010	12 Aug 2010	10 Sep 2010	17 Nov 2010
1432	07 Dec 10	15 Feb 2011	01 Aug 2011	30 Aug 2011	06 Nov 2011
1433	26 Nov 11	04 Feb 2012	20 Jul 2012	19 Aug 2012	26 Oct 2012
1434	15 Nov 12	24 Jan 2013	09 Jul 2013	08 Aug 2013	15 Oct 2013

and state-run tourist attractions, such as museums, close. Newspaper websites (p36) are the quickest way to find details when this occurs. If a public holiday falls on a weekend (ie Friday or Saturday), the holiday is usually taken at the beginning of the next working week.

The Islamic calendar starts at the year AD 622, when the Prophet Mohammed fled Mecca for the city of Medina. It is called the Hejira calendar (*hejira* means 'flight'). As it is a lunar calendar, it's roughly 11 days shorter than the Gregorian (Western) calendar, which means that Islamic holidays fall 11 days earlier each year. However, this is not a fixed rule, as the exact dates of Islamic holidays depend upon the sighting of the moon at a particular stage in its cycle. This can be as informal as a group of elderly imams being taken on a night-time drive into the desert to confer on whether or not the new moon is visible. This is why Islamic holidays are not announced until a day or two before they occur, and why they differ from country to country.

Ramadan

This is the month during which Muslims fast during daylight hours. They must also refrain from sex, swearing, smoking or any other indulgence. This is to clean the mind and body to better focus on the relationship with Allah.

During Ramadan, government offices ease back to about six hours' work (well, attendance) a day. Bars and pubs are closed until 7pm each night, live music is prohibited and dance clubs are closed throughout the month. Camel racing ceases too. Some restaurants do not serve alcohol during this month. Everyone, regardless of their religion, is required to observe the fast in public (see boxed text, p117).

For visitors interested in Islam or religion in general, this is a fascinating time to visit Dubai. If you walk the backstreets of areas such as Satwa at *iftar*, you'll see mosques with mats and carpets laid out with food ready for mosque attendees, and witness the streets come to life – well into the wee hours.

INTERNET ACCESS

Dubai is extremely well wired and you should have no trouble getting online. The internet is accessed through a proxy server that blocks pornography, gay-interest sites, websites considered critical of Islam or the UAE's leaders, dating and gambling sites, drug-related material and the entire Israeli domain. To the irritation of the country's huge foreign workforce, peer-to-peer and Voice over Internet Protocol (VoIP) software such as Skype is banned in the UAE.

Nearly every hotel and hotel apartment offers in-room internet access, either broadband or wireless, although rates are usually extortionate (Dh40 to Dh60 per hour is not uncommon); sometimes it's more economical to prepay for 24 hours.

A cheaper way to connect is through Etisalat Hotspots, which is available at all branches of Starbucks, Barista and Coffee Bean & Tea Leaf, as well as at major shopping malls and various restaurants and cafes (see www.etisalat.ae for the full list). You gain access by buying a prepaid card from the venue itself, or by using your credit card. Enter your card number and mobile phone number in the fields provided, and you'll be sent an access code by text message. Internet access costs Dh15 for one continuous hour, Dh30 for three continuous hours, Dh80 for six hours over a 30-day period and Dh120 for 12 hours over a 60-day period. Some restaurants and cafes also offer wi-fi access, sometimes free with purchase. Dubai Mall (p72) and BurJuman Centre (p96) both offer free wi-fi access, although you need a UAE mobile phone number to use it.

If your laptop is not wi-fi-enabled, you can still access the internet via Etisalat's Dial 'n' Surf service by dialling ☎ 500 5555; all you need is a modem and a phone line. No account number or password is needed. It is charged at 12 fils per minute directly to the telephone you are connected to, but do check with your hotel if there's an additional charge.

If you don't own a computer, nearly all hotels have business centres, and internet cafes charge as little as Dh2 per hour for access. The following are a bit pricier, but pleasant and reliable:

Al-Jalssa Internet Café (Map pp62–3; ☎ 351 4617; Al-Ain Shopping Centre, Al-Mankhool Rd; per hr Dh10; ☯ 8am-midnight) Thirty high-speed stations with webcam and headsets; wi-fi available too.

F1 Net Café (Map pp76–7; ☎ 345 1232; 1st fl, Palm Strip Shopping Centre, Jumeirah Rd; per 30/60min Dh8/15; ☯ 10am-10pm Sat-Thu, 2.30-10pm Fri) Opposite Jumeirah Mosque.

LEGAL MATTERS

Drugs in Dubai are simply a bad, bad idea. The UAE has a small but growing drug problem, and the authorities are cracking down hard on it. The minimum penalty for possession of even trace amounts is four years in prison, and the death penalty is still on the books for importing or dealing in drugs (although in fact it usually ends up being a very long jail term; see boxed text, below). Jail sentences for being involved in drugs by association are also fairly common. That means that even if you are in a room where there are drugs, but are not partaking, you could be in as much trouble as those who are. The secret police are pervasive, and they include officers of many nationalities.

There are also import restrictions for prescription medications that are legal in most countries, such as diazepam (Valium), dextromethorphan (Robitussin), fluoxetine (Prozac) and anything containing codeine. Check with the UAE embassy in your home country for the full list. If you need to take such medications, carry the original prescription and a letter from your doctor.

Other common infractions that may incur a fine, jail time or even deportation include drinking alcohol in an unlicensed public place; buying alcohol without a local licence; writing bad cheques; unmarried cohabitation; and public eating, drinking and smoking during daylight hours in Ramadan. Another big no-no is sexual or indecent public behaviour. Although Dubai has the most tolerant social codes in the Middle East, police can still crack down on people appearing to push the limits. In 2008, the case of the British non-married couple caught having sex in the sand outside the Jumeirah Beach Hotel made headlines around the world (they were convicted, fined and slapped with a three-month jail sentence which was suspended on appeal). At the time of writing, another British couple is appealing a one-month prison term after conviction for kissing passionately in public.

If arrested, you have the right to a phone call, which you should make as soon as possible (ie before you are detained in a police cell or prison pending investigation, where making contact with anyone could be

DRUGS: ZERO TOLERANCE

We can't shout the following words loudly enough: do not attempt to carry illegal drugs into Dubai! In fact, even if you're not attempting to import drugs, you should double-check that there isn't the faintest speck of anything illegal anywhere in your baggage or on your person. You must also ensure that medicines and drugs legal in your country are legal in Dubai before travelling with them. If you have illegal substances in your bloodstream, this still counts as possession too, and a urine test could see you found guilty. Several drugs available over the supermarket counter in other countries are banned substances in the United Arab Emirates (UAE).

The following cases illustrate just how unforgiving Dubai's drug laws are:

- A British tourist was arrested at Dubai airport after 0.03g of cannabis, an amount smaller than a grain of sugar and invisible to the human eye, was detected on the stub of a cigarette stuck to the sole of his shoe. He was sentenced to four years in prison.
- A British TV producer was arrested and held for possessing the health supplement melatonin, which is taken to alleviate jet lag and is legal in the UK and Dubai. After being cleared of importing an illegal substance, he was held for over a month without charges in a Dubai prison while the rest of his possessions were tested.
- A Saudi man was sentenced to four years in prison after a tiny, dried-up leaf of Qat (a mild stimulant, which is legal in Yemen) was found on his clothing.
- A Swiss man was reportedly imprisoned after customs officials found three poppy seeds on his clothes. These had fallen off a bread roll he ate at Heathrow.
- A British woman was held in custody for two months before UAE customs officers accepted that the codeine she was using for her back problem had been prescribed by a doctor.
- BBC1 radio host and drum 'n' bass DJ Grooverider was sentenced to four years in prison after 2.16 grams of cannabis was found in his luggage upon arrival at the airport. (He was released after 10 months.)

difficult). Call your embassy or consulate first so they can get in touch with your family and possibly recommend a lawyer.

Dubai Police has established a Department of Tourist Security (☎ 800 4438; ☽ 24hr) to help visitors with any legal complications they may face on their trip.

MAPS

The free *Dubai at a Glance* map is usually available from the Department of Tourism & Commerce Marketing (DTCM) welcome desks (see p195) and hotel concierges. Bookshops, petrol stations, supermarkets and hotel shops also stock maps. The most current and accurate maps are published by Explorer; its *Dubai Mini Map* (Dh18) provides a large fold-out overview map with detailed maps of key areas. For more detail, invest in the *Dubai Map* (Dh45) or the comprehensive *Dubai Street Atlas* (Dh145).

MEDICAL SERVICES

There are pharmacies on just about every street in Dubai. See the daily newspapers for a list of pharmacies that are open 24 hours, or call ☎ 223 2323. As a visitor you will receive medical care, but you will be charged for it, so don't leave home without travel health insurance. The standard of medical services is quite good.

For house calls, contact Health Call (☎ 363 5343; http://health-call.com; per visit Dh600-800), which will send out Western-trained doctors around-the-clock.

The following government hospitals have 24/7 emergency rooms:

Al-Wasl Hospital (Map pp64-5; ☎ 219 3000; Oud Metha Rd, south of Al-Qataiyat Rd, Za'abeel)

Dubai Hospital (Map pp52-3; ☎ 219 5000; Abu Baker al-Siddiq Rd, near cnr Al-Khaleej Rd)

Rashid Hospital (Map pp64-5; ☎ 337 4000; off Oud Metha Rd, near Al-Maktoum Bridge, Bur Dubai)

For non-urgent care, contact the following or ask your consulate for a referral:

Al-Zahra Medical Centre (Map pp70-71; ☎ 331 5000; www.al-zahra.com; Al Safa Tower, Sheikh Zayed Rd, near Emirates Tower Metro station)

American Hospital (Map pp64-5; ☎ 336 7777, emergency ☎ 309 6877; www.ahdubai.com; opposite Mövenpick Hotel, Oud Metha) Has a walk-in clinic (no appointment needed) open 10am to 5pm daily, as well as a 24-hour emergency room.

Dubai London Clinic (Map pp76-7; ☎ 344 6663; www.dubailondonclinic.com; Jumeirah Rd, Umm Suqeim; ☽ 8am-7pm Sat-Wed, 8am-5pm Thu)

MONEY

The UAE dirham (Dh) is divided into 100 fils. Notes come in denominations of five, 10, 20, 50, 100, 200, 500 and 1000. There are Dh1, 50 fils, 25 fils, 10 fils and 5 fils coins. The coins only show the denomination in Arabic, so it's a great way to learn. The UAE dirham has been pegged to the US dollar since the late 1980s at a mid-rate of approximately US$1 = Dh3.679.

ATMs & Credit Cards

There are globally linked ATMs all over Dubai at banks, shopping malls and at the upmarket hotels. Visa, MasterCard and American Express are widely accepted at shops, hotels and restaurants throughout Dubai and debit cards are accepted at bigger retail outlets.

Changing Money

If you need to change money, exchange offices tend to offer better rates than banks. A bunch of them cluster near the Deira Gold Souq (market), especially along Sikkat al-Khail St, Naif Rd and around Baniyas Sq, and in Bur Dubai near the *abra* (water taxi) stations. Reliable exchanges include Al-Rostamani (☎ 295 6777; www.alrostamaniexchange.com) and UAE Exchange (☎ 229 7373; www.uaeexchange.com), with multiple branches around town at locations including Mall of the Emirates, Dubai International Airport and Ibn Battuta Mall.

Currencies of neighbouring countries are all recognised and easily changed, with the exception of the Yemeni rial. American Express (Map pp64-5; ☎ 408 2222; ground fl, Hermitage Bldg, Za'abeel Rd, Karama; ☽ 8.30am-5pm Sat-Thu) is next to the main post office.

Tipping

By law, only food and beverage outlets in hotels are entitled to tack a service charge (usually 10%) onto bills. Independent restaurants are not officially permitted to do so, although many seem to thumb their nose at the regulation. Unfortunately, the service charge rarely ends up in the pockets of the person who served you, which is why it's nice to give them a few extra dirham in cash if they did a good job. For more details, see p107.

NEWSPAPERS & MAGAZINES

English-language newspapers in Dubai include the free *7 Days* (www.7days.ae – amusingly published six days a week), the government-owned and infuriatingly obsequious *Emirates Business 24/7* (www.business24-7.ae), the high-design weekly tabloid *Xpress* (www.xpress4me.com), and the long-established dailies (*Gulf News*, *Khaleej Times* and *Gulf Today*). In 2008 the Abu Dhabi government launched *The National*, the region's most ambitious English-language daily newspaper to date, with a staff of around 180 international journalists. For more on the local media, see p36.

International newspapers and news magazines such as the *International Herald Tribune* and *The Economist* are fairly easy to find, though expensive and sometimes several days or a week out of date. *The Times* is the first UK newspaper to print a daily Dubai edition and the *Financial Times* publishes a Middle East edition.

Foreign newspapers are available in larger bookshops and hotels as well as Spinneys and Choithrams supermarkets. *Time Out Dubai* is produced weekly and has detailed listings and stories on upcoming events. It costs Dh7, although you'll find it free in Dubai's better hotel rooms. *What's On* is the other listings monthly and costs Dh10, although it's a lot tamer than the competition.

ORGANISED TOURS
Creek Cruises

For details of dinner cruises, see p107.

Tour Dubai (Map pp52-3; ☎ 336 8407; www.tour-dubai.com; tours adult/child Dh130/90, dinner cruises Dh225/125; ☺ tours 11.30am, 1.30pm, 3.30pm, 5.30pm, dinner cruise 8.30pm) Departs close to Radisson Blu Hotel in Deira. One-hour Creek tours aboard a dhow with pre-recorded English commentary. The two-hour dinner cruise includes a buffet, soft drinks and taped music; alcohol is available.

Bus Tours

Big Bus Company (Map pp64-5; ☎ 340 7709; www.bigbustours.com; 24hr tickets adult/child/family Dh220/100/540, 48hr tickets Dh285/130/700) These 'hop on, hop off' city tours aboard open-topped double-decker buses are not a bad way for Dubai first-timers to get their bearing. Buses travel along two interlinking routes: the red City route (1¾ hours without getting off) and the blue Beach route (2½ hours). Buses make 21 stops at major malls, beaches and landmarks (eg Gold Souq, Burj al-Arab, Burj Dubai, Dubai Creek). They depart roughly every 20 minutes between 9am and 5pm daily and come with taped commentary in – count 'em – eight languages. Tickets also include a Dhow Creek cruise, a souq walking tour and *abra* ride, entry to the Dubai Museum and Sheikh Saeed al-Maktoum House, and shopping discounts at Wafi Mall and Mercato Mall. Tickets are sold online, on the bus or at hotels. Pick up a flyer or check the internet for pick-up points.

Wonder Bus Tours (Map pp62-3; ☎ 359 5656; www.wonderbusdubai.net; BurJuman Centre, cnr Khalid bin al-Waleed (Bank St) & Trade Centre Rds, Bur Dubai; tours adult/child/family Dh125/85/390) Twice a day (actual times depend on the tide) this amphibious bus drives down to the Creek, plunges into the water, cruises for an hour and then drives back onto land and returns to the BurJuman Centre.

PHOTOGRAPHY

Dubai loves technology, so memory cards, batteries and other accessories for digital cameras are available in big supermarkets, at shopping malls and in electronics stores. If you take video or photographs of airports, government offices, military and industrial installations, you will arouse suspicion and could get into trouble. Also, ask permission before photographing Muslim women.

The best spots for photography, especially early and late in the day, tend to be near the Creek, where you can capture dhows, *abras*, historical buildings and Dubai's most colourful city scenes. Lonely Planet's *Urban Travel Photography* by Richard I'Anson will help you get the best results. The UAE uses the PAL video system.

POST

Your hotel should be able to send mail for you, but otherwise stamps are of course available at local post offices operated by Emirates Post (☎ 600 599 999; www.emiratespost.com). A letter to Europe costs Dh4.75, while a postcard costs Dh3 and a 1kg parcel costs Dh95.50. Rates to the US or Canada are almost identical: Dh5.50 for letters, Dh3 for postcards and Dh97 for the 1kg parcel. Mail generally takes about a week to 10 days to Europe or the USA and eight to 15 days to Australia.

Major post offices:

Al-Musallah Post Office (Map pp62-3; ☺ 8am-2pm Sat-Thu, 5-9pm Fri) At Al-Fahidi Roundabout in Bur Dubai.

Al-Rigga Post Office (Map pp54-5; ☺ 8am-8pm Sat-Thu, 5-9pm Fri) Near the Clock Tower Roundabout.

Central Post Office (Map pp64–5; Za'abeel Rd; ☻ 8am-8pm Sat-Thu, 5-9pm Fri) On Bur Dubai side of the Creek in Karama.

Dubai International Airport (Map pp54–5; ☻ 24hr) Near Gate 18 of Terminal 1.

Jumeirah Post Office (Map pp76–7; ☻ 8am-8pm Sat-Thu, 5-9pm Fri) On Al-Wasl Rd, near 13 St.

Satwa Post Office (Map pp76–7; Al-Satwa Rd; ☻ 8am-8pm Sat-Thu, 5-9pm Fri)

Courier Service

If you need to send something in a hurry, contact the following courier agencies for office locations and hours:

Aramex (☎ 600 544 000; www.aramex.com)

DHL (☎ 800 4004; www.dhl.co.ae)

FedEx (☎ 800 4050; www.fedex.com)

UPS (☎ 800 4774; www.ups.com)

RADIO

The quality of radio programming in Dubai is improving (particularly talk radio), but it's generally a cringe-worthy and ad-saturated affair wherever you point the dial.

BBC Worldwide (87.9) Broadcasts from 9am to 6pm.

Channel 4 FM (104.8) Contemporary Top 40.

Dubai Eye (103.8) News, talk and sports.

Dubai FM (92) Classic hits from the '80s, '90s etc, as well as dance and lounge at weekends.

Emirates Radio 1 (104.1) Popular music.

Emirates Radio 2 (99.3) Eclectic programming.

It's worth searching through the dial, as there are stations playing Hindi, Arabic and Indian regional music, and stations where you can hear recitations of the Quran – very soothing when you're stuck in Dubai's horrific traffic.

RELOCATING

If you like Dubai so much you don't want to leave, you may not have to. In most cases, relocating to Dubai is easy. To secure a three-year residency permit, you need either an employer to sponsor you (see Work, p197), a spouse with a job who can sponsor you, or ownership of freehold property, which comes with a renewable residency permit.

It seems almost inconceivable that 20 years ago foreign workers in Dubai were eligible for a 'hardship allowance' – financial compensation for having to live in a boring, conservative and unbearably hot place. Back then, working hours were short and salaries were high. Today some people will accept a drop in salary to experience the much-feted 'Dubai dream', despite the fact that inflation is on the rise, rents are still sky-high (though they've dropped as much as 40% since the economic downturn) and wages haven't increased in years (and are now on a par with salaries in the West). For many, these conditions are offset by the fact that the salary is tax free, and that myriad perks are still considered standard in many expat packages, such as a relocation allowance, annual plane tickets home, housing, health insurance, kids' education allowance and long, paid holidays.

These days many people are moving to Dubai for reasons that are less to do with financial reward, and more to do with job satisfaction and being part of the developments that are taking place in the region. The opportunities for career progression are fantastic. Competition exists, but it's nowhere near as tough as it is back home. Whereas the expat of the oil-boom days was in his or her 40s or 50s, white, middle class, and more than likely worked in oil, gas, petroleum, construction, nursing, teaching or foreign relations, times have changed. The new expats come in all ages, races, nationalities and classes, and the work itself is more glamorous, with the most coveted opportunities being in tourism, hospitality, marketing, PR and advertising, real-estate development, project management, architecture, interior design, fashion and entertainment. While the opportunities are fantastic, the work culture can be intense. Late nights and weekends in the office are commonplace and it can be tricky achieving the right work–life balance.

While Dubai may not be as culturally active as many other cities (there's very little theatre, live music or quality cinema), it's easier to get noticed if you are a budding playwright, actor, musician or film director. The opportunities to travel from Dubai are fantastic, with the Indian subcontinent, Eastern Europe, East Africa and all of the Middle East accessible within a few hours' flying time. And then there's the fine dining, the beaches, the desert trips at weekends, the inspiring multiculturalism and the chance to learn about the Arab World and Islam.

For a detailed guide to relocating to the Gulf, see Lonely Planet's *Oman, UAE & Arabian Peninsula* guide. For information on long-term rentals, see p153.

SAFETY

On the whole, Dubai is a very safe city, but you should exercise the same sort of caution with your personal safety as you would anywhere. Due to Dubai's location at the heart of the Gulf, the US Department of State and British Foreign Office both warn travellers of a general threat from terrorism.

One very real danger in Dubai is bad driving. We also don't recommend that you swim, water ski or jet-ski in the Creek. The tides in the Gulf are not strong enough to flush the Creek out on a regular basis, so it is not a clean waterway, despite what the tourist authorities might tell you. Also, be careful when swimming in the open sea. Despite the small surf, currents can be very strong and drownings are not uncommon.

SMOKING

Dubai has a comprehensive smoking ban that essentially extends to all public places, with the exception of nightclubs and enclosed bars. Shopping malls, hotels, restaurants and cafes may have designated smoking rooms but these must be clearly marked, properly ventilated and cannot be entered by people aged under 20 years. Hotels have rooms where smoking is permitted. The fine for lighting up in a nonsmoking area can range from Dh1000 to Dh8000. There are also fines for getting caught throwing cigarette butts into the street. In 2009 the ban was extended to include *sheesha* smoking in parks, beaches and public recreation areas.

TELEPHONE

The UAE has an efficient communications system that connects you with anywhere in the world, even from the most remote areas. Etisalat was the sole operator until du came on the scene in 2007, but as both are government-owned, prices have not budged much. Note that Skype is blocked in the UAE, although many people manage to get around this by downloading a proxy bypass or VPN. Do a Google search for instructions.

Local calls (within the same area code) are free. Coin phones have been almost completely superseded by cardphones. Phonecards are available in various denominations from grocery stores, supermarkets and petrol stations – do not buy them from street vendors.

To phone another country from the UAE, dial ☎ 00 followed by the country code. If you want to call the UAE, the country code is ☎ 971. The area code for Dubai is ☎ 04, though if you are calling from outside the UAE you drop the zero.

Directory enquiries (☎ 181)
International directory assistance (☎ 151)

Faxes

Practically all hotel receptions or business centres will be able to send and receive faxes. Alternatively, most typing and photocopying shops also have fax machines you can use.

Mobile Phones

The UAE's mobile phone network uses the GSM 900 MHz and 1800 MHz standard, the same as Europe, Asia and Australia. Mobile numbers begin with either 050 (Etisalat) or 055 (du). If you don't have a worldwide roaming service, consider buying a prepaid SIM card, eg at Dubai Duty Free at the airport, at any Etisalat office or at licensed mobile phone shops. The excellent-value Ahlan Visitor's Mobile Package lasts 90 days, costs Dh60 and includes Dh25 of credit. Domestic calls cost Dh0.50 a minute and international calls are priced at Dh2.50 a minute. Domestic text messages cost Dh0.30, international ones Dh0.90. Recharge cards in denominations of Dh25, Dh50, Dh100, Dh200 and Dh500 are sold at grocery stores, supermarkets and petrol stations – once again, do not buy them from street vendors.

TIME

Dubai is four hours ahead of GMT. The time does not change during the summer. Not taking daylight saving into account, when it's noon in Dubai, the time elsewhere is as follows:

City	Time
Auckland	8pm
London	8am
Los Angeles	midnight
New York	3am
Paris & Rome	9am
Perth & Hong Kong	4pm
Sydney	6pm

TOILETS

The best advice is to go when you can. Public toilets in shopping centres, museums, restaurants and hotels are Western style and are generally well maintained. Those in souqs and bus stations are usually only for men. Outside of the cities you might have to contend with 'hole in the ground' loos at the back of restaurants or petrol stations. Muslims are quite fastidious about cleanliness, which is why you'll always find a hose and nozzle next to the toilet, which is used to rinse yourself before using the toilet paper.

TOURIST INFORMATION

The Department of Tourism & Commerce Marketing (DTCM; ☎ 223 0000; www.dubaitourism.ae) operates 24-hour information kiosks in the Terminal 1 and 3 arrivals areas of Dubai International Airport, as well as booths at the following malls: Deira City Centre (Map pp54-5), BurJuman (Map pp62-3), Wafi Mall (Map pp64-5), Ibn Battuta (Map pp82-3) and Mercato Mall (Map pp76-7). These are officially open from 10am to 10pm, although we frequently found them unstaffed, leaving you to pick through a meagre assortment of flyers and brochures by yourself.

TRAVELLERS WITH DISABILITIES

Dubai has made a big effort in recent years to improve its services for people with disabilities. The Department of Tourism & Commerce Marketing (DTCM; ☎ 223 0000; www.dubaitourism.ae) website includes a Special Needs Tourism section, which contains information on wheelchair-accessible parks, heritage sites, cinemas, malls and tour operators.

The airport is well equipped with low check-in counters, carts, automatic doors, lifts and quick check-in. Dubai Taxi (☎ 208 0808, 224 5331; www.dubaitaxi.ae) has special vans with wheelchair lifts for Dh50 per hour, but they must be ordered 24 hours in advance. Some local buses and all water taxis are wheelchair-accessible. Dubai Metro has lifts and grooved guidance paths in stations and wheelchair spaces in each train compartment. Most parking areas in town contain spaces for drivers with disabilities.

Top-end hotels are the ones most likely to have rooms with extra-wide doors and spacious bathrooms; however it's best to discuss your particular needs when making a reservation. For other venues, call ahead to find what access to expect. Wheelchair ramps, for instance, are still a rarity, even in public buildings and at tourist attractions;

exceptions include the Dubai Museum and Heritage Village.

VISAS

Entry requirements to the UAE are in constant flux, which is why you ought to double-check all information in this section with the UAE embassy in your home country.

At the time of writing, citizens of 34 developed countries, including nearly all of Western Europe plus Australia, Brunei, Canada, Hong Kong, Japan, Malaysia, New Zealand, Singapore, South Korea and the USA, get free on-the-spot visas on arrival in the UAE at air, land and sea ports. Officially, these cost Dh100, but the fee was not being collected. Visas are also supposedly valid for 30 days and non-renewable. In practice, though, they appear to be valid for 60 days (even if the stamp in your passport says 30!).

If you're a citizen of a country not included in the list above, a visit visa must be arranged through a sponsor – such as your Dubai hotel or tour operator – prior to your arrival in the UAE. The non-renewable visas cost Dh100 and are valid for 30 days. Citizens of Gulf Cooperative Council (GCC) countries only need a valid passport to enter the UAE and can stay as long as they want. It is generally not possible to enter with an Israeli passport, but there's no problem entering the UAE with an Israeli stamp in a non-Israeli passport.

Note that passports must be valid for at least six months from the date of arrival.

Visa Extensions

Visit visas can be extended once for 30 days by the Department of Immigration & Naturalisation (Map pp62-3; ☎ 398 0000; Sheikh Khalifa bin Zayed Rd, near Bur Dubai Police Station) for Dh500 and a fair amount of paperwork. You may be asked to provide proof of funds. It's much easier, and usually cheaper, to leave the country for a few hours and head back for a new stamp. People have

VIS-À-VIS OMAN

If you are from one of the 34 countries eligible to get an on-the-spot visa at Dubai airport, you won't need to obtain a separate visa for Oman. Everyone else has to apply in advance at the Omani embassy in Abu Dhabi. If you are visiting Oman on a tourist visa, these same nationalities can enter the UAE by land, air or sea without visa charges.

been known to stay in Dubai for a year or more simply by flying out to Bahrain, Doha, Muscat or Kish (an island off the Iranian coast) every two months and picking up a new visa on their return.

Visas can only be extended in the city or emirate you arrived in, so if you landed in Sharjah, you can't get your visa extended in Dubai.

WOMEN TRAVELLERS

Many women imagine that travel to Dubai and within the UAE is much more difficult than it actually is. No, you don't have to wear a burka (headscarf or veil). Yes, you can drive a car. No, you won't be constantly harassed. In fact, Dubai is one of the safest Middle East destinations for women travellers. It's totally fine to take cabs, stay alone in hotels (although you may want to avoid the fleabag hotels in Deira and Bur Dubai) and walk around on your own in most areas. Having said that, this does not mean that some of the problems that accompany travel just about anywhere in the world will not arise in Dubai as well, such as unwanted male attention and long, lewd stares, especially on public beaches. Try not to be intimidated, and appear self-confident. For a few simple techniques on how to avoid harassment, see below.

Although prostitution does not officially exist, authorities do little to suppress the small army of 'working women' catering to both expats and Emiratis in clubs, bars and on the backstreets of Deira and Bur Dubai. In terms of dress, they're often indistinguishable from other women, which is confusing to the men and opens up the possibility of respectable women being solicited erroneously. While

this can be offensive, just imagine how embarrassed the guy must feel about his mistake.

Attitudes towards Women

Some of the biggest misunderstandings between Middle Easterners and Westerners occur over the issue of women. Half-truths and stereotypes exist on both sides: many Westerners assume that all Middle Eastern women are veiled, repressed victims, while a large number of locals see Western women as sex-obsessed and immoral.

Traditionally, the role of a woman in the region is to be a mother and matron of the household, while the man is the financial provider. However, as with any society, the reality is far more nuanced. There are thousands of middle- and upper-middle-class professional women in the UAE who, like their counterparts in the West, juggle work and family responsibilities.

The issue of sex is where the differences between the cultures are particularly apparent. Premarital sex (or indeed any sex outside marriage) is taboo, although, as with anything forbidden, it still happens. Emirati women are expected to be virgins when they marry, and a family's reputation can rest upon this point. The presence of foreign women provides, in the eyes of some Arab men, a chance to get around these norms with ease and without consequences. Hence the occasional hassle.

What to Wear

Even though you'll see plenty of Western women in skimpy shorts and tank-tops in the shopping malls and other public places, you should not assume that it's OK to do so.

TOP 10 TIPS FOR WOMEN TRAVELLERS

- Wear a wedding ring – it will make you appear less 'available'.
- If you're unmarried but travelling in male company, say that you're married rather than girlfriend/boyfriend.
- Avoid direct eye contact with men (dark sunglasses help).
- Don't sit in the front seat of taxis unless the driver is a woman.
- On public transport, sit in the women's section towards the front.
- If you need help for any reason (directions, etc), ask a woman first.
- If dining alone, eat at Western-style places or ask to be seated in the 'family' section.
- It's perfectly acceptable for women to go straight to the front of a queue (eg at banks or post offices) or ask to be served first before any men that may be waiting.
- If someone follows you in his car, take a picture of his licence plate or just get your mobile phone out (if it doesn't have a camera, just pretend it does).
- If you're being followed, go to the nearest public place, preferably a hotel lobby. If this doesn't discourage them, ask the receptionist to call the police, which usually makes them slink away.

While they're too good a host to actually say anything, most Emiratis find this disrespectful. Despite Dubai's relative liberalism, you are in a country that holds its traditions dear. When it comes to beach parties and nightclubs almost anything goes, but take a taxi there and back.

Generally speaking, dressing 'modestly' has the following advantages: it attracts less attention to you; you will get a warmer welcome from locals (who greatly appreciate your willingness to respect their customs); and it'll prove more comfortable in the heat. Dressing modestly means covering your shoulders, knees and neckline. Baggy T-shirts and loose cotton trousers or over-the-knee skirts will not only keep you cool but will also protect your skin from the sun. If you travel outside Dubai, keep in mind that everywhere else in the UAE is far more conservative.

WORK

You can pre-arrange work in the UAE, but if you enter the country on a visit visa and then find work, you will have to leave the country for one day and re-enter under your employer's sponsorship.

If you have arranged to work in Dubai you will enter the country on a visit visa sponsored by your employer while your residence visa is processed. This process involves a blood test for HIV/AIDS and lots of paperwork. Those on a residence visa who are sponsored by a spouse who is in turn sponsored by an employer are not officially permitted to work. This rule is often broken, and it is possible to find work in the public or private sector. If you are in this situation, remember that your spouse, and not the company you work for, is your sponsor. One effect of this is that you may only be able to apply for a tourist visa to another Gulf Arab country with a consent letter from your spouse. In some cases you will need to be accompanied by your spouse, who has company sponsorship. Similarly, if you

want to apply for a driving licence, you will also need a consent letter from your spouse.

If you obtain your residence visa through an employer and then quit because you've found something better, you may find yourself under a six-month ban from working in the UAE. This rule is designed to stop people from job-hopping.

If you are employed in Dubai and have any work-related problems, you can call the Ministry of Labour Helpline (☎ 800 665) for advice.

Finding Work

While plenty of people turn up in Dubai on a visit visa, decide they like the look of the place and then scout around for a job, this isn't really the most effective way to go about it. First, most employees are on a contract that's generally for three years. Secondly, there are a lot of sums to be done before you can really figure out whether the amount you're offered is going to make financial sense. Things such as a housing allowance, medical coverage, holidays and schooling (for those with kids) have to be taken into account before you can decide.

Target who you want to work for and try to set up meetings before you arrive. Email and follow up with a phone call or two. Employers in Dubai are very fond of people with qualifications. However, it's of little consequence which higher learning establishment you attended. Teachers, nurses and those in engineering are highly valued in Dubai and are well paid.

The *Khaleej Times* and the *Gulf News* publish employment supplements several times a week. When you find a job, you will be offered an employment contract in Arabic and English. Get the one in Arabic translated before you sign it.

Business Aid Centre (☎ 337 5747; www.bacdubai.com)

SOS Recruitment Consultants (☎ 396 5600; www.sosrecruitment.net)

Arabic is the official language of the UAE, but English is also widely understood. Despite the prevalence of English, you'll find that locals appreciate travellers trying to speak Arabic, no matter how muddled you may think you sound. Learn a few basic Arabic phrases (eg greetings and civilities) before you go. For a more in-depth guide to the language than that included in this chapter, get a copy of Lonely Planet's compact but comprehensive *Middle East* phrasebook. It covers the predominant languages and Arabic dialects of the region and includes script throughout.

SOCIAL
Meeting People

Hello/Welcome.
marhaba
Peace be upon you.
al-salaam alaykum
Peace be upon you. (response)
wa alaykum e-salaam
How are you?
kay fahlak?
Good, thanks.
zein, shukran
Goodbye.
fI'man ullah or ma'al salaama
Goodbye. (response)
alla ysalmak (to a man)
alla ysalmich (to a woman)
Goodbye.
hayyaakallah (to a man)
hayyachallah (to a woman)
Goodbye. (response)
alla yhai'eek (to a man)
alla yhai'eech (to a woman)
Please.
min fadhlak (to a man)
min fadhlich (to a woman)
Thank you (very much).
shukran (jazeelan)
You're welcome.
al-afu
Excuse me.
lau tismah (to a man)
lau tismahin (to a woman)
Yes.
na'am
No.
la'
If God is willing.
insha'allah
Do you speak English?
titkallam ingleezi?

Do you understand (me)?
hal bitifhaam (alay)?
I understand.
ana fahim (by a man)
ana fahma (by a woman)
I don't understand.
ana mu fahim (by a man)
ana mu fahma (by a woman)

Could you please …?	mumkin min fadhlak …?
repeat that	a'id hatha
speak more slowly	takalam shwai shwai
write it down	iktbha lee

Going Out

What's on …?	maza yahdos …?
locally	mahaleeyan
today	al-yom
tonight	al-layla
this weekend	fee nihayet hatha alesboo'a

Where are the places to eat?
wayn el mahalat al-aakl?

PRACTICAL
Question Words

How?	chayf?
How many?	cham?
What?	shu?
When?	mata?
Where?	wayn?
Who?	mnu?

Numbers & Amounts

0	sifr
1	wahid
2	ithneen

3	thalatha
4	arba'a
5	khamsa
6	sitta
7	sab'a
8	thimania
9	tis'a
10	ashra
11	hda'ash
12	thna'ash
13	thalatha'ash
14	arba'ata'ash
15	khamista'ash
16	sitta'ash
17	sabi'ta'ash
18	thimanta'ash
19	tisi'ta'ash
20	'ishreen
21	wahid wa 'ishreen
22	ithneen wa 'ishreen
30	thalatheen
40	arbi'een
50	khamseen
60	sitteen
70	saba'een
80	thimaneen
90	tis'een
100	imia
101	imia wahid
102	imia wa-ithneen
200	imiatain
300	thalatha imia
1000	alf
2000	alfayn
3000	thalath-alaf

Days

Monday	yom al-ithneen
Tuesday	yom al-thalath
Wednesday	yom al-arbaa'
Thursday	yom al-khamis
Friday	yom al-jama'a
Saturday	yom as-sabt
Sunday	yom al-had

Banking

I want to …	ana areed an …
cash a cheque	asref el-chek
change money	asref beezat
change travellers cheques	asref chekat siyaheeya
Where's the nearest …?	wayn aghrab …?
ATM	alet saref/sarraf alee
foreign exchange office	maktab al-serafa

Post

Where is the post office?
wayn maktab el-bareed?

I want to send a …	ana areed an arsell an …
fax	faks
parcel	barsell/ta'rd
postcard	beetaga bareediya
I want to buy …	ana areed an ashtaree …
an aerogram	reesala jaweeya
an envelope	zaref
a stamp	tab'eh bareed

Phones & Mobiles

I want to buy a (phone card).
ana areed ashtaree (beetaget hatef)
I want to make a call (to …).
ana areed an atsell (bee …)
I want to make a reverse-charge/collect call.
ana areed tahweel kulfet al-mukalama ila al-mutagee

Where can I find a/an …?	wayn mumkin an ajed …?
I'd like a/an …	ana areed …
adaptor plug	maakhaz tawseel
charger for my phone	shahen leel hatef
mobile/cell phone for hire	mobail leel ajar
prepaid mobile/ cell phone	mobail moos baq aldaf'
SIM card for your network	seem kart lee shabaket al-itsalaat

Internet

Where's the local internet cafe?
wayn magha al-internet?

I'd like to …	ana abga an …
check my email	chayk al-emayl malee
use the internet	ahsaal ala khat internet

Transport

When does the … leave?	mata yamshi …
When does the … arrive?	mata yusal … (m) mata tusal … (f)
boat	il-markab (m)
bus	il-bas (m)
plane	il-tayara (f)
train	il-qittar (m)

When's the first/last bus?
mata awal/akha bas?
When's the next bus?
mata il-bas al-thani?
Is this taxi free?
anta fathee?
Please put the meter on.
lau samaht shagal al-addad
How much is it to …?
bcham la …?
Please take me to (this address).
lau samaht wasalni la (hadha elonwan)

FOOD

Can you recommend a …?	mumkin an tansahanee ala …?
bar/pub	baar
cafe	magha
restaurant	mata'am

Is service/cover charge included in the bill?
hal al-fattoora tashmole al-khadma aidan?

breakfast	futtoor
lunch	ghadha
dinner	asha
snack	akal khafif
eat	kol
drink	ishrab

EMERGENCIES

It's an emergency!
halet isa'af!
Could you please help me/us?
mumkin an toosaadnee min fadhlak?
Where's the police station?
wayn marekaz al-shurta?

Call …!	etasell bil …!
a doctor	tabeeb
an ambulance	sayyaret al-isa'af
the police	shurta

HEALTH

Where's the nearest …?	wayn aghrab …?
(night) chemist	saydalee (laylee)
dentist	tabeeb asnan
doctor	tabeeb
hospital	mustashfa

I have (a) …	ana andee …
diarrhoea	is-haal
fever	sukhoona
headache	suda or waja' ras
pain	alam/waja'

GLOSSARY

This glossary contains a list of terms you may hear on your travels through Dubai. For food terms you'll commonly find in the city, check out the Lebanese Food Lingo 101 (p112) and Farsi Food (p108) boxed texts.

abeyya – (also abaya) woman's full-length black robe
abra – small, flat-decked boat; water taxi
adhan – call to prayer
agal – headropes used to hold a gutra in place
al-housh – courtyard
areesh – palm fronds used to construct houses
asr – mid-afternoon
attar – perfume
ayyalah – Bedouin dance
azan – call to prayer

baiti – romantic Arabic poetry style
barasti – traditional Gulf method of building palm-leaf houses; house built with palm leaves
barjeel – wind tower; architectural feature of masayf houses designed to keep the house cool
bateel – young shoot of date-palm plant

Bedouin – (plural Bedu) a nomadic desert dweller
burj – tower
burka – a long, enveloping garment worn in public by Muslim women
corniche – seaside road
dabar – cheap eatery
dalla – traditional copper coffeepot
dhow – traditional sailing vessel of the Gulf
dhuhr – noon
dishdasha – man's shirt-dress
dosa – flat grilled bread
eid – Islamic feast
fajr – dawn
falaj – traditional irrigation channel

ghatic – large tree like a weeping willow
Gulf Cooperation Council (GCC) – members are Saudi Arabia, Kuwait, Bahrain, Qatar, Oman and the UAE
gurdwara – Sikh place of worship
gutra – white headcloth

habban – Arabian bagpipes
hajj – Muslim pilgrimage to Mecca

halal – meat from animals killed according to Islamic law

hammam – bathhouse

hammour – common species of fish in Gulf waters

haram – forbidden by Islamic law

hawala – written order of payment

Hejira – meaning 'flight'; the Islamic calendar is called the Hejira calendar

imam – prayer leader, Muslim cleric

insha'alla – 'if Allah wills it'; 'God willing'

isha'a – twilight

jasr – drum covered with goatskin, which is slung around the neck and hit with sticks

jebel – hill, mountain

kandoura – casual shirt-dress worn by men and women

khaleeji – traditional Gulf-style music

khanjar – traditional curved dagger

khor – inlet or creek

liwa – traditional dance performed to a rapid tempo and loud drumbeat; it is usually sung in Swahili and most likely brought to the Gulf by East African slaves

luban – frankincense

maghrib – sunset

majlis – formal meeting room or reception area

Majlis, The – parliament

mandir – temple

manior – percussion instrument of a belt decorated with dried goat hooves

masayf – traditional summer house incorporating a *barjeel*

masgouf – fish dish

mashait – traditional winter house incorporating a courtyard

masjid – mosque

mathaf – museum

mihrab – niche in a mosque indicating the direction of Mecca

mimzar – oboe-like instrument

mina – port

muezzin – mosque official who sings the *azan*

mullah – Muslim scholar, teacher or religious leader

nabati – Arabic vernacular poetry

oud – wooden Arabian lute; also the wood used to burn with frankincense

qibla – the direction of Mecca, indicated in a mosque by the *mihrab*

Ramadan – Muslim month of fasting

sabkha – salt-crusted coastal plain

saruj – clay and manure building material mix

shayla – black veil

sheesha – tall, glass-bottomed smoking implement; also known as a water pipe or 'hubbly-bubbly'

sheikh – venerated religious scholar, tribal chief, ruler or elderly man worthy of respect

sheikha – daughter of a *sheikh*

souq – market

tafila – Arabic poetry written in prose style

talli – ancient Nubian art

tamboura – harplike instrument with five horse-gut strings that are plucked with sheep horns

tolah – a measure of perfume; 12mL or 12g

Trucial States – former name of the United Arab Emirates; also called Trucial Coast and Trucial sheikdoms

umrah – little pilgrimage

wasta – influence gained by connections in high places

wind tower – *barjeel*; architectural feature of *masayf* houses designed to keep the house cool

wudu – practice of ritual washing before daily prayer

BEHIND THE SCENES

THIS BOOK

This 6th edition of *Dubai* was written and researched by Andrea Schulte-Peevers. The 5th edition was written by Matthew Lee and John A Vlahides and the 4th edition by Terry Carter and Lara Dunston. This guidebook was commissioned in Lonely Planet's Melbourne office, laid out by Cambridge Publishing Management, UK, and produced by the following:

Commissioning Editors Emma Gilmour, Sasha Baskett

Coordinating Editors Catherine Burch, Dianne Schallmeiner

Coordinating Cartographer Anthony Phelan

Coordinating Layout Designer Paul Queripel

Managing Editor Liz Heynes, Melanie Dankel

Managing Cartographer Adrian Persoglia

Managing Layout Designer Celia Wood

Assisting Editors Michala Green, Caroline Hunt, Kim Hutchins, Ceinwen Sinclair

Assisting Cartographers Fatima Basic, Diana Duggan, David Kemp, Alex Leung, Mandy Sierp, Andrew Smith

Cover Pepi Bluck, lonelyplanetimages.com

Internal Image Research Aude Vauconsant, lonelyplanetimages.com

Colour Designer Julie Crane

Indexer Marie Lorimer

Project Managers Eoin Dunlevy, Glenn van der Knijff

Language Content Laura Crawford

Thanks to Sasha Baskett, Helen Christinis, Michelle Glynn, Jane Hart, Lisa Knights, Katie Lynch, Lyahna Spencer

Cover photographs Ibn Battuta Mall, Andalusia, Dubai, UAE, Walter Bibikow/JAI/Corbis (top); Group of men in the desert, Dubai, UAE, Caro/Alamy (bottom)

All images are copyright of the photographer unless otherwise indicated. Many of the images in this guide are available for licensing from Lonely Planet Images: www.lonelyplanetimages.com.

THANKS

ANDREA SCHULTE-PEEVERS

A heartfelt *shukran* to the following people whose help, advice, support, encouragement and insights were invaluable during my research: Rashmi Chittal, Anka Patel, Elizabeth Hansen, Maria Basziszta, Ulrike Baumann, Lisa Carusone, Neil Rumbaoa, Clare Dunford, Sana Khan, Angela Bak, Vivienne Gan, Bénédicte Flouriot, Nadir Bendjedah, Manal El Matni, Stephanie Khouy, Sanaz Ghahremani, Ruth Hulat, Tatyana Khan, Florance Stankova, Stephanie AbouJaoude, Nazlee Tayob, Fernanda Makhoul, Inga Schwer, Helen Spearman, Jessica Parry, and Jason and Imeson from Ohm Records. Special thanks to my colleague John Vlahides for so generously sharing his experiences and contacts, to commissioning editor Emma Gilmour for entrusting me with this gig, and to the entire Lonely Planet team responsible for producing this kick-ass book. Last but not least, the biggest thanks go to David, my loyal companion in love and life.

THE LONELY PLANET STORY

Fresh from an epic journey across Europe, Asia and Australia in 1972, Tony and Maureen Wheeler sat at their kitchen table stapling together notes. The first Lonely Planet guidebook, *Across Asia on the Cheap*, was born.

Travellers snapped up the guides. Inspired by their success, the Wheelers began publishing books to Southeast Asia, India and beyond. Demand was prodigious, and the Wheelers expanded the business rapidly to keep up. Over the years, Lonely Planet extended its coverage to every country and into the virtual world via lonelyplanet.com and the Thorn Tree message board.

As Lonely Planet became a globally loved brand, Tony and Maureen received several offers for the company. But it wasn't until 2007 that they found a partner whom they trusted to remain true to the company's principles of travelling widely, treading lightly and giving sustainably. In October of that year, BBC Worldwide acquired a 75% share in the company, pledging to uphold Lonely Planet's commitment to independent travel, trustworthy advice and editorial independence.

Today, Lonely Planet has offices in Melbourne, London and Oakland, with over 500 staff members and 300 authors. Tony and Maureen are still actively involved with Lonely Planet. They're travelling more often than ever, and they're devoting their spare time to charitable projects. And the company is still driven by the philosophy of *Across Asia on the Cheap*: 'All you've got to do is decide to go and the hardest part is over. So go!'

BEHIND THE SCENES

OUR READERS

Many thanks to the travellers who used the last edition and wrote to us with helpful hints, useful advice and interesting anecdotes: Erik Leenders, Shaila Mahomed, Mladen Nikolic, Peter Pereira, Paul Rulkens, Dee Taylor

SEND US YOUR FEEDBACK

We love to hear from travellers – your comments keep us on our toes and help make our books better. Our well-travelled team reads every word on what you loved or loathed about this book. Although we cannot reply individually to postal submissions, we always guarantee that your feedback goes straight to the appropriate authors, in time for the next edition. Each person who sends us information is thanked in the next edition and the most useful submissions are rewarded with a free book.

To send us your updates – and find out about Lonely Planet events, newsletters and travel news – visit our award-winning website: lonelyplanet.com/contact.

Note: We may edit, reproduce and incorporate your comments in Lonely Planet products such as guidebooks, websites and digital products, so let us know if you don't want your comments reproduced or your name acknowledged. For a copy of our privacy policy visit lonelyplanet.com/privacy.

BEHIND THE SCENES

Notes

INDEX

A

abras 60, 182, **7**
Abu Dhabi 24, 25, 27, 42
Abu Dhabi International
  Airport 179-80
accidents 184
accommodation 152-65,
  see also hotels, Sleeping
  subindex
  B&Bs 152
  Bur Dubai 156-9
  costs 153-4
  Deira 154-6
  Jumeirah 161-2
  New Dubai 163-5
  online booking service
    153
  rentals 153
  reservations 153
  Sheikh Zayed Road
    159-61
activities 139-49, 168-71,
  *see also individual
  activities*, Sports &
  Activities *subindex*
air travel 178-80
  airports 27, 178-80
Al Serkal Cultural
  Foundation 61, 67
Al-Ahmadiya School 56,
  58, **7**
Al-Ain 173-5
Al-Ain Oasis 174
Al-Jahili 174
Al-Maktoum International
  Airport 180
Al-Mamzar Beach Park 78
Al-Mateena 56
Al-Quoz 73-4

Al-Safa Park 79
alcohol 32, 106, 126, 128
amusement parks, *see*
  Entertainment *subindex*
animal attractions, *see*
  Sights *subindex*
animals 33-4, 171, 173
antiques 98, 99
Aquaventure 81
Arabian Gulf 33
architecture 38-41
area codes 194, *see also
  inside front cover*
art fairs 16
art galleries 41-2, *see also*
  Sights *subindex*
arts 41-4, *see also
  individual arts*
ATMs 191

B

B&Bs 152, *see also* Sleeping
  subindex
babysitting 186
Badiyah 176
barasti 39-40
bargaining 89
bars 126, 127-32, *see also*
  Entertainment *subindex*
  Bur Dubai 128
  Deira 127
  Jumeirah 130-1
  New Dubai 131-2
  Sheikh Zayed Road
    128-30
Bastakia Quarter 61, 67, **7**
bathrooms 194-5
beaches 78
Bedouin people 91-2, 168
birds 33-4, 176
boat tours 60, 107, 146, 192
boat travel
  abras 60, 182
  water taxis 183
books, *see also* literature,
  Shopping *subindex*
  book fair 17
  carpets 89
  children, travel with 186
  history 21, 22
  off-road driving 170
bull-butting 176

Bur Dubai 46, 60-8, **62-5**
  accommodation 156-9
  bars 128
  eating 111-14
  itineraries 48-9
  shopping 94-8
  walking tour 67-8
Bur Dubai Souq 61, 68, **8**
Burj al-Arab 38, 79, 161, **4**
Burj Dubai, *see* Burj Khalifa
Burj Khalifa 26, 38, 69
bus tours 192
bus travel 18, 180, 183
  water buses 183-4
business hours 186, *see also
  inside front cover*
  restaurants 186
  shops 89, 186

C

cafes, *see also* Eating
  subindex
  sheesha cafés 135-6
call to prayer 158
camels
  camel market 175
  racing 148
  riding 170, **12**
  souvenirs 101, **8**
camping 168
car travel 35, 181-2, 184
  accidents 184
  drink-driving 182-3
  hire 168, 170, 181-2
  off-road driving 168,
    170
  parking 182
  road rules 182
  road tolls 181
carbon offset 179
carpets 90, 101, *see also*
  Shopping *subindex*
books 89
censorship 37, 42-3
children, travel with 186,
  see also Entertainment
  subindex
  babysitting 186
  restaurants 113
cinema 42-3, 126, 136-7,
  see also Entertainment
  subindex

film festivals 16-17,
  42, 136
climate 15, 186-7
climate change 179
clothes 32, *see also*
  Shopping *subindex*
  dress codes 32, 196-7
  sizing chart 100
clubs 126, 132-4, *see also*
  bars, Entertainment
  subindex
conservation, *see*
  environment
conservatism 15, 29
consulates 187-8
cosmetic surgery 144
cosmetics, *see* Shopping
  subindex
costs 17
  accommodation 153-4
  alcohol 106, 128
  eating 106
courier services 193
courses
  cultural 187
  language 187
courtyard houses 39, 61, 66
credit cards 191
Creekside Park 66-7
cricket 148, 149
cruises 146
  abra cruises 60
  dinner cruises 107, 192
cultural foundations 61,
  66, 67
culture 3, 28-9, 30
  courses 187
  festivals 15, 95
currency exchange 191
customs regulations 187

D

dance 43-4
dates 96, 176
day trips 171-7
Deira 46, 50-9, **50**, **52-5**
  accommodation 154-6
  bars 127
  eating 108-10
  itineraries 48-9
  shopping 93-4
  walking tour 57-9

INDEX

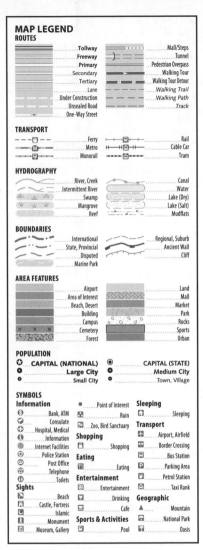

MAP LEGEND

ROUTES

.... Tollway
.... Freeway
.... Primary
.... Secondary
.... Tertiary
.... Lane
.... Under Construction
.... Unsealed Road
.... One-Way Street

.... Mall/Steps
.... Tunnel
.... Pedestrian Overpass
.... Walking Tour
.... Walking Tour Detour
.... Walking Trail
.... Walking Path
.... Track

TRANSPORT

.... Ferry
.... Metro
.... Monorail

.... Rail
.... Cable Car
.... Tram

HYDROGRAPHY

.... River, Creek
.... Intermittent River
.... Swamp
.... Mangrove
.... Reef

.... Canal
.... Water
.... Lake (Dry)
.... Lake (Salt)
.... Mudflats

BOUNDARIES

.... International
.... State, Provincial
.... Disputed
.... Marine Park

.... Regional, Suburb
.... Ancient Wall
.... Cliff

AREA FEATURES

.... Airport
.... Area of Interest
.... Beach, Desert
.... Building
.... Campus
.... Cemetery
.... Forest

.... Land
.... Mall
.... Market
.... Park
.... Rocks
.... Sports
.... Urban

POPULATION

○ .... CAPITAL (NATIONAL)
● .... Large City
● .... Small City

◉ .... CAPITAL (STATE)
● .... Medium City
○ .... Town, Village

SYMBOLS

Information
⑤ .... Bank, ATM
◎ .... Consulate
⊕ .... Hospital, Medical
❶ .... Information
@ .... Internet Facilities
⊗ .... Police Station
⊖ .... Post Office
☎ .... Telephone
⊕ .... Toilets

Sights
🏖 .... Beach
🏰 .... Castle, Fortress
☪ .... Islamic
▮ .... Monument
🏛 .... Museum, Gallery

● .... Point of Interest
🔲 .... Ruin
🔲 .... Zoo, Bird Sanctuary

Shopping
🔲 .... Shopping

Eating
🔲 .... Eating

Entertainment
🔲 .... Entertainment
🔲 .... Drinking
🔲 .... Cafe

Sports & Activities
🔲 .... Pool

Sleeping
🔲 .... Sleeping

Transport
🔲 .... Airport, Airfield
🔲 .... Border Crossing
🔲 .... Bus Station
🔲 .... Parking Area
🔲 .... Petrol Station
🔲 .... Taxi Rank

Geographic
▲ .... Mountain
🔲 .... National Park
🔲 .... Oasis

Published by Lonely Planet Publications Pty Ltd
ABN 36 005 607 983

Australia (Head Office)
Locked Bag 1, Footscray, Victoria 3011,
☎ 03 8379 8000, fax 03 8379 8111,
talk2us@lonelyplanet.com.au

USA 150 Linden St, Oakland, CA 94607,
☎ 510 250 6400, toll free 800 275 8555,
fax 510 893 8572, info@lonelyplanet.com

UK 2nd fl, 186 City Rd, London, EC1V 2NT,
☎ 020 7106 2100, fax 020 7106 2101,
go@lonelyplanet.co.uk

MIX
Paper from
responsible sources
FSC™ C021741
www.fsc.org